by the same editors

Social Work Theories in Action
Mary Nash, Robyn Munford and Kieran O'Donoghue
ISBN 978 1 84310 249 6
eISBN 978 1 84642 100 6

of related interest

Relationship-Based Social Work, Second Edition
Getting to the Heart of Practice
Edited by Gillian Ruch, Danielle Turney and Adrian Ward
Foreword by David Howe
ISBN 978 1 78592 253 4
eISBN 978 1 78450 543 1

Innovations in Social Work Research
Using Methods Creatively
Edited by Louise Hardwick, Roger Smith and Aidan Worsley
ISBN 978 1 84905 585 7
eISBN 978 1 78450 145 7

Relationship-Based Research in Social Work
Understanding Practice Research
Edited by Gillian Ruch and Ilse Julkunen
ISBN 978 1 84905 457 7
eISBN 978 1 78450 112 9

New Theories for
SOCIAL WORK PRACTICE

• • • •

Ethical Practice for Working with Individuals, Families and Communities

EDITED BY ROBYN MUNFORD AND
KIERAN O'DONOGHUE

FOREWORD BY JIM IFE

Jessica Kingsley *Publishers*
London and Philadelphia

First published in 2019
by Jessica Kingsley Publishers
73 Collier Street
London N1 9BE, UK
and
400 Market Street, Suite 400
Philadelphia, PA 19106, USA

www.jkp.com

Copyright © Jessica Kingsley Publishers 2019

Library of Congress Cataloging in Publication Data
A CIP catalog record for this book is available from the Library of Congress

British Library Cataloguing in Publication Data
A CIP catalogue record for this book is available from the British Library

ISBN 978 1 78592 158 2
eISBN 978 1 78450 426 7

Printed and bound in Great Britain

We dedicate this book to Merv Hancock (1926–2016), a social work leader in Aotearoa New Zealand, in recognition of his contribution to critical thinking on social work theory and practice. Merv, thank you for reminding us of the importance of history, of context, and that at the heart of practice is social justice. Thank you for your wisdom, humility and inspiration over many years.

Thank you to the contributors and the publishing team. We hope this book is an opportunity for practitioners to reflect on their practice and on the knowledge which informs this practice.

Contents

Foreword

JIM IFE

We are living at a time of significant change.

Multiple crises – ecological, economic, social and political – loom in the near future, and in some measure they are already part of our experience. Climate change is real and is affecting people's lives in many nations. Globalization and neoliberal ideology have together created a global economy that is both inequitable and unsustainable. We are reaching, and indeed have overshot, the ecological limits to growth, with devastating consequences not only for humans but also for the non-human world. There is a growing global realization that we cannot go on as we have been, and that in confronting the future the one thing of which we can be sure is that it will not be a simple continuation of the present, even though alternative futures are still hard for many people to imagine.

In such a world of uncertainty, how should social workers practise? Given the vulnerabilities of many already disadvantaged groups, the increasing precarity of people's lives, and the obscene levels of inequality we now see globally and nationally, it would seem that social workers are going to be more needed than ever in the coming decades. The principles of social justice and human rights, and the emphasis on relationships, that are foundational for social work, will be very important in this period of crisis and change. But the organizational structures in which social workers can practise, and the forms that this practice might take, are far from clear. It is in that context that this book makes an important contribution.

In adapting to a new and uncertain future, there is a temptation to discard the old and start again. This, for social work, would be a serious mistake. While the future will undoubtedly throw up new challenges and require new ways of practising, it is also true that social workers have developed considerable experience in working for social justice, and in strengthening relationships at all levels: family, community and society.

This experience will be important in shaping a future for social work, and social workers can and should use their expertise – in both theory and practice – as a basis for future and evolving forms of alternative social work. Indeed, it can be argued that social work skills, theory and values have much to contribute to the wider society. One common theme among many writers concerned with ecological or economic crisis is the importance of community; if there is to be a way forward for humanity, it will require strong, resilient and sustainable communities, and in this regard social workers have much to contribute. Social workers cannot afford to be apologetic about their professional knowledge and skills, but rather should recognize that they have expertise that others are looking for, and that social work can play a pivotal role at this historic moment. The chapters in this book provide a strong basis for building the newly emerging social work. They recognize the importance of existing social work knowledge and practice wisdom, and show how the new social work can emerge from the best of the old.

The continuing erosion of the commons – whether in terms of land, public space, education, intellectual property, human services or cultural practices – is reinforced by the politics and economics of neoliberalism, where everything possible is commodified and placed in private ownership, to be used for private profit rather than human flourishing. The impact of this on human (and indeed non-human) community is serious, and it is important for social workers to find ways to push back against continuing neoliberal commodification and to emphasize the importance of relationships and of community as what give meaning and significance to life. This emphasis on relationship, and relational reality, is central to social work practice, and this is reflected in many of the chapters of this book. The strong community traditions of Aotearoa New Zealand, evident to many visitors to that country, and central to the way social work has been conceptualized there, represent a particularly strong focus for future social work, and here Aotearoa New Zealand has much to teach the rest of the world about community-based social work.

The centrality of service recipients or communities is another major theme of this book. In an era so dominated by Western modernity, with its top-down traditions and its embrace of managerialism, this is indeed a radical position. Social workers are well aware of the inadequacy of many programmes designed by academics, managers or political leaders, and imposed on families or communities who have little or no say in the matter. Such practice both disempowers those we would rather be seeking to empower, and also further alienates them from the very structures and institutions that are supposedly designed to *help*. The importance of people actually having significant agency in determining the nature of the services they need, and being able to articulate their own hopes and aspirations rather than these being assumed by well-meaning bureaucrats or managers, has been consistently advocated by social workers in many different settings, and is another strong theme of the chapters in this book. In this way, social workers can join, and indeed lead, the challenge against the top-down thinking that has been so characteristic of many approaches to *intervention* (a word that social workers should use only with extreme caution).

Increasing ecological awareness has underlined the importance of the principle of diversity. Whether in agricultural, biological or human fields, diversity is more sustainable, and indeed necessary for life and for communities to thrive. Modernity has bred an obsession with similarity or uniformity, often motivated by a limited view of effectiveness or efficiency. It may be easier to deal with or manage a community of sameness rather than a community of difference, but it is from communities of difference that people can flourish. Rather than the traditional labour saying of *in unity is strength*, the ecological principle is *in diversity is strength*. The value of diversity is now recognized across many different fields, from agriculture to genetics to microbes to cultures, to human communities.

This principle applies also to social work. Diversity is central to good social work practice, and social workers have considerable experience in promoting diversity as a positive to be supported, rather than as a problem to be managed. The emphasis on diversity in many of the chapters of this book is again an indication that the book is dealing with emerging issues that are central to social work practice. Diversity is seen as a problem rather than a strength in many societies, leading to xenophobia, racism and a reluctance to support programmes of multiculturalism. It is shown particularly in attitudes to refugees and asylum seekers. At this time, social work's commitment to diversity is of particular relevance, and should be a strong point of advocacy by social workers in many different contexts.

Indigenous knowledge is particularly important for contemporary social work. This is not just so that non-indigenous workers can engage in culturally appropriate practice with indigenous people, important though this is. Of more significance is the contribution indigenous knowledge and worldviews can make in helping humanity move beyond narrow anthropocentric Western modernity, which is proving ecologically disastrous and is destroying not only human community, but the very physical world that sustains humanity, as well as rendering many other species extinct. Those of us who are social workers from Western cultural backgrounds need to recognize that our cultural traditions, which inevitably inform our social work, are unsustainable, colonial and racist.

They are not a basis for good social work practice committed to social justice and human rights.

For increasing numbers of people worldwide, the insights of indigenous worldviews represent a way forward, whether it be from the indigenous peoples of Aotearoa New Zealand, Australia, the Pacific, North America, Latin America, Africa, Asia or the Arctic. Social workers, internationally, have recognized this, with the inclusion in the Global Definition of Social Work of *indigenous knowledge* as a core component of social work knowledge. Social work in Aotearoa New Zealand has been at the forefront of recognition of the value of indigenous knowledge and the deep incorporation of this into social work theory and practice, and the discussion of indigenous cultural knowledges and traditions in this book represents a particularly significant contribution to social work well beyond Aotearoa New Zealand.

The incorporation of indigenous knowledge is not the only area where Aotearoa New Zealand social work is at the cutting edge of social work knowledge and practice development. The emphasis on community structures, community development, and community as a basis for social work has a long tradition in Aotearoa New Zealand, more so than in many other Western nations. This is significant for the future development of social work internationally; the need for strong community-based structures and processes means that the experience developed by social workers will have much to teach social workers elsewhere in the Western world, where community structures are eroded and where social work has become too influenced by individually oriented clinical models of practice which, while of obvious value in some cases, cannot serve as a viable basis for future practice for more than a small minority of those needing social work services. While the importance of community is well recognized by social workers in other cultural contexts, Aotearoa New Zealand is perhaps the leading Western nation in understanding social work practice in this way. In addition, there has also been a recent revival of a more radical or critical tradition in Aotearoa New Zealand social work, all too often lacking in other Western nations, which is another reason why the emerging ideas in this book will be of interest well beyond national boundaries.

With a future promising uncertainty, precarity, crisis and change, it is impossible to forecast just how that instability will play out. Social work, if it is to remain relevant and if it is to make a contribution to newly emerging social, economic, ecological and political orders, will need above all high levels of creativity, imagination and thinking that is *outside the square*. There are many potential sources of creative inspiration and imagination for social work beyond its traditional knowledge base, such as art, music, drama, poetry, film, social media and, most importantly, the wisdom of those people and communities with whom we work. The old ways of thinking and working will not necessarily be what is needed in the newly emerging practice environment. Social workers will be able to draw on their insights and practice experience in ways that will contribute to a better world, but they will also need to be open to the unexpected, to making the most of unanticipated opportunities, and to dare to dream. In that context, this book, bringing together newly emerging forms of understanding and practice, represents an excellent place to start; though at this time no one knows where those journeys will end.

Jim Ife

Introduction

ROBYN MUNFORD AND KIERAN O'DONOGHUE

The genesis for this book comes from our previous edited text, *Social Work Theories in Action*, which explored fields of practice and presented an integrated framework for practice.

This 2005 book was well received by practitioners, educators and students, who appreciated the focus on an integrated framework for practice that situated the practitioner and client in a working relationship where theory and action meet in a dialogical interaction. This new book extends these ideas and explores emerging theories for social work practice. It explores the core values, knowledge, and skills of social work practice in diverse fields of practice. It captures the expanding role of social work into new sites of practice and the need for different approaches that encourage social work educators and practitioners to think differently about practice. To this end, the book foregrounds current challenges and alternative ways of thinking about knowledge and practice, such as the positioning of cultural knowledge and lived experience. This thinking has contributed to transforming social work practice and the ways in which social work services are able to respond to the needs of diverse populations. This emerging thinking positions the *client* at the centre of decision making and change processes and encourages practitioners to interrogate the nature of helping relationships and the roles of the social worker and the client. In different ways, each of the chapters explores these ideas and the challenges to traditional thinking about the nature of social work practice and the helping relationship.

The book is aimed at both students (undergraduate and postgraduate professional social work programmes) and practitioners. While it is primarily focused on social work students and practitioners, it has relevance for other helping professions, such as support work in health, mental health, disability, and youth work. The book is aimed at an international audience and the theory, literature and case scenarios have relevance for practice globally. This introduction presents some of the key issues and ideas that are explored in the book. The discussion concludes with an overview of the book and a brief introduction to each of the chapters.

Issues and ideas

This book is informed by the changes that are happening in social work theory and practice internationally. Of interest is generating an understanding of how the international definition of social work (International Federation of Social Workers (IFSW) 2014) is given effect in different contexts. This definition promotes social justice, human rights, collective responsibility and respect for diversities as core principles of social work practice. Context is a central theme and involves social workers seeking out local knowledge and solutions. For example, in Aotearoa New Zealand the reclaiming of indigenous practice approaches has been a major focus for social work education and practice. While social workers recognize the importance of global perspectives and international connections, they acknowledge the significance of their unique place in the world and the ways in which this shapes their social work practice.

A social work pioneer in Aotearoa New Zealand, Merv Hancock, reminds us of the importance of context in understanding the relationship between the individual and their social milieu (Interview with Merv Hancock (Munford and Nash 1994, p.9)):

> For me, social work is a profession, a community of people who share a common goal of always seeking new ways to assist people. A part of this is that social work takes seriously the social context in which it finds itself. At certain times the profession has to attend very closely to the needs of the individual, and at other times to the social order.

As this quotation emphasizes, social and community workers attend to the immediate needs of individuals, families, and communities, while building an understanding of social change and the relationship between personal issues and the broader social and political context. Globally, social workers have embraced the challenge of working at both the personal and political level and have sought to understand the connection between private troubles and public issues.

Over the last decade, there have been contextual changes resulting in rising inequality and poverty; dehumanization, radicalization, and terrorism; environmental instability; a growing digital divide; an interconnected globalized world dominated by trade, economic productivity, efficiency and outcomes; and, the increasing demand and rising costs of healthcare, food, shelter and other basic necessities. These changes are most apparent in stories about a lack of affordable housing; unemployment; exploitative work contracts; children going to school without breakfast, lunch or adequate clothing; and people being subjected to displacement, discrimination, suspicion, disrespect, abuse and violence.

We live in an increasingly digital world but the effects of this development are mixed. On the one hand, it provides an unprecedented ability to share information, bring people together to provide support for each other (via Twitter, Facebook, E-advocacy, E-therapy online petitions and support groups). However, on the other hand, it has increased individuals' vulnerability (particularly, young people) to issues such as cyberbullying, cyberstalking, as well as the risk that one's life, feelings, success and reputation are harmed in a click of a mouse or a tweet. In the workplace, the digital society has created opportunities for new forms of surveillance, recast the boundaries between the personal and the professional, and challenged the construction of privacy and confidentiality.

The development of big data, analytics and application of actuarial methods for identifying those most at risk or in need of investment, together with evidence-based, evidence-informed, evidence-guided practice can be seen as an extension of the *what works* discourse from the 1970s. These developments have a direct impact on social work practice: practice becomes more specialized and focused towards the commissioners' or funders' agendas, with the increased expectations of the use of evidence and the attainment of set outcomes.

An evidence and outcomes agenda is in contrast with the reflective, relational, strengths and communitarian heart of social work that emphasizes the artistry of practice within the uncertainty of the here and now. This takes place in a face-to-face meeting in relationship, where there is a focus on the hopes, dreams and possibilities for the future and the interconnectedness of people with each other and their families, significant others and communities. The paradox of our times is that better outcomes rely on good processes, practices, relationships, resourcing and community support (Dale, Mooney and O'Donoghue 2017).

As the chapters illustrate, social workers have developed intentional and evidence-informed practice approaches that enable them to work in partnership with clients to effect change at the individual level while working on wider social and community change strategies to challenge structural disadvantage such as inequality, marginalization and impoverished material conditions. A cornerstone of practice is the analysis of lived experience and the deconstruction of discourses that frame human suffering as an individual experience resulting from personal deficits. This practice requires social workers to work at multiple levels and generate insights into the complexity of social situations. Working successfully with complexity enables social workers to understand the nature of social relations at many levels, at the policy level and in the everyday practice of social work and the lived experiences of those we work alongside. Central to this practice is hooking into strengths and capacities, finding out what has worked in the past and building on these to find the spaces for change. It is about acknowledging the capacities of individuals to create knowledge and understanding of their own experiences. This involves interrogating the discourses that construct individuals and groups in particular ways, that subjugate their knowledge, and that position them at the margins, for example the historical treatment of disabled people and their exclusion from decision making about services and support.

Each chapter offers a fresh perspective on the role of social work practice in diverse settings. The chapters present emerging thinking on social work practice and encourage readers to critically reflect on the relevance of these ideas for their practice. Developments in specific practice areas are explored: models for working with children, young people and families; new ideas in the mental health and disability fields of practice; effective practice with resettled refugees; and practice with older people. The idea of strengths and relational practice and the importance of developing authentic helping partnerships and alliances is a dominant theme in all of these chapters. There is a focus on ecological perspectives as they offer an understanding of the dynamic interplay between systems and the interaction between individuals and their environments (Bronfenbrenner 1977). An important theme throughout the book is the connection between micro and macro levels of practice and developing collective responses to addressing enduring challenges. Several chapters explore these ideas and present the emerging thinking in community development practice, including green social work and responsive social work practice in disaster work, which underlines the importance of establishing collaborative relationships with other professionals. Emerging thinking in practice approaches is presented: indigenous approaches to practice; social work practice in Pacific communities; developing effective cross-cultural practice and integrative body–mind practice. Current thinking on informed and ethical practice and the importance of supervision in ensuring that practice remains responsive to the diverse needs of clients are also focused on in this book. This discussion offers readers an opportunity to reflect on their supervision practice and on the strategies they can use to resolve ethical dilemmas in everyday practice.

Overview of chapters

The book is divided into four key parts as described below. The chapters we have selected have currency in both Aotearoa New Zealand and internationally and together address the multi-levelled nature of social work practice. Each chapter explores the theory and literature pertinent to the particular field of practice and presents examples of practice. The challenges and current debates in the respective fields of practice are presented and cover a broad remit, including: how to enact the core values of the profession such as promoting social justice and human rights; how to uphold practice that responds to psychosocial issues while confronting structural conditions; how to ensure the voices and knowledge of service users are at the centre of practice; and, how to adopt strengths and relational practices when funding for services is fragmented and uncertain. Each chapter concludes with reflection questions as an opportunity for the reader to critically reflect on their practice and identify how the ideas presented can contribute to their work.

Working with Individuals and Families in their Environments

Part 1 presents emerging thinking on social work practice with individuals and families who have faced adversity. It explores key themes such as wellbeing, identity, and the importance of place, a sense of belonging, and forming enduring connections within families and communities. A central theme is that of citizenship; the chapters offer interesting insights into how social workers work alongside clients to challenge invisibility and advocate for recognition. The cornerstone of this work is the promotion of strategies that enable clients to experience meaningful support that enables them to contribute to their communities. A key element of this practice is to support clients to enact agency and to participate fully in community life. Helping relationships present an opportunity for clients who have been excluded and marginalized to have voice and to have their knowledge and capacities respected. This involves clients leading decision-making processes for determining plans and interventions.

In the first chapter, Jackie Sanders and Robyn Munford present a model of practice for working with vulnerable youth. The PARTH model emerged out of the findings of an Aotearoa New Zealand longitudinal study of youth who had experienced chronic exposure to adverse childhood experiences (ACE). The study explored their service experiences, their key transitions, and their strategies for locating support and resources to mitigate the effects of harmful events and environments. The PARTH model draws on Positive Youth Development (PYD) approaches and defines the core elements of effective practice. The model provides a way for social workers to develop meaningful encounters with vulnerable youth that can lead to better outcomes.

The second chapter by John Pinkerton, John Canavan and Pat Dolan explores family support and social work practice. This chapter examines the emerging theories in this field of practice and demonstrates the interweaving of social work and family support. The discussion foregrounds the social ecology of family life as the core concern of social work practice with children and their carers. Family support is positioned as an effective intervention in social work practice with families. The chapter examines the key elements of family support practice and practitioners' capacity to connect and kindle the psychosocial resources within a family's social ecology.

Jay Marlowe explores social work practice with resettled refugees in Chapter 3. The chapter discusses recent theories and models that inform the multiple ways that social workers can effectively work with refugees. It situates the discussion within a global context and considers current challenges and emerging issues for practice in local contexts and internationally. The chapter presents a model of practice that contains the key elements for achieving successful resettlement experiences, including meaning-making and building connections. This model has a strong foundation in social justice practice and posits a central role for social workers in facilitating citizenship and promoting strategies that ensure the upholding of human rights.

In the next chapter, Garth Bennie and Sara Georgeson also explore ideas about citizenship and examine new models of practice for supporting disabled people to live meaningful lives and to be fully included in community life. There are major shifts in thinking that are reframing disability support. This transformation is informed by principles that challenge power relations and promote choice and control. The changes have implications for social work practice and for practitioners who do not have lived experience of disability. The chapter explores these challenges and the ways in which practitioners can negotiate new social work roles, relationships and power dynamics.

Next, Malcolm Golightley and Gloria Kirwan explore social work practice and mental health. They argue for consideration of the global trends and critical debates that have influenced the theoretical foundation on which modern mental health services are based. They also strongly encourage social workers to reflect on the contribution they make to this field of practice. The chapter explores emerging frameworks of practice which are situated within a human rights perspective and are informed by strengths-based approaches. Central to these approaches is the assertion of the consumer voice and the adoption of a recovery model that recognizes that knowledge gained from lived experience should inform diagnosis and treatment processes.

In the final chapter in this section, Polly Yeung considers social work with older people. The chapter explores the current discourses of ageing and debates about how to effectively meet the needs of a growing older population. The chapter is organized around two approaches to service delivery, Sen's capability approach and the person-centred approach. These approaches incorporate important roles for social workers who provide interventions that recognize the diverse experiences of older people and enable them to maintain control over their lives, including being involved in decisions about care and support.

Developing Communities

Part 2 explores the connection between individual experience and wider community issues. Historically, social workers have embraced an emancipatory ethic in their practice (VanderPlaat 2016) and have contributed to social action and wider social change projects. They have joined social movements and worked in civil society and at the political level to challenge oppressive discourses, policies, systems and structures. The first chapter by Robyn Munford and Jackie Sanders presents a model for transformative practice in community organizations: community-led development. This is a collective response to intractable social issues and the chapter explores the key role community organizations can have in forming partnerships with community members to turn resistance into sustained social change projects. This practice demonstrates that small and local change initiatives can lead to substantive positive social change. A key element of this practice is working collaboratively and building alliances across organizations and networks in order to harness the strengths and capacities of communities.

The next chapter by Lena Dominelli also explores social work practice at multiple levels and the important role social workers have in social change projects. The chapter examines green social work practice in urban spaces and presents insights into the challenges confronting social workers in this critical field of practice. Green social work adopts a holistic approach that takes account of the needs of people, the earth and physical environment, and the power relations that exist in socio-economic and political systems. The chapter locates green social work within a social justice approach that recognizes the interdependencies between people and their physical, social, political, economic and cultural environments as part of an interconnected ecosystem.

Kathryn Hay, in the final chapter in Part 2, explores social work practice in disaster work. The chapter examines the central elements of this emerging field of practice and argues that social workers have knowledge and skills (such as psychosocial interventions, advocacy, community organizing and policy design) which are relevant to all phases of disaster management. Social workers' skills in working at multiple levels with vulnerable populations and in collaboration with others are particularly pertinent to disaster management work. This chapter promotes an integrated response to disaster work that situates practice with individuals within a collective response to disaster management. Underpinning this approach is a commitment to social justice and processes for realizing human rights.

Practice Approaches

Part 3 presents practice approaches that embrace a common theme, that of respectful and culturally responsive social work practice. In Aotearoa New Zealand, this is framed as mana-enhancing practice. The first chapter by Paulé Ruwhiu explores this practice and presents a framework that foregrounds indigenous knowledge and locates indigenous voices and cultural understanding at the centre of practice. This approach to achieving wellbeing focuses on strengths, growth, and the promotion of an identity and self-determination that is derived from a sense of belonging and creating strong connections with whānau (family), place and iwi (tribe). While the focus in this chapter is on social work practice in Aotearoa New Zealand, it has much relevance for social work internationally, as it embraces the core concepts of relational practice, the importance of context and history, and the promotion of respectful practice that recognizes the central place of values and beliefs in helping relationships.

The second chapter by Tracie Mafile'o extends these ideas and explores social work with Pacific communities. The chapter provides fresh perspectives on relational practice as a cornerstone of effective practice with diverse communities. Pacific values and beliefs and their contribution to relational practice are explored and provide a framework for practice and a process for practitioners to critically reflect on their practice. An important focus is on the partnerships between social workers and clients and the potential relational practice has to strengthen connections, build a sense of belonging and enhance the support networks and strategies that achieve transformative change within communities.

The next chapter by Rosaleen Ow extends the idea of culturally relevant, nuanced and sensitive social work practice. This chapter explores cross-cultural social work practice and examines the key elements of building genuine and authentic practice relationships with diverse cultural groups. The key components of cross-cultural practice are explored, including cultural awareness, cultural competence, cultural safety, and the emerging concept of cultural humility. Cross-cultural social work practice is located within sound ethical practice and promotes an *ethic of care*. This chapter offers important insights into how social workers can promote culturally relevant practice and address the challenges and tensions that arise in this intentional approach to practice.

The chapter by Sylvia Chan, Cecilia Chan and Celia Chan presents a holistic approach to social work practice and explores the interrelatedness of spiritual, natural and human dimensions. This approach, the Integrative Body-Mind-Spirit approach (IBMS), focuses on achieving holistic wellbeing for clients who are facing major life crises such as terminal illness. The chapter presents a model for practice that actualizes the body–mind–spirit approach: the IBMS Process Model, which involves the five stages of engaging, nurturing, shifting, integrating and transforming (ENSIT). Of importance in this model is practitioner self-care, which is a core element in this holistic approach to social work practice and the achievement of wellbeing.

Informed and Ethical Practice

Part 4 includes two chapters that explore informed and ethical practice. The discussion underlines the importance of intentional practice and the key role of critical reflection in social work practice. The first chapter by Kieran O'Donoghue explores supervision and evidence-informed practice. The chapter reviews the history of social work supervision theory and the central role supervision has played in achieving evidence-informed practice. A focus of this chapter is the presentation of an evidence-informed supervision model that guides practitioners' critical reflection on their supervision practice. This model focuses on the construction of supervision and includes the key elements of the supervision alliance and interactional processes. The model provides a framework for the supervision of practitioners and for the supervision of practice with clients.

The final chapter by Donna McAuliffe and Lesley Chenoweth explores ethical decision making in social work practice. The chapter draws on the premise that social workers have a responsibility to uphold important principles of social justice and human rights. A central focus of this chapter is an examination of the ways in which knowledge of ethics and ethical decision making is integrated into social work education programmes. The authors explore current thinking on the teaching of ethical theory and its location in the curriculum in order to examine how well practitioners are prepared to develop a deep understanding of social work ethics and ethical decision making in practice.

References

Bronfenbrenner, U. (1977) 'Toward an experimental ecology of human development.' *American Psychologist 32*, 7, 513–531.

Dale, M., Mooney, H. and O'Donoghue, K. (2017) *Defining Social Work in Aotearoa.* Palmerston North, New Zealand: Massey University Press.

International Federation of Social Workers (IFSW) (2014) *Global Definition of Social Work.* Accessed on 04/09/2018 at www.ifsw.org/what-is-social-work/global-definition-of-social-work.

Munford, R. and Nash, M. (1994) *Social Work in Action.* Palmerston North, New Zealand: Dunmore Press.

VanderPlaat, M. (2016) 'Activating the sociological imagination to explore the boundaries of resilience research and practice.' *School Psychology International 37*, 2, 189–203.

• Part 1 •

WORKING WITH INDIVIDUALS AND FAMILIES IN THEIR ENVIRONMENTS

Chapter 1

PARTH Practices and Better Outcomes: Creating 'Lucky' Encounters between Social Workers and Vulnerable Youth

JACKIE SANDERS AND ROBYN MUNFORD

Introduction

The concept of vulnerability is increasingly shaping global academic debates, government responses and programme development for youth who face major challenges in navigating a safe path to adulthood (Gorur 2015). As yet there is no commonly agreed definition of vulnerability (Rizvi 2015) and there is debate about its usefulness as a concept because of its ambiguity and stigmatising potential (Becroft 2016; Cole 2016; Foster and Spencer 2011). For instance, some have adopted a universal definition, arguing that the simple fact of being dependent makes youth inherently vulnerable (Daniel 2010). Others consider that vulnerability should only be used to define particular sub-groups of youth who confront atypical levels of risk (Gorur 2015; Felitti *et al.* 1998; Smyth 2013; Walker and Donaldson 2010).

In our research (the Youth Transitions Research programme, see www.youthsay.co.nz), we adopted this latter approach: vulnerability as exposure to atypically high, non-normative levels of risk across multiple life domains that compromised youth capacity in reaching their full potential. Many of these risks were beyond the direct control of youth themselves and their vulnerability was thus compounded by restricted availability of adults who could help them positively address these multiple challenges. This definition of vulnerability has two key elements: high levels of complex risks and reduced likelihood of positive outcomes (Gorur 2015). It highlights the critical importance of adults taking decisive action to address the risks that create vulnerability and this is where it becomes important to understand what types of intervention make a difference.

While it is clear that chronic exposure to adverse childhood experiences (ACE) makes children and young people vulnerable to poor outcomes, there is less clarity concerning the characteristics of effective interventions (Metzler *et al.* 2017; Walker and Donaldson 2010). Relatively few programmes have been subjected to evaluations using the randomised controlled trials (RCTs) that would conclusively establish efficacy (Mitchell 2011; Thurston 2016). Despite this, the call for *evidence* to support claims of programme efficacy is strong as governments have become increasingly unwilling to fund programmes without such proof (Thurston 2016). Indeed, rather than a developmental asset, some have suggested service delivery can exacerbate vulnerability and thus there is a pressing need to understand the characteristics of successful interventions (Mitchell 2011).

In the face of these challenges, Positive Youth Development (PYD) theory has provided a framework that draws together many of the ideas regarding how to most effectively work with vulnerable youth. While PYD emerged out of the youth development field, it has much relevance for social work (Metzler *et al.* 2017). This chapter outlines the core components of PYD and this discussion provides a context for elaborating on a model of effective social work practice (PARTH) which emerged from our longitudinal study of vulnerable youth in Aotearoa New Zealand. The chapter concludes with questions for reflection.

Positive Youth Development (PYD): a framework for effective practice

Emerging during the 1980s out of dissatisfaction with deficit-focused approaches PYD has created a platform for a fundamentally new way of thinking about and working with young people (Benson *et al.* 2007; Lerner 2005). PYD provides a framework for harnessing the strengths and capacities inherent in all youth, for creating opportunities so that all youth can thrive and for responding to the challenges posed by chronic exposure to harm. PYD is a strengths-based, ecological theory which defines youth as competent social actors who must be actively involved in the programmes designed to support their development (Benson *et al.* 2007; Lerner 2005). Rather than problems to be fixed, PYD defines all youth as having the potential to develop into caring, responsible contributors to society, given relevant and meaningful support. PYD programmes feature the *Big Three* characteristics: 'positive and sustained relationships with competent, caring adults; the development of life skills, and opportunities for youth engagement and empowerment' (Sanders, Munford and Liebenberg 2017, p.202).

PYD and resilience

The ecological and strengths focus of PYD has a good fit with contemporary approaches to resilience (Benson *et al.* 2007). Resilience is a multi-faceted, socio-ecological construct that includes individual factors, family/caregiving factors and extra-familial factors, including relationships outside the family (for example, with friends, teachers and service providers), as well as community, cultural and spiritual resources that enable individuals to respond positively to significant challenges (Masten 2014). In this sense, it provides a valuable framework for social work with vulnerable youth because of the emphasis on working with youth in their social context. A particularly important facet of resilience is that it is malleable; it changes over time as young people's lives change. Resilience manifests itself differently in different social, cultural and historical contexts (Masten 2014). These characteristics make resilience particularly useful to PYD-informed social work interventions which also emphasize culturally and contextually responsive practices (Munford and Sanders 2011).

PYD and relationships

According to PYD, positive development becomes possible when adults create nurturing and enabling relationships with youth. The international research consistently points to the protective and promotive roles that a positive, enduring relationship with at least one committed adult has in terms of outcomes for vulnerable youth (Dewar and Goodman 2014; Fallis 2012). There is evidence that the quality of the social work relationship is a stronger determinant of successful outcomes than the individual characteristics of the young person, their family or the challenges they face (Bastiaanssen *et al.* 2014; DuMont, Widom and Czaja 2007; Liebenberg, Sanders and Munford 2016). From a PYD perspective, the social worker has the potential to be a critical developmental resource (Munford and Sanders 2016a). The social worker–youth relationship may be the first time the young person experiences a trustworthy, reliable, committed relationship with an adult (Everall and Paulson 2002; Ruch, Turney and Ward 2010). However, strong, committed, positive relationships do not happen spontaneously (Duncan, Miller and Sparks 2004). Building this relationship is an intervention in its own right and one that needs careful attention (Kroll 2010; Ruch *et al.* 2010). When practitioners use

PYD practices they come from a position of genuine respect, hold high aspirations for the young person and create opportunities for them to exercise personal agency and develop life skills. These practices result in better outcomes (Jobe and Gorin 2013; McLeod 2007; Sanders and Munford 2014; Sanders *et al.* 2017; Walker and Donaldson 2010).

PYD, culture and context

From a PYD perspective, human development is a bi-directional process which involves individuals influencing and being influenced by their contexts (Benson *et al.* 2007). These processes of mutual influence vary according to the specific social and cultural context and this means that social workers need to understand the particularities of young people's lives (Benson *et al.* 2007). In our research, the developmental process was characterized by significantly different configurations of risks and resilience for Māori (the indigenous population) and Pākehā youth (white New Zealanders) (Sanders *et al.* 2017). In terms of practice, what this means is that while nurturing relationships with caring adults are common features of PYD practices, these relationships and the opportunities they create manifest themselves differently in different cultures and contexts (Benson *et al.* 2007).

This contextually specific facet of positive development requires that adults provide access to contextually and culturally relevant and meaningful resources and developmental opportunities (Lerner 2004). Positive youth development in this sense is a collective endeavour that is potentiated by well-functioning communities that can provide resources that are culturally and socially relevant. This has implications for policy, because communities need to be enabled to create the empowering and facilitative social environments that provide positive developmental opportunities for youth to develop into contributing, caring, confident, competent adults (Lerner 2004, 2005). The task of PYD-informed social work then becomes ensuring that positive culturally and socially relevant and meaningful resources are available to youth.

PYD and risks

The pervasive, negative impact which chronic risk exposure during childhood has on outcomes in adulthood is now well established (Felitti *et al.* 1998; Metzler *et al.* 2017). Adverse childhood experiences have a profound impact on children's brain development and on later outcomes

(Felitti *et al.* 1998; Metzler *et al.* 2017). Disrupted attachments and relationships that are neglectful, exploitive or abusive cause trauma for children (Ruch *et al.* 2010). Of particular relevance during adolescence, exposure to chronic risk and trauma and an absence of positive, nurturing adults compromises the key adolescent developmental processes of identity development and the development of a positive sense of agency (Bulanda and Byro Johnson 2016). These negative impacts transfer across generations, intensifying vulnerability to negative outcomes for each subsequent generation so exposed (Merrick, Leeb and Lee 2013). Young people exposed to significant, enduring risks miss out on key normative childhood experiences; their childhoods end prematurely and, in this sense, are compressed. These young people also shoulder adult responsibilities early and this means that their transitions to adulthood are accelerated (Stein, Ward and Courtney 2011).

Key tasks for social workers wanting to provide meaningful help are to directly involve the young person in decision making and to provide numerous opportunities for them to learn to make pro-social decisions and to practise decision making. In this way, the intervention becomes the safe place where young people try out new ways of managing their lives and, critically, where they are supported to try again when things go wrong.

PARTH: an approach to social work practice with vulnerable youth

While enduring, positive, caring adult relationships make a positive difference for vulnerable young people (Dewar and Goodman 2014), in our research it was also clear from young people's narratives that there was an element of *luck* in terms of whether or not practitioners worked in ways that made such a relationship possible (Munford and Sanders 2015, 2016a, 2016b). The proposition that it might simply be *the luck of the draw* that made the difference between good and poor outcomes for vulnerable youth is of great concern. Intervention in a young person's life should significantly weight the odds in favour of a good outcome. The PARTH model responds to this challenge and distils the common characteristics of *lucky* encounters. PARTH defines the core elements of effective practice and in so doing provides a way for social workers to develop meaningful encounters with vulnerable youth that can lead to better outcomes. The key components of this model are discussed below and case studies (using pseudonyms) derived from the research are used to illustrate key points.

P – passion, perseverance, patience, perspective

The first six months was basically like holding onto the tail of a tiger. I had read the case notes and talked to some of the professionals who had been involved in Anthony's life. By the time I became involved, he was 14, angry and very self-reliant. It seemed to me that we would get nowhere until I could prove to him that I would stay the distance. I needed to show that I would take everything he threw at me, and just keep calmly coming back to him to start again. If someone didn't get alongside him, I was afraid that he was going to end up killing someone. Everyone had let this boy down, from his earliest days, the adults around him, whether they were whānau (family), workers, whoever, basically he had not been anyone's priority and his behaviour reflected that sense of huge isolation and aloneness, of being passed from pillar to post, with no one being consistently there for him. The professionals were very focused on his behavior and trying to control that, but I thought, if I could provide some stability then the behaviour would subside, because he wouldn't need it anymore. So my task as I saw it was to persevere, show him he was very important to me, and also to reflect back to him the positive aspects of who he was, that I could see, so that he could start to build a new, positive story about himself. I just kept reminding myself that if I had been in Anthony's shoes, I might have reacted in the same ways as he did. (Timoti, Anthony's social worker)

By definition, work with vulnerable youth is challenging and requires energy, commitment and the willingness to keep seeking solutions even in the most difficult situations. A passionate orientation helps workers to persevere and persist. As Timoti noted, it is a reminder not to give up but rather to be determined to make a positive difference. Young people noticed when workers were passionate about their work. The young person below highlights the fact that passion and perseverance do not necessarily call for exceptional efforts, but rather for everyday acts of genuine commitment:

You just have to be there for the person, like the extra mile like how [my social worker] said 'If you don't txt me I'll find you' and she did find me, took me to [a cafe]... And she just talked to me and said 'it's got to stop' [drug use] but she talked to me on my level when she was talking to me, she wasn't talking to me as this person that had to do their job, I was real to her, it helped.

Perspective is also important. Timoti's approach highlights that when workers define young people's behaviours as adaptations to their challenging environments they can create interventions that directly address the suffering that underpins this risky or troubling behaviour. So, for instance, in our research we noted how Josie was arrested for stealing from a supermarket. She explained that she had stolen sanitary products because her family had not provided these things. Josie's experiences of not having her material resource needs met by her family collided with 'structurally blind' welfare and justice systems that did not recognize the limited alternatives available to her (Goshe 2015, p.44). Accordingly, the system defined stealing as an indicator of delinquency rather than the best choice she could make in her circumstances. Interventions are more effective when social workers understand the internal logic that underpins individual youth behaviours that on the outside may appear maladaptive. Perspective also includes understanding how particular cultural meaning systems and social contexts shape behaviours (Benson *et al.* 2007).

Passion, patience, perseverance and perspective highlight the need for social workers to pay attention to their own emotional engagement in the support relationship. As Timoti suggested, successful support occurs when social workers genuinely appreciate the life the young person has lived and the skills they have developed in managing challenging lives.

A – adaptability, agility, action oriented, agency

I was lucky I guess, because my Carly (social worker) was based at school. She must have done a lot of fast talking to my teachers to get me back. I was actually kicked out for [fighting, stealing and selling drugs at school]. But when we had the meeting with the school bosses, Carly just argued and argued for me, she said stuff, stuff about me, my strengths, I didn't realize she saw those things. She got them to let me go back to school for a trial, she would supervise me and work with my teachers. I could go to her room whenever I needed to, so I had somewhere to go when I was losing it. She put [herself] on the line for me… No one had ever done that before. She got me helping her to work with younger kids at school who were [struggling]. It made me feel really good to help someone else, instead of being the person who was always in trouble, always the problem. (Jenna on her social worker)

While the impact of trauma on adolescent development is now well recognized and policies and practices increasingly emphasize trauma-related work (Cohen, Mannaruni and Deblinger 2006; Poole and Greaves 2012), the impact of structural factors on the capacity of young people to thrive is less well recognized, but equally important (Goshe 2014). Some vulnerability arises from youth behaviours, from exposure to trauma and dangers in the family (Gorur 2015; Rizvi 2015). However, neighbourhoods, social, political and economic systems also cause, contribute to or exacerbate trauma and so practice needs to directly address these factors as well (Goshe 2014; Metzler *et al.* 2017). As Jenna's account highlights, agile, action-oriented practice that looks for solutions in non-traditional places is required, and this includes collaborative work across disciplinary boundaries (Collins 2001).

Exclusion from education is a structural factor that creates vulnerability and risk (Coleman 2016; Lumby 2012; Sanders, Munford and Liebenberg 2016a; Sanders, Munford and Thimasarn-Anwar 2016b). While vulnerable young people find it hard to keep attending school, as Jenna's situation illustrates, schools also find it difficult to accommodate these students (Sanders and Munford 2015; Sanders *et al.* 2016a). In terms of practice, both the young person and the school need to be supported. Sometimes, this can mean advocating for extended time in a foster care placement because longer periods in care are linked with better educational outcomes (Collins 2001). In other cases, this may mean finding a place in an alternative educational programme to provide most of the educational input, while actively supporting re-integration into mainstream classrooms, perhaps on a sessional basis in a subject area where the young person has a particular interest. Alternatively, as in Jenna's situation, when a social worker advocates for the strengths of the young person, is willing to support teachers and provide supports for students who will otherwise be expelled, it is possible to return to mainstream classrooms.

At its most fundamental level, PARTH is about providing developmentally appropriate interventions with adolescents. This means providing opportunities for personal agency and autonomy. While it is important to encourage an active helping partnership with youth, practitioners can struggle to relinquish control and this can be particularly acute in mandated work (Walker and Donaldson 2010). However, even in mandated interventions, social workers can still encourage autonomy and agency. When the young person is not able to choose whether or not the service is involved in their life, they can still have choices about some aspects of the intervention, and practitioners can always ensure they listen to and respect the young person's perspectives (Liebenberg *et al.* 2016; Walker and Donaldson 2010).

Regardless of the setting, the priorities are to find opportunities for the young person to be an active decision- and choice-maker, and to be clear and transparent about those areas where such collaboration is not possible. Indeed, when programmes use collaborative rather command-and-control approaches, young people are more likely to see professional involvement as a positive resource (Benson *et al.* 2007; Collins 2001).

For instance, rather than punishing or controlling her, Jenna's social worker asked her to help with younger students, giving her responsibility in the process. The social worker also recognized that there would be times when Jenna needed to be able to leave the classroom without risking being punished and she made her office available for this purpose. Combined, these practical strategies recognized Jenna as a competent autonomous person who was an active partner in finding relevant and meaningful solutions. It also gave her responsibility and a sense of value. Our research indicated that these types of interventions resulted in better longer term outcomes (Sanders and Munford 2014; Sanders *et al.* 2017).

R – relationships based on respect and reciprocity, they are relevant and responsive

> Hine was raised by her grandmother from birth until her grandmother died when Hine was ten. The fact that child protection services allowed her first social worker to stay part of the process throughout the agency's seven-year involvement made a major difference. When she was placed out of the district, her social worker kept in touch by phone and regularly visited her. This relational continuity was of major importance to Hine. All her family members had abandoned Hine, leaving her with no strong kin relationships to call on once her grandmother died. She described her social worker as her 'government mummy'.
>
> Interviewer: What stands out as the best thing that someone's done for you?
>
> Hine: My social worker. I love her so much she's just pure awesomeness… I can't really explain it. She's always been there, she's like a real mummy. She's my government mummy. She's really cool. I am still in contact with her even though I am not with [service] anymore.

Positive, nurturing relationships between adults and youth are a central focus of PARTH and are critical to creating meaningful interventions with young people. Hine describes a support relationship that features genuine care and respect. Our research clearly identified that outcomes were better when practitioners provided positive, empowering and respectful interventions that recognized that the crises that brought them into services were embedded in longer term, chronic issues (Liebenberg *et al.* 2016; Sanders *et al.* 2017). Effective interventions were characterized by positive, enduring relationships between the social worker and young person that addressed both the crisis episode and the underlying issues (Munford and Sanders 2015, 2016a, 2016b; Stevens *et al.* 2014).

Family and peer relationships are often ignored in interventions with vulnerable youth (Walker and Donaldson 2010). Indeed, even when they are considered it is often because they are seen as exacerbating the risks around vulnerable youth (Collins 2001). The lack of attention given to the positive potential of family and friends is perplexing because services abruptly end for many young people as they age out of systems and then tend to gravitate back to their families and peer networks (Collins 2001; Noble-Carr and Woodman 2016; Walker and Donaldson 2010). PARTH recognizes the importance of relationships across the domains of young people's lives (such as family, peers, community and education). Family and friends constitute important protective resources, they assist young people in making sense of their experiences and they play important roles in the process of identity formation (Bulanda and Byro Johnson 2016). Without such positive, enduring relationships, young people create identity out of loss and negative relational experiences (Noble-Carr and Woodman 2016). For these reasons, it is critical to support relationships that are culturally relevant and meaningful by strengthening family and wider relational networks that will endure beyond the intervention.

The relational component of the PARTH model reminds practitioners of the need to build the capacity to care in the adults around the young person so that they can become an enduring, positive presence once the intervention has ended (Munford and Sanders 2016a). While PARTH is a youth-centred approach, this does not mean that family and other key relationships should be ignored. Being youth centred might mean working closely with a parent for a significant period of time and spending relatively little or no time with the young person. There is strong evidence that whole-family approaches are the most effective way of reducing risk factors because they increase the protective factors that support sustainable change (Walker and Donaldson 2010). Assisting parents to better meet their children's emotional needs is one very direct way of addressing the trauma, loss and the longing for strong family relationships that characterize the narratives of vulnerable youth (Noble-Carr and Woodman 2016).

The relevant aspect of the PARTH model reminds practitioners to respond to the very real daily challenges that vulnerable youth confront such as food and safe shelter. When young people are expected to make major changes in their lives, the strategies and resources we make available to them must be relevant, realistic and sustainable; they must manifestly improve the young person's circumstances. In this regard, addressing material deprivation and the way that structural factors marginalize youth is important. In Aotearoa New Zealand, culturally relevant work draws on manaakitanga (Munford and Sanders 2011), a respect-based process that intentionally demonstrates care and concern for others. Manaakitanga creates emotionally and physically safe places that are welcoming, caring and engender a sense of belonging.

T – time, trust, transparency, thresholds, transitions

> Maggie's school counsellor (Naomi) recognized that she was the only adult Maggie trusted. Naomi understood the importance of a trustworthy relationship with an adult during Maggie's transition from school to university. Maggie explains: '[by the last year at school] I was living with my counsellor. I couldn't have finished school otherwise. I still keep in contact with her; she still makes the time for me. It is incredible she did that.' While counsellors cannot take home all the vulnerable youth they meet, Naomi recognized that without this continuity Maggie would struggle to make a successful transition to university. Naomi responded by providing the support Maggie needed to achieve this transition. (Maggie and her school counsellor)

The quantity and quality of time is important. While the length of interventions should vary depending on youth need, it is important for practitioners to have sufficient time to establish the relationship and to create opportunities for critical learning moments (Scott and O'Neil 1996). Because vulnerable young people have experienced disruption and uncertainty throughout their childhoods, time has another meaning that highlights the importance of predictability, routine and structure (Noble-Carr and Woodman 2016; Stevens *et al.* 2014). Naomi demonstrated the importance of providing *containment*, a safe environment within which Maggie could learn coping skills and begin to articulate a different future to work towards (Shuttleworth 1991).

Trust-based relationships are the cornerstone of effective practice with vulnerable young people. They are transparent and involve young people in decision making. Trust is enhanced when practitioners explain why and how decisions are made. Building trusting relationships takes time, and organizations and policies need to explicitly allow for these time-intensive processes to occur (Stevens *et al.* 2014). Trust also calls for collaboration between the practitioners involved with the young person and their family (Walker and Donaldson 2010).

Service thresholds, entry criteria and waiting lists can delay interventions and result in young people being exposed to more harm; they can also undermine youth confidence that services will respond to their needs. Social workers have an advocacy role here in terms of ensuring that interventions are timely and respond to the unique needs of the young person (Cappelli *et al.* 2016; Coleman 2016).

Transitions between services and transitions out of services to independence need careful planning and management to ensure the best outcomes (Collins 2001). Transitions are critical moments in the lives of vulnerable young people, whether they are developmental, as in Maggie's case, or are changes in circumstances or movements between or out of services. Naomi understood that Maggie had experienced significant loss throughout her childhood and had been let down by adults and that this made her particularly vulnerable during this key transition (Noble-Carr and Woodman 2016). Ideally, transition planning comprises an integral part of the intervention right from the assessment and plans should be modified as circumstances change. In Maggie's case, there were no other responsible adults available to her to support this critical transition and Naomi's willingness to go beyond her role as a counsellor enabled Maggie to transition well to university and begin to write a new story for herself.

H – honesty, humility, a hopeful orientation

> Jazmine met Jayne, the group home parent, and was initially suspicious of her and her intentions. Jazmine said: 'Jayne was different to the other foster parents; she was really quiet, to start with I thought it was coz she was hiding things from me, that shit was about to happen. But she just kept on asking me what my goals were, what I wanted to be, where I wanted to go and then she would say, 'I am going to hold that dream for you and if you like we can work towards it together.' I thought it was shit, to be honest. But she just kept doing things like that and whenever things turned ugly, she would just keep reminding me of those dreams. … She also said to me right from the beginning, 'If something is going to change, I will tell you. If I can't do something, I will tell you. If I promise you something, I won't let you down.' You don't really believe this when you have been a foster kid. But after four years, now I look back she meant everything she said and she didn't say anything to me that she didn't mean. I still go back and see her; she is the one person through all my growing up who I could rely on. (Jazmine on her foster parent)

Young people told us that they appreciated it when practitioners were honest with them and gave them clear information about what was going to happen, even when this may have been a decision or outcome they did not want (Munford and Sanders 2016b). It is common for vulnerable youth who are clients of major service systems to experience being let down by the adults who are responsible for their care (Driscoll 2011). When practitioners withhold information or do not keep their promises, they resemble the unreliable adults in young people's own worlds (Driscoll 2011). Social workers can make a positive difference in young people's lives when, like Jayne, they keep their word and do what they say they will do. These practitioners are also honest about their limitations, and when difficult decisions have to be made they are honest about these.

As Anthony's social worker explained, humility calls for practitioners to recognize that if they were in the young person's shoes they might well make the same choices. Naomi demonstrated humility by holding her expertise lightly and being willing to step out of her role as a counsellor when she realized she could make a greater difference for Maggie by providing her with a safe place to live. In Aotearoa New Zealand, humility is often enacted through the culturally tuned concept of Ako (Munford and Sanders 2011). Ako encourages practitioners to recognize that the expertise and knowledge young people bring to the intervention is critical to sustainable change. Jayne illustrated Ako by not only holding Jazmine's hopes but also by making them the centre of her support, something she kept returning to in conversation with Jazmine. To be effective, practitioners must engage with the young person's story; this has both objective and subjective components – hearing what is said and emotionally connecting with the meaning of those experiences as they were experienced by the young person. The helping relationship is a place where young people can gain the confidence to talk about their dreams. A key social work task is supporting youth to access the resources and skills they need to work towards these dreams. Jazmine's account clearly demonstrated that holding hope and a positive vision for the future are important roles for the practitioner (Bulanda and Byro Johnson 2016; Handley *et al.* 2009).

Challenges

PARTH provides a set of orientations that social workers can use when supporting vulnerable youth. It is based on youth reports of the types of support relationships that work best for them. PARTH raises some challenges for social workers, particularly around being able to make the time available to build the strong, positive relationships young people said they needed. Caseload pressures can interrupt good relationship-building practices, particularly in the early stages of the intervention when the social worker will need to *prove* that they are available and will respond to the young person. Funding needs to ensure that time is available for these aspects of the work. PARTH calls for strong collaborations between professionals, and social workers may find it challenging to draw other professionals into the helping alliances; these professionals may feel that it is the social worker's job alone. However, social workers cannot do PARTH alone; PARTH requires collaborative, community effort. Vulnerability is created and sustained when multiple systems of influence fail to create opportunities for young people. This raises policy and organizational challenges because communities often struggle to provide the resources young people need. If social workers are to effectively utilize PARTH practices, communities need to be adequately resourced.

Conclusion

Adolescence is an opportunity to have a positive impact on adulthood outcomes, and there are therefore pressing reasons to understand how vulnerability accumulates during childhood and then manifests itself in different facets of youth lives. Exposure to multiple risks during childhood compromises positive development. It impacts negatively on developing brains. Positive development occurs when youth have a sense of belonging, being useful, competent, valuable and powerful. It is not only what social workers do in their work with vulnerable young people but also how they do it that creates the possibility of change. The PARTH orientations provide a framework which social workers can use to guide how they do their work of intentionally supporting young people's positive development.

Reflection questions

- Why do relationships matter? Describe the characteristics of effective practitioner–youth relationships.

- Why is it important for practitioners to identify people in youth networks that are positive and supportive?

- Describe the challenges a practitioner might face in trying to draw adults from young people's own networks into the support process. What sorts of strategies might help here?

- Why does resilience have a good conceptual fit with PYD? Why do PYD approaches work well with vulnerable young people?

- Are risks or strengths more important in PYD interventions? Explain your answer.

- Give some examples of individual and contextual risks. Explain what types of PYD responses would be appropriate to each type of risk.

- Why are autonomy and agency important in interventions with youth? What sorts of practices encourage youth autonomy?

- Why is it important to understand youth culture and context?

References

Bastiaanssen, I., Delsing, M., Kroes, G., Engels, R. and Veerman, J. (2014) 'Group care worker interventions and child problem behavior in residential youth care: Course and bidirectional associations.' *Children and Youth Services Review 39*, 48–56.

Becroft, A. (2016) *Ministry for Vulnerable Children Name 'Stigmatising and Labelling'.* Accessed on 02/06/2017 at www.stuff.co.nz/national/faces-of-innocents/82699004/ministry-for-vulnerable-children-name-stigmatising-and-labelling.

Benson, P., Scales, P., Hamilton, S. and Sesma, A. (2007) 'Positive Youth Development: Theory, Research, and Applications.' In W. Damon, R. Lerner and E. Pearson (eds) *Handbook of Child Psychology* (6th edition, vol. 1). Hoboken, NJ: John Wiley & Sons.

Bulanda, J. and Byro Johnson, T. (2016) 'A trauma-informed model for empowerment programs targeting vulnerable youth.' *Child and Adolescent Social Work Journal 33*, 303–312.

Cappelli, M., Davidson, S., Racek, J., Leon, S. *et al.* (2016) 'Transitioning youth into adult mental health and addiction services: An outcomes evaluation of the Youth Transition Project.' *Journal of Behavioural Health Services and Research 43*, 4, 597–610.

Cohen, J., Mannarino, A. and Deblinger, E. (2006) *Treating Trauma and Traumatic Grief in Children and Adolescents.* New York, NY: The Guilford Press.

Cole, A. (2016) 'All of us are vulnerable, but some are more vulnerable than others: The political ambiguity of vulnerability studies, an ambivalent critique.' *Critical Horizons 17*, 2, 260–277.

Coleman, C. (2016) *Did We Miss the Boat? The Need for a Paradigm Shift in Policy and Service Provision for Youth and Young Parents Transitioning from the Youth Services System in the Canadian Province of Newfoundland and Labrador.* Grand Forks, ND: University of North Dakota.

Collins, M. (2001) 'Transition to adulthood for vulnerable youths: A review of research and implications for policy.' *Social Services Review 75*, 2, 271–291.

Daniel, B. (2010) 'Concepts of adversity, risk, vulnerability and resilience: A discussion in the context of the "Child Protection System".' *Social Policy & Society 9*, 2, 231–241.

Dewar, L. and Goodman, D. (2014) *Literature Review: Best Practices in Transitioning Youth out of Care, Successful Transitions, Success as Adults.* Toronto, ON: Children's Aid Society of Toronto Child Welfare Institute.

Driscoll, J. (2011) 'Making up lost ground: Challenges in supporting the educational attainment of looked after children beyond Key Stage 4.' *Adoption & Fostering 35*, 18–31.

DuMont, K., Widom, C. and Czaja, S. (2007) 'Predictors of resilience in abused and neglected children grown-up: The role of individual and neighbourhood characteristics.' *Child Abuse & Neglect 31*, 255–274.

Duncan, B., Miller, S. and Sparks, J. (2004) *The Heroic Client: A Revolutionary Way to Improve Effectiveness Through Client-Directed, Outcome-Informed Therapy*. San Francisco, CA: Jossey-Bass.

Everall, R. and Paulson, B. (2002) 'The therapeutic alliance: Adolescent perspectives.' *Counselling and Psychotherapy 2*, 2, 78–87.

Fallis, J. (2012) *Literature Review: The Needs of Youth Transitioning from Protective Care and Best Practice Approaches to Improve Outcomes*. Winnipeg, Manitoba, Canada. Report for the General Child and Family Services Authority.

Felitti, V., Anda, R., Nordenberg, D., Williamson, D. *et al.* (1998) *Vulnerable Youth: Background and Policies*. Washington, DC: Congressional Research Service.

Foster, K. and Spencer, D. (2011) 'At risk of what? Possibilities over probabilities in the study of young lives.' *Journal of Youth Studies 14*, 1, 125–143.

Gorur, R. (2015) 'Vulnerability: Construct, Complexity and Consequences.' In K. ti Riele and R. Gorur (eds) *Interrogating Conceptions of 'Vulnerable Youth' in Theory, Policy and Practice*. Rotterdam: Sense Publishers.

Goshe, S. (2015) 'Moving beyond the punitive legacy: Taking stock of persistent problems in juvenile justice.' *Youth Justice 15*, 1, 44.

Handley, K., Horn, S., Kaipuke, R., Maden, B. *et al.* (2009) *The Spinafex Effect: Developing a Theory of Change for Communities*. New Zealand: Families Commission.

Jobe, A. and Gorin, S. (2013) '"If kids don't feel safe they don't do anything": Young people's views on seeking and receiving help from Children's Social Care Services in England.' *Child and Family Social Work 18*, 429–438.

Kroll, B. (2010) 'Only Connect…Building Relationships with Hard-to-Reach People: Establishing Rapport with Drug-Misusing Parents and their Children.' In G. Ruch, D. Turney and A. Ward (eds) *Relationship-Based Social Work: Getting to the Heart of Practice*. London: Jessica Kingsley Publishers.

Lerner, R.M. (2004) *Liberty: Thriving and Civic Engagement among America's Youth*. Thousand Oaks, CA: Sage.

Lerner, R. (2005) *Promoting Positive Youth Development: Theoretical and Empirical Bases*. White paper prepared for: Workshop on the science of adolescent health and development. Washington DC: National Research Council.

Liebenberg, L., Sanders, J. and Munford, J. (2016) 'A Positive Youth Development Measure of service use satisfaction for youth: The 13-item Youth Services Satisfaction Measure (YSS-13).' *Children and Youth Services Review 71*, 84–92.

Lumby, J. (2012) 'Disengaged and disaffected young people: Surviving the system.' *British Educational Research Journal 38*, 2, 261–279.

McLeod, A. (2007) 'Whose agenda? Issues of power and relationship when listening to looked-after young people.' *Child and Family Social Work 12*, 278–286.

Masten, A. (2014) 'Global perspectives on resilience in children and youth.' *Child Development 85*, 1, 6–20.

Merrick, M., Leeb, R. and Lee, R. (2013) 'Examining the role of safe, stable, and nurturing relationships in the intergenerational continuity of maltreatment – introduction to the special issue.' *Journal of Adolescent Health 53*, 5, S1–S3.

Metzler, M., Merrick, M., Klevens, J., Ports, K. and Ford, D. (2017) 'Adverse childhood experiences and life opportunities: Shifting the narrative.' *Children and Youth Services Review 72*, 141–149.

Mitchell, P. (2011) 'Evidence-based practice in real-world services for young people with complex needs: New opportunities suggested by recent implementation science.' *Children and Youth Services Review 33*, 207–216.

Munford, R. and Sanders, J. (2011) 'Embracing the diversity of practice: Indigenous knowledge and mainstream social work practice.' *Journal of Social Work Practice 25*, 1, 63–77.

Munford, R. and Sanders, J. (2015) 'Components of effective social work practice in mental health for young people who are users of multiple services.' *Social Work in Mental Health 13*, 5, 415–438.

Munford, R. and Sanders, J. (2016a) 'Foster parents: An enduring presence for vulnerable youth.' *Adoption & Fostering 40*, 3, 264–278.

Munford, R. and Sanders, J. (2016b) 'Finding meaningful support: Young people's experiences of "risky" environments.' *Australian Social Work 69*, 2, 229–240.

Noble-Carr, D. and Woodman, E. (2018) 'Considering identity and meaning constructions for vulnerable young people.' *Journal of Adolescent Research 33*, 6, 672–698.

Poole, N. and Greaves, L. (2012) *Becoming Trauma Informed*. Toronto, ON: Centre for Addiction and Mental Health.

Rizvi, F. (2015) 'Foreword.' In K. ti Riele and R. Gorur (eds) *Interrogating Conceptions of 'Vulnerable Youth' in Theory, Policy and Practice*. Rotterdam: Sense Publishers.

Ruch, G., Turney, D. and Ward, A. (2010) *Relationship-Based Social Work: Getting to the Heart of Practice*. London: Jessica Kingsley Publishers.

Sanders, J. and Munford, R. (2014) 'Youth-centred practice: Positive youth development practices and pathways to better outcomes.' *Children and Youth Services Review 46*, 160–167.

Sanders, J. and Munford, R. (2015) 'Fostering a sense of belonging at school – five orientations to practice that assist vulnerable youth to create a positive student identity.' *School Psychology International 37*, 2, 155–171.

Sanders, J., Munford, R. and Liebenberg, L. (2016a) 'The role of schools in building resilience of at risk youth.' *International Journal of Educational Research 80*, 111–123.

Sanders, J., Munford, R. and Thimasarn-Anwar, T. (2016b) 'Staying on track despite the odds: Factors that assist young people facing adversity to continue with their education.' *British Journal of Educational Research 42*, 1, 56–76.

Sanders, J., Munford, R. and Liebenberg, L. (2017) 'Positive youth development practices and better outcomes for high risk youth.' *Child Abuse and Neglect 69*, 201–212.

Scott, D. and O'Neil, D. (1996) *Beyond Child Rescue: Developing Family-Centred Practice at St Luke's*. Sydney: Allen and Unwin.

Shuttleworth, J. (1991) 'Psychoanalytic Theory and Infant Development.' In L. Miller, M. Rustin, M. Rustin and J. Shuttleworth (eds) *Closely Observed Infants*. London: Duckworth.

Smyth, P. (2013) 'A different approach to high-risk youths.' *Social Work Today 13*, 6, 10.

Stein, M., Ward, H. and Courtney, M. (2011) 'Editorial: International perspectives on young people's transitions from care to adulthood.' *Children and Youth Services Review 33*, 12, 2409–2411.

Stevens, K., Munford, R., Sanders, J., Liebenberg, L. and Ungar, M. (2014) 'Change, relationships and implications for practice: The experiences of young people who use multiple services.' *International Journal of Child, Youth and Family Studies 5*, 3, 447–465.

Thurston, J. (2016) 'What works: A new model of public service delivery?' *Practice: The New Zealand Corrections Journal 4*, 65–68.

Walker, J. and Donaldson, C. (2010) *Intervening to Improve Outcomes for Vulnerable Young People: A Review of the Evidence*. Research Report DFE-RR078. London: Department for Education.

• Chapter 2 •

Family Support and Social Work Practice

JOHN PINKERTON, JOHN CANAVAN AND PAT DOLAN

Introduction

As has been well established, no family life occurs in isolation. Building on that simple premise, this chapter considers how social work practice with children and families can ensure that social environment is considered not only as a contributory factor to deficits and difficulties but also as a source of potential strength and solutions. Arguably, this family support perspective has been at the core of social work since its origins. Yet it continues to prove extraordinarily difficult for social work practitioners to turn it into effective everyday practice. The challenge for social workers wishing to engage in family support practice is to grasp its breadth beyond their professional role while at the same time understanding how in accord it is with social work. Meeting that challenge has to include recognizing the difficulties posed for family support practice by the predominance of child protection as the contemporary driving logic behind most social work practice with families, whether that means identifying and managing risk to individual children, through national surveillance and intervention systems, or the provision of social protection for large scale populations, as promoted by global development agencies such as UNICEF (The United Nations Children's Fund).

This chapter aims to interweave social work and family support by focusing on the social ecology of family life as the core concern of social work practice with children and their carers. This concern requires expression at all five phases of the social work process: preparation, assessment, planning, intervention and evaluation (Parker 2017). Family support requires that the focus on family social ecology is held whatever the immediate goal of social work intervention (Gilligan 2000).

An ecological model of family support along with ten family support principles (Canavan, Pinkerton and Dolan 2016) will be set out as the basis on which to assess needs and to plan interventions selected from a 'diverse "tool kit" of skills and approaches' (Frost, Abbott and Race 2015, p.3). The importance of enlisting and mobilizing social support to reinforce and build resilience and social capital within the social ecology of the family will be stressed as the key goal of practice. Working through relationships will be presented as the core component of the work, with the personal encounter between social worker and family members emphasized as the axis of practice, enabled and constrained by the organizational, cultural and structural context (Thompson 2017).

Family support landscape

A core feature of social work practice is attention to process. Faced with the urgency of need it is both difficult and yet essential to attend to what will always be an unfolding of a beginning, middle and end to the work of creatively and effectively linking provision to need. To help discipline practice and to aid the social worker in managing what can be an overwhelming urge to reach out prematurely for an end goal, the social work process can usefully be considered as having five sequential phases: preparation, assessment, planning, intervention and evaluation. Preparation requires tuning in (Douglas and McColgan 1999) to the field of work so as to understand what it is that the social worker has available to bring to the encounter with a service user. Tuning in to family support is where social work practice in this field must begin.

In recent decades, family support has gained and maintained, despite some waxing and waning in influence, an important place among the key organizing concepts of child welfare policy and practice used by a variety of occupational groups in a range of countries (Canavan *et al.* 2016). Globally, family support practice is firmly rooted in rights discourses and in particular, the United Nations Convention on the Rights of the Child (UNCRC) – an international human rights treaty that grants all children and young people a comprehensive set of rights (United Nations 1989). Not only does the UNCRC direct practice towards a child's right to family life and parenting (Articles 9, 10 and 18), but all three of the central domains it covers – that is, protection, participation and provision – are directly relevant to family support practice.

From a review of recent literature and web sources it would be easy to think that this interest in family support is relatively new and linked to the development of early intervention and prevention programmes, driven by the imperatives of evidence-based practice – transparent methods, proven achievement of outcomes and cost effectiveness. In anglophone countries of the Global North there has been an expansion in the development and use by a range of agencies and types of staff of such programmes as Sure Start (Belsky *et al.* 2006), Incredible Years (Webster-Stratton and Reid 2010), Triple P parenting (Sanders 2012) and Signs of Safety (Turnell and Murphy 2017). However, that expansion needs to be seen as building on earlier programmes, such as Parent Effectiveness Training, and Family Group Conferencing (Connolly and Mason 2014), which draw on a greater range of national experiences and broader traditions of practice. This wider perspective reveals a family support literature that provides a deep and growing international pool of experience and understanding (Canavan, Dolan and Pinkerton 2000; Churchill and Sen 2016; Daly *et al.* 2015; Davies 2012; Devaney 2017; Dolan, Canavan and Pinkerton 2006; Featherstone 2006; Frost *et al.* 2015; Katz and Pinkerton 2003; Statham and Smith 2010).

Many family support programmes are designed as interventions based on the ages and stages of psychosocial child development. In particular, they reflect an appreciation of the importance of investing in the first three years of life to provide a sound platform for later development (Heckman 2006). Such early childhood development programmes are concerned with enhancing parenting skills and enriching children's experiences to promote normative development, in particular school readiness. A good example of those programmes is Sure Start in the UK.

Internationally, there are numerous parenting programmes alongside a growth in other forms of family support (Daly *et al.* 2015). However, these developments are regionally uneven. Some countries have introduced new policies and practices and in others, there has been a re-orientation or re-framing of existing provision (Daly *et al.* 2015). UNICEF has identified family support as a strategy in violence prevention and is testing out programmes in the Global South (see Cluver *et al.* 2016). Developments are led in some countries by the state and in others by non-government organizations or faith-based organizations. In some countries, family support means meeting needs as basic as food, water and shelter along with access to education and health services. In others, family support is about advancing the social and psychological needs of both children and their parents. Many programmes focus on positive parenting and include teaching skills in managing specific issues that arise during childhood and adolescence.

In the latency years, alongside the role of schools in providing opportunities for sporting and leisure activities, there are specific family support programmes. Examples are Experience Corps/Wizard of Words, which focus on literacy support, involving semi-formal support by older volunteers, and the Incredible Years programme, which targets behavioural issues for children in this age group by working with children and parents (Fives *et al.* 2013; Webster-Stratton and Reid 2010). In relation to early, middle and late adolescence, there is a range of programmes including youth mentoring, youth development projects, and mental and sexual health initiatives. These are based in both schools and community settings. Other programmes target specific issues. Alateen, for example, supports young people dealing with alcohol addiction in their family. There are also support services for young carers. Family members living with a disability may receive services focused on sustaining and enhancing their lives and ensuring they have their rights upheld and full access to community living.

There are various modes of family support delivery. It can involve focusing on the needs of a single individual within a family with a human services worker providing one-to-one skills training or counselling, arranging peer-to-peer mentoring, or engaging the individual in group work. The family itself may be the focus for change, with some variation of family therapy being provided. In addition to help in the home, school or community can provide sites for the different modes of delivery and can themselves be the target of change. The provision of programmes in school settings is increasing, including school-based peer-to-peer mentoring (Dolan and Brady 2012). Many schools offer social and personal health programmes, but young people often prefer services to be delivered outside both home and school. This can be in a non-stigmatizing setting such as a drop-in youth cafe where a targeted programme on sexual health or substance abuse can be delivered in a discreet manner.

For adolescents with particular mental health issues, community adolescent mental health services are increasingly available with attention given to outreach. Many young people have access to youth clubs along with more targeted youth programmes available to them locally in community settings. Those settings may be community development projects or a community-based social service centre/clinic. The Communities That Care programme addresses issues for children and parents through localized but targeted support interventions.[1] The underlying ethos of the programme is that families who have issues should not be segregated or stigmatized. As typically family problems are occurring within their local community, it is the obvious site for seeking and implementing solutions.

---

1   www.blueprintsprograms.com/factsheet/communities-that-care.

Many of the more recent family support programmes have been developed by helping professionals, such as psychologists and social workers. These tend to be outcomes focused, targeting behavioural change on the part of parents and carers and children and young people. Many are manualized and require professionally qualified practitioners to implement them with attention to programme fidelity (Frost and Dolan 2012; Frost *et al.* 2015). Some of these include the explicit use of logic models and theories of change. This psychosocial learning approach can appear rigid, with its sequential unfolding of assessment, intervention, monitoring of progress, managed closure and evaluation of success under the direction of an 'expert' practitioner. However, there is usually also a strong emphasis on the wider supportive functions of the programme and on the relationship skills and empathy of the practitioner delivering it.

One final point to note is the importance of not allowing only the evaluated, licensed, and well-marketed programmes to determine the parameters of family support. There are numerous local and regionally developed programmes in existence which also need to be recognized for their effectiveness and usefulness to families. A government-commissioned review of such family support programmes and projects in Ireland drew attention to their common components (Brady, Dolan, and Canavan 2004). The key factor central to success was not some aspect of service design but 'leadership' provided by an identifiable member of staff. These individuals, most typically a project leader, were found to act as advocate and champion for both the service and the service users alike. Family support is always contingent on the individuals, both human services workers and family members, their circumstances and their relationships at particular points in time (McCormack 2012). This includes relationships within and across organizations. Family support practice requires boundary-spanning leadership that is effective in working across disciplines and organizations (Canavan *et al.* 2016; Williams 2013).

Theorizing family support

Two things should stand out from this tuning into the existing field – the range and the flexibility of what can be encompassed by the term family support. Those two characteristics have been crucial to ensuring the usefulness and longevity as an organizing concept within the child welfare field. However, that range and flexibility have also been its major weakness. To date, family support has lacked sufficient theoretical, empirical and programmatic coherence to set a strengths-based child welfare agenda against the prevailing deficit logic of child protection. Rather, the concept has been used to articulate aspects of more or less compatible policy and practice – a role it has played alongside, and at times in competition with, the concepts of prevention and early intervention. It has covered up significant orientations to policy and practice. Protection from risk is not necessarily the same as promotion of support (Canavan *et al.* 2016).

To some extent, those different orientations to family support reflect different occupational perspectives. That should not distract from acknowledging that within social work itself there is a very real tension between a social justice vision of solidarity with families in straitened circumstances and the technocratic pursuit of classification and management of risk within failing families. Since the days of the Charity Organization Society and the Settlement movement at the turn of the 20th century (Payne 2005), that tension has played out, often creatively, according to time and place, arriving at provisional, relatively temporary, and sometimes hotly contested, resolution (Devaney and Spratt 2009; Munford and Sanders 2017).

> Social work with children and families reflects a fundamental tension between Family Support and child protection… This tension is present in legislation, governmental guidance, agency policy and individual practice. The resolution of that tension, whether it be at policy level and the way services are designed and delivered, or within an individual social worker's practice, is what shapes the services children and families receive. (Nelson 2005, p.21)

Individual social workers need to reflect on where their own position is on that tension and how it is informed by their values, knowledge, skills and practice experiences. As yet there is no distinct family support theory to help inform that critical reflection. There is, however, a wide range of relevant theory informing the various expressions of family support. In one way, that is an inductive strength, encouraging lived experience to determine theoretical articulation. It encourages theoretical flexibility through pursuit of theory that seems likely to be most helpful in describing and analysing particular instances of family support.

However, such eclecticism begs the question of how theories get to be candidates for selection and plays down the theoretically informed, deductive aspect of reflective practice. While family support is not yet a distinct theory in its own right, there are four core constructs, each with an associated theoretical base, that usefully complement each other in a manner that provides a coherent theoretical foundation. The four constructs are social ecology, resilience, social support and social capital (Canavan *et al.* 2016).

Social ecology

Social ecology directs attention to 'the ways in which people and their habitats shape and influence one another through a process of reciprocal interactions between individuals and groups and their immediate and wider environments' (Jack 1997, p.109). It emphasizes the multiple dimensions to be considered in understanding psychosocial development – physical, social, economic and cultural environments as well as personal attributes. It also considers the multiple levels at which processes of development play out – within the individual, the immediate family, informal groups and formal organizations. Perhaps most importantly, it has at its core a concern to give cognisance to the complexity of the cumulative impact of processes and events over time, expressed at both biographical and historical scale.

This perspective is most clearly set out in the influential work of Urie Bronfenbrenner (1979), which is well known for its powerful image of the developing child nested in four interlocking, interdependent systems. The first of these, the micro-system, is where close relationships are experienced, positive and negative, with parents and siblings, extended family, friends and neighbours. Where these micro-systems engage or overlap, they collectively constitute the meso-system. For example, a child's meso-system might comprise her immediate family, the school which she attends, and the neighbourhood football club of which she is a member. Beyond the meso-system there lies the exo-system, in which the child has no direct involvement but is affected by it through the ramifications of the influence it has over the first two systems. A parent's workplace and local political institutions may be key constituents of the exo-system, providing enrichment or impoverishment to the meso- and micro-systems. The fourth and overarching system is the macro-system. Here the spheres of law, politics, culture and the economic order establish the ideological and material master pattern of the whole social formation in which a person's development takes place.

Resilience

At the core of resilience as an organizing concept is the recognition that children and young people can achieve good outcomes in the face of significant adverse conditions through the interplay of risk and protective factors, internal and external. There is no one agreed definition of resilience. However, whatever the emphasis in the different definitions of resilience, either implicit or explicit, in all of them are concerns with development, adaptation and outcomes, coping with threats and adversity, individual and environmental interaction, and supportive and undermining factors (Canavan 2007).

To move away from any lingering association of resilience with an individual's character traits and to make it applicable across cultures, the definition usefully emphasizes that it refers to relationships within a process of navigation and negotiation:

> In the context of exposure to significant adversity, whether psychological, environmental, or both, resilience is both the capacity of individuals to navigate their way to health-sustaining resources, including opportunities to experience feelings of wellbeing, and a condition of the individual's family, community and culture to provide these health resources and experiences in culturally meaningful ways. (Ungar 2008, p.225)

Situated and de-centred in this way, resilience becomes more a characteristic of the social ecology of which the individual is a part, rather than just of the individual. That said, even with that definition it remains the case that resilience can only be measured in terms of outcomes achieved by an individual relative to what was expected.

Resilience is associated with a range of factors amenable to intervention and change: a secure attachment with another person; having positive relationships with friends; a positive experience in some particular aspect of their life; feeling in control over decisions in life; being given the chance of a 'turning point', such as a new opportunity or a break from a high-risk situation. Resilience is often conceptualized in relation to these risk and protective factors: 'those characteristics, variables, or hazards that, if present for a given individual, make it more likely that this individual, rather than someone selected at random from the general population, will develop a disorder' (Mrazek and Haggerty 1994, p.12). Protective factors, however, 'reduce the likelihood of problem behaviour either directly or by mediating or moderating the effect of exposure to risk factors' (Arthur et al. 2002, p.576). Whatever the experiences in earlier life there is still the opportunity of introducing protective factors at later stages. Provision of such opportunities through family support can help build resilience and counter previous disadvantage (Gilligan 2009). Indeed, there is even evidence of steeling effects in which successful coping with stress or adversity at an early stage in life can lead to improved functioning and increased resistance to stress/adversity later on (Rutter 2012).

Social support

Social support is both the perception and the actuality of having assistance available from other people. In the main, this support is accessed from the central helping system found in the micro- and meso-systems of the informal networks of nuclear and extended family and to a lesser extent friendships (Canavan *et al.* 2000; Cutrona 2000). It is generally only when that support is perceived or experienced as weak, non-existent or incapable of offering help when required, that a person will turn, or be directed, to formal sources of support. This is not to counterpoise the informal and the formal as an either/or choice. Informal support has the advantage of being non-stigmatizing, offered at no cost and available as and when needed. There are, however, types and degrees of need where professional help is clearly required (Gardner 2003). Thus, formal support can both supplement and complement the informal. It can even, for short periods, substitute it.

There are specific kinds and qualities of support available to families. Four main types of support have been identified (Cutrona 2000): concrete support, which relates to practical acts of assistance between people; emotional support, which comprises acts of empathy, listening and generally being there for someone when needed; advice support, which goes beyond the advice itself to the reassurance that goes with it; esteem support, which centres on how one person rates and informs another of their personal worth.

In addition to noting the different types of support, it is important to recognize that there are variations in the quality of support. That is expressed in three major ways. First, closeness expresses the extent to which support can be assumed and given because of mutual affection between partners, near family members and long-established friends. A second dimension is reciprocity that involves activity whereby help is exchanged equally between people, and ensures that a person does not feel beholden to another. There is a comfort and security that goes with knowing that the exchange of support is available if and when it is needed. The third dimension is durability, which relates to the contact rates and length of time people are known to each other. Ideally, reliable members are those who are known for a long period, are nearby to offer help, and typically are in no way intrusive. Understanding the types and qualities of support in play is crucial to assessing family situations and planning ways for mobilizing and strengthening resources.

Social capital

Although still a contested and developing concept (Field 2003), social capital can helpfully be defined as 'the sum of the resources, actual or virtual, that accrue to an individual or a group by virtue of possessing a durable network of more or less institutionalized relationships of mutual acquaintance and recognition' (Bourdieu and Wacquaint quoted in Henderson *et al.* 2007, p.12). Those networks of support consolidate into social capital. Three different types of social capital have been identified in the literature: bonding social capital connects people with similar characteristics in relationships of solidarity based on shared experiences and values. Bridging social capital extends those relationships through making connections between one bonded network and another different one. Bonding social capital constitutes a kind of sociological superglue, whereas bridging social capital provides a sociological WD-40 (Putnam 2000 quoted in Barry 2012, p.56). There is also linking social capital, which is a relationship between an individual and a figure of power outside their informal networks, such as a local politician or a formal service provider of health, education or social care.

It is important to recognize that all forms of social capital are based on active contact and carry with them moral obligations:

> [Social capital is] developed in our relationships, through doing things for one another and the trust that we develop in one another. It helps in bonding fragmented social life; in the bridging of communities to places and contacts beyond their immediate environment and in the linking of people to formal structures and agencies that they may need for help with opportunities for education and employment. (Catts and Ozga quoted in Allan and Catts 2012, p.6)

Family support interventions can be seen as a form of social capital building (Broadhead, Meleady and Delgado 2008). Thus, social capital can be viewed as developmental assets realized through effective social support. For some families, realizing this personal potential will require additional formal family support interventions aimed at bolstering the type and quality of social support available to them in their social ecology, in effect linking capital. It is important to recognize that there can be negative features to social capital. It can exclude as well as include and reinforce oppressive hierarchies of power within social networks based, for example, on age, gender and class.

Integrated social ecology

It is clear that these four theories are connected and share common elements; for example, the link between social support enlistment through mobilizing bonding and bridging social capital in order to build resilience (Canavan *et al.* 2016). This is represented in Figure 2.1 as the social ecology of family support. Children and young people require the support of immediate family. Family rests on the support of extended family, which in turn draws on wider informal networks of friends, neighbours and community. These various sources of informal support provide bonding capital that in turn needs to be able to access a wide range of formal institutions within the statutory, community, voluntary and private sectors to establish bridging and linking capital to meet educational, health and recreational needs and give expression to rights. Statutory, community, voluntary and private sectors require support from national policy and legislation, which is in turn increasingly underwritten by global conventions and institutions (Canavan *et al.* 2016). The arrows in Figure 2.1 are to indicate a dynamic at play within and across all the layers of the social ecology of family support. That dynamic expresses and determines the interconnections, characteristics and direction of change within the social ecology as well as over historical and biographical time.

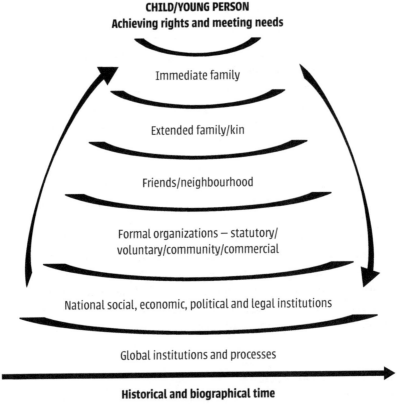

Figure 2.1: The social ecology of family support

Family support practice

Informed by the social ecology of family support, it is possible to arrive at a definition of family support:

> Family Support is both a style of work and a set of activities; which reinforce positive informal social networks through integrated programmes; combining statutory, voluntary, community and private services, primarily focused on early intervention across a range of levels and needs with the aim of promoting and protecting the health, wellbeing and rights of all children, young people and their families in their own homes and communities, with particular attention to those who are vulnerable or at risk. (Canavan *et al.* 2016, p.20)

Combining the seven layers of family support (see Figure 2.1) in a single definition makes for an unwieldly sentence but very importantly underscores the integrated nature of family support. All seven elements should have equal attention and all need to be present. The definition also needs to be underpinned by a set of ten practice principles:

- Child centred: focus on the wishes, feelings, safety and wellbeing of children.

- Needs led: bringing together assessed and expressed needs with the minimum intervention required.

- Strengths based: mindful of resilience as a characteristic of the lives of many children and families.

- Socially inclusive: addressing issues around ethnicity, disability and rural/urban communities.

- Partnership based: including children, parents, other carers, professionals and communities.

- Informal network focused: utilizing and strengthening informal support networks.

- Easily accessed: facilitating self-referral and multi-access referral paths.

- Responsive and flexible: attending to location, timing, setting and changing needs, incorporating both child protection and out-of-home care.

- Collaborative in development: involving service users and providers in the planning, delivery and evaluation.

- Evidence informed: building in measures of success based on research and case-specific outcomes indicators to judge progress and improve services.

The definition and practice principles express a social justice vision of solidarity with families in straitened circumstances. That vision sits well with the emancipatory tradition within social work (Thompson 2017). It also challenges social workers to assess the social ecologies of families they are engaged with in a way that identifies the resilience to be found in individual family members and their relationships within the whole of the family social ecology, including the meso- and macro-systems (Jack and Gill 2010a; Jack and Gill 2010b). Through informed planning and skilled intervention, resilience can be supported and mobilized or be protected and strengthened by additional resources.

The required additional support can be specific family support resources (Frost *et al.* 2015). For example, in Northern Ireland, family support hubs have been developed as an interagency and intersectoral mechanism to enable the matching of family support provision to individual and family need (Health and Social Care Board/Social Care Institute for Excellence 2016). Hubs are not bricks and mortar places but an organizational mechanism with dedicated staff, regular meetings and a website. They facilitate professional and self-referral to a wide range of services, providing both practical and more intensive support. They have provided a platform to reinstate the centrality of the voluntary and community sector in the delivery of support services, which are accessible, timely, flexible and non-stigmatizing. The growing awareness of hubs has encouraged families to seek help when issues emerge, secure in knowing services are only delivered via the hub where there is informed consent and families can engage voluntarily.

However, it is equally important to recognize that family support interventions by social workers draw on the mainstream of their practice. In reviewing a set of four family support cases, which included high-risk child-protection concerns involving maternal rejection, drug dependency, parental disability, identity confusion and disruptive acting-out behaviour, a Scottish social worker identified six central common themes: building relationships; subjectivity (use of self); thresholds and boundaries (multi-agency working); collaboration with family members; avoiding dependency; and clarifying objectives (McCormack 2012). These are all mainstream social work practice themes:

> Interventions with the individual can work to increase self-esteem, self-worth, coping skills, autonomy and competence, or attempt to decrease psychic discomfort. Interventions in families and groups can work to enable the members to recognize and change their interactions and patterns of communication. Alternatively, interventions into the environment can work to increase the adaptive fit for individuals, such as attempting to reduce and eliminate discrimination, oppression and prejudices, and increase opportunities for individuals and groups to actively engage with the environment to meet their specific needs. (Teater 2014, p.26)

Case study: Anne

Anne is a lone parent with three young boys, aged 18 months, 3 years and 7 years old. She lives in a small rural village in a very run-down home and is living on a very low income. She has limited contact with her family and even less with her neighbours, some of whom distrust her because of her excessive drinking and apparent neglect of her children. Anne was reported by a neighbour to the child welfare authorities following the neighbour witnessing a 'slapping attack' on the 3-year-old by the mother. The case was allocated for social work assessment, and other incidents of physical and emotional abuse involving all three children were uncovered. Removal of the children from Anne's care was considered but deferred to explore community-based options.

From the outset Grainne, the social worker allocated the case, judged that Anne was committed and emotionally close to her children, as they were to her, but was struggling with her parenting responsibilities and her problem drinking. Anne pleaded with Grainne to be allowed keep her children and vowed she would reform. Grainne framed her relationship with Anne as a problem-solving partnership between adults with a shared commitment to the safety and wellbeing of the children. She made clear her, and her agency's, view that the existing situation could not be allowed to continue and that the required changes would need help from outside the immediate family. While unhappy about having a social worker involved with her and the children, Anne was at the same time relieved, seeing it as an opportunity to stop things getting worse.

A local voluntary organization provided a family group conferencing service and so Grainne advocated for the family and got a meeting convened quickly. A previously estranged sister of Anne's and an empathic neighbour, whose child was a close friend of Anne's eldest boy, were identified to help develop and implement a safety plan for the children and a change plan for Anne. As a result of these plans, Anne now attends a support group addressing problem drinking (as it is in a nearby town her bus fare is paid for), has a part-time job in the local supermarket two mornings a week, leaving her children with her sister, and is attending a parenting plus programme run by a local family centre organised for her by Grainne. She also goes weekly to a mother and toddlers club in the local library.

Grainne makes regular home visits to work with Anne on her change plan, acknowledging the setbacks as well as the progress. Grainne also makes unplanned home visits and liaises with the school to check on the children's safety and welfare. The plan is now for her to withdraw from involvement after what will have been nine months of engagement with the family, leaving Anne with confidence in her coping skills, routine in her family care, reliable informal support, an improved income and knowledge about how to get formal support if required.

Future challenges

The reflective nature of family support practice demands ongoing attention to the development of the field and, in particular, the challenges to be faced. Some of these challenges are elaborated here, beginning with the ongoing tension between child protection and family support. While no policy or practice choice is 'easy', there is a tendency to opt for the more risk averse as seeming to offer greater defences for the worker, the child welfare organization and the state. As a practice choice, an orientation towards family support as opposed to procedural child protection means carrying more of the immediate risk for all concerned, balancing the risk to the child with the supports and strengths in their existing ecology. Understanding and managing that tension requires commitment, knowledge and skills to ensure the realization of children's rights as the goal of family support.

In this chapter, the argument has been presented that family support is not vague – that it can be built on interrelated sets of theories, a definition and principles for practice. In an era of rhetorical commitment to evidence-based practice or at least evidence-informed practice, family support needs to provide its evidentiary basis. One aspect of this is to demonstrate the value of the theories in practice. A body of robust studies is required that test the value of focusing on resilience and social support, of working with an ecological frame and working to build social capital within the specific frame of social work. Ultimately, studies of practice that illustrate these theoretical orientations working in tandem and resulting in positive changes in the lives of children and parents will be key.

Family support practice is integrated practice; it is multi-agency practice; it is multidisciplinary practice. Therefore, successful working together between professionals and volunteers, between agencies and between professionals, is a basic requirement. However, we know that in spite of the many studies and scholarly contributions, and the exhortations and guidance that these offer, this requirement is often not achieved. A further challenge relates to the currently highly bureaucratic nature of child protection social work practice and associated proceduralization, detailed record keeping and the requirements of desk-based work. Because of its overriding emphasis on relationships, family support practice means spending time with people, in their communities, seeing what their relationships are like and building relationships with them – the weight-bearing beam of the change process.

A positive challenge for family support practice is using technology as part of its toolkit – for example, the use of smartphone apps in supporting positive parenting; using FaceTime and related technologies when distance and limited resources constrain face-to-face interactions. For practitioners, easily accessed databases that provide information on local services, community and voluntary activity are already available (in Northern Ireland: www.cypsp.org/information-support). Also for families themselves, new technologies to help them identify and access available support are easily imagined as part of future practice.

Family support practice must also be alive to new needs reflecting macro-system trends of globalization and related demographic, cultural, social structural and policy shifts. For example, what does family support practice look like in societies where 'beanpole families' (families with strong ties, few children, usually living at a distance from each other) are the norm; what does it look like with migrant, refugee and asylum-seeking families? While the theory, definition and principles outlined in this chapter should be sufficient to explore those questions, it is essential to be open to new practice experience requiring rethinking of any aspect of how family support is understood at this point in time.

Conclusion

This chapter has presented an interweaving of social work and family support based on acknowledging the centrality to both of social ecology, resilience, social support and social capital. Together they provide a basis for the social work process as applied to family support. While acknowledging the range of work that now features in the family support landscape, programmes do not make the worker, so perhaps the most important contribution of social work to family support is its traditional and contributing commitment to relationships. Successful family support is strongly connected to the capacity of practitioners to connect and kindle the psychosocial resources within a family's social ecology – the core work of professional social work. Formal family support programmes have an important place among those resources, but they have to be grounded in the informal relationships between individuals both within and between the informal and formal networks of support. Family support and social work are fitted, but not reducible, to each other because they share attention to the process of mobilizing psychosocial resources through helping relationships. They both provide and promote support through a managed and negotiated partnership process of preparation, assessment, planning, intervening and evaluating. Undergirding that is a shared commitment to respectful, empathic, human solidarity.

Reflection questions

- Where does the right to family life feature in your understanding of children's rights and of the tensions between family support and child protection?

- What skills do you have, what methods are you competent in and what programmes do you know about that could comprise your family support 'toolbox'?

- How do the ten family support practice principles help you understand the approach the social worker took in the case study?

- How do the four key concepts of social ecology, resilience, social support and social capital help you to understand the positive changes achieved in the case study?

References

Allan, J. and Catts, R. (2012) *Social Capital, Children and Young People*. Bristol: Policy Press.
Arthur, M.W., Hawkins, J.D., Pollard, J., Catalano, R.F. and Baglioni, A.J. (2002) 'Measuring risk and protective factors for substance use, delinquency and other adolescent behaviours: The Community that Care youth survey.' *Evaluation Review 26*, 6, 575–601.
Barry, M. (2012) 'Social Capital in the Lives of Young Carers.' In J. Allan and R. Catts (eds) *Social Capital, Children and Young People*. Bristol: Policy Press.
Belsky, J., Melhuish, E., Barnes J., Leyland, H.E. and Romaniuk, H. (2006) 'Effects of Sure Start local programmes on children and families: Early findings.' *British Medical Journal 332*, 7556, 1476.

Brady, B., Dolan, P. and Canavan, J. (2004) *Working for Children and Families: Exploring Good Practice*. Galway: Child and Family Research and Policy Unit, Western Area Health Board/National University of Ireland Galway.

Broadhead, P., Meleady, C. and Delgado, M.A. (2008) *Children, Families and Communities: Creating and Sustaining Integrated Services*. Maidenhead: Open University Press.

Bronfenbrenner, U. (1979) *The Ecology of Human Development*. Cambridge, MA: Harvard University Press.

Canavan, J. (2007) 'Resilience: Cautiously welcoming a contested concept.' *Child Care in Practice 14*, 1, 1–7.

Canavan, J., Dolan P. and Pinkerton, J. (2000) *Family Support: Direction from Diversity*. London: Jessica Kingsley Publishers.

Canavan, J., Pinkerton, J. and Dolan, P. (2016) *Understanding Family Support: Policy, Practice and Theory*. London: Jessica Kingsley Publishers.

Churchill, H. and Sen, R. (2016) 'Intensive family support services: Politics, policy and practice across contexts [themed section].' *Social Policy and Society 15*, 2, 251–336.

Cluver, L., Lachman, J.M., Ward, C., Gardner, F. *et al.* (2016) 'Developing a parenting programme to prevent child abuse in South Africa: A pre-post pilot study.' *Research on Social Work Practice 27*, 7, 758–766.

Connolly, M. and Mason, J. (2014) 'Private and public voices: Does family group conferencing privilege the voice of children and families in child welfare?' *Journal of Social Welfare and Family Law 36*, 4, 403–414.

Cutrona C.E. (2000) 'Social Support Principles for Strengthening Families.' In J. Canavan, P. Dolan and J. Pinkerton (eds) *Family Support: Direction from Diversity*. London: Jessica Kingsley Publishers.

Daly, M., Bray, R., Bruckauf, Z. and Byrne, J. (2015) *Family and Parenting Support: Policy and Provision in a Global Context*. Florence: UNICEF Office of Research.

Davies, M. (2012) *Social Work with Children and Families*. London: Palgrave Macmillan.

Devaney, C. (2017) 'Promoting Children's Welfare through Family Support.' In P. Dolan and N. Frost (eds) *The Routledge Handbook of Global Child Welfare*. London: Routledge.

Devaney, J. and Spratt, T. (2009) 'Child abuse as a complex and wicked problem: Reflecting on policy developments in the United Kingdom in working with children and families with multiple problems.' *Children and Youth Services Review 31*, 6, 635–641.

Dolan, P. and Brady, B. (2012) *A Guide to Youth Mentoring: Providing Effective Social Support*. London: Jessica Kingsley Publishers.

Dolan, P., Canavan, J. and Pinkerton, J. (2006) *Family Support as Reflective Practice*. London: Jessica Kingsley Publishers.

Douglas, H. and McColgan, M. (1999) 'Preparation for contact: An aid to effective intervention.' *Care: The Journal of Practice and Development 7*, 2, 53–64.

Featherstone, B. (2006) 'Rethinking family support in the current policy context.' *British Journal of Social Work 36*, 1, 5–19.

Field, J. (2003) *Social Capital*. London: Routledge.

Fives, A., Kearns, N., Devaney, C., Canavan, J. *et al.* (2013) *Evaluation of the Effectiveness of Barnardo's Wizards of Words Reading Programme*. Dublin: Barnardo's.

Frost, N., Abbott, S. and Race, T. (2015) *Family Support*. Cambridge: Polity Press.

Frost, N. and Dolan, P. (2012) 'The Theoretical Foundations of Family Support.' In M. Davies (ed.) *Social Work with Children and Families*. Basingstoke: Palgrave.

Gardner, R. (2003) 'A National Evaluation of Family Support Services.' In I. Katz and J. Pinkerton (eds) *Evaluating Family Support: Thinking Internationally, Thinking Critically*. Chichester: John Wiley & Sons.

Gilligan, R. (2000) 'Family Support: Issues and Prospects.' In J. Canavan, P. Dolan and J. Pinkerton (eds) *Family Support: Direction from Diversity*. London: Jessica Kingsley Publishers.

Gilligan, R. (2009) *Promoting Resilience: Supporting Children and Young People Who Are in Care, Adopted or in Need*. London: British Association for Adoption and Fostering.

Health and Social Care Board/Social Care Institute for Excellence (2016) *Family Support Hubs in Northern Ireland*. London: Social Care Institute for Excellence.

Heckman, J.J. (2006) 'Skill formation and the economics of investing in disadvantaged children.' *Science 312*, 5782, 1900–1902.

Henderson, S., Hollan, J., McGrellis, S., Sharpe, S. and Thompson, R. (2007) *Inventing Adulthoods: A Biographical Approach to Youth Transitions*. London: Sage.

Jack, G. (1997) 'An ecological approach to social work with children and families.' *Child and Family Social Work 2*, 2, 109–120.

Jack, G. and Gill, O. (2010a) 'The Impact of Economic Factors on Parents or Caregivers and Children.' In J. Howorth (ed.) *The Child's World: The Comprehensive Guide to Assessing Children in Need* (2nd edition). London: Jessica Kingsley Publishers.

Jack, G. and Gill, O. (2010b) 'The Impact of Family and Community Support on Parents or Caregivers and Children.' In J. Howarth (ed.) *The Child's World: The Comprehensive Guide to Assessing Children in Need* (2nd edition). London: Jessica Kingsley Publishers.

Katz, I. and Pinkerton, J. (2003) *Evaluating Family Support: Thinking Internationally, Thinking Critically*. Chichester: John Wiley & Sons.

McCormack, J. (2012) 'Family Support Work in Practice.' In M. Davies (ed.) *Social Work with Children and Families*. Basingstoke: Palgrave.

Mrazek, P.J. and Haggerty, R.J. and Committee on Prevention of Mental Disorders, Institute of Medicine (1994) *Reducing Risks for Mental Disorders: Frontiers for Prevention Intervention Research*. Washington, DC: National Academy Press.

Munford, R. and Sanders, J. (2017) 'Child Welfare Practices in New Zealand.' In P. Dolan and N. Frost (eds) *The Routledge Handbook of Global Child Welfare*. London: Routledge.

Nelson, P. (2005) 'Social Work with Children and Families.' In S. Shardlow and P. Nelson (eds) *Introducing Social Work*. Lyme Regis: Russell House.

Parker, J. (2017) *Social Work Practice: Assessment, Planning, Intervention and Review*. London: Sage.

Payne, M. (2005) *The Origins of Social Work: Continuity and Change*. Basingstoke: Palgrave.

Rutter M. (2012) 'Resilience: Causal Pathways and Social Ecology.' In M. Ungar (ed.) *The Social Ecology of Resilience: A Handbook of Theory and Practice*. New York, NY: Springer.

Sanders, M.R. (2012) 'Development, evaluation and multidimensional dissemination of the Triple P – Positive Parenting Programme.' *Annual Review of Clinical Psychology 8*, 345–379.

Statham, J. and Smith, M. (2010) *Issues in Early Intervention: Identifying and Supporting Children with Additional Needs*. London: Department for Children, Schools and Families.

Teater, B. (2014) *An Introduction to Applying Social Work Theories and Methods* (2nd edition). Maidenhead: Open University Press.

Thompson, N. (2017) *Social Problems and Social Justice*. London: Palgrave Macmillan.

Turnell, A. and Murphy, T. (2017) *Signs of Safety Comprehensive Briefing Paper* (4th edition). Perth, Australia: Resolutions Consultancy Pty Ltd.

Ungar, M. (2008) 'Resilience across cultures.' *British Journal of Social Work 38*, 2, 218–235.

United Nations (1989) *United Nations Convention on the Rights of the Child (UNCRC)*. Accessed on 21/03/2018 at www.ohchr.org/EN/ProfessionalInterest/Pages/CRC.aspx.

Webster-Stratton, C. and Reid, M.J. (2010) 'Adapting the Incredible Years, an evidence-based programme, for families involved in the child welfare system.' *Journal of Children's Services 5*, 25–42.

Williams, P. (2013) 'We are all boundary spanners now?' *International Journal of Public Sector Management 26*, 1, 17–32.

• Chapter 3 •

Social Work with Resettled Refugees

JAY MARLOWE

Introduction

As protracted and recent conflicts continue globally, the number of forced migrants is now at record levels since World War II. The United Nations High Commissioner for Refugees (UNHCR 2017) states that in 2016 one person was forcibly displaced every three seconds, thus bringing the global total of people forcibly displaced to more than 65 million. The intense fighting across Syria, Iraq, Democratic Republic of Congo, South Sudan and other countries has significantly contributed to this increase over the past several years. The experience of forced migration means that people involuntarily leave behind important histories, relationships and opportunities. And as they cross international borders, there are powerful debates and contestations as to the responsibilities of receiving societies in providing a safe haven to those who have left much, if not everything, behind.

Heated local, national and international debates focus on the impact of resettling refuges in relation to social cohesion, capacities to integrate, national identity, the allocation of finite resources and potential implications for security and safety. Internationally, political parties have leveraged populist support where a 'politics of fear' (see Bogen and Marlowe 2015) has justified particular anti-immigration agendas and policies. Alongside these developments, the proliferation and accessibility of a wide range of digital communication technologies is transforming the structure and role of social networks. The use of these technologies raises additional questions about the ways people interact with others in places both proximate and distant.

The roles for social work related to refugee settlement are many. Social workers may find themselves working with refugees relative to physical health, mental health, housing, child welfare, language acquisition, community integration, employment and many other aspects that are part of settling in a new country (Valtonen 2008). Others may help inform various social policies and there is also a clear role for research that provides a basis to advocate for more meaningful forms of support and social change. This chapter explores recent theories related to the integration and the challenges of adapting to a new social reality in resettlement contexts. It provides a global context to consider the contemporary and fast-moving political, technological and social developments and to highlight the multiple ways that social work can effectively work with refugees.

Context and key terms

One of the principal tasks of the UNHCR is to oversee people's right to seek asylum from persecution, which is one of the 30 articles enshrined in the Universal Declaration of Human Rights. Though more than 190 member states have signed an agreement to this declaration, the treatment of people forcibly displaced represents one of the most contested political, social and economic issues in contemporary times. Numerous terms have emerged to describe people on the move, including: refugee, asylum seeker, boat person, illegal migrant, economic migrant, undocumented migrant, trafficked person – the list continues. As social workers, it is imperative that we understand what these terms mean and the powerful discourses through which the experiences of forced migration are understood and embraced.

In general, the wider society (and often politicians and the media) fail to distinguish the differences between refugees, asylum seekers and other terms used to describe forced migrants. A *forced migrant* is a person who has left their home or country of habitual residence *involuntarily*. This involuntary decision may relate to a variety of factors that might be economic, climate related, social or political. When a person is forcibly displaced for reasons related to persecution (often political), this is where people are able to claim certain protections under the refugee convention. A person may seek refugee status because it provides certain protections from states signatory to the 1951 Convention relating to the status of refugees. Article 1 of *The 1951 Convention Relating to the Status of Refugees* (United Nations 1951) defines a *refugee* as:

> a person who is outside her or his country of nationality and who is
> unable or unwilling to return to that country due to a well-founded fear of

persecution because of a person's race, religion, nationality, membership of a particular social group or political opinion.

The process of crossing international borders in the case of refugees and asylum seekers is known as forced migration because the well-founded fear of persecution means that they must leave because their safety is at risk. Within this definition, it is necessary to acknowledge that a refugee can be anyone. The term does not represent a particular class, ethnic background, regional location, religion or other marker of identity – anyone can be a refugee.

An *asylum seeker* is a person who is seeking refugee status and has crossed the border of their country of habitual residence. For countries signatory to the United Nations 1951 Convention, until a person's claim for refugee status has been determined, they cannot be sent back to their country of habitual residence. This is a legal principle known as *non-refoulement*.

A *stateless person* is someone who is not recognized as a citizen by any state. The UNHCR (2017) estimates that there are more than ten million people in this situation, across more than 75 countries, who often live in precarious circumstances. *Unaccompanied minors* are young people under the age of 18 who do not have a parent or responsible adult to care for them. In 2016, more than 75,000 unaccompanied minors applied for asylum, with the majority going to Germany (more than 35,000); most of these young people came from Afghanistan. These young people can be particularly vulnerable to trafficking and exploitation as they seek asylum.

And finally, there are *internally displaced people*. An internally displaced person is someone who has been forced to flee their home (often due to armed conflict, persecution or a disaster) but has not crossed an internationally recognized state border. This group (sometimes known as IDPs) is often forgotten about when there is a stronger focus on Europe, North America and Australasia's response to forced migrants arriving at the associated borders. Internally displaced people, by far, make up the greatest proportion of forced migrants globally. The UNHCR (2017) states that there are more than 40 million internally displaced people and these can often be extremely vulnerable due to the challenges of ensuring safety and security in places that are within, or near, zones of high conflict.

As social workers, we must understand what these different terms mean so that it is possible to have accurate debates about what should constitute local to international responses to forced migration. In numerous countries, the policies for working with refugees, asylum seekers, unaccompanied minors and other groups of migrants can be very different, raising concerns of oppressive social policies (see Bloom and Udahemuka 2014; Briskman, Latham and Goddard 2008). Social work has an important role in voicing such concerns. Alongside this structural focus, work in the forced migration area also requires recognizing the rich diversity that forced migrants bring with them; this clearly brings the profession's commitments to human rights and social justice to the fore as forced migrants seek safety and a new home. Now that these key terms have been defined, it is possible to consider the main theories and social work approaches that relate to working in the forced migration field.

Theoretical challenges and debates in the field

Public debates about forced migration are often not well informed and can have significant ramifications related to realising socially just outcomes and processes in response to what is often referred to as the 'refugee crisis'. In particular, Bogen and Marlowe (2015) note a shifting political discourse of viewing those seeking asylum from persecution as being *at risk* to *a risk*. This means that, rather than focusing on the need to protect Afghans escaping persecution from the Taliban or the plight of Yazidis fleeing the terror of Islamic State, the predominant debate is on whether welcoming refugees means that receiving states and their associated societies are themselves safe and secure. This discourse incorrectly conflates refugees with terrorism and makes it difficult to garner political support for global solutions. It also shifts the focus from protecting the vulnerable to the economic costs and burden that settling refugees can mean for a receiving society.

Social work has an important role to respond to such claims and to ensure that public debate is informed by sound evidence. If the wider society's understandings and political debate are largely focused on refugees as a security risk, then these understandings can negatively impact on refugees' opportunities to participate as peers in civil society (Pupavac 2008). Some of the major debates are now highlighted.

Welcome versus deterrence

There are heated discussions that occur at professional and policy levels that relate to *welcome versus deterrence*. This particular debate asks the question: does providing policies that provide safety and support, and that are welcoming to refugees, inadvertently create the contexts where refugees are more willing to take a chance to come to countries in Europe, North America and elsewhere? Those supporting the deterrence approach note that not all migrants are forcibly displaced by persecution and that some (often referred to as 'economic migrants') are just looking for a better quality of life. Others argue that making it difficult to cross national borders and settle actively encourages refugees to look for solutions closer to home and not take dangerous passage across the Mediterranean and Andaman Seas, for instance. In 2016, the International Organization for Migration estimated, on its Missing Migrants Project website, that there were nearly 5000 migrant deaths in the Mediterranean among people who were seeking asylum and more than 7000 deaths recorded worldwide.[1]

However, there are groups that argue that we should take a more welcoming stance to forced migrants and that we should be looking for ways to protect them further rather than focusing on ways to keep them out or to discourage their movements. Germany is an example of this and has settled more than 1 million asylum seekers over the last few years. While Europe is focused at the moment on the 'refugee crisis', it is worth noting that there were numerous countries during both world wars that offered Europeans safe haven. For social work, there is a need to engage in such debates and understand the ways in which history and politics intersect to better ensure socially just outcomes and processes in relation to forced migration.

Agency versus structure

The *agency versus structure* debate concerns whether the struggles of refugees can be related to individual/group-level decisions (agency) or are the outcome of structural forms of oppression and disadvantage. The social work literature provides helpful guidance in this area as it explicitly links the experience of people's private pains to public issues (Mills 1959). Social workers need to be able to provide a critical analysis of structure when common statistics are reported about refugees that focus on their unemployment rates, costs to society and other negative discourses that may create a moral panic about refugees. A number of social work writers who take an anti-oppressive stand and a commitment to human rights provide some helpful guidance (see Dominelli 2008; Ife 2012; Thompson 2012).

There are some inspiring examples of how social workers have addressed structural forms of racism and exclusion as these relate to refugees (Bloom and Udahemuka 2014; Briskman *et al.* 2008). Being aware of such case studies provides a basis to think about the ways in

---

1   http://missingmigrants.iom.int.

which powerful structures can be critiqued and questioned in a manner more likely to be safe for the practitioner, their organization and also the clients whom they work alongside. This debate is obviously much broader and applicable to the wider society and highlights the need for social workers to think about practice from micro, meso and macro levels (see Nash 2005).

Vulnerabilities and capacities

The term 'refugee' is often conceptualized within a deficit-focused frame. Social work's commitment to strengths-based practice provides a helpful reframing here that also acknowledges that refugees bring with them incredible forms of resilience, knowledge and skills that have helped them to survive and thrive in both forced migration contexts and after settling into a new country. My work in relation to the Canterbury earthquakes in Aotearoa New Zealand, for example, highlighted that refugees often had remarkable strategies and forms of resilience that helped them to cope with the unanticipated events related to disasters (see Marlowe and Bogen 2015). This perspective was often missed by those tasked with disaster recovery, particularly because refugees are largely viewed as passive victims. Others have highlighted how an overemphasis on negative mental health outcomes for refugees has pathologized them as damaged people (Pupavac 2008).

These deficit-focused perspectives mean that practitioners can miss opportunities to understand and acknowledge how experiences of trauma can also provide opportunities for growth (Calhoun and Tedeschi 2014; Simich and Andermann 2014). The balancing act for social work is to simultaneously consider people's vulnerabilities *and* capacities/strengths. This is not about privileging one over the other but about understanding how these operate within people's wider ecological context.

Human and climate induced displacement

Increasingly, countries are examining the relevance of the Refugee Convention for climate change where people are forcibly displaced by rising sea levels, desertification and environmental situations (Docherty and Giannini 2009). Because the refugee definition requires a well-founded fear of persecution, it is difficult to include *environmental* refugees because climates, of themselves, do not persecute people, even though the evidence of climate change through human activity is compelling. Thus, the contemporary ways that people are forcibly displaced must be considered alongside the 1951 definition and represent possibly one of the most pressing questions over displacement in the decades to come. For social work, climate change represents an important ongoing and future agenda as the intersections between sustainability, social justice and human rights come together from local to international levels.

Local and transnational mobilities (and constraints)

The field of mobility studies (see Urry 2007) shows that, while the movement of humans is part and parcel of human history, the speed at which people can now travel and communicate is unprecedented. Through air travel, sending remittances and engaging with social media, people can remain connected to friends and family overseas instantaneously and continuously (see Marlowe 2018). The focus on the practices of transnational family, friendship, and even community, heralds relatively new ways of maintaining significant connections over distance. The associated literature acknowledges these new social practices and highlights how people can remain committed to more than one place (Collins 2009; Madianou and Miller 2013). There is a tension here, however. If a person can maintain intimate connections with friends and family overseas through social media applications, this raises questions about people's commitments to local places.

The rise of social media and increasing global connectivity means that people can maintain relationships through applications such as Skype, Facebook, Viber, Snapchat, WhatsApp and many others. The usability, accessibility and affordability of such digital communications means that, although only 1 percent of the world's refugees may be resettled, they can still maintain quite powerful relationships with those living in their countries of origin and in the wider diaspora (see UNHCR 2016). For many resettled refugees, opportunities for family reunification (where they can bring members to them on a permanent basis) remain very difficult and limited (Choummanivong, Poole and Cooper 2014). In this sense, there are some that have written about transnationalism as an *enduring* solution for refugees (Long 2014). These developments are particularly important recognizing again that only 1 percent of refugees worldwide will have the chance to resettle. Social media have the potential to connect such diaspora; the UNHCR (2016) notes in its report, *Connecting Refugees*, that the sites of displacement are finding increasing access to affordable technologies and internet connectivity. Social workers may consider the ways in which to bring transnational family into their work, for example through social media. There is also a role in helping to inform and critique policies that focus on refugees and what support (or lack thereof) relates to the accessibility, usability and affordability of digital technologies.

A key question that emerges for social work, then, is: how do the affordances of social media impact on refugees' participation in and commitment to their sites of resettlement? It may be that having contact with family overseas provides the basis for refugees' wellbeing and engagement in civic forms of practice (education, work, voting, sport, etc.) in their country of resettlement. Alternatively, it might be that these ongoing transnational links could discourage such forms of activity. This question is not limited to just refugees and migrants, but to a world which is increasingly connected and mediated by digital devices and wireless connectivity. The ways in which social work considers practice within a transnational remit represents another professional future that could significantly shape the ways in which practice is envisaged.

A case study to assist in thinking about the intersections of refugee resettlement and social work practice now follows.

Case study: Practice application

Jenny is a health social worker based in a hospital setting whose role is to assist patients' transition back into their homes after major surgery. One of her clients, Arif, is a man from Syria who resettled as a refugee in Australia two years ago. His journey to Australia is one that includes significant experiences of trauma, including being detained in a prison for three years because of his political views. He has just received news that a biopsy shows evidence of cancer and his doctor suggests that he should consider chemotherapy as soon as possible. However, Arif speaks little English and seems to be more concerned with bringing his family who are living in a refugee camp in Jordan to Australia. When Arif was told about his medical situation, there was not an interpreter present. He appears to be depressed and disoriented. He is a religious man but feels quite isolated because there are not many Syrians who live close by and having sufficient financial resources is a real struggle. He tells Jenny through an interpreter that he will not worry about his medical issues until he has been reunited with his family.

It becomes clear in this case study that the work with Arif is not just about ensuring that he is able to return home after his biopsy. There are multiple issues that present related to his situation within Australia and also with his transnational family. The hospital that Jenny works for may define the scope of her work in fairly clear ways that demarcate the aspects of practice she can focus on and what other aspects she may need to refer on to another agency. Moreover, she finds herself working in multidisciplinary environments where social work perspectives may struggle to advocate in situations where biomedical perspectives (focusing on diagnosis, treatment and cure) can take precedence over more holistic ways of knowing.

There are many such examples where an overemphasis on post-traumatic stress disorder, depression and other mental illnesses arising from past trauma become the primary (even sole) focus of treatment at the expense of a broader analysis that considers the intersections of social policy, inequality, discrimination, and power (see Marlowe 2018). Social work is well placed to respond to these wider concerns.

Within this case study, there are a number of practice-related questions that need further consideration:

1. What is the role of gender in this interaction? For some groups, gender roles may be strictly defined and can impact on professional encounters.

2. What strengths and capacities might Arif possibly have? How can these be mobilized in this situation?

3. What are the implications of limited English proficiency and the use of interpreters?

4. How does social work best function in multidisciplinary environments and how can alternating views be constructively discussed and, at times, challenged?

5. What are a social worker's roles and responsibilities when working with a person who has significant ongoing transnational relationships? How could this social worker assist with Arif's concerns?

6. It is also apparent that the social worker needs to be reflexively aware of their *own* history – one that powerfully informs values, beliefs and actions. What assumptions does the social worker carry that relate to their understandings of refugees and forced migration?

These are complex questions but ones which are 'difficult to think but good to think' and relate to our commitments to social justice (see Finn and Jacobsen 2003, p.66; Irizarry *et al.* 2015). The following section presents important considerations for social work practice that relate to this case study and refugee resettlement more broadly.

Refugee resettlement and emerging social work practice

This chapter focuses predominantly on resettlement contexts as these are often where the social work profession is most active. This is not to say, however, that social work does not have a role in other situations. There are three durable solutions that the UNHCR identifies for refugees: (1) voluntary repatriation; (2) local integration; and (3) resettlement. The notion of something that is *durable* suggests a condition that is lasting and thus provides a reasonable sense of safety and security from the fear of persecution. The first durable solution, *voluntary repatriation*, represents a situation when refugees are able to safely return home. In recent years, there have been examples of voluntary repatriation in places such as Afghanistan, Ivory Coast and Sri Lanka. This solution, however, is not available in many countries where ongoing conflicts continue, sometimes for decades.

The second durable solution is *local integration*, which involves the gradual inclusion of refugees into a neighbouring country of asylum (see UNHCR 2017). While this is something that is difficult to qualify and quantify, there are numerous examples of Burmese people living in Bangkok, Colombians in Ecuador and South Sudanese people settling in places such as Nairobi, Cairo and Kampala.

Finally, *resettlement* is defined by the UNHCR (2015, p.51) as the 'transfer of refugees from the country in which they have sought asylum to another State that has agreed to admit them as refugees, granting them permanent settlement and the opportunity for eventual citizenship'. Less than 1 percent of the world's refugees will have chances to resettle in places such as the United States, Canada, United Kingdom, Scandinavia, Australia, Aotearoa New Zealand and the 30 other countries that have formal refugee resettlement programmes. In fact, the UNHCR (2017) notes that developing regions host more than 84 percent of the world's refugees. Although the people who are resettled represent the minority of populations of concern worldwide, resettlement offers a durable solution whereby people can begin a new life with (relative) human rights protections. Social workers can play an important role in ensuring that such rights are realized.

Once refugees resettle, they begin the complex task of crafting a new social existence in a new receiving society – a process often referred to as *integration*. While the definition of integration can be contested, it can be understood as a process of adapting to a new host society without losing or foregoing one's own cultural identity and history. It is also important to recognize that integration outcomes are not only about a refugee's actions and aspirations, but also require an analysis of the opportunities afforded by the host society (and its institutions) and the associated welcome it provides.

One of the most-cited models that captures this complexity is put forward by Ager and Strang (2008). They introduce ten domains that refugees (and the host society) must negotiate and navigate under four themes, as follows:

- *Means and markers*: employment, housing, education and health.

- *Social connection*: social bonds, social bridges, social links.

- *Facilitators*: language and cultural knowledge, safety and stability.

- *Foundation*: rights and citizenship.

Each of these themes will now be elaborated on further as it relates to refugee resettlement and the associated implications for social work practice.

Means and markers: employment, housing, education and health

Social work's commitment to holistic practice means that work related to housing, employment, education and health is not viewed in isolation. This is of critical importance for refugees as each of these *means* are intimately linked with one another, as was illustrated clearly in the Arif case study. The need to consider the links between health, housing, education, employment and other everyday experiences is critical for developing deeper understandings of people's situations and effective social work practice. It also requires that social workers are adept in working with multidisciplinary teams and with organizations that may have little or no training about working with refugees.

Ensuring that people from refugee backgrounds are provided with adequate housing can be a critical challenge – particularly if they are resettled in places where there is a shortage of housing stock. In such situations, there are financial implications for whether refugees can afford to live in certain areas and there can also be a wider societal perception (often misguided) that argues that 'we' should be housing 'our' own before providing refugees with housing. Such debates highlight an important role that social work has in responding to such discussions which usually focus on the economic costs of settling refugees in the first few years (Fozdar and Hartley 2013). There have been recent reports from recognized economists that settling refugees can actually be good for the society through economic returns and in the other ways that refugees can contribute (see Hugo 2014; Legrain 2016).

The international literature shows that refugees often have higher rates of both unemployment and underemployment when compared with the general population (Searle *et al.* 2012). While this can partly be explained by the fact that refugees must adjust to a new social reality and possibly learn the receiving society's language, it must also be recognized that refugee resettlement is not just about the decisions that individuals make. It is the receptiveness and the welcome that the wider society and its institutions make to providing meaningful settlement opportunities. Numerous studies now show evidence of a segmented labour market where refugees are not afforded opportunities to work even though they have the skills and desire for work (Colic-Peisker and Tilbury 2006; O'Donovan and Sheikh 2014). Again, this is where social work's commitments to anti-discriminatory practice can provide nuance to the agency/structure debate and cast light on existing forms of structural inequality and disadvantage.

Social workers can also play an important role in education for forced migrants. Children of refugee backgrounds may have had significantly interrupted education and may find it challenging to be placed with their age-matched cohort (see Valtonen 2008). Adults may also have had limited education and, at times, might not be literate in their first or preferred language. These dynamics indicate that supporting the schooling and educational experiences of people from refugee backgrounds means social workers might need to ensure that teachers and principals are aware of the associated challenges. At the same time, it is also important that refugees are not positioned within a deficit-focused lens as there are many examples of where refugees have excelled and flourished in educational contexts and have gone on to make significant contributions to their country of settlement and to the peace-building process in their country of origin.

And finally, health plays a central role in refugees' wellbeing and opportunities for meaningful integration. As the case study illustrated, there were numerous issues for Arif to think through, including family reunification, cancer diagnosis, lack of belonging, past traumas and the provision of interpreters. The focus on health is usually related to its mental and physical aspects, although social workers should continue to think of health in very broad ways that also incorporate other aspects associated with wellbeing. One of the most common assumptions about refugees is that they are traumatized (Marlowe 2018; Pupavac 2008). While there is little debate that most refugees have *experienced trauma* through their forced migration journey, it does not necessarily mean that they are automatically *traumatized* people. There are some tensions here. In general, rigorous studies that look at the mental health of refugees show an increased risk factor for the development of post-traumtic stress disorder, depression, anxiety and, to a lesser degree, schizophrenia (Fazel, Wheeler and Danesh 2005; Hollander *et al.* 2016; Porter and Haslam 2005). What is sometimes lost in these discussions is that still *the vast majority of refugees do not show the associated symptoms for such diagnoses.* Thus, the focus often missed is: why is it that so few refugees present with serious mental health concerns when this is considered alongside the experiences that they have had to endure?

In relation to physical health, refugees can present with a range of health issues from spending years (if not decades) in refugee camps where it can be difficult to maintain good physical health in contexts with limited food resources, medical supplies and medical intervention. For these reasons, refugees can sometimes present with chronic health conditions. The health report by Mortensen, Rainger and Hughes (2012) provides an excellent overview of some of the common mental and physical health conditions that refugees present with for further reference.

Social connection: bonding, bridging and linking social capital

As social workers consider the various settlement domains related to housing, employment, health and education, it is clear that achieving practical outcomes is intimately tied to people's connections with family, friends, the wider society and institutions. The social connection theme focuses on Putnam's (2000) theory of 'social capital' that identifies and describes the different types of relationships that individuals, communities and institutions create: bonding, bridging, and linking.

The notion of capital refers to a resource, so 'social capital' basically refers to the social resources that people are able to draw on for a variety of reasons. *Bonding* relationships occur between individuals of the same (refugee/ethnic/socio-economic/demographic) community, whereas *bridging* relationships are associations created between individuals from different ethnic (socio-economic/demographic) communities. Thus, bonding capital is created when individuals and groups within a community are able to connect and support each other, and utilizes the intrinsic assets and strengths of a community for action. Bridging capital is developed when one community combines its assets and resources with those of other communities (Putnam 2000).

The *bonding* forms of connection can be very important for social work practice. As was clear in the Arif case study, the lack of having other people around him who shared a common language and culture made understanding and navigating his current concerns more challenging. The need to adjust to a new social reality with unfamiliar social constructions and practices related to parenting, community, work, happiness, gender roles and many others means that the acculturation process is one that can take time for refugees. This process may require navigating gender roles and adjusting to a new legal context. Children often learn languages more quickly than their parents (Valtonen 2008). Community groups defined by ethnicity might or might not be all that cohesive in resettlement contexts. At times, an ethnically defined community might be placed quite far apart in urban settings where securing housing is difficult. These situations provide a basis, particularly through community development models of social work practice, to ensure that bonding forms of capital can be strengthened and realized (see Ife 2012).

Even once a refugee is resettled, they generally have very limited forms of *bridging* capital that connect them to opportunities, resources and information. Social workers can help facilitate these connections by working to encourage local communities to meet one another and by encouraging refugees to engage with various forms of civic life. As Putnam (2000, pp.22–23) famously stated, bonding capital is good for 'getting by' and bridging capital is good for 'getting ahead' through a network of ties that connect people to new opportunities.

This social connection theme also relates to the relations that people have with institutions – *linking* capital. It is here that a refugee's relationship with state institutions and non-government organizations can either help facilitate a successful integration experience or can possibly impede it. Returning to the case study, Jenny must also consider the immediate and broader contexts when working with Arif that include the social work profession, hospital and multidisciplinary teams and government institutions that develop policies related to people's lived experiences.

The role of social work in advocating and brokering to connect people to these institutions can be incredibly important. However, there are other times when social workers must take social action and respond to oppressive structures that discriminate against particular groups of people (both overtly and in tacit ways). This work is more easily said than done, but there are numerous examples now of social workers challenging powerful institutions (see Briskman *et al.* 2008).

Facilitators: language and cultural safety

The means and markers theme, along with the social connections outlined earlier, is powerfully linked to considerations of language and cultural safety and stability – the facilitators. While this may not be surprising, the need for social workers to ensure that they are working in a culturally responsive way that honours people's language(s) and history is paramount. This will mean that, as a social worker, you are adept at working with interpreters and understand the subtleties that can occur, often defined at levels that include gender, age, ethnicity and other cultural factors (see Nash 2005). It might also require consulting with elders or cross-cultural workers to ensure that social work practice does not unintentionally silence people's experiences, concerns and/or aspirations. Recognizing that a 'refugee' does not represent a specific cultural background, ethnicity, religion, class or other identifier means that social workers must embrace culturally responsive practice to ensure that our work is accessible and adaptable to context.

Foundation: rights and citizenship

Finally, the last theme of Ager and Strang's (2008) integration framework is the foundation of rights and citizenship. This foundation clearly places commitments to human rights and social justice at the core of our work. While it might be that some aspects of social work practice will focus predominantly (perhaps even exclusively) on the 'mean and markers' level or on social connection, the need to locate this work within a broader structural frame is imperative.

A helpful way to look at this foundation theme is through the lens of human rights. Numerous social work authors have written about how a commitment to human rights informs our profession generally (Connolly and Ward 2008; Ife 2012) and in relation to refugees specifically (Marlowe and Humpage 2016). Basically, the idea of *foundation* is that the other themes of means/markers, social connections and facilitators cannot be realized if there is no foundation of human rights that supports the realization of the other three themes. Having a strong foundation in the ways that social workers can work from a rights-based perspective is an important base to begin working with people from refugee backgrounds. Within the associated case study, the right to family, work, health, education, an interpreter and others can help articulate a language for social work to advocate for particular services and support that may not otherwise be realized.

Conclusion

This chapter began with an overview of forced migration and defined a number of key terms. In focusing predominantly on refugee resettlement, it presented some of the main theories related to integration and social work practice. Regardless of the field of practice, social workers will find themselves working with people who are from refugee backgrounds. It is imperative that social workers are aware of some of the main considerations related to successful settlement and that, in many ways, the needs, hopes and aspirations of people from refugee backgrounds are much the same as people in the wider society. Recognition of the history that people carry with them, including their dreams and aspirations, is an important first step in developing effective social work practice.

Reflection questions

- What are your assumptions when you hear the words 'refugee' or 'asylum seeker'? What words and images come to mind and allow you to think through the associated discourses that inform these understandings?

- How can social workers understand potential vulnerabilities that refugees might have (internal and external) and yet maintain a strengths-based focus that also recognizes people's agency and capacities to respond to adverse events?

- What is social work's role in responding to public debate about local to global concerns on forced migration?

- In what ways can we think about transnational social work practice which is often based in local contexts?

- How can we evaluate our own practice to better ensure that we are working towards outcomes that allow resettled refugees the opportunities to exercise voice and the agency to pursue the aspirations that they have in their new receiving country?

Websites and other resources

- Refugee Council of Australia: www.refugeecouncil.org.au/getfacts/statistics.

- United Nations High Commissioner for Refugees: www.unhcr.org.

- See the International Organization for Migration's *Missing Migrant Report* website that details total migrant deaths for people trying to find asylum in another country: http://missingmigrants.iom.int.

References

Ager, A. and Strang, A. (2008) 'Understanding integration: A conceptual framework.' *Journal of Refugee Studies 21*, 2, 166–191.

Bloom, A. and Udahemuka, M. (2014) '"Going through the doors of pain": Asylum seeker and convention refugee experiences in Aotearoa New Zealand.' *Kōtuitui: New Zealand Journal of Social Sciences Online 9*, 2, 70–81.

Bogen, R. and Marlowe, J. (2015) 'Asylum discourse in New Zealand: Moral panic and a culture of indifference.' *Australian Social Work* 1–12. doi:10.1080/031240 7X.2015.1076869.

Briskman, L., Latham, S. and Goddard, C. (2008) *Human Rights Overboard: Seeking Asylum in Australia.* Melbourne: Scribe Publications.

Calhoun, L.G. and Tedeschi, R.G. (2014) *Handbook of Posttraumatic Growth: Research and Practice.* London: Routledge.

Choummanivong, C., Poole, G.E. and Cooper, A. (2014) 'Refugee family reunification and mental health in resettlement.' *Kōtuitui: New Zealand Journal of Social Sciences Online 9*, 2, 89–100.

Colic-Peisker, V. and Tilbury, F. (2006) 'Employment niches for recent refugees: Segmented labour market in twenty-first century Australia.' *Journal of Refugee Studies 19*, 2, 203–229.

Collins, F.L. (2009) 'Connecting "home" with "here": Personal homepages in everyday transnational lives.' *Journal of Ethnic and Migration Studies 35*, 6, 839–859.

Connolly, M. and Ward, T. (2008) 'Human Rights and Culture.' In M. Connolly and T. Ward (eds) *Morals, Rights and Practice in the Human Services.* London: Jessica Kingsley Publishers.

Docherty, B. and Giannini, T. (2009) 'Confronting a rising tide: A proposal for a convention on climate change refugees.' *Harvard Environmental Law Review 33*, 349–403.

Dominelli, L. (2008) *Anti-Racist Social Work.* New York, NY: Palgrave Macmillan.

Fazel, M., Wheeler, J. and Danesh, J. (2005) 'Prevalence of serious mental disorder in 7000 refugees resettled in western countries: A systematic review.' *The Lancet 365*, 9467, 1309–1314.

Finn, J. and Jacobsen, M. (2003) 'Just practice: Steps toward a new social work paradigm.' *Journal of Social Work Education 39*, 1, 57–78.

Fozdar, F. and Hartley, L. (2013) 'Housing and the creation of home for refugees in Western Australia.' *Housing, Theory and Society* 1–26. doi:10.1080/14036096.2013.830985.

Hollander, A.-C., Dal, H., Lewis, G., Magnusson, C., Kirkbride, J.B. and Dalman, C. (2016) 'Refugee migration and risk of schizophrenia and other non-affective psychoses: Cohort study of 1.3 million people in Sweden.' *British Medical Journal 352.* https://doi.org/10.1136/bmj.i1030.

Hugo, G. (2014) 'The economic contribution of humanitarian settlers in Australia.' *International Migration 52*, 2, 31–52.

Ife, J. (2012) *Human Rights and Social Work: Towards Rights-Based Practice.* Cambridge: Cambridge University Press.

Irizarry, C., Marlowe, J.M., Hallahan, L. and Bull, M. (2015) 'Restoring connections: Social workers' practice wisdom towards achieving social justice.' *British Journal of Social Work 46*, 7, 1855–1871.

Legrain, P. (2016) *Refugees Work: A Humanitarian Investment that Yields Economic Dividends.* Accessed on 15/ 07/ 2017 at www.opennetwork.net/wp-content/uploads/2016/05/Tent-Open-Refugees-Work_V13.pdf.

Long, K. (2014) 'Rethinking "Durable" Solutions.' In E. Fiddian-Qasmiyeh, G. Loescher, K. Long and N. Sigona (eds) *The Oxford Handbook of Refugee and Forced Migration Studies*. Oxford: Oxford University Press.

Madianou, M. and Miller, D. (2013) *Migration and New Media: Transnational Families and Polymedia*. London: Routledge.

Marlowe, J. (2018) *Belonging and Transnational Refugee Resettlement: Unsettling the Everyday and the Extraordinary*. London: Routledge.

Marlowe, J. and Bogen, R. (2015) 'Young people from refugee backgrounds as a resource for disaster risk reduction.' *International Journal of Disaster Risk Reduction 14*, 2, 125–131.

Marlowe, J. and Humpage, L. (2016) 'Policy Responses to Refugees in New Zealand: A Rights-Based Analysis.' In J. Maidment and E. Beddoe (eds) *New Zealand Social Policy for Social Work and Human Services: Diverse Perspectives*. Christchurch: Canterbury University Press.

Mills, C. (1959) *The Sociological Imagination*. London: Oxford University Press.

Mortensen, A., Rainger, W. and Hughes, S. (2012) *Refugee Health Care: A Handbook for Professionals*. Accessed on 15/07/2017 at www.health.govt.nz/publication/refugee-health-care-handbook-health-professionals.

Nash, M. (2005) 'Responding to Settlement Needs: Migrants and Refugees and Community Development.' In M. Nash, R. Munford and K. O'Donoghue (eds) *Social Work Theories in Action*. London: Jessica Kingsley Publishers.

O'Donovan, T. and Sheikh, M. (2014) 'Welfare reforms and the refugee resettlement strategy: An opportunity to achieve meaningful employment outcomes for New Zealanders from refugee backgrounds?' *Kōtuitui: New Zealand Journal of Social Sciences Online 9*, 2, 82–88.

Porter, M. and Haslam, N. (2005) 'Predisplacement and postdisplacement factors associated with mental health of refugees and internally displaced persons: A meta-analysis.' *Journal of the American Medical Association 294*, 5, 602–612.

Pupavac, V. (2008) 'Refugee advocacy, traumatic representations and political disenchantment.' *Government and Opposition 43*, 2, 270–292.

Putnam, R. (2000) *Bowling Alone: The Collapse and Revival of American Community*. London: Simon & Schuster.

Searle, W., Prouse, E., L'Ami, E., Gray, A. and Grune, A. (2012) *New Land, New Life: Long-Term Settlement of Refugees in New Zealand. Main Report*. Wellington, New Zealand: Ministry of Business, Innovation and Employment. Accessed on 13/01/2017 at www.dol.govt.nz/research/migration/pdfs/new-land-new-life-longterm-settlement-refugees main-report.pdf.

Simich, L. and Andermann, L. (eds) (2014) *Refuge and Resilience: Promoting Resilience and Mental Health Among Resettled Refugees and Forced Migrants* (Vol. 7). New York, NY: Springer.

Thompson, N. (2012) *Anti-Discriminatory Practice* (5th edition). New York, NY: Palgrave Macmillan.

UNHCR (2015) *UNHCR Global Resettlement Statistical Report 2014*. Geneva: United Nations High Commissioner for Refugees. Accessed on 15/07/2017 at www.unhcr.org/pages/4a16b1676.html.

UNHCR (2016) *Connecting Refugees: How Internet and Mobile Connectivity Can Improve Refugee Well-Being and Transform Humanitarian Action*. Geneva: United Nations High Commissioner for Refugees. Accessed on 15/07/2017 at www.unhcr.org/publications/operations/5770d43c4/connecting-refugees.html.

UNHCR (2017) *Global Trends: Forced Displacement in 2016*. Geneva: United Nations High Commissioner for Refugees. Accessed on 15/07/2017 at www.unhcr.org/globaltrends.

United Nations (1951) *The 1951 Convention Relating to the Status of Refugees*. Geneva: United Nations High Commissioner for Refugees. Accessed on 15/07/2017 at www.unhcr.org/1951-refugee-convention.html.

Urry, J. (2007) *Mobilities*. Cambridge: Polity Press.

Valtonen, K. (2008) *Social Work and Migration: Immigrant and Refugee Settlement and Integration*. Farnham: Ashgate Publishing.

Chapter 4

Negotiating New Disability Practice Contexts: Opportunities and Challenges for Social Workers

GARTH BENNIE AND SARA GEORGESON

Introduction

There are major paradigm shifts under way that are reframing how disability is understood. Disabled activists internationally have led conversations about disability that promote a human rights approach to disability (Shakespeare 2014). In 2006, the United Nations finalized the Convention on the Rights of Persons with Disabilities (United Nations 2006) and the Optional Protocol (negotiations included disabled people from UN member states). The Convention confirms that disabled people have the right to self-determination in all aspects of their lives: to not be discriminated against, to live in the community with their family, to access universal services including health and education, to have employment and economic security, and to access additional supports to enable them to fully participate as citizens in society. The challenges from disabled activists over the last three decades and the development of the UN Convention have required a significant rethink in how disability support and services are understood internationally (New Zealand Disability Support Network 2015, 2016; United Nations 2006).

The New Zealand Disability Strategy 2016–2026 outlines how government will implement the Convention, addressing areas that require legislative as well as policy changes and new initiatives. Specifically, Outcome 7: Choice and Control requires that 'Disabled people are consulted on and actively involved in the development and implementation of legislation and policies concerning supports and services that are both specific to them and for the mainstream' (Ministry of Social Development 2016, p.37). There is currently focus on transforming the Aotearoa New Zealand disability service system based on an approach called 'Enabling Good Lives'.

'Enabling Good Lives' embraces notions of choice and control along with the advent of personalized budgets and is already having emancipatory and empowering impacts on how disabled people and families see the world of support services and funding (Anderson, Ferguson and Janes 2014; Anderson, Janes and Pope 2015; Elder-Woodward 2016; Were 2016, 2017). As a result, markedly different roles and new relationships are being demanded from practitioners and, increasingly, practitioner roles are being filled by disabled people as part of an emerging services by and for disabled people/families paradigm.

However, these changes can also be a double-edged sword as the language of individualization, self-direction, and personalized budgets is readily adopted (some would say appropriated) in an economic and social policy context which is dominated by neoliberal narratives. These narratives regard disabled people as social investment liabilities alongside the ever-present prospect of government austerity (Brookes *et al.* 2015; Runswick-Cole and Goodley 2015). Unintended consequences can emerge as disabled people and families find themselves as a new cohort of consumers in a complex and ever-changing provider market place (Jackson 2005), with a degree of purchasing power constantly under threat from the possibility of government austerity measures. These measures make the possibility of the *good life* just as elusive as it has always been (Power 2014). For disabled people and family members in newly acquired practitioner roles there is the prospect of some challenging dynamics to navigate in a newly emerging service system that they were instrumental in advocating for, but which may struggle to realize its original intentions. An example involves practitioners being required to operate within all too familiar financial constraints that impact on their ability to meet the needs and aspirations individuals have identified in their plans.

For current practitioners who do not have lived experience (as disabled people or family members) there are some emerging uncertainties about future roles and how the social work profession needs to respond to the shift in power relations brought about by service system transformation. There is a consequent need to reassess the training and preparation of social work practitioners internationally who intend to work in these newly emerging service settings and to ask some searching questions about who should be driving the content and future development of qualifications and training (Jeon *et al.* 2015; Williams, Porter and Marriott 2014).

The 'Enabling Good Lives' programme is presented as a case study of emerging disability theory and practice. To explore how new social work roles, relationships and power dynamics might be negotiated by practitioners, including those with and without lived experience of disability, it is useful to describe key roles in the current service system and then to explore emerging theories that inform the 'Enabling Good Lives' principles and consequent system transformation. This provides a context for a discussion of new and emerging roles and how social workers (with and without lived experience of disability) might contribute in the transformed service system that is envisaged for Aotearoa New Zealand. Other challenges that are likely to occur from this system transformation will be explored, and some reflection questions are posed at the end of the chapter for the reader to ponder their position and ability to respond to significant system changes.

Current roles in the service system

While the focus of the discussion here is on the Aotearoa New Zealand disability service system, similar service developments are being experienced internationally. For example, in Australia the National Disability Insurance Scheme was launched in July 2013 (Australian Government 2013), following years of discussion about the need for a major reform of disability services.

As in many other jurisdictions, there are a number of roles in the current disability service system in Aotearoa New Zealand where social workers have traditionally been employed. Key tasks in these roles include providing information, advocacy, referral/intake, assessment, planning and service coordination, and family support. Disability-specific service providers frequently employ people with social work backgrounds as field officers or service coordinators who provide support to access information and services. Needs Assessment and Service Coordination (NASC) agencies are specific providers funded by government to act as the gateway for access to funded services in a specified locality (Ministry of Health 2015). The focus here is assessment for eligibility for funded services and coordination support to access services once eligibility is determined. Needs assessors and service coordinators often come from social work backgrounds.

The current service system in Aotearoa New Zealand is characterized by procedures for assessing eligibility for a pre-determined menu of services based on a set of historical assumptions about what disabled people and families need and when. Providers are contracted (and bulk funded) to provide these services based on rigid service specifications. The opportunity for disabled people and families to think and plan outside existing services is limited due to other options not being available in their region, or where providers cannot provide supports that go beyond the parameters of the service specifications in their contracts (Ministry of Health 2017). Social workers are frequently employed in this system in gatekeeping roles where key tasks are focused on assessment and determination of eligibility for funded services and then coordinating access to these.

The system is slow to respond to innovation and the best that some people experience is being on a waiting list for a service that, ultimately, may only be a limited version of what they really need or want. The system is entirely orientated to conceptualizing what people need only in terms of highly specified and pre-determined services, thus home supports are bundled as hours for home management, personal care and/or supported independent living and are largely delivered in the person's home. Disabled people and families also experience multiple assessment and planning processes, once to get access to the service system as a whole and then again with each service provider they subsequently encounter. The primary contractual relationship (and therefore locus of control) in the system is that between the government and the service provider, not between the disabled person/family and the service provider.

In this system, those in social work roles are overwhelmingly people without lived experience of disability and are more often than not regarded by disabled people and families as access guardians acting either on behalf of individual providers or on behalf of the state in terms of access to the system. If they are seen as advocates and allies it is usually framed in the context of support for gaining eligibility and access to existing services, not in imagining or creating a personalized or bespoke vision of what a *good life* might entail. For example, a person may request an allocation for support so they can participate as a volunteer at the community library only to be told that the only way they could be supported is to attend the library as part of a group activity. Nevertheless, there are some roles where advocacy and being an ally are to the fore, particularly with non-government organizations that do not provide government-contracted services. Such organizations are few in number and, as not-for-profit organizations, they rely on donations and operate on a fee-for-service basis, enabling them to be independent.

Emerging theories: enabling good lives and system transformation

The notion of personalized or individualized support directed by disabled people and/or families has been a narrative within and around disability services in jurisdictions such as the UK and Canada, as well as in Aotearoa New Zealand, for almost a generation (Kendrick 2009; Ministry of Health 2011). A theory of person-directed support has its origins in a drive to de-institutionalize community services based on the now widespread recognition that disabled people so often tend to be *in* and not *of* the community. They are passive recipients of pre-determined service options and not active, contributing and participating citizens pursuing their own personal vision of what a *good life* might be (DeCarlo 2016). Central to these initiatives has been the choice and control that is assumed to flow from having access to a personal budget, either directly or indirectly, through an agent of some kind.

Internationally, various models and approaches have been promulgated to translate these concepts into practice, often with variable levels of success (Kendall and Cameron 2013; Junne and Huber 2014; Mitchell, Brooks and Glendinning 2015; Moran *et al.* 2011; Salsberg *et al.* 2014). Much of this work has often occurred in isolated pockets due to the emergence of local leadership, and any success has usually been in spite of rather than because of the administrative and funding systems that support disability services. Where a *whole-system* approach has been developed, it has usually been limited to specific localities or restricted to specific funding components or cohort populations of the service system. These initiatives have often functioned as demonstrations and pilots that are tacked on to the existing system. Many have foundered or not moved to more widespread implementation due to bureaucratic inertia and the administrative challenges associated with scaling things up and the perceived financial risks associated with doing so (PricewaterhouseCoopers 2012). These perceived financial risks come in the form of either increased costs to the service system as a whole or the political risks associated with the possibility that disabled people and families will misspend or squander tax payers' money.

Nevertheless, despite these challenges, since 2003 the Aotearoa New Zealand context has seen a base of experience develop around the use of personal budgets through the Ministry of Health (for people disabled through non-injury related causes). This has been through the trialling and implementation of individualized funding, with coaching and other support offered through host agencies (Ministry of Health 2011).

However, the scope and availability of these options has meant that the overall uptake to date has been little more than 10 percent of the potentially eligible population. Like other jurisdictions, national scale implementation has been limited to specific population cohorts or funding components of the system.

An example of system-wide change is the establishment of the National Disability Insurance Scheme (NDIS) in Australia (Australian Government 2013). A transformation that is national in scale, it attempts to bring together a theory of person-directed support with system architecture that supports and encourages this in practice. This is a response to a system that was emphatically regarded by nearly everyone as broken. Implementation of the scheme is creating widespread turbulence and varying degrees of uncertainty for all participants, including disabled people, families, service providers and the administrators of the scheme. While there are some promising developments, the scheme will clearly take some time to embed so that all key stakeholders can participate with confidence (Green and Mears 2014; National Disability Services 2017).

Disabled people, service providers and policy makers in Aotearoa New Zealand have also developed similar aspirations. While there is not the same sense of a *burning platform* as experienced in Australia, there has been a gathering momentum and consensus that some kind of step change is needed if the disability service system is going to be more responsive and enable a person-directed approach in practice.

In 2008, a Select Committee Inquiry (Social Services Committee 2008) was held as a response to some serious shortcomings in the disability service system. It found that the system was not orientated to serving the interests of disabled people or families. System change was needed if their choice and control over what happened with disability services and supports was to be central.

A Ministerial Working Group was established in 2011 and developed a vision they called 'Enabling Good Lives'; this initiative was underpinned by a set of eight fundamental principles:

1. Self-determination – disabled people are in control of their lives.

2. Beginning early – investing early in families and supporting aspirational thinking about what they want for their child.

3. Person-centred – supports that are directed by, and are tailored to, an individual's needs.

4. Ordinary life outcomes – living an everyday life in everyday places.

5. Mainstream first – support to access mainstream services before specialist disability services.

6. Mana-enhancing – a Maori (indigenous) concept referring to respecting and recognizing a person's abilities and contribution.

7. Easy to use – supports that are simple to use and flexible.

8. Relationship building – supports build and strengthen relationships between disabled people, family and community.

(Cabinet Social Policy Committee 2017)

In 2012, the government signalled the prospect of fundamental change to the disability service system in the section of the New Zealand Disability Action Plan headed 'Shared result: Transform the disability support system' which is informed by the 'Enabling Good Lives Principles'.[1] An 'Enabling Good Lives' National Leadership Group was established to provide guidance and oversight. This group was made up primarily of disabled people and family members; it still exists today. These developments collectively established the links between 'Enabling Good Lives' (as a theory of change) and 'System Transformation', the leadership role of disabled people and families, and the support of government for change.

Since 2012 a number of pilots, demonstrations, and trials have sought to test various elements of what a transformed system might look like. As the result of this activity and several evaluations, along with a consideration of international experiences, some basic building blocks of a transformed system were arrived at which were in turn used as the basis for some initial high-level design work. This work has provided the central components of a transformed system (Anderson *et al.* 2014, 2015; Cabinet Social Policy Committee 2017; Were 2016, 2017). Further detailed design work continues to be undertaken. The new system was implemented in the MidCentral region of New Zealand's North Island[2] on 1 October 2018, and will be followed by staged implementation across the rest of the country from 2020.

Throughout the design phase, the role of disabled people and family members has been to the fore. A co-design and co-governance approach was adopted whereby a specific proportion of roles was reserved for disabled people and family members on all working groups looking at

---

1 See www.enablinggoodlives.co.nz/about-egl/enabling-good-lives-context/long-term-change-september-2012, accessed on 17/09/2018.

2 See www.midcentraldhb.govt.nz/AboutMDHB/Pages/Geographic-Area-and-Population.aspx, accessed on 17/09/2018.

both design and implementation (Cabinet Social Policy Committee 2017). This has not been without its challenges in terms of sourcing enough people with the time, experience and knowledge to contribute. However, it is also providing an enormous opportunity for a large group of people with lived experience to explore the world of disability policy and service development for the first time. Having disabled people and families as active and integral participants in both co-design and co-governance has established a bedrock not only for the design of a transformed system, but also for its implementation and ongoing operation.

Some essential components of a transformed service system informed by the 'Enabling Good Lives' principles are now emerging:

- *Independent facilitation-based support and planning* that actively supports self-direction so that disabled people have greater choice and control over their lives and support. A process that supports and encourages disabled people and families to imagine and navigate different futures that are not constrained by the current service system. People are considered in their wider context, not just in terms of formal support services.

- *Personal budgets* that are drawn from cross-government pooled funding that enables flexibility and self-directed purchase of supports and services.

- *A range of management options* that enables a person to determine how much or how little self-management they undertake in relation to their personal budget, and creates opportunities to easily change management options over time.

- *Accountability arrangements* that are proportionate to the size of a personal budget.

- *Investing in disabled people and families* so that they can participate in a transformed system with confidence and know how to maximize their choice and control.

- *A community facilitation and community building approach* that actively assists and supports disabled people to be valued and contributing citizens with an everyday life in everyday places. An approach that does not merely assimilate but changes the nature of the *mainstream* community so that it responds readily to diversity.

- *Access to independent advocacy* for those people who do not have families and personal networks or who rely on others to support their communication and decision making. Independent advocacy is focused entirely on the best interests of the person.

- *Co-governance arrangements and protocols that involve disabled people and families* at regional and national levels in the design, operation and evaluation of the service system.

Collectively, these components offer both a theoretical and practical framework for understanding the rationale for change and how it might be implemented. In addition, they signal that new skills and approaches are required by practitioners working in the disability sector, and that entirely new roles will need to be developed.

New roles: contribution, partnership and negotiation

Given the components of a transformed service system, assumptions can be made about the opportunities social work practitioners might assume and regard as simple variations on current roles. For example, facilitation and navigation roles, independent advocacy roles, professional development roles and participation in evaluation activities. Such assumptions would be mistaken for two reasons:

1. The notion of co-governance means that increasing numbers of disabled people and family members themselves will be looking to assume practitioner and leadership roles in these very same areas – as well as in the delivery of support services – and thus demanding access to resources that can enable them to do so.

2. The concept of self-direction means that not all current (and mostly non-disabled) practitioners will easily adapt to an environment where the power and decision making are shifting from those who deliver services to those who use (and purchase) services. There is a significant difference between providing support *to* or *for* disabled people and walking alongside someone where the decision making about what, who, how and when rests with the person. New relationship dynamics and ways of thinking and working are required.

This is not to suggest that all social workers will struggle with what is essentially a paradigm shift in the dynamics of power that frame disability support and services. There is no doubt that given the origins of social work and its commitment to social justice and the challenging of marginalization and inequality, many social workers will already have an embedded understanding of these changing relations of power. These social workers are largely seen by disabled people and family members as allies in their struggle for access to appropriate support and services. However, there will be a number of social workers who are challenged by the territory of change and how to traverse a new landscape of roles and relationships.

Non-disabled social work practitioners will be required to negotiate their way through a system that increasingly features services *by and for* disabled people. Lived experience as either a disabled person or family member will more frequently become a prerequisite for roles that have traditionally been regarded as the domain of (mostly) non-disabled social workers, as facilitators, planners, coordinators, evaluators and trainers as well as leadership roles in management and governance. There are readily observable parallels to these developments in the wider Aotearoa New Zealand context. We have seen the widespread emergence over the past two decades of Kaupapa Maori services – these are education, social and health services *by Maori, for Maori* (Pipi *et al.* 2004). Whānau Ora is a Kaupapa Maori approach that is based on the premise that whānau (extended family) should be directly resourced so that they can make the critical decisions about supports and services. A navigator provides a support role to explore possibilities and put together a plan (and a budget) that reflects the whānau's decision making and priorities (New Zealand Productivity Commission 2015). There are some very clear similarities between this approach and the concept of independent facilitation and access to personal budgets envisaged for the disability system transformation project.

The emergence of a practitioner workforce made up of disabled people and family members with lived experience does not mean that current (and largely non-disabled) social workers in the disability field are going to be entirely displaced. What it will mean is that the recruitment of social workers will increasingly be in the hands of either disabled people and family members themselves (through their personal budgets as users, and therefore a growing cohort of employers) or because disabled people and family members will be in leadership and governance roles with employing organizations. There will be times when there will be an explicit preference for someone with lived experience. An example is the independent facilitation role which is envisaged as the new front end or entry point to the disability service system. A recurring theme expressed by many (but not all) disabled people and family members is the need for this first point of contact to be a peer, someone with whom they can identify as having a similar lived experience.

The contribution of social workers without lived experience will need to focus increasingly on a *negotiation* to partner and collaborate with this emerging group of practitioners who do have lived experience. Central to this will be the need to create empowering environments where disabled people and family members are welcomed, can explore and take the opportunity to prepare, train and be supported into roles traditionally reserved for non-disabled practitioners. Creating empowering environments means organizing, designing and structuring learning and working environments that remove access barriers to the participation of disabled people and family members (Schalock and Verdugo 2013).

In preparing practitioners for disability practice contexts, social work training programmes need to consider how they ensure that courses and qualifications are accessible to disabled people and family members. Their participation in these programmes is critical to establishing a sustainable core of qualified social work practitioners with lived experience. Prioritizing the appointment of academics who are disabled or who have lived experience as family members to key roles in relevant course development and delivery is another critical dimension to ensuring that collaboration and partnership are embedded into leadership roles in these programmes. Having people with lived experience in these roles sends powerful messages around relevance and accessibility to aspiring practitioners and academics who are disabled. Equal opportunity and affirmative action approaches could be developed to address current inequities, both for students and staff, in social work education programmes.

In Aotearoa New Zealand, the employment rates of people with lived experience working in disability service settings where social work roles occur is about the same as for the general labour market, even in those agencies where disability employment services are the focus of delivery (Te Pou o te Whakaaro Nui and New Zealand Disability Support Network 2016). Participation in leadership, management and governance roles occurs at an even lower rate. The same can be said of government agencies where the focus of activity is disability-related policy and services. Disability services focused on areas like advocacy, audit and evaluation tend to follow the same trend. Undertaking accessibility audits and the meaningful implementation of diversity programmes with a disability focus are urgent priorities in these contexts. There are a range of well-established approaches that could be drawn on to address current shortfalls, including prioritizing students with lived experience for practicums, internships and leadership development initiatives (for management and governance roles), and promoting equal employment opportunity policies and affirmative action programmes. Again, seeing people with lived experience in frontline social work roles as well as in leadership and governance roles collectively sends important signals about shifts in power and the likely relevance of services for disabled people and families.

Both government and non-government employers can also reposition power dynamics by ensuring that people with lived experience are trained and supported into advisory, audit and evaluation roles within their agencies so that the voices of those who use services and programmes are central to decision making about their design and quality. These opportunities can often be the beginning of a career in the disability sector (and lead to training and qualifications in areas like social work) or could be employment opportunities as the result of undertaking such training.

A natural extension to having these opportunities is that disabled people and family members develop the skills and knowledge needed to establish and run their own programmes. Those who currently hold the power (funding, contracts, knowledge and skills) have important roles to play in facilitating and supporting the development of services by and for disabled people and family members.

Social workers without lived experience (in frontline and leadership and training roles) also have a critical role to play in developing this capability and capacity, as the transfer of knowledge and skills is a transfer of power. For example, practitioners could work alongside and partner with practitioners who have lived experience, supporting the acquisition of social work knowledge and skills (for example, through peer supervision and co-facilitation of services). Educators in social work training programmes could partner in both the transfer of existing knowledge and the creation of new social work theory and knowledge relevant to practice in disability service settings. Finally, social work leaders and managers could structure learning and work environments to be accessible and accommodating to students and employees with lived experience.

Future challenges

The changes being undertaken in 'system transformation' in Aotearoa New Zealand are significant and have relevance for other countries that are also planning system-wide transformation. As we have observed in the Australian scenario with the introduction of the NDIS, there are a number of future challenges at many levels that practitioners need to be prepared for.

Social workers who do not have the lived experience of disability will be required to negotiate a practice arena where the relations of power are shifting. This will be an ongoing challenge and the extent of this challenge will depend on the practitioner's understanding of the changes that are occurring around them and their ability to adapt to and accept a new status quo. Taking the time to reflect on and understand why these changes are occurring and what imperatives are driving them is essential. Doing so will shed light on new values, practices and approaches. Participating in opportunities that support this reflection and learning will be important. This can come in the form of seeking out supervision arrangements that challenge current values and practices and expose the practitioner to new ways of thinking. It will be important for those in social work roles to take up opportunities afforded through concepts like Communities of Practice (New Zealand Disability Support Network 2015, 2016) where facilitated groups of practitioners can learn about, implement and reflect on new approaches. It will also be important to have access to retraining through short courses and qualifications that anticipate the changing practice landscape.

These possibilities for new learning assume that such opportunities will be available. This kind of supporting infrastructure has long been overlooked as a critical component of system redesign, particularly when it comes to embedding innovation as everyday practice. In Aotearoa New Zealand, there is currently some effort to review disability-focused qualifications so that they anticipate and reflect the principles, practices and theoretical underpinnings of 'Enabling Good Lives'. These reviews are also looking at the knowledge and competencies needed to operate in a person-directed paradigm where the focus is on facilitation and community building. There is a need for social work internationally to keep up with the new thinking and practice in education and training if it is to continue to have, and be seen to have, relevance to those in the disability sector.

Another challenge is the development of the role of independent facilitation as the new front end to a transformed disability service system. This role is receiving a lot of attention not only because of its pivotal importance, but also because of the variety of views about who can be an independent facilitator, what constitutes independence and what kind of training and support is needed for the role. How this role is constructed and deployed in a transformed disability system is particularly relevant because it is one that will have a strong interest from those with social work backgrounds. Aside from one's view on what qualifications and training may or may not be needed, the role is a highly nuanced one requiring a rare blend of values, interpersonal skills and knowledge – about the service system, about community and about the impact of a disabling society.

Independent facilitation requires that one is able to walk alongside individuals and families in a way that enables as much self-direction as possible, but also exposes a person and family to new possibilities and a potential future that has not hitherto been considered. This process can create levels of discomfort and new experiences of dissatisfaction about one's current circumstances, confusion and a sense of powerlessness, but also the opportunity for positive change and a different future. Walking alongside people where they may start with new insights (enlightenment), move towards an understanding that things could change (emancipation) and then decide to exercise more choice and control (empowerment) can be truly transformative (Freire 1970). A practitioner undertaking a facilitation role, in relation to this process, should be guided by a coherent theoretical model of social change that clearly informs and guides practice.

Initiating and supporting people through such a process in an empowering way that respects the current values and worldview of the individual and family is paramount. It is also an enormous privilege and responsibility. The absence of the right approach and values framework can easily result in the imposition of the facilitator's values and worldview or that of the organization they work for, leading to disorientation, disempowerment and a perpetuation of power and control by others in the lives of disabled people and families. It is essential, then, that the independence of the role is about being free not only of the vested interests of organizations (funders and providers), but also of the imposition of the values and worldview of the facilitators themselves. There is a fine balance between respecting people's values and lives and gently introducing new ideas, alternative ways of seeing their world and imagining new possibilities; and then ensuring there is support and respect for a journey of personal or family change that can have unexpected and unforeseen consequences. Thus, independent facilitation is not just about independence from the vested interests of organizations, but also about independence from the vested interests of practitioners in these roles, with regard to how or with whom they are employed. This is a challenge that will be equally relevant for practitioners with and without lived experience.

As with any discussion about vested interests, it will be interesting to see how this narrative about the role of independent facilitation plays out in the context of system transformation. Central to resolving the embedded issues will be some kind of validation process or protocol that ensures the integrity of the role in relation to its perceived and actual independence.

It will be important for those in social work roles to participate in this dialogue. A validation process should ensure exposure to the required values frameworks, ethics, principles, skills and knowledge that underpin the role. The construction of this role and the capability of the practitioners involved are central to the success of system transformation. It will be essential to strike a balance between avoiding the creation of yet another imposed professionalized elite in the lives of disabled people and ensuring that there is a capable and diverse workforce in these roles.

A final challenge worth canvassing is the ethical dilemmas that may confront practitioners with lived experience. Having managed to overcome barriers to training and access to employment opportunities in a newly transformed system they will need to navigate some inevitable realities where the newly emerging system is struggling to match its original aspirations, especially if they have been instrumental in supporting or designing that system. While people may have more choice and control at one level, there will still be rules and guidelines around how and on what personal budgets are spent. These constraints may be the result of system design shortfalls, changing policy imperatives, but also of wider economic changes where government austerity measures could be implemented. Poor market stewardship on the part of the state could also lead to an overly complex marketplace of service providers, with the range and quality as variable as ever.

While navigating such dilemmas would not just be the province of practitioners with lived experience, their ability to straddle the boundary between the aspirations of disabled people and families (and their allies) and the constricting imperatives of the state could be especially challenging. In these circumstances, practitioners can opt for roles where the boundaries are more blurred or where the role is constructed as advocacy or activism. Where the practitioner (with and without lived experience) is on the boundary itself, the power of deeply embedded reflective practice, solid supervision and ethical coherency will be paramount. Examples of boundary roles include those involving decision making about personal budgets, policy and regulatory design, the rationing of resources and broader decisions about eligibility.

While 'Enabling Good Lives' and the 'system transformation' it is informing have the potential to be a step change in how disabled people and families access supports and services, it will not in and of itself transform wider society. One of the 'Enabling Good Lives' principles is *mainstream first*, which speaks to the imperative of participation in the mainstream rather than in services, and the need to build and change communities so that barriers to access are removed. Having access to independent facilitation and a personal budget will not, on its own, transform society in disabled people's interests.

As with other jurisdictions that have engaged in transformational change in partnership with disabled people, there are wider and deeply imbedded structural issues at work in Aotearoa New Zealand society that create the experience of being disabled. These include the lack of affordable and accessible housing; the absence of accessible transport options; an education system that struggles to be inclusive; and deeply rooted income inequality (New Zealand Disability Support Network 2016). Comprehensive legislative and regulatory developments are required to address these issues and make it possible for disabled people to actually exercise their citizenship rights. Organizations and groups focused on initiatives that seek to address these shortcomings are also opportunities where those with social work backgrounds may have much to offer.

Conclusion

This chapter has described a practice context in Aotearoa New Zealand that is in the midst of major transformation where both practitioners and disabled people are having to increasingly negotiate new roles and relationships based ultimately on a shift in power. This experience parallels developments in other jurisdictions that are aimed at transforming power relations in disability support. The debates and dilemmas for social work practitioners (with and without lived experience of disability) have been explored in the context of a rapidly evolving landscape of service provision where disabled people themselves are forging new roles and relationships with the service system. Some guidance has been offered on how practitioners can navigate this new landscape.

Reflection questions

- Can you identify roles in the disability service system where social workers can have an important role to play? To what extent are these roles on the boundary where the aspirations of disabled people and families meet the state's imperative for rules and regulations about funding and eligibility?

- Reflect on your own values and approaches in relation to the concept of being *person directed*. What changes do you think you might need to consider in relation to how you engage and work with disabled people and their families? Are there new frameworks and models that you need to explore?

- What roles in a transformed disability service system would be most compatible with your values, skills and goals?

- Reflecting on a social work education programme you are or have been enrolled in, how accessible is it for disabled people and family members aspiring to be social workers? Are there currently any students with lived experience of disability? What changes can you think of that would make the programme more accessible?

References

Anderson, D., Ferguson, B. and Janes, R. (2014) *Enabling Good Lives Christchurch Demonstration: Phase 1 Evaluation Report*. Wellington, New Zealand: Office for Disability Issues.

Anderson, D., Janes, R. and Pope, P. (2015) *Enabling Good Lives Christchurch Demonstration: Phase 2 Evaluation Report*. Office for Disability Issues. Accessed on 28/02/2018 at www.odi.govt.nz/nz-disability-strategy/other-initiatives/enabling-good-lives.

Australian Government (2013) *National Disability Insurance Scheme Act 2013*. No. 20. Australia: Australian Government.

Brookes, N., Callaghan, L., Netten, A. and Fox, D. (2015) 'Personalisation and innovation in a cold financial climate.' *British Journal of Social Work 45*, 86–103.

Cabinet Social Policy Committee (2017) *Disability Support System Transformation: Overall Approach*. Accessed on 28/02/2018 at www.odi.govt.nz/assets/New-Zealand-Disability-Strategy-files/Disability-Support-System-Transformation-Overall-Approach.pdf.

DeCarlo, M.P. (2016) *Implementation of Self-Directed Supports for Individuals with Intellectual and Developmental Disabilities: A Political Economy Analysis*. Richmond, VA: Virginia Commonwealth University School of Social Work.

Elder-Woodward, J. (2016) 'Disabled people's independent living movement in Scotland: A time for reflection.' *Ethics and Social Welfare 10*, 3, 252–266.

Freire, P. (1970) *Pedagogy of the Oppressed*. New York, NY: Herder and Herder.

Green, J. and Mears, J. (2014) 'The implementation of the NDIS: Who wins, who loses?' *Cosmopolitan Civil Societies Journal 6*, 2, 3915.

Jackson, R. (2005) *Who Cares? The Impact of Ideology, Regulation and Marketisation on the Quality of Life of People with an Intellectual Disability*. Sheffield: Centre for Welfare Reform. Accessed on 27/02/2018 at www.centreforwelfarereform.org.

Jeon, H., Mahoney, K., Loughlin, D.M. and Simon-Rusinowitz, L. (2015) 'Multi-state survey of support brokers in cash and counselling programs: Perceived roles and training needs.' *Journal of Disability Policy Studies 26*, 1, 24–32.

Junne, J. and Huber, C. (2014) 'The risk of users' choice: Exploring the case of direct payments.' *German Social Care, Health, Risk & Society 116*, 7–8, 631–648.

Kendall, S. and Cameron, A. (2013) 'Personalisation of adult social care: Self-directed support and the choice and control agenda.' *British Journal of Learning Disabilities 42*, 264–271.

Kendrick, M.J. (2009) 'Some lessons concerning agency transformation towards personalized services.' *International Journal of Leadership in Public Services 5*, 1, 47–54.

Ministry of Health (2011) *Evaluation of Individualised Funding Following the Expansion to New Host Providers*. Accessed on 28/02/2018 at www.health.govt.nz/system/files/documents/publications/evaluation-individualised-funding-oct11.pdf.

Ministry of Health (2015) *Disability Support Services: Needs Assessment and Service Coordination (NASC) Organisations*. Fact Sheet. Accessed on 28/02/2018 at www.health.govt.nz/system/files/documents/topic_sheets/needs-assessment-service-coordination-organisations-mar15.pdf.

Ministry of Health (2017) *Disability Information and Advisory Services and Needs Assessment and Service Coordination Review – A Proposed Design and Framework*. Accessed on 08/02/2018 at www.health.govt.nz/system/files/documents/publications/dias-nasc-review-proposed-design-framework-jan17.pdf.

Ministry of Social Development (2016) *New Zealand Disability Strategy 2016–2026*. Accessed on 28/02/2018 at www.odi.govt.nz/assets/New-Zealand-Disability-Strategy-files/pdf-nz-disability-strategy-2016.pdf.

Mitchell, W., Brooks, J. and Glendinning, C. (2015) 'Carers' roles in personal budgets: Tensions and dilemmas in front line practice.' *British Journal of Social Work 45*, 1433–1450.

Moran, N., Glendinning, C., Stevens, M., Manthorpe, J. *et al.* (2011) 'Joining up government by integrating funding streams? The experiences of the individualized budget pilot projects for older and disabled people in England.' *International Journal of Public Administration 34*, 4, 232–243.

National Disability Services (2017) *State of the Disability Sector Report*. Australia: National Disability Services: NDS. Accessed on 28/02/2018 at www.nds.org.au/news/state-of-the-disability-sector-report-2017-reflects-sector-under-pressure.

New Zealand Disability Support Network (2015) *Investing for Innovation and Quality: A Sector Briefing from NZDSN, the New Zealand Disability Support Network*. Wellington, New Zealand: NZDSN.

New Zealand Disability Support Network (2016) *Transformation, Inclusion and Citizenship: A Sector Briefing from NZDSN, the New Zealand Disability Support Network*. Wellington, New Zealand: NZDSN.

New Zealand Productivity Commission (2015) *Appendix C Case Study: Whānau Ora*. Accessed on 28/02/2018 at www.productivity.govt.nz/sites/default/files/social-services-final-report-appendix-c.pdf.

Pipi, K., Cram, F., Hawke, R., Hawke, S. *et al.* (2004) 'A research ethic for studying Māori and iwi provider success.' *Social Policy Journal of New Zealand Te Puna Whakaaro 23*, 141–153.

Power, A. (2014) 'Personalization and austerity in the crosshairs: Government perspectives on the remaking of adult social care.' *Journal of Social Policy 43*, 829–846.

PricewaterhouseCoopers (2012) *Planning for a Sustainable Disability Sector*. Accessed on 03/05/2018 at www.dss.gov.au/sites/default/files/documents/05_2014/fahcsia_sector_capacity_report_november_2012.pdf_-_adobe_acrobat_pro.pdf.

Runswick-Cole, K. and Goodley, D. (2015) 'Disability, austerity and cruel optimism in big society: Resistance and the disability commons.' *Canadian Journal of Disability Studies 4*, 2, 162–186.

Salsberg, C., Watson, N., Beresford, P. and Schofield, P. (2014) 'Personalization of health care in England: Have the wrong lessons been drawn from the personal health budget pilot?' *Journal of Health Services Research and Policy 19*, 3, 183–188.

Schalock, R. and Verdugo, M.A. (2013) 'Intellectual and developmental disabilities: The transformation of disabilities organizations.' *Intellectual and Developmental Disabilities 51*, 4, 273–286.

Shakespeare, T. (2014) *Disability Rights and Wrongs Revisited*. London and New York, NY: Routledge.

Social Services Committee (2008) *Inquiry into the Quality of Care and Service Provision for People with Disabilities.* Accessed on 28/02/2018 at www.parliament.nz/resource/en-nz/48DBSCH_SCR4194_1/cb220d2e3ba25dc33dec0b28b29b30578d110dd5.

Te Pou o te Whakaaro Nui and New Zealand Disability Support Network (2016) *The New Zealand Disability Support Workforce: 2015 Survey of NZDSN Member Organisations.* Auckland, New Zealand: Te Pou o te Whakaaro Nui.

United Nations (2006) *Convention on the Rights of Persons with Disabilities and Optional Protocol.* Accessed on 28/02/2018 at www.un.org/disabilities/documents/convention/convoptprot-e.pdf.

Were, L. (2016) *Summary Evaluation Report Phase One Enabling Good Lives Waikato Demonstration.* Office for Disability Issues. Accessed on 08/02/2018 at www.odi.govt.nz/nz-disability-strategy/other-initiatives/enabling-good-lives.

Were, L. (2017) *Enabling Good Lives Waikato Phase Two Evaluation Summary Report.* Office for Disability Issues. Accessed on 28/02/2018 at www.odi.govt.nz/nz-disability-strategy/other-initiatives/enabling-good-lives.

Williams, V., Porter, S. and Marriott, A. (2014) 'Your life, your choice: Support planning led by disabled people's organisations.' *British Journal of Social Work 44*, 1197–1215.

Note

The views expressed in this chapter are those of the authors and not necessarily those of the New Zealand Disability Support Network (NZDSN). No endorsement is implied by NZDSN.

Chapter 5

Social Work and Mental Health

MALCOLM GOLIGHTLEY AND GLORIA KIRWAN

Introduction

Worldwide, thousands of social workers are involved in the delivery of a rich tapestry of services in the field of mental health. However, the field of mental health care is in flux (Bracken 2014). The near universal increased awareness and acceptance of mental distress has resulted in greater demands on services and professionals. The diversity of social work practice is unified by long-held social work principles and practices, including a commitment to non-judgemental, inclusive and participatory ways of engaging with service users and working in ways which support service users to find their own solutions. The commitment to participatory practice is widely shared by social workers in all settings, transcending global borders and cultures.

A number of challenges and debates lie within the wider mental health field and these are taking place within a context of deinstitutionalization, increased recognition of service user rights and the development of recovery-informed practices. The increased international attention to the promotion of human rights within healthcare systems has prompted mental health services to work within *recovery-focused, participation-based* and *multidisciplinary* frameworks. This chapter considers how social work can position itself within these debates while staying faithful to its basic ethical and practice principles.

The literature shows that mental health social work involves a wide range of different approaches, practised in a diverse range of settings and with service users from children to older people (Golightley and Kirwan 2017). It is not possible to outline all of the different practice approaches that social workers are utilizing and developing in mental health settings across the world. Instead, we examine the principles of social work which underpin practice and we suggest that these principles provide a sound base from which social work can create a distinctive role in the field of mental health service provision across many regions of the globe.

Global trends in mental health policy and service provision

At an international level, recognition of the association between population health outcomes (including mental health outcomes) and social justice has been increasingly discernible in recent decades. This recognition of the relevance of democratic ideals, such as equal access to health care, fair distribution of social resources and the rights of individuals to voice their views, is reflected in the World Health Organization's *Alma Alta Declaration* in 1978 (WHO 1978) which consolidated the commitment to *health for all* in the global health discourse. In tandem with this rights-based objective of access to health care, there is heightened awareness of the benefits of including health users as active participants in their interactions with health services (Nabatchi and Leighninger 2015). The locus of power and expertise, exclusively held by the medical professions for so long and often characterized by a medical model, has thus become more dispersed and there exists an acknowledgment that population health can improve if individual citizens and local communities are enlisted as key actors in their own health trajectories. The active participation of people using health services has become politically desirable as well as improving population health outcomes (Golightley 2017). In other words, the participation of service users has come to be regarded as a health determinant in itself. The elevation of the role of individual health service users has not been lost on the field of mental health care and increasingly there is a call for greater consultation with and participation of mental health service users in the design, delivery and evaluation of mental health services.

Following on from the *Alma Alta Declaration*, the later *Jakarta Declaration* (WHO 1997) further developed the relationship between citizenship and health care by promoting the concept of consumer empowerment through individual participation (Priority No. 4) as a means to advancing global healthcare goals (Kilian *et al.* 2003). Thus, over time, the individual is recast as an *empowered* shaper of health outcomes, a role that reflects wider political efforts, beyond the realm of health care, to deliver on democratic and rights-based ideals.

These rights-informed ideals, such as equality of opportunity and fair distribution of resources, can also be discerned in the mental health strategy of the World Health Organization as articulated in the *Mental Health Action Plan 2013–2020* (WHO 2013). This plan incorporates the biomedical model of mental illness, alongside a social model that recognises connections between mental wellbeing and external 'social, cultural, economic, political and environmental factors' which can arise within the wider life context of individuals (WHO 2013, p.7). By reiterating the importance of consultation and collaboration with users of mental health services, the plan puts empowerment central to progressive, rights-based mental health care. Notably, it also positions mental health service user empowerment as a reparative response to the negative historical experiences of many mental health service users and the continued 'widespread human rights violations and discrimination experienced by people with mental disorders' (WHO 2013, p.7).

The recasting of *psychiatric patients* as agentic, self-determining *mental health service users* replaces the traditional medical model conceptualization of *patients* as people who are passive, incapable of making informed decisions and who are in constant need of monitoring and care (which at times can include coercive treatment and deprivation of liberty). Although not totally free from critical debate, social work has developed approaches that support and advance client self-determination within a partnership-based worker–client relationship. Preserving the dignity of the individual, through non-judgemental and strengths-based approaches, has been central to the aims of social work for many generations of social work practice – often working with marginalized groups regardless of whether this was fashionable (Compton and Galaway 1999). In this respect, social work is ahead of the newly discovered participation curve in the field of mental health and has built up a substantial body of knowledge, theory and skills on how to work in partnership with service users, including involuntary service users, in ways which maximize individual potential but also accommodate professional responsibility and address issues of risk and public accountability.

The mental health statements by the World Health Organization can be viewed as a response to the global demand for mental health treatment. For example, a systematic analysis of research on mental disorders in the European Union estimated a prevalence of 27.4 percent in 2005 (Wittchen and Jacobi 2005), a figure which was raised to 38.2 percent in a follow-up study published in 2011 (Wittchen *et al.* 2011). Globally, mental disorders account for 13 percent of the 'total global burden of disease', although this figure is likely to be higher in low- to middle-level income countries. Shortfalls in access to appropriate levels or forms of treatment in many parts of the world means there is often a reliance on institutional-based psychiatric care despite the evidence exposing its shortcomings (WHO 2012, p.1).

Increased awareness and raised expectations might also account for some of the increases in demand for services. Research by Mojtabai *et al.* (2011) indicates that a constellation of attitudinal, financial and structural factors can play a role in determining if, when or how individuals seek assistance from mental health services. It has become more socially acceptable to seek help for mental disorders, and the importance of good mental health to the economy and country as a whole is recognized (Ministry of Health 2016; Xiandong 2017).

While the changes are positive and encouraging, the effects of austerity and neoliberalism, especially in Europe, have in different ways propped up existing ways of working. This has altered the context within which social workers are trained and practise, resulting in rationing of scarce resources and an apolitical approach. Within this global context, we find considerable variation in the current status and representation of mental health social work. According to the National Association of Social Workers (NASW 2017), 60 percent of mental health services are provided in the United States of America by clinical social workers. This is not replicated in many other countries, where the numbers of mental health social workers remain low compared with other professional groups such as psychiatrists and nurses. Economic, political and policy factors in different countries can influence the head count of social workers within mental health services and this in turn affects how mental health social workers articulate their relevance and core functions (Wilson and Kirwan 2007). However, the changing nature of mental health care, fuelled in many respects by the philosophical shifts in favour of social justice, deinstitutionalization and the recovery model, present mental health social work with opportunities for establishing a more firmly embedded foothold within the field of mental health service provision.

Mental health care is undergoing significant changes in tandem with rising levels of mental health problems in society. As such, the field of mental health social work is one in which the profession has potential to make important contributions in the lives of mental health service users who often are at the receiving end of prejudice, stigma and marginalization in addition to their struggle with the disabling symptoms of different mental disorders and forms of mental distress. We now discuss some contemporary issues, such as debates about the causes of mental disorders, the rights of mental health service users and the future for recovery-based approaches to treatment and care as an example of the application of social work practice.

Causes of mental illness

Just over two hundred years ago, the acceptance that *madness* had a biological basis significantly altered societal attitudes towards people suffering with symptoms of mental distress and prompted greater understanding of the disabling impact of mental illness on the individual. In the period of modernity, the biomedical model had something of a *hero* status (Hyde, Lohan and McDonnell 2004, p.106) because it had usurped the previously held interpretation of mental symptoms as expressions of deviance and exposed the degrading nature of punitive confinement of people affected by mental health problems that was widely condoned in earlier eras. The rise of psychiatry brought with it a reconstruction of *madness* as illness, thus rendering it more socially acceptable, amenable to treatment and a suitable object of scientific research (Conrad and Schneider 1985).

Consequently, ongoing investment worldwide in research is now devoted to progressing knowledge in the field of mental health. The role played by non-biological factors in the development of mental symptomatology is increasingly being recognized. It is, therefore, a field of science surrounded by contested theories alive to potential progress in the discovery of explanations and cures for different forms of mental distress.

Critics of bio-determinist theories of mental illness point to the weak scientific base of psychiatry and its failure to map the biological causes of different mental disorders. Their voices are critical of the pathologizing of human reactions to the challenges of living (Kirk and Kutchins 1994; Rapley, Moncrieff and Dillon 2011; Timimi 2014). Alternative perspectives expose the part played by non-medical factors in the onset of mental illness, including psychological factors (Bentall 2004; Bentall *et al.* 2009), structural factors such as ethnicity, gender or class (Rogers and Pilgrim 2014), and factors arising from personal life experiences such as exposure to abuse, homelessness, trauma or isolation (Hammersley *et al.* 2008; Humphreys and Thiara 2003; Johnstone 2011; McKenzie, Whitley and Weich 2002). Sociological studies have exposed the limitations of institutional psychiatric care (Goffman 1961) and the long-term negative implications for individuals of being labelled (Rogers, Pilgrim and Lacey 1993). Foucault's (1954, 1965) theories of governance and social control have served to expose the risk management role which modern psychiatry carries out on behalf of society, involving the containment of individuals labelled as dangerous (see also Cohen 2013; Rose 1998). Concerns are expressed by some commentators about the extensive use of pharmacological remedies to the neglect of other more social or psychological remedies (Moncrieff 2011; Whitaker 2005).

If social work is to establish a realm of expertise, it needs to engage with these theoretical debates surrounding mental illness in society. This is not an altogether straightforward exercise, and Lacasse and Gomorry (2003, p.385) highlight divergence of opinion within the social work profession, leading to what they describe as 'intellectual tension' in the field of social work. This tension can be experienced by individual social workers employed within mainstream, multidisciplinary systems of mental health care where they find it difficult to reconcile the traditional psychiatric paradigm with their knowledge of the part played by non-biological factors in the trajectory of mental disorders (Maddock 2015). It is in the area of *the social* that social work should feel most comfortable given the social science basis of social work theory and knowledge. Social work has a wide practice base, which includes effective interventions to address problems in the environment of the individual, harnessing the support of family and community networks as well as tackling social exclusion, marginalization and the impact of social problems (Berzoff and Drisko 2015; Weiss-Gal and Welbourne 2008). However, social work needs to continue to build the evidence base that highlights the effectiveness of these interventions in mental health treatment contexts.

More targeted attention is also required to foster critical debates on mental health within social work. The social work curriculum, in most developed countries, has been criticized for its emphasis on the biomedical model of mental health and the lack of attention to alternative paradigms. Writing with reference to the American context, Lacasse and Gomorry (2003, p.400) lament what they regard as the lack of 'professional self-confidence to forge our own separate perspective, even based on the existent well-tested science that often contradicts much that is asserted to be factual by institutional psychiatry'. In other regions, social work students are under-exposed during their social work education to the critical debates within the field of mental health. This creates the danger that many social workers remain unclear on the extent to which social and structural factors – arguably the bread and butter of the social work profession – are fundamentally relevant to the services they provide to mental health service users. Gaps in the social work evidence base weaken the potential for the social work profession to identify and assert its skill base within the changing landscape of mental health service provision.

Mental health and human rights

At an international level, there is mounting action to promote the human rights of people with disabilities, including those suffering with mental disorders. Vanhala (2015) suggests that disability is no longer trapped in a medical discourse and there is greater awareness of the influence of social and political factors in how disability is defined, experienced by individuals and treated by society. While in the past, society's role regarding its responsibilities towards people with disabilities (including people experiencing mental illness) was heavily framed in paternalistic notions, there is now a shift in favour of rights-based, anti-discriminatory and empowering perspectives.

Ngui *et al.* (2010) provide an interesting discussion of the global context of mental disorders and health inequalities. They point out that ideas of social justice in the field of mental health can only be achieved by addressing what they describe as the 'underlying determinants' (p.236) of mental health problems which include, they suggest, 'fair, equitable, and ethical distribution of resources inclusive health and primary care policies, and strengthened legal and human rights protection for people living with mental disorders and their families' (p.237). In addition, they identify other issues that are also relevant to any advancement of the rights of mental health service users, including ethical research, ethical standards of treatment provision, adequate investment in services and appropriate resource allocation. Their paper also alludes to other rights-related issues, which social workers should be especially attentive to, including the relationship between poverty and mental disorders, as well as the marginalization of people from employment and social life when they are labelled as mentally unwell.

While Ngui *et al.* (2010) highlight the plight of people suffering from mental distress in developing countries or countries where mental health care is afforded low political priority, they also place a spotlight on the consequences of low investment in richer countries. For example, they mention how policies of deinstitutionalization, rolled out without adequate funding for community-based alternatives, can lead to phenomena which are not in the interests of people suffering from mental disorders, such as inappropriate incarceration of people with mental disorders in prisons, and increased rates of mentally unwell people presenting to homeless services. They conclude by suggesting that rights-informed systems of mental health care must provide the services people need and must address issues of societal inequality, discrimination, and stigma.

Social work has long championed the fairer distribution of resources in society, as well as anti-discriminatory and inclusive policies. The global agenda for social work (Jones and Truell 2012) highlights the commitment of social work to progress the ideals of distributive justice and anti-oppressive policies worldwide. The field of mental health is a landscape in which social work is well positioned to progress a human rights agenda at macro, mezzo and micro levels in support of the messages from the service user population which have gone too long unheard. For social work, the importance of working at societal/policy (macro level), in addition to work with individuals (micro level) and communities (mezzo level), is familiar territory. Its relevance is emphasized by Littrell and Lacasse (2012) who see a role for social work in challenging health policies which fail to deliver alternatives to medication-only treatments. They believe social workers could be more active in shaping the research agenda in the field of mental health. In support of this point, the academic social work literature is heavily weighted, in terms of mental health social work at the micro level. It is unclear if this reflects the actual focus of social work in the field of mental health but it is likely that more macro-level action could be carried out by social workers to tackle the structural and economic inequalities.

We explore how social work can position itself within the emerging trends and current debates by exploring a specific way of working.

Recovery as social work intervention

Nearly 30 years ago one of the authors of this chapter (you'll have to guess which one) carried out a small research project in a northern city in England to see what mental health patients (service users) wanted from a service.[1] The main message that emerged was a simple one: 'they wanted to be listened to', which formed the title of the report. More recently this was echoed in an article written from a rural Australian perspective (Hyde, Bowles and Pawar 2015), which had a sub-heading that stressed the importance of listening and communication: 'I just wish they would listen to me'. Both of these quotes are from service users, which although separated by 30 years carry the same message. Fast forward to 2017 and surprisingly these sentiments are still relevant.

If service users are not being listened to, the question becomes: how do we facilitate the service user voice or is it that their voice is not being listened to by the right person? Being listened to is a core part of being empowered, an idea that has an interesting history tracing its origins back to the world of community involvement with planning (Arnstein 1969). Such ideas have over the years steadily gained momentum. One example in the UK is the need for social work education to involve service users and carers in the design of social work courses. Service users are also involved in a wide

---

1   You probably guessed it was Golightley, M. (1985) *If Only They Would Listen: The Case for a Community Orientated Mental Health Service.* Lincoln: University of Lincoln (no longer available).

variety of key independent and voluntary organizations in the UK such as MIND, SANE and Shaping Our Lives, which, in addition to support for local user groups, also provide pressure group activities and high-quality data and information about mental health (see also Leff and Warner 2006).

A unifying message emanating from mental health service user movements is the rejection of pessimistic prognoses for people afflicted by different forms of mental disorders and the call for greater acknowledgment that people can survive and thrive while simultaneously coping with debilitating mental symptoms. This backlash against paternalistic and pessimistic approaches in mental health treatment has become associated with two rallying concepts. The first comes directly from the Disability Rights Movement, which has championed the phrase, *nothing about us without us*, a call which captures the push for inclusive and participatory modes of service delivery. The second rallying call has been the idea that people must not be defined by their disability, but supported to realize their personal goals in life. In the mental health arena, this has been framed as the recovery model and its arrival has highlighted the extent to which past practices in psychiatric treatment have been limited to symptom control, risk management and a void of positive messages to service users regarding their prognosis.

The concept of recovery, with its roots in the 1960s (Amering and Schmolke 2009), further developed by Anthony (1993), Deegan (2002) and others, has gained increasing credence in recent years, bringing with it the belief that there is potential for positive life change in the absence of total cure. Watts (2012) describes mental health recovery as a *re-enchantment with life* and a process through which the individual moves towards the achievement of positive personal goals from an empowered as opposed to an oppressed position. The discourse around recovery has been developed largely out of the lived experience of people with mental health problems who resist being defined solely in terms of their psychiatric diagnosis. Recovery is not just about the individual and usually is a combination of factors, some personal, some social and some political (Williams, Almeida and Knyahnytska 2015). Personal recovery involves the service user in an evaluation of what is helpful to them at that particular time. Social factors are just as complex, and effective recovery might mean the need for a purposeful social role or job with some evidence that entering mainstream employment may correlate more closely with clinical recovery than medical treatment (Tew *et al.* 2012). Of course, in these days of austerity, especially in Europe, political processes need to reduce marginalization and stigma and to claim respect and entitlements. The following case study represents a typical referral to a mental health service where the social work intervention is informed by a recovery approach.

Case study: Peter

Peter, aged 24 years, has been referred to the mental health team you work with by his local doctor. Peter's symptoms include auditory hallucinations and persecutory beliefs, which he explains have been building up over the past six months. Peter has a job in a restaurant as a trainee chef and before the onset of these symptoms he enjoyed his work, which he tells you gave him an outlet for his artistic and creative talents. However, over the past year or so he has found the long hours in the restaurant to be quite exhausting and it has also reduced his availability to meet with his friends in the evening and to socialize. As a result, he feels he has become increasingly socially isolated. About four weeks ago he phoned the restaurant to say he was unwell and would not be coming into work that night. He has not been in touch with his employer since then and is unsure if he still has a job.

Peter lives with his parents and younger brother, John. They have been very worried about his behaviour recently and report to your team that he has stayed mainly in his bedroom for the last four weeks and often becomes irritated when they try to talk to him. They became very concerned when he stopped eating meals in recent weeks because he believed his food was poisoned. Eventually, they persuaded Peter to see his doctor and the initial assessment suggested that a social work intervention along the lines of the recovery model was indicated and so a referral was initiated.

You may wish to think about some of the questions that follow in relation to this chapter in general and the case study in particular:

1. What additional information is relevant for you to collect as part of your social work assessment of Peter?

2. How can Peter participate in the assessment of his needs? What can you do to assist his participation?

3. What strengths can you identify in Peter's situation and how can these strengths contribute to any work you plan to do with Peter?

4. How can the members of your multidisciplinary team contribute to your assessment of Peter's situation?

For many service users, the recovery approach provides a readymade alternative to the traditional biomedical model on which many current services have been based. It also provides a connection with ideas of personal empowerment and participation – perspectives which generally emphasize the individual service user's right to be consulted and involved in treatment plans and decisions that are directly related to their care. Several Canadian studies have highlighted how recovery theory helps services focus less on what the service user cannot do and more on strengths and resilience as the most likely route to recovery (see, for example, Hurley and O'Reilly 2017). Although there isn't one single definition of recovery, it usually signifies that the service user can live with hope, meaning and purpose while dealing with the impact of mental illness (Khoury and Rodriguez del Barrio 2015; Williams *et al.* 2015).

While the recovery model has heralded a new departure in psychiatric treatment, much is familiar to social work practice. Indeed, the work of Saleebey (1992, 1996) spawned what has come to be referred to as the strengths model in social work theory and a perspective which is used by social workers in many areas of practice around the world. This was developed from evaluations of social work interventions to assist community-based living for people suffering with persistent and severe mental health problems, and there has been widespread interaction between strengths-based and recovery-oriented theory over many decades (Rapp 1998; Rapp and Goscha 2012).

The rise of the recovery model has brought with it an increased recognition of the need to listen to the views and experiences of service users in terms of understanding their needs, identifying gaps or problems in services and for working towards the humane provision of services (Borg and Kristiansen 2004). We suggest that listening to what service users want and being guided by social work principles are two sides of the same coin. But can social work go further? McCubbin and Cohen (1996) highlight the power disparities between service users and the monolithic professional discourses that control the services they engage with. Social work, with its commitment to advocacy and empowerment, can play a role in helping service users amplify their views and influence how services can become more attentive to their needs. By applying the components of participatory approaches, social work can effectively enable service users to feel valued, listened to and supported in their recovery pathway (Verhaeghe and Bracke 2011).

Challenges

Recovery as a concept is not entirely unproblematic and professional-led recovery based on the notion of getting better rightly comes in for criticism with the suspicion that this is the colonization of service user empowerment for purposes other than those it was intended for (Davies and Gray 2017). If this is the case then the themes of powerlessness and injustice that some authors (Davies and Gray 2017; Tew *et al.* 2012) suggest co-exist alongside mental illness might be exacerbated by paternalistic services based on the professional as an *all-knowing expert*.

In the era of techno-rational management, driven by the need to measure improvement, recovery could become yet another performance objective. The narrative around service user involvement in mental health services has been developed and made more challenging by the increase in specialized services and the variety of providers. Service users when they are at their most vulnerable can be the recipients of an array of mental health interventions. Indeed, the survivor movement has played a significant role in helping the embryonic service user movement to flourish. At the same time, of course, social workers are asked to engage more deeply with service users, provide more services and, as a consequence of austerity do this more efficiently and often with fewer resources. Social workers need to be empowered so as to become more creative and to resist traditional approaches where they appear unhelpful. Another tension is evident when the service user has to accept that they have a mental disorder in order to establish eligibility for services – something that can deter those who feel that all they need is support (Gwinner, Knox and Brough 2013).

Thus a type of splitting is taking place within the recovery discourse leading Pilgrim (2008, p.295) to describe it as a 'polyvalent concept', because within the medical model it has been re-invented as a new clinical tool, the success of which can only be measured by qualified clinicians who assess service user progress across clinically decided targets of behaviour and wellbeing. Despite the hope raised by the recovery model, service user groups continue to agitate for greater recognition of the subtle forms of control which they experience, including the lack of consultation and involvement in decisions related to their treatment, lack of recognition of their capacity to contribute to those decisions and the ongoing pervasive discrimination towards people with mental health problems in the wider society (McCubbin and Cohen 1996).

Recovery may be in danger of becoming colonized by clinical perspectives, prompting the suggestion by Roberts and Wolfson (2004) that it is clinicians or service providers who need to recover! Social work needs to appreciate the potential for clinical versions of recovery to obscure the original inclusive agenda of the strengths-based recovery model. Social workers need to advocate for service users to be respected as important participants in the processes of diagnosis and treatment planning because of their knowledge of mental illness gained through personal experience.

Conclusion

Some practice-related issues raise difficult questions for the profession. For example, how should the profession respond to the unresolved debates about the cause(s) of mental distress? If it attaches itself to a social model of disability, how can social work then mediate its role in services based on the medical paradigm? While there is an ever-increasing expectation that professionals, including social workers, will identify and contain risk, there is a strong push for the promotion of patient autonomy, participation and outcomes-based service delivery (Cohen and Timimi 2008). Reconciling these competing expectations presents something of a high wire act for social work and the implications of advocating for service user autonomy and independence while simultaneously acting in the role of risk manager are difficult to reconcile (Kirwan 2015).

A final observation is that the state of flux in which the field of mental health currently finds itself paradoxically offers social work the opportunity for cementing its role within this field and asserting its leadership potential in the development of services that are perceived as useful by those who need them most. These times of change in the field of mental health open up many possibilities for how services are delivered and this chapter has displayed many examples of the alignment between well-established social work practices and the emerging themes in mental health care. The profession is well placed to assert its expertise in the development of participatory-based therapeutic interventions which overtly reject paternalistic approaches to treatment and which aim instead to promote the dignity and social inclusion of all who experience the challenge of mental distress and ill-health.

Reflection questions

- Are service users being listened to or is it that they are not being taken seriously?

- What do you think are the advantages and disadvantages of the recovery model and why?

- What social work principles and practice skills are aligned with a recovery model?

References

Amering, M. and Schmolke, M. (2009) *Recovery in Mental Health: Reshaping Scientific and Clinical Possibilities*. Chichester: Wiley-Blackwell.

Anthony, W.A. (1993) 'Recovery from mental illness: The guiding vision of the mental health service system in the 1990's.' *Psychological Rehabilitation Journal 16*, 4, 11–23.

Arnstein, S.R. (1969) 'A ladder of citizen participation.' *Journal of the American Institute of Planners 35*, 4, 216–224.

Bentall, R.P. (2004) 'Abandonning the Concept of Schizophrenia: The Cognitive Psychology of Hallucinations and Delusions.' In J. Read, L.R. Mosher and R.P. Bentall (eds) *Models of Madness: Psychological, Social and Biological Approaches to Schizophrenia*. London: Routledge in association with The International Society for the Psychological Treatments of the Schizophrenias and Other Psychoses.

Bentall, R.P., Rowse, G., Shryane, N., Kinderman, P. *et al.* (2009) 'The cognitive and affective structure of paranoid delusions: A transdiagnostic investigation of patients with schizophrenia spectrum disorders and depression.' *Archives of General Psychiatry 66*, 3, 236–247.

Berzoff, J. and Drisko, J. (2015) 'What clinical social workers need to know: Bio-psycho-social knowledge and skills for the twenty first century.' *Clinical Social Work 43*, 263–273.

Borg, M. and Kristiansen, K. (2004) 'Recovery-oriented professionals: Helping relationships in mental health services.' *Journal of Mental Health 13*, 5, 493–505.

Bracken, P. (2014) 'Towards a hermeneutic shift in psychiatry.' *World Psychiatry 13*, 3, 241–243.

Cohen, B.M.Z. (2013) 'The Power of Madness: A Marxist Critique of Social Constructionism.' In H. Goodman, B.V. Russo and J. Zózimo (eds) *Beyond These Walls: Confronting Madness in Society, Literature and Art*. Oxford: Interdisciplinary Press.

Cohen, C.I. and Timimi, S. (eds) (2008) *Liberatory Psychiatry: Philosophy, Politics and Mental Health*. Cambridge: Cambridge University Press.

Compton, B.R. and Galaway, B. (1999) *Social Work Processes*. Belmont, CA: Wadsworth.

Conrad, P. and Schneider, J.W. (1985) *Deviance and Medicalization: From Badness to Sickness*. Columbus, OH: Merrill Publishing Company.

Davies, K. and Gray, M. (2017) 'The place of service-user expertise in evidence-based practice.' *Journal of Social Work 17*, 1, 3–20.

Deegan, P.E. (2002) 'Recovery as a self-directed process of healing and transformation.' *Occupational Therapy in Mental Health 17*, 3–4, 5–21.

Foucault, M. (1954) *Madness. The Invention of an Idea*. Paris: Presses universitaires de France.

Foucault, M. (1965) *Madness and Civilization: A History of Insanity in the Age of Reason*. New York, NY: Vintage Books.

Goffman, E. (1961) *Asylums: Essays on the Social Situation of Mental Patients and Other Inmates*. Englewood Cliffs, NJ: Prentice-Hall.

Golightley, M. (2017) *Social Work and Mental Health* (6th edition). London: Sage.

Golightley, M. and Kirwan, G. (eds) (2017) *International Reflections on Approaches to Mental Health Social Work*. Oxford: Routledge.

Gwinner, K., Knox, M. and Brough, M. (2013) 'Making sense of mental illness as a full human experience: Perspectives of illness and recovery held by people with a mental illness living in the community.' *Social Work in Mental Health 11*, 2, 99–117.

Hammersley, P., Read, J., Woodall, S. and Dillon, J. (2008) 'Childhood trauma and psychosis: The genie is out of the bottle.' *Journal of Psychological Trauma 6*, 2–3, 7–20.

Humphreys, C. and Thiara, R. (2003) 'Mental health and domestic violence: "I call it symptoms of abuse".' *British Journal of Social Work 33*, 209–226.

Hurley, D.J. and O'Reilly, R.L. (2017) 'Resilience, mental health and Assertive Community Treatment.' *Social Work in Mental Health 15*, 6, 730–748.

Hyde, A., Lohan, M. and McDonnell, O. (2004) *Sociology for Health Professionals in Ireland.* Dublin: Institute of Public Administration.

Hyde, B., Bowles, W. and Pawar, M. (2015) '"We're Still in There" – Consumer Voices on Mental Health Inpatient Care: Social Work Research Highlighting Lessons for Recovery Practice.' *British Journal of Social Work 45* (suppl_1), i62–i78.

Johnstone, L. (2011) 'Can Traumatic Events Traumatize People? Trauma, Madness and "Psychosis".' In M. Rapley, J. Moncrieff and J. Dillon (eds) *De-medicalizing Misery: Psychiatry, Psychology and the Human Condition.* Basingstoke: Palgrave Macmillan.

Jones, D. and Truell, R. (2012) 'The global agenda for social work and social development: A place to link together and be effective in a globalized world.' *International Social Work 55*, 4, 454–472.

Khoury, E. and Rodriguez del Barrio, L. (2015) 'Recovery-oriented mental health practice: A social work perspective.' *British Journal of Social Work 45* (suppl_1), i27–i44.

Kilian, R., Lindenbach, I., Löbig, U., Yhle, M., Petscheleit, A. and Angemeyer, M.C. (2003) 'Indicators of empowerment and disempowerment in the subjective evaluation of the psychiatric treatment process by persons with severe and persistent mental illness: A qualitative and quantitative analysis.' *Social Science and Medicine 57*, 6, 1127–1142.

Kirk, S.A. and Kutchins, H. (1994) 'The myth of the reliability of DSM.' *The Journal of Mind and Behavior 15*, 1–2, 71–89.

Kirwan, G. (2015) 'Risk Management and Challenges for Services and Workers.' In R. Sheehan and J. Ogloff (eds) *Working in the Forensic Paradigm: Cross-Discipline Approaches for Policy and Practice.* London: Routledge.

Lacasse, J.R. and Gomory, T. (2003) 'Is graduate social work education promoting a critical approach to mental health practice?' *Journal of Social Work Education 39*, 3, 383–407.

Leff, J. and Warner, R. (2006) Social Inclusion of People with Mental Illness. Cambridge: Cambridge University Press.

Littrell, J. and Lacasse, R. (2012) 'Controversies in psychiatry and DSM-5: The relevance for social work.' *Families in Society: The Journal of Contemporary Social Services 93*, 4, 265–269.

Maddock, A. (2015) 'Consensus or contention: An exploration of multidisciplinary team functioning in an Irish mental health team context.' *European Journal of Social Work 18*, 2, 241–261.

McCubbin, M. and Cohen, D. (1996) 'Extremely unbalanced: Interest divergence and power disparities between clients and psychiatry.' *International Journal of Law and Psychiatry 19*, 1, 1–25.

McKenzie, K.J., Whitley, R. and Weich, S. (2002) 'Social capital and mental health.' *British Journal of Psychiatry 181*, 4, 305–308.

Ministry of Health (2016) *The Office of the Director of Mental Health Annual Report 2015.* Wellington, New Zealand: Ministry of Health.

Mojtabai, R., Olfson, M., Sampson, N.A., Jin, R. *et al.* (2011) 'Barriers to mental health treatment: Results from the National Comorbidity Survey Replication (NCS-R).' *Psychological Medicine 41*, 8, 1751–1761.

Moncrieff, J. (2011) 'The Myth of the Antidepressant: An Historical Analysis.' In M. Rapley, J. Moncrieff and J. Dillon (eds) *De-medicalizing Misery: Psychiatry, Psychology and the Human Condition.* Basingstoke: Palgrave Macmillan.

Nabatchi, T. and Leighninger, M. (2015) *Public Participation for 21st Century Democracy.* Hoboken, NJ: John Wiley & Sons.

National Association of Social Workers (NASW) (2017) *Mental Health.* Washington, DC: National Association of Social Workers. Accessed on 14/12/2017 at www.socialworkers.org.

Ngui, E.M., Khasakhala, L., Ndetei, D. and Weiss Roberts, L. (2010) 'Mental disorders, health inequalities and ethics: A global perspective.' *International Review of Psychiatry 22*, 3, 235–244.

Pilgrim, D. (2008) '"Recovery" and current mental health policy.' *Chronic Illness 4*, 295–304.

Rapley, M., Moncrieff, J. and Dillon, J. (eds) (2011) *De-medicalizing Misery: Psychiatry, Psychology and the Human Condition*. Basingstoke: Palgrave Macmillan.

Rapp, C.A. (1998) *The Strengths Model: Case Management with People Suffering from Severe and Persistent Mental Illness*. New York, NY: Oxford University Press.

Rapp, C.A. and Goscha, R.J. (2012) *The Strengths Model: A Recovery-Oriented Approach to Mental Health Services*. New York, NY: Oxford University Press.

Roberts, G. and Wolfson, P. (2004) 'The rediscovery of recovery: Open to all.' *Advances in Psychiatric Treatment 10*, 1, 400–409.

Rogers, A. and Pilgrim, D. (2014) *A Sociology of Mental Illness* (5th edition). Buckingham: Open University Press.

Rogers, A., Pilgrim, D. and Lacey, R. (1993) *Experiencing Psychiatry: Users' Views of Services*. London: Macmillan in association with MIND Publications.

Rose, N. (1998) 'Governing risky individuals: The role of psychiatry in new regimes of control.' *Psychiatry, Psychology and Law 5*, 2, 177–195.

Saleebey, D. (1992) *The Strengths Perspective in Social Work Practice*. White Plains, NY: Longman.

Saleebey, D. (1996) 'The strengths perspective in social work practice: Extensions and cautions.' *Social Work 41*, 3, 296–305.

Tew, J., Ramon, S., Slade, M., Bird, V., Melton, J. and Le Boutillier, C. (2012) 'Social factors and recovery from mental health difficulties: A review of the evidence.' *British Journal of Social Work 42*, 3, 443–460.

Timimi, S. (2014) 'No more psychiatric labels: Why formal psychiatric diagnostic systems should be abolished.' *International Journal of Clinical and Health Psychology 14*, 208–215.

Vanhala, L. (2015) 'The diffusion of disability rights in Europe.' *Human Rights Quarterly 37*, 831–853.

Verhaeghe, M. and Bracke, P. (2011) 'Stigma and trust among mental health service users.' *Archives of Psychiatric Nursing 25*, 4, 294–302.

Watts, M. (2012). Recovery from 'Mental Illness' as a Re-Enchantment with Life: A Narrative Study. Doctoral thesis. Dublin: University of Dublin, Trinity College. Accessed on 19/07/2017 at www.tara.tcd.ie/bitstream/handle/2262/77083/Michael%20Watts%20PhD%20Thesis.pdf?sequence=1&isAllowed=y.

Weiss-Gal, I. and Welbourne, P. (2008) 'The professionalization of social work: A cross-national exploration.' *International Journal of Social Welfare 17*, 281–290.

Whitaker, R. (2005) 'Anatomy of an epidemic: Psychiatric drugs and the astonishing rise of mental illness in America.' *Ethical Human Psychology and Psychiatry 7*, 1, 23–35.

WHO (1978) *Report on the International Conference on Primary Care, Alma Alta*. Geneva: World Health Organization.

WHO (1997) *Jakarta Declaration on Leading Health Promotion into the 21st Century. The Fourth International Conference on Health Promotion: New Players for a New Era – Leading Health Promotion into the 21st Century*. Geneva: World Health Organization. Accessed on 15/12/2017 at www.who.int/healthpromotion/milestones_jakarta.pdf.

WHO (2012) *Global Burden of Mental Disorders and the Need for a Comprehensive, Coordinated Response from Health and Social Sectors at the Country Level*. Report by the Secretariat to the 65th World Health Assembly. A65/10. Geneva: World Health Organization. Accessed on 15/12/2017 at http://apps.who.int/gb/ebwha/pdf_files/WHA65/A65_10-en.pdf?ua=1.

WHO (2013) *Mental Health Action Plan 2013–2020*. Geneva: World Health Organization. Accessed on 15/12/2017 at www.who.int/mental_health/publications/action_plan/en.

Williams, C.C., Almeida, M., Knyahnytska, Y. (2015) 'Towards a biopsychosociopolitical frame for recovery in the context of mental illness.' *British Journal of Social Work 45* (suppl_1), i9–i26.

Wilson, G. and Kirwan, G. (2007) 'Mental health social work in Northern Ireland and the Republic of Ireland: challenges and opportunities for developing practice.' *European Journal of Social Work 10*, 2, 175–191.

Wittchen, H.-U. and Jacobi, F. (2005) 'Size and burden of mental disorders in Europe: A critical review and appraisal of 27 studies.' *European Neuropsychopharmacology 15*, 357–376.

Wittchen, H.-U., Jacobi, F., Rehm, J., Gistavsson, A. *et al.* (2011) 'The size and burden of mental disorders and other disorders of the brain in Europe 2010.' *European Neuropsychopharmacology 21*, 9, 655–679.

Xiandong, W. (2017) 'Objectives of China and the global mental health plan.' *Shanghai Archives of Psychiatry 29*, 2, 111–112.

Chapter 6

Social Work with Older People

POLLY YEUNG

Introduction

Older people are the fastest growing segment of the population worldwide (World Health Organization 2012). Given this ageing population, it is anticipated that the need for aged care will also increase; hence, social workers are becoming more exposed and involved with older clients, their carers and families. The significance of social work practice with older people is underlined by the challenges of changing health and human services and the influences of the marketization of welfare and the emphasis on individual responsibility. Understanding the factors that contribute to longevity and predict optimal ageing, whether it is in the community or in residential care for older people, is central to social work scholarship and practice.

This chapter contextualizes the discussion of social work with older people by providing a brief overview of the demographic and socio-political context of older people in Aotearoa New Zealand. It addresses a range of key issues, including the current discourses of ageing, that impact on, and intersect with, meeting the needs of a growing older population. It then explores how Sen's capability approach and the person-centred care approach provide important frameworks for social work practice and interventions that support the health and wellbeing of older people. Two case studies are introduced in this chapter to enable readers to explore the complex nature of ageing. These stories illustrate experiences of ageing in relation to social and family life, physical health and mobility, and emotional and mental health.

An ageing population

According to the United Nations (UN) report, *World Population Ageing 2013*, ageing is defined as 'the process that results in rising proportions of older people in the total population' (United Nations 2013, p.3). The world's population is rapidly ageing and the number of people aged 65 and over is projected to be two billion by 2050 (United Nations 2009). By 2050, the segment of those 80 years and older will be 31 percent, up from 18 percent in 1988 (Organisation for Economic Co-operation and Development 1988). The nature of being old is also changing, particularly in developed countries, as people have longer life expectancy, rising standards of living, better health and are more likely to have a longer retirement period (MacKean and Abbott-Chapman 2012). In Aotearoa New Zealand, the ageing population (65+) is projected to grow to 1.28–1.37 million in 2041 (Statistics New Zealand 2014). By 2025, the number of people aged over 65 will surpass children aged 14 years and under, and this gap is likely to continue to widen (Ministry of Social Development 2015). Among people aged 65 years and over, 17.1 percent of them identified as European, followed by 5.6 percent Maori, 4.7 percent Asian and 2.4 percent Pacific people (Statistics New Zealand 2013a). While the current trend demonstrates the wide variance in the ethnic groups in New Zealand among older cohorts, Dyson (2002) argues that older ethnic minority group members are expected to increase substantially over the next decades, particularly among older Maori and Pacific peoples. Maori and Pacific peoples have also been reported to have poorer health than other ethnic groups (Ministry of Health 2007).

The rapid ageing of the population is not unique to Aotearoa New Zealand as the same trend can be seen internationally. This trend brings significant fiscal and economic challenges, particularly with regards to housing, transportation, healthcare and the distribution of resources related to health and wellbeing. The Aotearoa New Zealand government spends more on funding its universal healthcare system than some other Organisation for Economic Co-operation and Development countries such as Hungary and Greece, and also has a higher than average proportion of long-term care residents, most of whom are aged 80 and over (Organisation for Economic Co-operation and Development 2015). According to the research by Broad *et al.* (2015), for nearly 40 percent of people aged 65 and over, the place of death occurred in residential aged care. The rising demand of late-life care services among older people has created much debate in Aotearoa New Zealand. The government and policy makers have identified issues and future challenges in managing age-related illness and disease and the implications for the health and disability workforce who deliver care to older people (Anderson-Wuf 2017).

Discourses of ageing

The impact of demographic change has attracted an increased focus on older people within public and social policies as it affects demand and expenditure on adult social and healthcare. The World Health Organization (2002) has recommended that the focus on older people be shifted from care to independence, participation and wellbeing, by promoting *active ageing*. Theoretical frameworks, such as healthy ageing (Hansen-Kyle 2005), productive ageing (Bass, Caro and Chen 1993) and successful ageing (Rowe and Kahn 1997), emphasize 'the importance of maintaining and fostering the physical and mental wellbeing of people as they age' (Buys and Miller 2006, p.2). The emphasis on the reduction of disease and disability in order to maintain active engagement in life in later life is strongly associated with the ability to be fully involved in decision making (Boudiny 2013). In Aotearoa New Zealand, the government has developed the *Positive Ageing Strategy* (Ministry of Social Development 2015) and the *Health of Older People Strategy* (Ministry of Health 2002) to ensure older people can live as independently as possible in their own homes by being active and responsible for their own wellbeing. While the notion of healthy or positive ageing may be considered as a response to a deficit model of ageing based on disengagement, dependency and ageism (Stephens, Breheny and Mansvelt 2015), the promotion of an active later life is of primary economic and social importance given the ageing population. This has informed social policy internationally with the focus being on reducing the financial cost of health and welfare for older people while maximizing their contribution to society (Stenner, McFarquhar and Bowling 2011). The context of social work is therefore challenged by an unprecedented change in demography and the ongoing legitimization of the reduction in state welfare spending favoured by governments with neoliberal economic ideologies that individualize responsibility for retaining independence in later life (Lloyd *et al.* 2014; Martinson and Minkler 2006).

The discourses of healthy and successful ageing have generated considerable debate and have been critiqued as being oppressive and as marginalizing older people, most notably those ageing with physical and cognitive disabilities, who cannot live up to the ideal construct of being active and independent (Stephens *et al.* 2015). Some researchers (Pinquart and Sorensen 2000; Yeung and Breheny 2016) have argued that subjective wellbeing is an important component of successful ageing as it concerns a positive evaluation of one's own life, including life satisfaction, happiness and quality of life, which is much more important than focusing on supporting older people to avoid disease and disability. Existing research has reported that chronic illness and multi-morbidity are features of ageing that can restrict participation by negatively influencing wellbeing (Martinson and Berridge 2015); however, older age and poor physical health do not determine wellbeing. Studies of older people show that subjective wellbeing is not just affected by health but by many other factors such as socio-demographic characteristics, including race, gender and class (Hsu 2012; Murtagh and Hubert 2004), life course socio-economic factors (Niedzwiedz *et al.* 2014), material and economic conditions (Netuveli *et al.* 2006; Usui, Thomas and Durig 1985) and social and family relationships (Xavier *et al.* 2003).

Based on the above arguments, there is a need to go beyond illness and disability as the basis of wellbeing in older age and to include the role of supportive environments in improving positive psychosocial states that contribute to subjective wellbeing (Martinson and Berridge 2015). Healthy ageing need not be determined by the health status or physical functioning of older people, but can be conceptualized in terms of keeping their lives purposeful and the capability to live well in later life (Stephens *et al.* 2015). Researchers (for example, Alpass *et al.* 2007; Breheny and Stephens 2010; Willets 2010; Yeung and Breheny 2016) have argued that current discourses have constructed demographic changes and ageing in particular ways. For example, older people have been divided into two groups: healthy older people who should be encouraged to actively participate and take responsibility for their wellbeing, and dependent older people viewed primarily as recipients of care. To address these criticisms, Bowling (2007, p.275) suggests that a model of successful ageing would need to be 'sensitive to difference in opportunities to age successfully and to variations in values between cultures'.

Practice approaches

It is critical that the social work profession takes a strong stance to advocate effectively for the wellbeing and social equality of vulnerable populations. This section introduces two frameworks that inform social work practice with older people: (1) The capability approach and (2) Person-centred practice.

Sen's capability approach

Currently healthy ageing policy and interventions tend to focus on the responsibility of individuals to achieve good physical health and can underplay the impact of people's broader circumstances. The capability approach by Sen (2010) proposes the need to move beyond raw measurements, such as utility or income, to a focus on practical and societal conditions that allow or restrict choice in how to live one's life. Human dignity and human rights are closely linked with the notion of the capability approach. Sen's (1992, 2000) capability approach provides a way to integrate physical changes of ageing, environmental influences and psychosocial effects by focusing on what older people themselves value in regards to healthy ageing. It differs from the traditional approaches of evaluating wellbeing, which focus on measures of income, material goods and assets. The capability approach understands wellbeing in terms of functioning, which focuses on what individuals are able to do and be, and the freedom they have to exercise their own agency to pursue the lives they aspire to and value. Paying attention to capability is particularly important for understanding the health of older people who have different levels of functional capacity as they age. In this way, they are supported to create their own version of what constitutes optimal wellbeing and quality of life (Yeung and Breheny 2016).

Drawing on the capability approach, Welch Saleeby (2007) has modelled the relationship between determinants of wellbeing (see Figure 6.1). In this model, commodities and their characteristics reflect a person's life situation (environmental, personal factors and physical functioning). Personal factors (for example, economic wellbeing, disability/chronic illnesses) and environmental factors (for example, accessibility, stigma and attitude) play integral roles in facilitating or limiting functioning. With this focus on capability, attention is shifted from our constructions of ageing based on individual responsibility for wellbeing to the ways that social and environmental contexts can influence the achievement of functioning. For example, Yeung and Breheny (2016) used Welch Saleeby's model of the capability approach to explore the determinants of wellbeing among older people living on their own.

A capability perspective indicates that even in the context of chronic conditions and poor mental and physical health, increased capabilities can lead to greater wellbeing. Sen's (1985) notion of capabilities concerns people's abilities to achieve those *beings and doings* that people have reason to value in life. These *beings and doings* can range from basic functioning, such as being well nourished, visiting people at any time, to more complex functioning, such as having control over decision making

(Breheny *et al.* 2013). The capability framework distinguishes itself from other traditional approaches, which have a narrower evaluation of one's life. Sen (2004) and Morris (2009) argue for holistic approaches that promote understanding of context-relevant capabilities identified by older people rather than just by professionals. As Terzi (2005, p.206) states, 'attention should be given to individual conceptions of wellbeing, and to their interplay with political, social and cultural settings, thus, ultimately, with conditions that may influence choice and reasoning'.

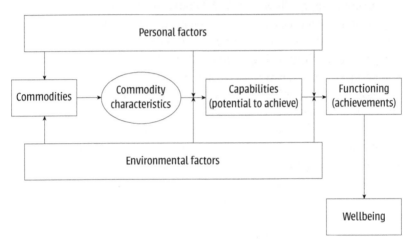

Figure 6.1: Welch Saleeby's model of the capability approach

If healthy ageing is perceived as an absolute state (achieved only when certain physical criteria are reached), then as people become older and frailer, they will face increasing challenges in meeting expectations that are grounded in physical health. The capability approach places older people, their real opportunities to be, and their freedom of choice, at the centre of a multidimensional approach to wellbeing, including the capability to be well nourished, to be in a good health, and to be able to take part in the life of the community (Sen 2000). The capability approach to healthy ageing should be seen as the outcome of an interaction between personal characteristics (e.g., ability/disability, skills, gender, age), economic and social resources and assets (e.g., financial security, social norms, racism) and the environment (e.g., neighbourhood, existence of a transportation system, infrastructure). These resources enable individuals to achieve wellbeing through facilitating practical opportunities. Such approaches challenge the dominant discourses of healthy ageing, which neglect the impact of inequalities such as socio-economic status and the structural barriers that shape the health status of people throughout their life course (Lloyd *et al.* 2014; Stephens *et al.* 2015; Pond, Stephens and Alpass 2010).

The application of Welch Saleeby's model positions healthy ageing as a matter of social justice, and redresses inequality and discrimination. It is important to recognize and support the diverse experiences of older people and work against framing disadvantage in later life as due to personal failures (Liang and Luo 2012). The capability approach connects with the social work core value of social justice by examining the importance of challenging and removing social systems and institutions that limit a person's opportunity to choose a life of their own value (Alkire 2005). Social workers have an important role to play in reframing healthy ageing by empowering the voices and experiences of older people and in supporting them to seek or redefine purpose in life and to expand their capability to achieve what they value in later life. At the core of the social work profession is its critical and political roots and the transformation of structures and systems that deepen economic, social, political and cultural inequalities. Given that the capability approach provides a strong theoretical lens of social justice it enables social workers to position themselves as active agents who engage in transformative and sustainable approaches to social change (Veal, King and Marston 2016).

The following case study introduces Judy, who wants to remain as independent as possible and continue to live in the community. As you read Judy's story, consider how the capability approach promotes an understanding of what matters the most to Judy's health and wellbeing and what roles social work and healthcare professionals can play in supporting Judy to live successfully in her own home for as long as possible.

Case study 1

Judy is 83 years old. She has lived by herself in her own three-bedroom home since her husband died 10 years ago. There are five steps at the back of the house and six in the front. She has two daughters; one lives overseas and one lives an hour's drive away. Since her husband died, Judy started learning Tai Chi and every Thursday morning drives 15 minutes to the community centre to practise with other people for an hour. Judy loves her independence and living on her own. In the last two years, she started developing some arthritis and can no longer climb up and clean windows. She cannot mow the lawn anymore but still tries to get out and about to work in her garden. Despite the arthritis, she remains active by using her walking stick to walk around the shopping mall and to the library with her friends. A few months ago, she had a fall on the slippery steps of her front porch. Although she did not suffer from any major injury, her daughter spoke to the hospital social worker and expressed serious concern about her mother no longer being able to look after herself and insisted that she should move into a residential aged care facility. Judy is really upset about her daughter's suggestion and says that she would hate living in a rest home where she would not have her privacy and freedom and be able to do what she wants. Judy also feels that no one has consulted her about what she wants and people just think she is old and useless.

Thinking of Welch Saleeby's model and being mindful that Judy is 83 years old and has some degree of fragility which is impacting on her mobility and makes her vulnerable, ask yourself the following questions:

1. How can social workers and other healthcare professionals support and enable Judy to remain within her own home while addressing her daughter's concerns around safety and other issues?

2. Judy's cultural identity has not been specified, but how does this influence your work with Judy and her daughter?

Person-centred approaches in social work with older people

Respect for people is at the core of person-centred approaches and is situated within Immanuel Kant's concepts of mutual respect and sympathetic benevolence (Richards 1981). Making sure that people are involved in and at the centre of decisions about their care is now embedded in multidisciplinary practice with older people (McCormack 2003). Relationships are essential when caring for older people, particularly for those who are frail or require extensive care and support. Person-centred care is not just about giving people whatever they want or providing information. It is about knowing the older person's life history and understanding the values held by those in helping relationships (Brown Wilson 2009).

The rapid ageing of the population in Aotearoa New Zealand means the need for aged residential care will also increase. Debates about the best way of ensuring high-quality care provision for vulnerable older people are increasingly important. The New Zealand *Health of Older People Strategy* (Ministry of Health 2002) underlines the need for planning for this growing service need. According to Statistics New Zealand (2013b), more than 30,000 older people are reported to be living in residential aged care (RAC) facilities, which is a 14.1 percent increase since 2006. As the demand for residential care grows, the need to ensure standards of care and quality of life in these settings becomes critical. Moving into residential care involves life changes that significantly impact on an individual's quality of life and wellbeing. For example, changes occur in social interactions and there is a need to adapt to issues affecting one's privacy, dignity and independence (Abley 2012; Brownie and Horstmanshof 2012; Yeung *et al.* 2016).

In response to increasing concerns and dissatisfaction among patients and their families about traditional nursing home practice, the delivery of care within the health system has been evolving (Rosher and Robinson 2005; Sharma, Bamford and Dodman 2015). A range of new models of care has been developed and implemented by some RAC facilities; these share a focus on person-centred care as 'an approach to the planning, delivery, and evaluation of healthcare that is grounded in mutually beneficial partnerships among healthcare providers, patients, and families' (Institute for Patient- and Family-Centered Care n.d.). For many older people, the transition from home to residential care may be a sudden, involuntary and disempowering experience due to their increasing dependence on facility staff for all aspects of their care (Rodgers and Neville 2007). In addition, residents do not always experience optimal quality of life, independence or self-direction (Petriwskj *et al.* 2016; Yeung and Rodgers 2017). Although many long-term care facilities have the ability to facilitate social interaction and offer activities, residents have expressed that a home-like environment, social relationships, having their privacy and dignity respected, and social support (or connectedness) are important for enhancing their quality of life (Oosterveld-Vlug *et al.* 2014; Ryan and McKenna 2015; Yeung and Rodgers 2017).

Relationships between staff, residents and their families have also emerged as fundamental to the experience of quality for care home residents. Research has emphasized that residents value staff being personal, which includes paying attention to the small details in care and having a caring attitude, rather than just focusing on the technical elements of care (Deutschman 2001; Ryan and McKenna 2015). Engaging the family in the residential care setting is also acknowledged to be important in enhancing the care of the older person (Gaugler 2006; Hamann 2014). Family members can maintain an ongoing relationship with their family member by overseeing the quality of care and by being fully involved in care decisions. Many families want to be part of the team where trust and mutual affection develop between families and staff (The Green House Project 2015). Although staff recognize the importance of working in this way, they often feel they have insufficient time to give to families (Hertzberg and Ekman 2000; Jones and Moyle 2016). Clearly, the importance of constructive staff–family relationships cannot be underestimated (Yeung and Rodgers 2017).

While the movement away from an institutional model of aged care to resident/person-centred care has been considered as an essential part of a culture change in the service provision of aged care in Aotearoa New Zealand, Australia and around the world (Hamann 2014; Petriwskyj *et al.* 2016; Yeung *et al.* 2016; Yeung and Rodgers 2017), care professionals including social workers can be overwhelmed by the structural and administrative challenges to providing genuinely person-centred care (Rockwell 2012). The social work code of conduct promotes the key principle of keeping the dignity of the client front of mind in a person-centred manner (see, for example, Social Workers Registration Board 2016). However, research has reported that social workers continue to face difficulties in practising within pre-existing medical models of care that focus on objective measurable tasks, rather than on the provision of care that is underpinned by a meaningful relationship based on respect and trust (Rockwell 2012; Yeung and Rodgers 2017).

Person-centred care in residential care services strives to focus on the person in what are essentially communal living care environments that are moving toward relationship-based care (Davies 2001; Nolan, Davies and Grant 2001). Rockwell (2012) has further suggested the need to combine person-centred practice with relationship-based care and relational autonomy to reflect the key ethos of social work practice for older people living in residential aged care facilities. Social workers are well positioned to facilitate this process given their skills in networking, advocacy, care coordination and strengths-based interventions. In relationship-based approaches, dependence and frailty are not perceived as creating the vulnerability which threatens a person's autonomy and dignity, but these approaches suggest that vulnerability occurs when a person is treated as dependent and is not supported to be involved in decisions about their care.

It is important to understand how the socio-cultural context and institutional structures in a residential facility may undermine a person's opportunity to exercise autonomy and maintain their dignity (Sherwin and Winsby 2011). Yeung and Rodgers's (2017) study on what matters most to residents' quality of life showed the importance of responding to both socio-psychological as well as physiological needs and encouraging the participation in activities that are individualized and meaningful. Such activities develop connectedness to other residents and staff, add quality to life, and do not simply fill in the resident's day. Being known and respectfully treated as a unique individual with personal preferences opens a pathway for relational autonomy, which acknowledges the central role of others in decision making, including social workers, who have a responsibility to engage older people's emotional experiences and offer clear guidance when they are confronting serious illnesses. Social workers are often strong advocates for the person-centred approach as its principles and values are central to their professional code of ethics. This means that social workers commit to establishing meaningful and purposeful relationships with individuals and their families or significant others to support them to manage and address difficulties and challenges. This is integral to residents' and familes' perceptions of quality of life and care in residential settings.

Another aspect that may undermine person-centred approaches is the contractual arrangements within care homes (Howe, Jones and Tilse 2013), which may create an ambiguous status for the residents. For example, the tension involved in trying to live an autonomous, private life, within a public environment dominated by routine and organizational structure, which can impact adversely on residents' satisfaction with care services and subsequently their overall quality of life (Cook, Thompson and Reed 2015). Relationship-based care involves communication and partnership between residents, families and staff, and this approach will enhance residents' quality of life. Cook *et al.* (2015) argue that older people who relocate to care facilities because they are no longer able to independently meet their fundamental human needs may sacrifice ontological security in favour of physical security. Therefore, to enable residents to regard care facilities as *home*, staff need to be focused on recognizing, acknowledging and supporting residents' aspirations to living in care, rather than existing in care.

The following case study of Julie and her husband David illustrates two key issues of ageing and aged care. The first one is about informal care as central to the experience of ageing for older people. As an older person's health deteriorates, it becomes very challenging to care for them at home, even with support services. It can also be difficult for family members who care for the person at home for an extended period of time to share the care with strangers. This leads to the second issue of family members experiencing strong feelings of grief and loss due to the difficulty in making the decision to admit a family member into residential care. Family members may want to contribute to the care of the relative after admission to a facility through involvement in care planning, decision making and sometimes in continuing to provide some hands-on care such as assisting with meals and drinks. Importantly, family members want their loved one to be recognized as an individual, and in keeping with a person-centred approach, they play an important role in helping staff to understand who the residents are and who they have been (Irving 2015).

Case study 2 ···

Julie is 75 years of age and her husband, David, is 81 years of age. Five years ago, they moved into a retirement village which is situated in a large residential aged care complex that provides a range of care options. Julie and David have two children, a daughter and a son, and both live in the same city. The grandchildren often visit Julie and David. Twelve months ago, David had a stroke which resulted in aphasia, serious mobility, and incontinence issues. Given that David's needs have become greater, he is now in the care home next to the retirement village where Julie continues to stay. David has been in care for four months and some of the nurses have noticed that Julie has been acting like a co-carer as she is in David's unit all day or with David in the dining or entertainment room. At times Julie insists on doing David's personal care and she seems to have withdrawn from her circle of friends who also live in the retirement village. She seldom participates in her favourite activities, gardening and playing bridge. Julie has also been reluctant to spend time with her grown-up children and grandchildren saying that she needs to look after David.

However, David seems to show signs of depression which is connected to his health deterioration and he also expresses feeling guilty that Julie is becoming like his carer rather than his wife. Since David has been admitted to the care home, Julie has lost a lot of weight and has started complaining about having constant headaches. Julie also complained to her daughter and the nursing director at the care home of staff treating her indifferently when she comes in and stays with David. Other staff members have said to the nursing director that Julie often instructs them on how to look after David and demands extra attention during their busy times. Julie's daughter has also been in touch with the nursing director about her mother's behaviour and declining health. The nursing director has decided to contact the care facility social worker to discuss Julie and David's situation.

It is not easy to care for a loved one and make the difficult decision to admit a family member into a care home. This can be complicated for a married couple like Julie and David when one person from the couple is admitted to a care home and is separated from their spouse. Consider these questions:

1. As a care facility social worker, how would you talk to Julie about her struggle to relinquish care after David was admitted into the care home?

2. What can you do to ensure Julie maintains a social and active lifestyle?

3. How would you encourage David to share his concerns and feelings with Julie?

4. How would you help Julie and David's children deal with the sudden changes that are happening to their parents?

5. In terms of person-centred and relationship-based care practice, how would you ensure that your practice embraces the principles of empathy, congruence and unconditional positive regard?

Emerging challenges in social work practice with older people

As the world's population is ageing, people over 65 will receive some form of long-term care services, including a broad range of personal care, health and social services. One of the challenges for social work practice is that the literature on care and the promotion of residents' wellbeing is *nurse centred*. International literature illustrates that social workers are employed across the continuum of long-term care in settings such as hospitals, nursing homes, and in primary care (Allen *et al.* 2007; Koren and Doron 2005; Petersen *et al.* 2016). Research conducted by Thornton (2012) in Aotearoa New Zealand has shown that district health boards do not consistently provide services such as social work to meet the transition and emotional needs of older people moving into residential facilities. This research also raised concerns about the wellbeing of older people and the provision of ongoing care and family involvement in care provision. Social workers' competencies and skills can be useful in addressing these concerns. McKenna and Staniforth's (2017) study reported that social work services can ensure that older people have adequate time to make informed choices about their future care needs and can also assist older people and their families to attend to psychosocial issues that are implicit in transitioning to late-life care.

The challenge for social workers is to be equal team members in multidisciplinary teams as they bring unique knowledge and skills. For example, Koenig *et al.* (2011) state that social workers can contribute to upholding residents' rights to independence and dignity and to support them to work with care staff within a person-centred care approach. Using strengths-based relational practices, social workers can support residents to have autonomy and to identify and pursue their needs and preferences (Rockwell 2012). Washburn and Grossman (2017) have further emphasized that to promote social work practice that is authentic and genuine, practice should be grounded in empathy (understanding the resident's perspective), congruence (respectful and consistent in service provision) and unconditional positive regard (valuing the person for who they are without judgement). Moreover, social workers can support residents and their families to resolve the feelings of grief and dislocation they may experience when they move to a care facility.

Social workers can also work at a macro level and advocate for families to have opportunities to raise their concerns and, alongside this, facilitate family engagement in decision making and in supporting their family member to fully participate in this decision making. Petersen *et al.* (2016) have further emphasized that social work practice can adopt community development approaches that provide a critical analysis of structural factors that have an impact on the provision of care, such as power, class, gender and ethnicity. These approaches can promote an inclusionary space of family caregiving that supports residents, their families, friends and staff to be fully involved in care decisions and in formulating policies and practices that can enhance people's wellbeing and quality of life.

Conclusion

The changes in the social welfare and healthcare system currently under way in Aotearoa New Zealand and internationally are unsettling and challenging. Demographic trends indicate that there will be a significant increase in demand for services due to the longer life expectancy of older people. It is important to consider that older people, like all age groups, need appropriate time and support to adjust to accepting disability, functional decline and the possibility of the need to accept services or leave their home and move into residential care. Social workers have an important role in supporting older people to maintain control over their lives and remain as active citizens. Older people have a unique set of experiences, abilities and capabilities which mean that a 'one size fits all' approach to care provision is inappropriate (Crawford and Walker 2008, p.12). The evidence suggests that issues of diversity and inequality in health in old age are important, as is knowing how psychosocial, socio-economic and structural factors impact on care options. While some researchers (e.g., Boudiny 2013) argue that promoting physical activity and healthy lifestyles for people of all ages is appropriate within the healthy ageing policies, an important question is how social and healthcare professionals and policy makers can ensure that the concept of active or successful ageing is inclusive for all people, including those who are frail, dependent and vulnerable.

Social workers in both community and residential settings have an important role in developing age-friendly environments and supportive services. They also have a role in confronting the dominant discourses of ageing that blame older people for not being able to maintain independence, participate actively and remain productive. Social work practice, with a focus on justice, human rights, empowerment and advocacy, has an important role in challenging structural barriers and inequalities, including private business models of healthcare provision that endanger the level of care provided to those who are most in need. Social work is in a position to have the knowledge and understanding to serve as a key source of communication, information and relationship-based continuity to provide the support necessary to older people and their families undergoing major life transitions.

Reflection questions

- Ageing is a complex phenomenon; thinking of the ideas presented in this chapter, reflect on what they mean for you as a social worker.

- Consider the current government policies in your country that encourage older people to be more proactive in their choices of healthcare. How will this change the healthcare system and impact on ageing within a diverse society?

- What are the key features of person-centred and relationship-based care approaches and how do these inform your practice as a social worker? How do these inform the processes for developing meaningful support that is responsive to the needs of older people?

References

Abley, C. (2012) 'Responding to vulnerability in old age: Patient-centred care.' *Nursing Standard 27*, 9, 42–46.

Alkire, S. (2005) 'Why the capability approach?' *Journal of Human Development 6*, 1, 115–135.

Allen, P., Nelson, H., Netting, F. and Cox, D. (2007) 'Navigating conflict: A model for nursing home social workers.' *Health & Social Work 32*, 3, 231–234.

Alpass, F., Towers, A., Stephens, C., Fitzgerald, E., Stevenson, B. and Davey, J. (2007) 'Independence, wellbeing, and social participation in an aging population.' *Annals of the New York Academy of Sciences 1114*, 1, 241–250. doi:10.1196/annals.1396.009.

Anderson-Wuf, J. (2017) 'The Profile of Older People in Australia and New Zealand.' In M. Bernoth and D. Winker (eds) *Healthy Ageing and Aged Care*. Melbourne, Australia: Oxford University Press.

Bass, S., Caro, F. and Chen, Y. (1993) *Achieving a Productive Ageing Society*. Westport, CT: Auburn House.

Boudiny, K. (2013) 'Active ageing: From empty rhetoric to policy tool.' *Ageing & Society 33*, 1077–1098.

Bowling, A. (2007) 'Aspirations for older age in the 21st century: What is successful aging?' *International Journal of Ageing & Human Development 63*, 263–297.

Breheny, M. and Stephens, C. (2010) 'Ageing in a material world.' *New Zealand Journal of Psychology 39*, 2, 41–48.

Breheny, M., Stephens, C., Alpass, F., Stevenson, B., Carter, K. and Yeung, P. (2013) 'Development and validation of a measure of living standards for older people.' *Social Indicators Research 114*, 3, 1035–1048.

Broad, J.B., Ashton, T., Gott, M., McLeod, H., Davis, P.B. and Connolly, M.J. (2015) 'Likelihood of residential aged care use in later life: A simple approach to estimation with international comparison.' *Australian & New Zealand Journal of Public Health 30*, 4, 374–379. doi:10.1111/1753-6405.12374.

Brown Wilson, C. (2009) 'Developing community in care homes through a relationship-centred approach.' *Health and Social Care in the Community 17*, 2, 177–186.

Brownie, S. and Horstmanshof, L. (2012) 'Creating the conditions for self-fulfilment for aged care residents.' *Nursing Ethics 19*, 6, 777–786.

Buys, L. and Miller, Y. (2006) 'The meaning of active ageing in older Australian: Exploring the relative importance of health, participation and security.' Accessed on 31/11/2016 at https://eprints.qut.edu.au/6671/1/6671.pdf.

Cook, G., Thompson, J. and Reed, J. (2015) 'Re-conceptualising the status of residents in a care home: Older people wanting to "live with care".' *Ageing & Society 35*, 8, 1587–1613.

Crawford, K. and Walker, J. (2008) *Social Work with Older People* (2nd edition). Exeter: Learning Matters/Sage.

Davies, S. (2001) 'The Care Needs of Older People and Family Caregivers in Continuing Care Settings.' In M.R. Nolan, S. Davies and G. Grant (eds) *Working with Older People and Their Families*. Buckingham: Open University Press.

Deutschman, M. (2001) 'Redefining quality and excellence in the nursing home culture.' *Journal of Gerontological Nursing 27*, 28–36.

Dyson, R. (2002) *Health of Older People Strategy: Health Sector Action to 2010 to Support Positive Ageing*. Wellington, New Zealand: Ministry of Health.

Gaugler, J. (2006) 'Family involvement and resident psychosocial status in long-term care.' *Clinical Gerontologist 29*, 4, 217–228.

Hamann, D. (2014) 'Does empowering resident families or nursing home employees in decision making improve service quality?' *Journal of Applied Gerontology 33*, 5, 603–623.

Hansen-Kyle, L. (2005) 'A concept analysis of healthy ageing.' *Nursing Forum 40*, 2, 45–47.

Hertzberg, A. and Ekman, S.L. (2000) '"We, not them and us?" Views on the relationships and interactions between staff and relatives of older people permanently living in nursing home.' *Journal of Advanced Nursing 31*, 3, 614–622.

Howe, A.L., Jones, A.E. and Tilse, C. (2013) 'What's in a name? Similarities and differences in international terms and meanings for older people's housing with services.' *Ageing & Society 33*, 4, 547–578.

Hsu, H.C. (2012) 'Trajectories and covariates of life satisfaction among older adults in Taiwan.' *Archives of Gerontology & Geriatrics 55*, 1, 210–216.

Institute for Patient- and Family-Centered Care. (n.d.) *What is Patient- and Family-Centered Health Care?* Accessed on 06/02/2016 at www.ipfcc.org/faq.html.

Irving, J. (2015) 'Beyond family satisfaction: Family-perceived involvement in residential care.' *Australasian Journal on Ageing 34*, 3, 166–170.

Jones, C. and Moyle, W. (2016) 'Staff perspectives of relationships in aged care: A qualitative approach.' *Australasian Journal on Ageing 35*, 3, 198–203.

Koenig, T., Hee Lee, J., Feilds, N. and MacMillan, K. (2011) 'The role of the gerontological social worker in assisted living.' *Journal of Gerontological Social Work 54*, 5, 494–510.

Koren, C. and Doron, I. (2005) 'Being a social worker in homes for the aged: The real, the ideal, and the gaps between.' *Journal of Gerontological Social Work 44*, 3/4, 95–114.

Liang, J. and Luo, B. (2012) 'Toward a discourse shift in social gerontology: From successful aging to harmonious aging.' *Journal of Aging Studies 26*, 3, 327–334.

Lloyd, L., Tanner, D., Milne, A., Ray, M. *et al.* (2014) 'Look after yourself: Active ageing, individual responsibility and the decline of social work with older people in the UK.' *European Journal of Social Work 17*, 3, 322–335.

MacKean, R. and Abbott-Chapman, J. (2012) 'Older people's perceived health and wellbeing: The contribution of peer-run community organisation.' *Health Sociology Review 21*, 1, 47–57.

Martinson, M. and Berridge, C. (2015) 'Successful aging and its discontents: A systematic review of the social gerontology literature.' *The Gerontologist 55*, 1, 58–69.

Martinson, M. and Minkler, M. (2006) 'Civic engagement and older adults: A critical perspective.' *The Gerontologist 46*, 3, 318–329.

McCormack, B. (2003) 'A conceptual framework for person-centred practice with older people.' *International Journal of Nursing Practice 9*, 202–209.

McKenna, D. and Staniforth, B. (2017) 'Older people moving to residential care in Aotearoa New Zealand: Considerations for social work at practice and policy levels.' *Aotearoa New Zealand Social Work 29*, 1, 28–40.

Ministry of Health (2002) *Health of Older People Strategy.* Wellington, New Zealand: Ministry of Health.

Ministry of Health (2007) *An Indication of New Zealanders' Health 2007.* Wellington, New Zealand: Ministry of Health.

Ministry of Social Development (2015) *2014 Report on the Positive Ageing Strategy.* Wellington, New Zealand: Office for Senior Citizens.

Morris, C. (2009) 'Measuring participation in childhood disability: How does the capability approach improve our understanding?' *Developmental Medicine and Child Neurology 51*, 92–94.

Murtagh, K.N. and Hubert, H.B. (2004) 'Gender differences in physical disability among an elderly cohort.' *American Journal of Public Health 94*, 8, 1046–1411.

Netuveli, G., Hildon, Z., Montgomery, S., Wiggins, R. and Blane, D. (2006) 'Quality of life at older ages: Evidence from English Longitudinal Study of Ageing.' *Journal of Epidemiological Community Health 60*, 357–363.

Niedzwiedz, C., Katikireddi, S., Pell, J. and Mitchell, R. (2014) 'Socioeconomic inequalities in the quality of life of older Europeans in different welfare regimes.' *The European Journal of Public Health 24*, 3, 364–370.

Nolan, M.R., Davies, S. and Grant, G. (2001) 'Integrating Perspectives.' In M. Nolan., S. Davies and G. Grant (eds) *Working with Older People and Their Families: Key Issues in Policy and Practice.* Buckingham: Open University Press.

Oosterveld-Vlug, M.G., Pasman, H.R.W., van Gennip, I.E., Muller, M.T., Willems, D.L. and Onwuteaka-Philipsen, B.D. (2014) 'Dignity and the factors that influence it according to nursing home residents: A qualitative interview study.' *Journal of Advanced Nursing 70*, 97–106.

Organisation for Economic Co-operation and Development (1988) *Aging Populations: The Social Policy Implications.* Washington, DC: OECD Publications and Information Centre.

Organisation for Economic Co-operation and Development (2015) *Health at a Glance 2015: OECD Indicators.* Paris: OECD Publishing. Accessed on 15/02/2017 at http://apps.who.int/medicinedocs/documents/s22177en/s22177en.pdf.

Petersen, M., Wilson, J., Wright, O., Ward, E. and Capra, S. (2016) 'The space of family care-giving in Australian aged care facilities: Implications for social work.' *British Journal of Social Work 46*, 81–97.

Petriwskyj, A., Parker, D., Wilson, C. and Gibson, A. (2016) 'What health and aged care culture change models mean for residents and their families: A systematic review.' *The Gerontologist 56*, 2, e12–e20.

Pinquart, M. and Sorensen, S. (2000) 'Influences of socioeconomic status, social network, and competence on subjective well-being in later life: A meta-analysis.' *Psychology & Aging 15*, 2, 187–224.

Pond, R., Stephens, C. and Alpass, F. (2010) 'Virtuously watching one's health: Older adults' regulation of self in the pursuit of health.' *Journal of Health Psychology 15*, 5, 734–743.

Richards, D. (1981) 'Rights and autonomy.' *Ethics 92*, 3–20.

Rockwell, J. (2012) 'From person-centered to relational care: Expanding the focus in residential care facilities.' *Journal of Gerontology Social Work 55*, 3, 233–248.

Rodgers, V. and Neville, S. (2007) 'Personal autonomy for older people living in residential care: An overview.' *Nursing Praxis in New Zealand 23*, 1, 29–36.

Rosher, R.B. and Robinson, S. (2005) 'Impact of the Eden Alternative on family satisfaction.' *Journal of the American Medical Directors Association 6*, 3, 189–193.

Rowe, J.W. and Kahn, R.L. (1997) 'Successful aging.' *The Gerontologist 37*, 433–440.

Ryan, A. and McKenna, H. (2015) 'It's the little things that count: Families' experience of roles, relationships and quality of care in rural nursing homes.' *International Journal of Older People Nursing 10*, 1, 38–47.

Sen, A. (1985) *Commodities and Capabilities*. Oxford: Oxford University Press.

Sen, A. (1992) *Inequality Re-examined*. Oxford: Clarendon Press.

Sen, A. (2000) *Social Exclusion: Concept, Application, and Scrutiny. Social Development Papers 2000*. No.1. Office of Environment and Social Development. Manila, Philippines: Asian Development Bank.

Sen, A. (2004) 'Dialogue. Capabilities, lists, and public reason: Continuing the conversation.' *Feminist Economics 10*, 77–80.

Sen, A. (2010) 'The mobile and the world.' *Information Technologies and International Development 6*, Special Issue, 1–3.

Sharma, T., Bamford, M. and Dodman, D. (2015) 'Person-centred care: An overview of reviews.' *Contemporary Nurse 51*, 2–3, 107–120.

Sherwin, S. and Winsby, M. (2011) 'A relational perspective on autonomy for older adults residing in nursing homes.' *Health Expectations 14*, 2, 182–190.

Social Workers Registration Board (2016) *Code of Conduct*. Accessed on 18/07/2016 at http://swrb.govt.nz/concerns-and-information/code-of-conduct.

Statistics New Zealand (2013a) *2013 Census Quickstats about People Aged 65 and Over*. Accessed on 06/07/2016 at http://archive.stats.govt.nz/Census/2013-census/profile-and-summary-reports/quickstats-65-plus.aspx.

Statistics New Zealand (2013b) *Living Outside the Norm: An Analysis of People Living in Temporary and Community Dwellings, 2013 Census*. Accessed on 08/09/2015 at http://archive.stats.govt.nz/Census/2013-census/profile-and-summary-reports/outside-norm.aspx.

Statistics New Zealand (2014) *Ageing Population Effects*. Accessed on 11/03/2017 at https://rcaforum.org.nz/sites/public_files/images/160426-ageing%20pop%20commentary.pdf

Stenner, P., McFarquhar, T. and Bowling, A. (2011) 'Older people and "active ageing": Subjective aspects of ageing actively.' *Journal of Health Psychology 16*, 467–477.

Stephens, C., Breheny, M. and Mansvelt, J. (2015) 'Healthy ageing from the perspective of older people: A capability approach to resilience.' *Psychology & Health 30*, 6, 715–731.

Terzi, L. (2005) 'A capability perspective on impairment, disability and special needs. Towards social justice in education.' *Theory and Research in Education 3*, 197–223.

The Green House Project (2015) *The Green House Project*. Accessed on 12/02/2016 at http://thegreenhouseproject.org.

Thornton, G. (2012) *Aged Residential Care Service Review*. Wellington, New Zealand: Thornton New Zealand. Accessed on 25/02/2017 at https://nzaca.org.nz/assets/Documents/ARSCR-Full-Report.pdf.

United Nations, Department of Economic and Social Affairs, Population Division (2009) *World Population Ageing 2009*. New York, NY: United Nations.

United Nations, Department of Economic and Social Affairs, Population Division (2013) *World Population Ageing 2013*. Accessed on 30/06/2016 at www.un.org/en/development/desa/population/publications/pdf/ageing/WorldPopulationAgeing2013.pdf.

Usui, W.M., Thomas, J.K. and Durig, K.R. (1985) 'Socioeconomic comparisons and life satisfaction of elderly adults.' *Journal of Gerontology 40*, 110–114.

Veal, D., King, J. and Marston, G. (2016) 'Enhancing the social dimension of development: Interconnecting the Capability Approach and applied knowledge of social workers.' *International Social Work*. doi.org/10.1177/0020872816651703.

Washburn, A.M. and Grossman, M. (2017) 'Being with a person in our care: Person-centred social work practice that is authentically person-centred.' *Journal of Gerontological Social Work*. doi.org/10.1080/01634372.2017.1348419.

Welch Saleeby, P. (2007) 'Applications of a capability approach to disability and the International Classification of Functioning, Disability and Health (ICF) in social work.' *Journal of Social Work in Disability & Rehabilitation 6*, 1–2, 21–232.

Willetts, D. (2010) *The Pinch: How the Baby Boomers Stole Their Children's Future and Why They Should Give It Back*. London: Atlantic Books.

World Health Organization (2002) *Active Ageing: A Policy Framework*. Accessed on 04/06/2013 at https://extranet.who.int/agefriendlyworld/wp-content/uploads/2014/06/WHO-Active-Ageing-Framework.pdf.

World Health Organization (2012) *Aging and Life Course*. Accessed on 24/03/2014 at www.who.int/ageing/media/infographics/en.

Xavier, F.M., Ferraz, M.P., Marc, N., Escosteguy, N.U. and Moriguchi, E.H. (2003) 'Elderly people's definition of quality of life.' *Revista Brasileira de Psiquiatria 25*, 1, 31–39.

Yeung, P. and Breheny, M. (2016) 'Using the capability approach to understand the determinants of subjective wellbeing among community-dwelling older people in New Zealand.' *Age & Ageing 45*, 2, 292–298.

Yeung, P. and Rodgers, V. (2017) 'Quality of long-term care for older people in residential settings: Perceptions of quality of life and care satisfaction from residents and their family members.' *Nursing Praxis in New Zealand. Journal of Professional Nursing 33*, 1, 28–43.

Yeung, P., Rodgers, V., Dale, M., Spence, S. *et al.* (2016) 'Psychometric testing of a person-centred care scale the Eden Warmth Survey in a long-term care home in New Zealand.' *Contemporary Nurse 50*, 176–190.

• Part 2 •

DEVELOPING COMMUNITIES

Chapter 7

Transformative Social Work Practice in Community-Based Organizations

ROBYN MUNFORD AND JACKIE SANDERS

Introduction

This chapter explores transformative social work practice in community-based organizations. While the discussion draws on practice examples from Aotearoa New Zealand, the theories and principles outlined have relevance for social work practice in community-based organizations internationally. Community-based organizations work at the local level and provide a range of services, such as social work, early childhood services, education programmes and family support. Many of the clients who use these services have been marginalized and excluded from full participation in their communities because of impoverished social and material circumstances and restricted access to resources and support. Community-based organizations are well placed to support transformative social work practice as they open up resources and expand opportunities through intensive work with clients across a number of integrated services.

Transformative social work practice involves challenging social injustice, working in partnership with clients to understand their lived experiences, and identifying social change strategies that enable communities to realize better futures. Community development approaches (Munford and Walsh-Tapiata 2005) are closely connected to transformative social work practice as they address immediate issues while working alongside groups to identify the dominant discourses, structures, policies and practices that require transformation.

Internationally, social workers have been challenged to understand issues of diversity, displacement and the impact of marginalization and of growing inequalities (Finn and Jacobson 2003; Nelson, Price and Zubrzycki 2017). This requires a commitment to building trust-based partnerships with clients and coming to a deep appreciation of the issues they face, including the factors that contribute to inequality and marginalization. It involves understanding local contexts, foregrounding indigenous knowledge and identifying strategies for constructing meaningful relationships between diverse cultural groups.

In Aotearoa New Zealand, transformative social work practice operates within a bicultural context (Munford and Sanders 2011) and requires recognition of the primary relationship between Māori as Tangata Whenua (the indigenous population and guardians of the land) and Tauiwi (others who came to Aotearoa New Zealand after Māori). The Te Tiriti o Waitangi (the Treaty of Waitangi) prescribes the relationship between Māori and Tauiwi (Ruwhiu 2009). Social workers have been challenged to reflect on the position of the Treaty in social work practice. The relationship between Māori and the Crown forms a critical nexus within which other cultural and social relationships need to be resolved. In recent times, the need to develop practice that responds to multicultural imperatives within this bicultural framework has also become an important part of social work practice. For example, communities of the Pacific Islands have a strong presence in Aotearoa New Zealand and have introduced a range of worldviews that have strengthened our practice (Mafile'o and Vakalahi 2017). Foregrounding cultural frameworks in practice has been a significant focus for social work and reflects global efforts to confront oppression and marginalization of specific groups such as indigenous peoples (Gray, Coates and Yellow Bird 2008). Transformative social work practice has had a key role in challenging the practices that marginalize cultural knowledge. It recognizes the importance of local and cultural knowledge in the construction of the practice of social work.

This chapter begins with a discussion of the emerging theories of transformative social work practice and explores one approach within transformative approaches: community-led development. It identifies the key elements of practice that guide social workers in their support of community-led social change processes. The discussion then moves to a presentation of a case study to illustrate the framework of practice in action. This is followed by a discussion of the challenges to transformative practice approaches. The chapter concludes with questions for reflection.

Emerging theory and practice

Transformative social work practice involves intervention at multiple levels. Social workers attend to the immediate needs of individuals, families and communities, while encouraging an understanding of the relationship between personal issues and the broader social and political context and the factors that facilitate social change. These social work approaches give effect to the international definition of social work (International Federation of Social Workers 2014), which promotes social justice, human rights, collective responsibility and respect for diversities as core principles of social work practice. The capacity to understand the connection between the personal and the structural has been perceived as one of the key strengths of social work (Ferguson and Lavalette 2006; Finn and Jacobson 2003; Munford and Sanders 2013; Nelson *et al.* 2017). At the centre of this practice is an understanding of the social conditions that have functioned to exclude and marginalize populations (Canavan 2008; VanderPlaat 2016).

Social workers, in their interactions with clients, are positioned as 'witness bearers' (Irizarry *et al.* 2016, p.1857) to social injustice, the impact of adverse social conditions, and social inequalities. Transformative social work practice promotes a critical analysis (Mezirow 2003; Weiss and Schott 2016; Witkin 2014) of these circumstances and of the factors that undermine democratic citizenship. Social workers work alongside clients to challenge the discourses, policies and structures that exclude citizens from fully participating in community life. In this way, social workers are able to respond to what Canavan (2008, p.5) has coined the 'concrete awfulness' (Canavan 2008, p.5) of everyday lives and to mitigate the 'real consequences' (p.5) of social inequality while working on a wider level to transform the policy and structures that create these social conditions.

Transformative social work practice embraces an 'integrative perspective' (Weiss and Schott 2016, p.3) that recognizes the complexity of lived experience and the need to work on multiple levels to address social issues. It draws on a range of approaches that are grouped under the rubric of emancipatory practice; such approaches explicitly focus on issues of social justice, on exposing power imbalances and on exposing the root causes of social issues (Dominelli 1998; Munford and Sanders 2013). These include *inter alia*: anti-oppressive practice, indigenous approaches, feminist social work, critical social work, and community development. This chapter focuses on one approach to transformative social work practice within community-based organizations: community-led development.

Community-led development

Community-led development can be classified within a range of approaches (community organization, community development, collective impact approaches) that support communities to work together to identify shared issues and to generate solutions that reflect local contexts and knowledge (Cabaj and Weaver 2016; Munford and Walsh-Tapiata 2005; Porter, Martin and Anda 2016). While there are multiple definitions of community-led development (Department of Internal Affairs 2017), central to these approaches is the self-determination of communities in identifying community issues and in determining the strategies to address these issues. Social workers in community-based organizations have an important role in working alongside clients to promote social change processes. This involves establishing partnerships with community members in order to craft strategies that address immediate concerns and that also confront intractable issues, such as inadequate access to material and social resources. Of significance is the commitment to an emancipatory ethic that challenges the discourses, which frame adversity and human suffering as a consequence of personal deficits (VanderPlaat 2016, p.198). At the cornerstone of this practice is connecting personal troubles with public issues, including exposing 'structural barriers' (VanderPlaat 2016, p.198) and the effects of 'punitive and marginalizing social policy and social discourse' (Nelson *et al.* 2017, p.604). This analysis of social conditions is a crucial first step in social change processes. Social workers then have a key role in encouraging people's belief that change is possible. This involves foregrounding the centrality of human agency and the transformative potential of social action (Munford and Sanders 2013). Importantly, social workers can provide a space for clients to hold hope and optimism that different futures can be realized (Porter *et al.* 2016).

Community-led development: key elements of practice
Establishing partnerships and naming the issue
Social change begins with the recognition that it is possible to confront the discourses and structures that determine everyday lives. Establishing partnerships is an important first step in social change processes and social workers in community-based organizations have a key role in facilitating these partnerships. In these trust-based partnerships, social workers demonstrate a deep respect for people's capacity to generate meaning about their own circumstances and to build an understanding of the connection between personal experience and the structural conditions that shape these experiences (Finn and Jacobson 2003; Irizarry *et al.* 2016; VanderPlaat 2016). Within these partnerships, consideration is given to how clients move from a position where they are perceived as passive recipients of services with little control over how services and support are delivered, to an active role in determining service responses.

Social workers can support clients to become what Porter *et al.* (2016, p.2) call 'agents of culture change' where they not only take on a role in defining more appropriate responses to their needs but also challenge the root causes of social conditions and the impact of these on their daily lives.

The process of naming the issue involves bringing people together to analyse an issue and to identify the possibilities for social change (Porter *et al.* 2016). It begins with social workers listening to the stories clients bring to helping relationships (Irizarry *et al.* 2016). Transformative practice embraces the belief that there is space for agency (Pallota-Chiarolli and Pease 2014) and for action, and that despite the overwhelming impact of social conditions on everyday life, people do engage in 'small acts of resistance' (Nelson *et al.* 2017, p.609). Social workers support clients to build on these acts of resistance at the individual level and transform them into wider social change processes. For example, a social worker supporting parents to access appropriate learning support for their disabled children facilitates these parents coming together to extend their individual advocacy for their children into a wider social change strategy. This strategy challenges schools to be more responsive to the learning needs of all disabled children and to embed access to appropriate learning support within their policies and practices.

In these social change processes, social workers support clients to take a lead role in defining an issue. Social workers offer a combination of practical and emotional support; the practical is concerned with providing tools for social change, such as tools for analysing issues and for reflecting on the *how* of social change processes. The emotional component involves mediating the personal effects of dealing with injustice (Pallotta-Chiarolli and Pease 2014; Pease *et al.* 2016) and the feelings of humiliation and despair caused when institutions are unresponsive and when social policies marginalize people (Irizarry *et al.* 2016; VanderPlaat 2016). Social workers can provide containment and a safe space for these feelings to be held while supporting clients to have agency, to challenge injustice and to hold hope that change is possible (Irizarry *et al.* 2016). This practice and the partnership between social workers and clients provides a strong foundation for creating a shared vision and for identifying change strategies.

Creating a shared vision and identifying change strategies

Social workers have a key role in working with community groups to create a shared vision and to identify social change processes. The process for creating a shared vision begins with the stories of personal experience and an exploration of the wider factors that shape this experience.

For instance, taking the example above of learning support for disabled children, parents come together to share their personal experiences and by identifying the common factors in these experiences they begin to develop a vision for how to transform the learning experiences for their children. Critical reflection processes are used to explore the possibilities for social change processes (Pallota-Chiarolli and Pease 2014). At the centre of these processes is reasserting how to enact agency and reiterating how small changes can have great effects, such as the first step in coming together to share stories of injustice, which then inform social change processes. Critical reflection processes also enable groups to identify how change processes operate at multiple levels. For instance, working on an individual level to ensure entitlement to services and support while using this information to work on a wider level to influence policy and the discourses that have created hardship and social inequality.

In working to create a shared vision and to identify change strategies, the social worker has a key role in encouraging people to reflect on the change process, to map progress and to find ways to maintain hope that goals can be achieved. An effective mechanism for maintaining the momentum of change is to engage in a process of 'crafting strategy' (Westley, Zimmerman and Patton 2006, p.141) which enables the group to harness both the 'intentional and spontaneous strategies' that emerge in change projects (p.25). This strategy is used to identify what is working well and to develop processes for extending these activities. It identifies catalysts for change and the critical moments in the change project that can be used to strengthen change endeavours. For example, community events are used to inform community members of progress and to encourage others to become involved. These activities promote broader social change, which incorporates the community's aspirations and values (Cabaj and Weaver 2016).

Social workers also have a key role in promoting 'generative' conversations (Porter *et al.* 2016, p.14) that enable group members to remain connected to the change process. They can assist with documenting change processes while ensuring that community members maintain leadership of the project. This is achieved by recognizing and valuing the experiences and knowledge of group members.

Sharing experience and knowledge to identify social change strategies

The sharing of experience and knowledge provides a foundation for determining social change strategies. At the core of this practice is the foregrounding of local knowledge and the recognition that wisdom comes from everyday life (Munford and Walsh-Tapiata 2005).

Transformative, participatory practices recognize that the only valid knowledge from which to initiate social change comes from the everyday understandings of those directly affected (VanderPlaat 2016). These practices create opportunities for community members to participate in the creation of the discourses that define them rather than being the 'disenfranchised subjects of privileged discourses which talk *about* them' (p.198). Social workers have an important role in supporting community members to bring local knowledge into change processes. This practice includes building an understanding of the context of social life and the ways in which global and national issues and policies are played out in local communities.

Transformative practice requires an understanding of how relations of power operate in community settings. While a primary focus is on the negative consequences of power relations, a critical analysis of these relations also allows for an examination of the situations when community members are able to resist power relations and enact 'little practices of freedom' (Morley, Macfarlane and Ablett 2014, p.165). For instance, taking the example of parents advocating for learning support for their disabled children, these parents took advantage of international guidelines on the rights of disabled children to have access to education in mainstream settings. They were able to pressure local schools to be more responsive to their children's learning needs while building on these initiatives to effect wider change strategies.

Of importance in change endeavours is seeking opportunities to foreground local knowledge and expertise and providing space for an exploration of 'counter-narratives' (McKenzie-Mohr and Lafrance 2017, p.189). These 'counter-narratives' challenge the 'master narratives' (p.189) that have constructed knowledge and interpretation of experience in ways that result in the silencing of some voices. An example from Aotearoa New Zealand has been the silencing and undermining of indigenous knowledge within the 'master narratives' of colonization. Social workers have joined with others to challenge these narratives alongside dealing with the economic, social and political consequences of colonization and the loss of mana (respect) and recognition of Māori as Tangata Whenua (guardians of the land). An expression of the reclaiming of knowledge is embodied within Ako, an indigenous concept that intentionally recognizes and respects the rich and varied knowledge and expertise of community members (Munford and Sanders 2011). Ako has been used over generations as a critical dimension of Māori pedagogy and can be harnessed in social change processes to generate new thinking about complex issues. This concept reminds social workers of the reciprocal view of learning and teaching, giving and receiving. It underscores the critical significance of establishing relationships that respect and recognize difference and of intentionally creating spaces where diverse voices can be heard and contribute to change.

Social workers can use 'critical curiosity' (Irizarry *et al.* 2016, p.1861) to facilitate knowledge sharing. This sharing of experience and knowledge, the disruption of dominant discourses and reflection on the social processes operating within communities, enhances a community's sense of efficacy and brings members 'together in solidarity to mobilize for change' (McKenzie-Mohr and Lafrance 2017, p.202). These actions promote self-determination by enabling community members to have a voice, to be heard, and to actively participate in change processes.

With the facilitation of these knowledge-sharing processes, the multiple meanings of lived experience and interpretations of community issues are captured and these stories then provide a catalyst for change processes. In the telling of these stories, community members build confidence in forming alliances and in leading community change processes. In this way, the change process becomes self-sustaining.

Working collectively and promoting collaborative leadership

Collective processes in community-led development enable community members to work together to generate community solutions and imagine bold visions for the future (Cabaj and Weaver 2016). Relational practices are critical in community change endeavours and enable communities to achieve change that is meaningful and embedded within community contexts and experiences (Munford and Sanders 2011). These practices involve mutual respect and recognition that all community members have valid contributions to make. They provide a framework for working collectively and for promoting collaborative leadership in change processes. Collaborative practices help build social capital and by valuing everyone's contribution they increase the potential for innovative solutions to be found to address challenging issues. Working collectively is the essence of successful change projects in that it enables diverse knowledge, experience, values and skills to be harnessed in change processes. Collaborative leadership begins with community engagement and the creation of strong trust-based partnerships where people come together in authentic and constructive ways (Cabaj and Weaver 2016; Porter *et al.* 2016).

There is a clear role for social workers here in supporting these processes by facilitating activities that encourage community members to take the lead in change projects. A central focus of this role is establishing group processes that promote mutual support and group cohesion. A fundamental challenge is to ensure that the community remains at the centre of change projects and that group activities are inclusive and incorporate diverse perspectives (Cabaj and Weaver 2016). Of importance is maintaining energy levels; group members must work in a reflective cycle to remain focused on both short- and long-term goals.

Community-led development draws on emerging thinking in other models of social change that have articulated the core attributes of transformative practice. The idea of *communities of practice* (Wenger 1998) is one such approach that provides important insights into community change endeavours. *Communities of practice* seek opportunities for collective learning which sustain active participation in change projects. This is an iterative learning cycle where groups work together to learn new skills and explore new information that enhances change and that enables the group to make the most of change opportunities and possibilities (Porter *et al.* 2016). For instance, taking the example of parents working together to advocate for learning support for their disabled children within mainstream education settings, these parents engaged in collective learning which enabled them to learn new skills, such as how to prepare submissions and to present at public meetings, and this in turn strengthened group bonds and helped maintain the momentum for change. Each achievement along the way contributed to long-term goals and the vision for change.

Community-led development also has synergies with other community change approaches. Collective impact approaches use community change processes to address intractable issues such as homelessness (Cabaj and Weaver 2016). The foundational elements of collective impact approaches involve mobilizing resources by promoting relationships and alliances across all levels of the community, including community members, local organizations and national organizations that have an impact on community life (Cabaj and Weaver 2016). Common to all of these approaches is engaging in continuous communication to ensure that practices are inclusive and draw on the expertise of all participants. Central to sustaining the momentum for change is a commitment to a cycle of action and reflection. This is a collective process with two key elements: first, reflection on action including progress on short- and long-term goals, and second, reflection on group processes. The first element involves practices that notice and celebrate change. These practices harness emerging possibilities which strengthen the commitment to working together to address the challenges and the conflicts that arise in change processes. Social workers will often take on the role of an appreciative enquirer during the continuous cycle of action and reflection. They can pose questions that will enable the group to engage with the challenges, but also to bring to the surface both the strengths and resources within the community and the wider context (Porter *et al.* 2016).

Action and reflection cycles embolden social change agents to make *more* of opportunities by using prior successes to identify the possibilities for extending these successes and the positive impact of community change projects (Munford, Sanders and Maden 2012). With regard to reflection on group processes, the central focus is on ensuring that these remain inclusive, that community members maintain ownership of change projects and that all participants are able to actively participate. Social workers have an important role in helping to ensure that collaboration does not become an end in itself and that its purpose is clearly articulated; that is, to realize transformative community change while supporting individuals to access meaningful resources and support.

The cycles of action and reflection are central components of community change endeavours. They help communities maintain hope and optimism that real change is possible (Porter *et al.* 2016). The next section extends the discussion and presents a case study that illustrates transformative practice in action.

Transformative practice in action
Working together on a community issue: realizing positive futures

This case vignette presents an example of transformative social work practice in a community-based organization. It is a composite vignette that draws on practice in one community-based organization (identifying information has been changed in order to protect the anonymity of clients and community members). The vignette explores the experiences of families who lived in impoverished social and material conditions. It presents a community change project that focused on realizing positive futures for the children in this community. The families were exposed to harmful circumstances such as intergenerational violence and abuse and for them issues of safety were a major concern. These families dreamed of having better futures for their children. A major challenge for these families had been the struggle to gain access to services that were responsive and consistent. However, they reported that when they started attending activities and services at the community-based organization things improved, as they were able to access support for all family members, such as early childhood programmes, parenting support, after-school activities, social work support, and health services.

In working with these families over the long term, social workers had supported them to negotiate the effects of living in impoverished material and social circumstances. Families established trust-based relationships with social workers and were able to share their experiences of mediating the effects of being poor and of living on the margins. Central to these stories was the daily struggle to survive and to provide for their children. Also of importance was sharing stories with other families who were facing the same issues. These connections helped them make sense of their experiences and together they explored the structural conditions that shaped these experiences. The sharing of experiences with others enhanced their feelings of belonging as they came to learn that they were not alone in their struggles and that others were also facing these daily challenges (Finn and Jacobson 2003; Irizarry *et al.* 2016; VanderPlaat 2016).

Social workers worked with families on their immediate issues and together they came to a decision that a community approach would contribute to addressing these issues. A major concern was the struggles families faced in supporting their children to fully participate in education; *not fitting in* had significant implications for these children both academically and because opportunities for participation in extra-curricular activities were restricted, such as involvement in sports and cultural activities. Many of the children reported that they experienced discrimination at school because they lived in an area that was known as *dangerous and bad*. Several of the families had challenged schools to be more responsive to these issues and had advocated for education support and resources that would enable their children to feel safe at school and to be fully engaged in school activities. While this advocacy had achieved some success for individual children, the local schools had not embedded these into their educational practices, so positive responses were not sustained over the long term.

After exploring these issues with the social worker, the families decided to work on a change project that would focus on working with local schools to encourage them to adopt practices that were more inclusive for all children in the wider community. The community-based organization had a key role in supporting the change process by providing practical resources such as meeting spaces. Social workers also assisted group members to facilitate meetings and develop tools that would help participants in their decision making and in the identification of change strategies.

Creating a shared vision for change

Social change processes occur at multiple levels. Social work practice with families at the micro level – for instance in this example, helping families to negotiate for education resources and support for their children as individual challenges emerged – can then inform change processes at a wider level. In listening deeply to the stories families told about their aspirations for nurturing their children to have better learning opportunities, social workers were able to support families to direct their attention to a wider change process that focused on challenging and changing school practices. In group meetings, parents identified their vision for change. Social workers encouraged parents to share their stories of success; for example, where individual advocacy efforts had resulted in change for their children. The social workers then supported families to see that these small acts of resistance (Nelson *et al.* 2017) could be harnessed in a wider change project that achieved enduring change where individual responses became embedded in school practices.

In their meetings, the families shared stories of the other issues that they faced in their everyday lives, such as the consequences of inadequate financial resources and issues of violence in the wider community. While these were major challenges for many of the families, in sharing their stories they identified that gaining access to education and support for their children's learning had the potential to transform their children's lives. They decided that this would be the focus of their first efforts at community-level change. These families articulated that engagement in education would realize different futures for their children. They shared stories of older children who had been excluded from school and did not return to school; as a consequence of this exclusion from school, many of these young people were unable to find meaningful employment, several had addiction issues, some had joined gangs as a way to engender a sense of belonging and others were in prison.

As the group continued to meet to finalize their short- and long-term goals for change, they invited others who were also concerned about education issues to join their change project and in this way they were able to broaden the expertise of the group (Westley *et al.* 2006).

Sharing experience and knowledge

Successful social change projects harness the skills and knowledge of all group members. Given the central role of the community organization in supporting families across a number of service domains, social workers had deep knowledge about community life, both the challenges and the strengths. This meant they were well placed to support group members to mobilize their strengths and have the confidence to share their experiences, skills and knowledge. Of significance in the change project was the use of community events to publicize the project and to bring others on board. Personnel from the school were invited to these events so that they could gain new perspectives on community life. This included being involved in cultural events, which were significant for the community, events which strengthened connections across diverse groups and generated a sense of belonging (Munford and Walsh-Tapiata 2005). These events told a counter-story (McKenzie-Mohr and Lafrance 2017) of community life, a community that had been defined by outsiders as *troubled and dangerous*. These counter-stories foregrounded the coping capacities and strengths of the community, and school personnel were able to see these first hand.

The sharing of knowledge was intentionally enacted through the process of Ako (Munford and Sanders 2011), where group participants engaged in an iterative learning cycle that positioned them as both learners and teachers. This was a powerful process as it built members' confidence to develop change strategies. In these processes, they were able to *try out* change strategies. Importantly, these processes mirrored the policies and practices they wanted to see happen in school environments; an inclusive approach to learning where school personnel recognized the expertise of parents and in partnership with parents created positive learning environments that benefited all children. The process of Ako enabled parents to have a voice on issues where they had previously been silent. These changes enhanced their self-determination, and with the support of social workers, they gained confidence that they would be heard and that their experiences and knowledge would be valued. This in turn gave them the courage to extend the change project to involve other community members and these alliances strengthened the change processes.

Working together to achieve positive change

Successful change projects require collective and collaborative responses that are able to harness diverse knowledge and skills (Cabaj and Weaver 2016; Porter *et al.* 2016). As the project developed, families formed strong alliances with school personnel who were prepared to work with them. As they gained confidence in the change process, they invited others from outside the local community to share their experiences in transforming school environments.

The social worker had a key role in bringing information into the group so that members could use this to inform their change strategies and project goals – for example, learning about the national policy on school practices, including the expectation that schools needed to demonstrate how they positively responded to the needs of all learners. The group members were also able to discover examples from other locations where schools had successfully established positive learning environments by being creative in the way they used resources and how they constructed these environments to respond to the diverse needs of students. This was important learning for the families, as it gave them information on how to encourage schools to be more culturally responsive to the diverse ethnic backgrounds of the children in their school. The connections with other communities were critical learning moments (Westley *et al.* 2006) and helped maintain the momentum of the change project as families became confident that they were on the *right track* given that others had achieved significant and enduring change in learning environments. These opportunities for learning about other successful projects also extended the social capital of the group as this valuable information enabled them to have confidence that they could work with school personnel to effect change.

A collective approach and working with diverse interests, experience and knowledge generated many opportunities to make *more* and to harness possibilities in the change process (Munford *et al.* 2012). Action and reflection cycles were a central component of the change project and included two aspects: critical reflection on group processes and the monitoring of the achievement of project goals.

It is important that at all stages of change projects, the group processes remain inclusive and enable all participants to participate fully, including sharing leadership roles. The ownership of the change endeavour remains with the group and they lead key decisions on change processes. Social workers have a key role in promoting mana-enhancing (respectful) practices even when conflict emerges. This includes using their practice wisdom to support group members to feel safe in bringing personal stories into the public arena (Nelson *et al.* 2017).

In reflecting on the achievement of project goals, action and reflection cycles focus on noticing and celebrating change and building on this success. For example, a major achievement in this project involved creative thinking around the community event where school personnel were encouraged to attend; their attendance enabled them to gain fresh insights into community life and as a result they were more willing to become involved in the change project. Important alliances were established at this event and these enabled the group to work directly with those who had the power to implement new education policies and practices.

Action and reflection cycles enable participants to maintain a critical curiosity (Irizarry *et al.* 2016) throughout the change project so that the momentum for change is sustained. At the core of this practice is supporting group members to see that small achievements can have larger effects, such as bringing on board a teacher early in the process who had implemented positive learning environments and who acted as a key informant for the project. The strong foundation achieved in successful social change projects can be harnessed to support other social justice projects.

In this change project, success in working with the school to create positive and safe learning environments enabled the community to challenge the wider policies that undermined the ability of schools to be responsive to the diverse and particular education needs of the community. Success in this project also gave the group confidence to become involved in change projects on other issues, such as addressing community violence. The project also foregrounded the important role of the social worker and other practitioners in the organization in that they were able to scaffold the change project (Cabaj and Weaver 2016) by providing practical and emotional support to group members.

As this case vignette has demonstrated, transformative practice has the potential to enable communities to challenge structural barriers, to disrupt taken-for-granted discourses on community life, and to lead change projects that can realize different futures for community members.

Challenges

Transformative social work practice works with the immediate lived experiences of clients while supporting social change processes at a wider level. While this practice has the potential to transform everyday lives, this work can be difficult. A major challenge for social workers is to promote transformative practice while responding to tightly prescribed funding requirements that are focused on individual service responses to problems (Porter *et al.* 2016). Such approaches may prioritize clinical practice and short-term interventions. While these interventions are able to address some of the issues that clients bring to social work organizations, there are many issues (such as the consequences of living in impoverished social and material circumstances, and not having access to essential resources such as education, health and employment) which require a more systematic and sustained response that directs attention to the root causes of adverse social conditions (Porter *et al.* 2016). Transformative practice approaches can address these complex social issues; however, this means that community-based organizations need to make a sustained commitment to social justice practice (Irizarry *et al.* 2016). This is a major challenge for many community-based organizations where resources are scarce and are in demand for other programmes.

Another key challenge is concerned with the essence of social justice work and the linking of personal troubles to public issues (Irizarry *et al.* 2016; Nelson *et al.* 2017). It is challenging for clients who have been silenced, and blamed for the daily challenges in their everyday lives, to join social change initiatives. This practice requires a clearly defined theory of change that moves from an exclusive focus on service delivery to a focus on social action where the counter-stories (McKenzie-Mohr and Lafrance 2017) of clients inform change processes and where inclusive processes support these clients to be heard and to lead social change projects.

Conclusion

Practice that makes a difference requires social workers to be courageous in confronting inequality and marginalization and to speak up for social justice. Transformative social work practice aligns with recent calls for a more 'robust paradigm of critical social work' (Nelson *et al.* 2017, p.610) that can respond to complex global challenges. While the focus of this chapter has been on one example of transformative social work practice – community-led practice in community-based organizations – the ideas discussed have relevance for all social workers who aspire to being involved in social justice practice.

At the core of transformative practice is a focus on local solutions, and on communities leading change processes; of importance in these change processes is recognizing that small changes in local communities collectively contribute to large effects. Transformative practice requires collaborative leadership and the building of strategic alliances, which keep alive optimism that change is possible and can be enduring. This practice gives effect to the principles of the international definition of social work and the promotion of social justice, human rights and collective responsibility, and underlines the central role of social workers in supporting diverse populations to participate fully in their communities and to determine their own futures.

Reflection questions

- How does transformative social work practice align with the international definition of social work?

- Define the core attributes of community-led development and identify practice examples from your own experience to illustrate these.

- Identify the challenges in community-led development. How might social workers in community-based organizations respond to these?

- Discuss an example from your practice where you could work with community-led approaches.

- Why are action and reflection important in change processes?

References

Cabaj, M. and Weaver, L. (2016) *Collective Impact 3.0: An Evolving Framework for Community Change*. Waterloo, ON: Tamarack Institute.

Canavan, J. (2008) 'Resilience: Cautiously welcoming a contested concept.' *Child Care in Practice 14*, 1, 1–7.

Department of Internal Affairs (2017) *Community-Led Development Programme*. Wellington, New Zealand: DIA.

Dominelli, L. (1998) 'Anti-oppressive Practice in Context.' In R. Adams, L. Dominelli and M. Payne (eds) *Social Work: Themes, Issues and Critical Debates*. Basingstoke: Macmillan.

Ferguson, I. and Lavalette, M. (2006) 'Globalization and global justice: Towards a social work of resistance.' *International Social Work 49*, 3, 309–318.

Finn, J.L. and Jacobson, M. (2003) 'Just practice: Steps toward a new social work paradigm.' *Journal of Social Work Education 39*, 1, 57–78.

Gray, M., Coates, J. and Yellow Bird, M. (eds) (2008) *Indigenous Social Work Around the World: Towards Culturally Relevant Education and Practice*. Aldershot: Ashgate Publishing.

International Federation of Social Workers (2014) *Global Definition of Social Work*. Accessed on 04/09/2018 at www.ifsw.org/what-is-social-work/global-definition-of-social-work.

Irizarry, C., Marlowe, J.M., Hallahan, L. and Bull, M. (2016) 'Restoring connections: Social workers' practice wisdom towards achieving social justice.' *British Journal of Social Work 46*, 7, 1855–1871.

Mafile'o, T, and Vakalahi, H.F.O. (2017) 'Indigenous social work across borders: Expanding social work in the South Pacific.' *International Social Work* (Online first, 1–16). doi:10.1177/0020872816641750.

McKenzie-Mohr, S. and Lafrance, M.N. (2017) 'Narrative resistance in social work research and practice: Counter-storying in the pursuit of social justice.' *Qualitative Social Work: Research and Practice 16*, 2, 189–205.

Mezirow, J. (2003) 'Transformative learning as discourse.' *Journal of Transformative Education 14*, 1, 58–63.

Morley, M., Macfarlane, S. and Ablett, P. (2014) *Engaging with Social Work: A Critical Introduction*. Port Melbourne: Cambridge University Press.

Munford, R. and Sanders, J. (2011) 'Embracing the diversity of practice: Indigenous knowledge and mainstream social work practice.' *Journal of Social Work Practice 25*, 1, 63–77.

Munford, R. and Sanders, J. (2013) 'Assessment of Families.' In M.J. Holosko, C.N. Dulmus and K.M. Sowers (eds) *Social Work Practice with Individuals and Families: Evidence-Informed Assessments and Interventions*. Hoboken, NJ: Wiley.

Munford, R., Sanders, J. and Maden, B. (2012) 'Building Strengths in Families and Communities.' In J. Duncan and S. Te One (eds) *Comparative Early Childhood Education Services: International Perspectives*. New York, NY: Palgrave Macmillan.

Munford, R. and Walsh-Tapiata, W. (2005) 'Community Development: Principles into Practice.' In M. Nash, R. Munford and K. O'Donoghue (eds) *Social Work Theories in Action*. London: Jessica Kingsley Publishers.

Nelson, D., Price, E. and Zubrzycki, J. (2017) 'Critical social work with unaccompanied asylum-seeking young people: Restoring hope, agency and meaning for the client and worker.' *International Social Work 60*, 3, 601–613.

Pallotta-Chiarolli, M. and Pease, B. (2014) 'Recognition, Resistance and Reconstruction: An Introduction to Subjectivities and Social Justice.' In M. Pallotta-Chiarolli and B. Pease (eds) *The Politics of Recognition and Social Justice: Transforming Subjectivities and New Forms of Resistance*. London: Routledge.

Pease, P., Goldingay, S., Hosken, N. and Nipperess, S. (eds) (2016) *Doing Critical Social Work: Transformative Practices for Social Justice*. Sydney: Allen and Unwin.

Porter, L., Martin, K. and Anda, R. (2016) *Self-Healing Communities: A Transformational Process Model for Improving Intergenerational Health*. Princeton, NJ: Robert Wood Johnson Foundation.

Ruwhiu, L. (2009) 'Indigenous Issues in Aotearoa New Zealand.' In M. Connolly and L. Harms (eds) *Social Work: Contexts and Practice*. Melbourne: Oxford University Press.

VanderPlaat, M. (2016) 'Activating the sociological imagination to explore the boundaries of resilience research and practice.' *School Psychology International 37*, 2, 189–203.

Weiss, E.L. and Schott, E.M.P. (2016) 'Introduction.' In E.M.P. Schott and E.L. Weiss (eds) *Transformative Social Work Practice*. Thousand Oaks, CA: Sage.

Wenger, E. (1998) *Communities of Practice: Learning, Meaning, and Identity*. Cambridge: Cambridge University Press.

Westley, F., Zimmerman, B. and Patton, M.Q. (2006) *Getting to Maybe: How the World is Changed*. Toronto, ON: Random House.

Witkin, S.L. (2014) 'Change and deeper change: Transforming social work education.' *Journal of Social Work Education 50*, 4, 587–598.

Chapter 8

Green Social Work in Urban Spaces: Greening Urban Cityscapes through Green Social Work Practices

LENA DOMINELLI

Introduction

Green social work perspectives are useful in critiquing measures that exploit land and resources with little regard for the health and wellbeing of people, other living things and planet earth. Such exploitation is particularly marked in cities. Cities are becoming concreted over in the interests of maximizing land use, thereby stressing people and the physical ecosystem. Urban developers pressurize the physical environment by squeezing more and more people into small spaces, producing higher and higher apartment blocks and undermining the wellbeing of people, and plants and animals that formerly roamed over green fields before they became concreted land in a *hyper-urbanized* landscape (Dominelli 2012). The fire in Grenfell Tower in London in the summer of 2017 provides a horrific example of how profit maximization costs lives as well as emitting toxic substances into the atmosphere and local environment when combustible cladding burns. How much did this one fire add to greenhouse gas emissions (GHG) and other toxic substances emitted into the air and surrounding soil? These costs must be ascertained as they impact on the environment alongside the suffering and grief caused to people whose lives have been devastated.

This chapter considers the changing face of cities from a green social work perspective that subjects urban initiatives to critical scrutiny via a strengths-based approach that focuses on the health and wellbeing of people, other living things and planet earth. Green social workers have sought to green the city by critiquing measures that exploit land and resources with little regard for the long-term sustainability of people, other living things and the physical environment. This includes the promotion of holistic co-produced projects to green the environment, address social problems created by urban living and develop community gardens by redesigning car parks and rooftops to create food for local communities and transform practice in greener directions.

I reflect on examples of green social work practice where people have developed community gardens within cityscapes ranging from derelict building sites to allotments, transforming public perceptions of the urban environment. Other transformations have included the provision of: grassy green recreational spaces with trees and plants for enjoyment during leisure time; vegetable gardens that reduce food insecurity by supplying locally grown fresh fruit and vegetables; wildlife reservations that help safeguard biodiversity; restored degraded soils utilizing composting schemes; and multicultural neighbourhood activities to bring diverse people together and promote social cohesion. I also touch on other measures that cover built infrastructures and garbage collection. Greening cities can contribute to reductions in GHGs by challenging the unhealthy aspects of the urban jungle; promoting greening activities within it; enhancing resilience among community members and reducing the spread of bleak concrete landscapes. Greening cities can also be promoted as a therapeutic activity.

The world population is projected to rise up to about 12 billion by 2030 and this will create pressure on communities to release agricultural land for building purposes, and to raise the number of people housed per hectare of land. Skyscrapers stretching to higher and higher levels are deemed an acceptable solution to the dilemma of producing more houses per unit of land (Busch and Huang 2015). Those supporting this approach argue that high-density high-rise housing conserves land resources and is more efficient in delivering public utilities to the greatest number easily and cheaply. This is leading to more densely populated cities across the world, and I have termed this development *hyper-urbanization* (Dominelli 2012), a trend that I consider detrimental to people's wellbeing as well as that of the planet. The *small is beautiful movement* (Schumpeter 1973) stands as a counter to growing hyper-urbanization, even though population trends now reveal that in 2015 the majority of the world's inhabitants became urban dwellers.

In country after country, the expansion of cities as rural migration towards them grows has led to the growth of more slums as the built infrastructures of cities, especially with regards to housing, sanitation, utilities and jobs, prove inadequate in meeting demand. The United Nations (UN) has estimated slums to have grown to 860 million in 2010–2012 (Marx, Stoker and Suri 2013). The largest internal migratory movement from rural to urban areas occurs in the People's Republic of China, with millions of people leaving the countryside for cities. However, sub-Saharan Africa has more slum dwellers as a ratio of the population. From a green social work perspective, slum-dwelling constitutes a violation of people's human rights to shelter and poses questions for policy makers to assist in providing well-built housing and infrastructures for populations migrating to cities, or, alternatively, and preferred, is that rural areas are sensitively developed to provide sustainable, well-paid jobs within a green environmental framework. Green social workers can argue for such transformational shifts in policy directions.

Urbanizing the planet

As city after city is becoming concreted over, people are beginning to question the prioritization of higher and higher apartment blocks and loss of green fields for use by people, plants and animals. However, this strand of thinking ignores the possibility that small cities, self-sufficient in many activities and functions, would avoid the worst excesses of urbanization, including the centralization of services, and the concentration of cultural activities and employment opportunities in cities. These developments have various costs associated with them, including the long hours people spend commuting into work with the attendant traffic jams, pollution and extra energy costs.

Various green and sustainable initiatives seek to counteract such trends. Small, imaginative local community initiatives have formed green urban spaces (Campbell 1996). These have involved green social workers in devising renewable alternatives to fossil fuels, planting trees, plants and vegetables, conserving spots for wildlife, converting concreted spaces at ground and roof levels into green spaces for growing food for human consumption and encouraging the creation of wildflower gardens for birds, bees and insects. Community gardens have provided one vehicle for achieving these aims. These physical spaces have also been turned into therapeutic domains for rehabilitating human beings stressed by urban living, and rejected the planners' injunctions that turn green spaces into grey concrete and glass edifices.

Organizing the use of space and resources to meet people's needs forms an anthropomorphic view of the world and has given rise to the contemporary historical period humanity currently inhabits, known as the Anthropocene. This approach has involved people in making trade-offs between their demands for resources and the skills utilized to turn them into marketable goods. Social relations in contemporary societies are organized into a globalized capitalist system known as neoliberalism with an ideology that entitles men (primarily) to exploit natural resources to meet human needs as part of modernity. This accords priority to maximizing profit margins by using the speediest and cheapest means to extract nature's bounty and turn it into commodities or goods and services for sale. Modernity itself, sold as the *age of reason*, was underpinned by the belief that technological innovations would propel humanity forward and that planning and technologies could solve all human problems, including those caused by over-population and the super-exploitation of natural resources.

The earth is urbanizing rapidly, with the UN asserting that by 2015 over half (55%) of the planet's population lived in cities. Moreover, these consumed 80 percent of the world's energy and released most of the GHGs. Urbanized settlements will house 70 percent of the world's population by 2050. The Dutch group Arcadis has indirectly exposed the undesirability of urbanization. Its rankings of the world's most liveable cities use criteria that highlight factors that impact directly on people: the planet and profit. According to Arcadis, the four most liveable cities are in Europe – Frankfurt, London, Copenhagen and Amsterdam. The four least liveable cities include the world's two most populous nations – Mumbai (India), Wuhan (China), New Delhi (India) – and Nairobi (the worst city), which is on the African continent. These pessimistic figures do not augur well for the health of either people or the planet if urbanization is to proceed at its current hectic pace, especially in fast-growing and rapidly industrializing areas of the world like Asia and sub-Saharan Africa.

An optimistic approach to urban living is heralded in the *Vertical City*,[1] which argues that individuals living high in the sky can reduce their requirements for utilities infrastructures, including energy, water and sanitation, through individual initiatives such as using local, renewable energy sources, conserving water, reducing waste and eating locally produced food. These activities can be promoted in smaller cities, with less cost to the environment because energy is not consumed to take utilities from ground level to sky level. Besides costing more to build, what do these buildings add to GHG emissions? This question must be answered.

Within the framework of modernity, the problem of urbanization is deemed one that planners can solve, and a variety of movements

---

1   www.verticalcity.org.

have sought to find sustainable solutions to the problems produced by urbanization. Key notions include the concept of liveable space through environmentally friendly neighbourhoods such as the Garden City, the Neighbourhood Unit, Modernism, Neo-traditionalism, and Eco-urbanism (Sharifi 2016). For example, Ebenezer Howard, who established the Garden City idea amid the slums of Victorian London, was inspired by the notion of creating healthy, liveable and sustainable communities based on neighbourhoods. His concerns are similar to today's. However, current populations will have to address past failures to produce sustainable cities; for example, solving major problems created by climate change is a major global issue.

Sustainability is crucial to green, living cities. Alas, there is no agreed definition of its meaning among scholars. Yet, the belief in intergenerational equity and the integration of social, political, cultural, economic, organizational and environmental considerations are deemed inherent to the concepts about the city mentioned above (Brundtland 1986; Wheeler 2004; Dominelli 2012; Sharifi and Murayama 2014). Soil degradation in some decayed cityscapes also requires remediation. Interdisciplinary work on the subject has involved physical and social scientists addressing soil health, especially in brownfield sites. Moreover, soil scientists are beginning to develop links with social workers and their engagement with local communities is emerging. One such project involves Karen Johnson, at Durham University. She has led a project, ROBUST (regeneration of brownfield land using sustainable technologies), which has been able to restore carbon and other minerals in degraded soils. Such soil regeneration can also contribute to healthier lives for people by creating more solid ground on which to build infrastructures and grow crops.

Social work endeavours in greening urban spaces

Social workers have been involved in green or environmental initiatives since the inception of the profession. For example, Jane Addams organised waste recycling schemes through Hull House in Chicago's poverty-stricken slums. During the 1990s, the works of Besthorn (2012), Rogge (2000) and Ungar (2002) critiqued the way in which *the person in the environment* had concentrated largely on socio-economic, political and cultural systems to the detriment of the physical environment. Crucially, their work identified issues that had been neglected for some time. However, they failed to embed their critique in neoliberal capitalism's voracious appetite for people, energy and other physical and material substances to fuel its development and technological innovations. Additionally, they ignored the unequal power relations within which social and human development occurs. Green social workers seek to address both issues (Dominelli 2012).

Dominelli (2012, p.25) defines green social work as a 'holistic approach to social development' that takes account of the needs of people, the earth's flora, fauna and physical environment, the socio-economic and political systems within which social development occurs, and the power relations that exist between and among people, and between people, other living things and the earth as a holistic ecosystem. Moreover, green social workers examine the contexts that produce both natural and (hu)man-made disasters, and argue for the co-production of solutions to the problems raised by outdated modes of social development rooted in neoliberalism. They encourage locality-based egalitarian partnerships and interdisciplinarity wherein the physical and social sciences, arts and humanities holding scientific knowledge engage in dialogical exchanges with local/community and indigenous knowledges. This approach has redefined the *duty to care* from one that focuses only on people to one that encompasses all living things, the interdependencies between them and the physical environment (Dominelli 2012). If humanity cares for planet earth, it will care for humanity, and thus reinforce the mutuality of existence and not the dualism favoured by modernity.

Additionally, green social workers support the realization of environmental justice. Dominelli (2012) defines environmental justice as the right to live in a sustainable, healthy environment that enables all peoples to use the earth's resources to meet current needs without jeopardizing future generations' use of these, and while caring for the planet and all it contains. Therefore, environmental justice includes the duty to care *for* and care *about* others (and oneself) alongside caring for planet earth. Green social workers endorse environmental justice as a holistic and global responsibility embedded within social justice because it affirms interdependencies between peoples and their physical, social, political, economic and cultural environments as part of one whole, interconnected ecosystem.

The remit of green social work has no arbitrary limits. Its scope and scale are defined by those working on specific activities. Many green social work projects to date have focused on small neighbourhood-based communities. Spatial considerations linked to geographic communities, for example neighbourhoods, are associated with those expressed by other identity and interest communities located within the same geographical space. The size of a community in the 21st century can be enlarged significantly through the internet, which has created virtual communities that exist beyond traditional ideas of time and space. Such communities take rapidity of travel and communication for granted. These developments are positive in several respects, including that of bringing the world closer together. There are significant energy costs involved in maintaining the servers and computers utilized in making these possible and this can add environmental stresses that can contribute considerably to climate change. Nonetheless, holistic, transdisciplinary approaches to community development can produce transformative change, although much of this has occurred in rural areas, for example in Misa Rumi in Argentina where solar-powered stoves used for cooking and heating reduced carbon emissions by 80,000 tons, safeguarded the nearly extinct Yareta tree by eliminating the need for firewood, and allowed women to stop collecting firewood (Stott 2009). The island of Eigg in Scotland produces 90 percent of its energy from renewable wind, solar and hydro sources. It won the Gold Ashden Award for improving its energy efficiency (Chmiell and Battacharyya 2015).

Fortunately, community workers actively promote solar-powered electricity for both heating and cooking in diverse cities globally. For example, 20 American cities that represent about 0.1 percent of the USA's land area have 6.5 percent of that country's solar photovoltaic (PV) capacity (Pentland 2015). Moreover, a number of university-based social work students have initiated projects to green the land in urban communities and contribute to reducing food insecurity among marginalized communities. For example, a community garden at Monmouth University produced fresh fruit and vegetables to feed homeless people (Mama 2018). In other instances, practitioners, social work students and service users have greened specific buildings, including their own workplaces. For example, the Burnside Gorge Community Centre in Victoria, Canada, built a rooftop garden. This centre assists children and families experiencing child protection issues in turning their lives around. The building itself is green in that it meets the Leadership in Energy and Environmental Design (LEED) certification to platinum standard.

In other locations like Vancouver, Canada, community workers have promoted community initiatives that include replacing car parks with allotments for growing vegetables, and creating rooftop gardens. The construction of green high-rise buildings has been encouraged in countries as politically different as China, Singapore, and Qatar. Tower 101 in Taipei, Taiwan, illustrates a high-rise edifice that has acquired green credentials.

Having green rooftops makes an important contribution to greening the urban environment. However, it may be necessary to involve engineers in their creation if these are to be constructed properly and avoid roof collapses. This occurred in 2013 in Hong Kong's City University, Kowloon Tong campus and injured three people. Other issues that need to be addressed include the prevention of damp spots appearing in ceilings below the rooftop garden and roots penetrating the membranes that are designed to curtail their growth. Typically, a rooftop garden requires between six and nine layers of membranes to work effectively.

Green social work is transdisciplinary, which means that green social workers have to work with various people from other disciplines, including architects, engineers, chemists and biologists.

Despite successful cases, the issue of greenness and its relevance and implementation in cities remains problematic. Residents often complain about the lack of green urban environmental spaces where everyone can enjoy leisure and recreational activities, children can play and older people can exercise, sit and chat. These provisions are often bounded by existing cultural traditions and unequal social relations that impinge on the enjoyment of such initiatives and can often privilege men (Button 2017). Taking cultural and other local factors into account by working with local people and organizations provides the rationale behind green social work's commitment to locality-specific and culturally relevant approaches to greening the environment.

Regardless of land scarcity, most stakeholders agree that green spaces in cities contribute to human physical and mental wellbeing, provide urban havens for wildlife, add to the attractiveness of the cityscape and contribute to GHG reductions. Green social workers in urban areas deal with a range of issues other than greening rooftops. These are many and varied, but they cannot all be covered in one chapter, so key issues are highlighted here by focusing on the blurring of urban–rural boundaries, garbage reduction and recycling, and water harvesting and sanitation.

Urban issues requiring green solutions
Rurbanization: blurring the urban–rural boundaries
High-density urban environments have a range of problems to resolve that often rely on exploiting rural environments, often against the wishes of rural residents. The ensuing tensions exacerbate the urban–rural divide, instead of ensuring that the relationship between them is one of mutuality. Such developments can be captured by calling them *rurbanization* – the urbanization of rural areas. This carries with it associated air, soil and water pollution and higher GHG emissions, and encourages long commutes that clog up rural roads, thus adding to a country's carbon footprint and destroying the rural ambience of the areas concerned (Dominelli 2009).

Globally, the need for urban housing has meant that farmlands near cities have been sold to developers, often at inflated prices, but also against the wishes of the local rural populace. For example, land required to build road networks, including motorways such as the M40 out of London, comes at the expense of farmland. Equally pressing is the issue of land claims for the construction of high-density housing estates on the outskirts of villages, which usually have inadequate built infrastructures including schools, medical facilities, water, sanitation, power, communications and roads. Providing these facilities also gobbles up rural farmlands, taking them out of agricultural production forever. These developments also change the nature of existing villages. Garner (2017) describes the blurring of such boundaries in the USA.

Green social workers have been involved in mobilizing villagers against such developments, often working within existing local organizations, volunteering to undertake a range of tasks, including calling meetings, speaking at them, and assisting residents in completing forms to protest against these developments. Social workers have also been involved in supporting local residents in demanding community-based facilities, including minibuses, play areas and other amenities for local children. Such initiatives have been crucial in developing rural housing estates that cities have used to *dump* troubled families in; areas that lacked the resources that such families require.

Friends of Rural and Sustainable Environment (FORSE),[2] for example, has been conducting a lengthy battle against the construction of 4000 houses in rural south Warwickshire, England, where the nearby three villages have around 200 houses each and there are no social amenities, apart from a pub in two of the three villages. Poor existing infrastructures would be unable to deal with the additional demands associated with the predicted huge rise in population and providing them would require even more farmland, which initially had been designated as green-belt land, that is, land that is not to be used for development purposes. This development, would, as Garner (2017) demonstrated in her study, destroy the rural nature of that countryside for the existing villages by creating a small town of about 12,000 residents, but without the required amenities.

According to FORSE, local residents are aggrieved by this development because they have already had to accept the motorway, a landfill site in the area that receives waste from nearby towns and cities including Birmingham, and, more recently, a dual carriageway. This dual carriageway has been built to move vehicles taking workers to the Jaguar Land Rover

---

2   https://en-gb.facebook.com/FORSEgroup.

Centre near Lighthorne Heath off the motorway during peak hours and has also consumed farmland for road users. Now the firm is threatening to relocate elsewhere. The street lights along the length of the carriageway add to light pollution in a once rural area, known for its beautiful starlit skies. Moreover, changing industrialized farming practices in the area have undermined the network of underwater springs that previously nurtured the wet habitats of endangered species such as water voles and the great-crested newts.

Opposition to such developments has been overridden by local city or town planners and slightly modified versions are going ahead. Such encroachments on green-belt lands – lands which were theoretically set aside and protected from such development – augur ill for the remaining countryside in the UK. Rurbanization cushions developers' profits because it is cheaper for their developments to occur in greenfield sites rather than brownfield ones, which might involve de-contamination of derelict land.

Garbage reduction and recycling

Getting rid of waste produced by city dwellers is another urban issue that has implications for rural and other peripheral areas as the providers of land sites for disposing of the rubbish. A crucial problem in urban waste is plastic – bags and other forms of polythene packaging. Not only does their production use scarce fossil fuels – petroleum which could be usefully diverted to other purposes like making medicines – but plastic degrades slowly and causes danger to birds, fish and other marine life, and pollutes beaches and coastlines. Reducing consumption, separating the rubbish at source and recycling materials are some of the actions that green social workers have supported in countries including Sri Lanka and India.

The collapse of gigantic waste dumps in Colombo in Sri Lanka and Addis Ababa in Ethiopia in 2017, and Guatemala City in 2016, and landslides caused by dumps containing debris from large-scale construction sites in Shenzhen, China, in 2015, among other similar occurrences have led to the deaths of hundreds of people and the destruction of numerous dwellings located nearby. This is in addition to the nuisances of insects such as flies and mosquitoes, and vermin like mice and rats that normally accompany garbage-based sites.

The burial of debris from earthquakes and other natural disasters also presents huge problems of disposal that have no easy solutions. Moreover, the rubble arising from earthquakes and other natural disasters contains a mixture of substances, some of which are toxic and should be separated out, but this rarely occurs. Involving local people in the decisions made about such concerns and in recycling materials is essential. These also constitute tasks that can be facilitated by green social workers who encompass caring for people and the planet in their deliberations.

Some people earn their livelihoods by collecting, separating and recycling garbage. Whether such work should be encouraged is strongly contested, but this solution is not sufficient on its own. Waste reduction requires wider responses, including the ending of built-in obsolescence of household goods such as kettles, fridges, televisions and mobile phones, and the one-time use of plastic dishes, glasses, knives, forks, spoons and glass bottles, for a start. Repairing electrical goods rather than replacing them with the latest model of any gadget is a more earth-friendly approach to contemporary consumption patterns. However, achieving this aim impacts on profit margins, and unaccountable multinational corporations have little interest in following this course of action.

Green social workers can initiate discussions between the communities where such waste ends up and the companies that have their headquarters overseas. Holding companies accountable for the decisions company directors and investors make falls within the remit of green social work and could be a useful mobilization point for communities seeking sustainable development.

Water and sanitation

Supplying cities with clean drinking water and disposing of effluent are crucial issues for city planners and policy makers to address in order to avoid unequal access to water and sanitation infrastructures which impact most badly on poor people. The World Health Organization (WHO) calculated that 2.4 billion people had no or poor sanitation facilities at their disposal, and 940 million practised open defecation in 2015. This appalling statistic exists despite provision for their rectification being included in the Millennium Development Goals (MDGs), which ran from 2000 to 2015. Kulkarni, O'Reilly and Bhat (2017) describe the importance of access to such facilities for poor urban women in India. They highlight the importance of unequal power relations that are mediated by class, caste, economic status and various cultural traditions. Many poor women are assaulted when using public latrines in everyday life, and in refugee camps. Moreover, communities are unlikely to blame their own social relationships, but often assert that it is men from outside their own group that are responsible for these attacks. While stranger assault is especially relevant in war situations where attacking women's bodies is used as an instrument of war, stranger danger is not the only source of sexual and physical forms of violence against women. Green social workers engaging women in such settings can help them understand better the power dynamics behind such attacks and develop locality-specific and culturally relevant forms of self-defence.

Additionally, in Mumbai, a city inhabited mainly by marginalized groups, the local government has advised people to harvest their own water – usually rainwater – to deal with water scarcity. Doing this costs money, and so the middle classes are better able to take advantage of privatized solutions to a social problem. Nonetheless, globally, many children have benefited from the improved access to water and sanitation, leading to a drop in the number of children dying from diarrhoea from 2000 to 1000 per day between 2005 and 2015 (WHO 2015). These numbers must be reduced to zero. To achieve this goal in communities lacking these resources, green social workers can initiate activities built around the Sustainable Development Goals (SDGs), which replaced the MDGs and last from 2015 to 2030.

Water is a necessity of life. Without it, people would not be able to live. Women and children are the ones who spend excessive amounts of time fetching water for the household, and this consumes time and energy that could be put to other uses, including paid employment for women, and schooling for the children. These two groups also become responsible for disposing of the family's garbage and sewage waste. This, like procuring water, is another activity that is poorly valued, although it consumes a lot of time and burdens most women and children in society who are least empowered. Thus, class, gender and age are important factors deeply embedded in the social fabric that constrain access to publicly funded water and sanitation provisions. Green social workers ought to engage with the gendered dimensions of these issues and assist women in meeting community needs without further exploitation. *Doing no harm* is a critical ethical principle in green perspectives involving people and the environment (Dominelli 2012).

Carter, Dietrich and Minor (2017) make similar points about the importance of water, sanitation and hygiene in preventing the spread of diseases, including those likely to initiate global pandemics, including Ebola. This concern is also relevant in humanitarian aid situations. For example, poor hygiene meant that Haitians who had survived the earthquake disaster succumbed to the cholera epidemic when this disease was introduced by Nepalese troops who came to the country's assistance under the auspices of the UN. Haiti had not had a cholera outbreak for over 100 years and its occurrence in 2010, at a point in time when all the built infrastructures including governance structures and health facilities had collapsed, meant that it spread before the source of the outbreak – leaking sewage pipes at a UN base – could be acknowledged and repaired

(BBC News 2016). This event also identified the importance of ensuring that aid workers, whatever their source, are healthy and suggests that they should undergo health checks before they are admitted into already vulnerable populations and locations. Realizing this goal requires coordination and labour power, something that green social workers can provide.

Lessons acquired elsewhere, including the West, may be applicable if culturally adapted to such situations. The lack of either private provisions or public facilities and built infrastructures that covered the entire population in this regard was a lesson learned in Victorian Britain where the provision of running water and sanitation infrastructures to all homes through public health initiatives reduced illnesses and diseases spread by their absence, especially in poor urban homes. Collective action that transcended local class and other social divisions made a huge difference to public and individual health and wellbeing. These lessons provided by historical examples can also be made available to policy makers who insist on reinventing the wheel at the expense of poor people and the environment. Green social workers can facilitate this learning both within communities and outside them.

The therapeutic power of the environment and future challenges

Social workers have appreciated the therapeutic value of the environment for some time. However, many of these initiatives have been used primarily for young people, especially those living in urban areas who were in trouble with law enforcement agencies. Rehabilitation usually takes the form of building up young people's characters by taking troubled youths into the great outdoors and the wilderness. For example, Outward Bound courses to *build character* provide them with opportunities they would not otherwise have to improve self-confidence and develop further their social skills in relating to other people. Outward Bound is a UK charity that has existed since 1941.

The therapeutic value of such approaches, especially those labelled *intermediate treatment*, in the UK is well established, even though they do not work well for all young people. Such programmes aim to build young people's self-esteem, resilience, capacity to get along with others and to make decisions in a mature manner. For many, such activities turn their lives around.

Intermediate treatment lost favour in statutory social work in the UK in the 1990s, when a number of stories including that of 'Safari

Boy' highlighted how those who had had thousands of pounds spent on rehabilitating them through expensive character-building trips abroad (for example, on safari in Africa for this particular case) continued with their criminal careers soon afterwards (Gladdis 2012). The media's hysterical responses unfortunately did not address the issue that having spent time on an intermediate treatment, young people were returned to the inadequate environments that had proved unable to nurture them in the first place.

Such instances highlight the importance of holistic responses to troubled young people as advocated by green social workers who would seek to integrate them into other more sustaining communities and social relationships. This could involve engaging them in training, realizing employment opportunities and being rehoused. But this work requires resources in education, housing and employment that cater specifically for their needs. Sadly, this was not an option favoured by British policy makers then or now. They prefer deficit models of intervention that blame young people for their plight.

Urban gardens have also been used as therapeutic tools. For example, in war-torn Britain of the 1940s, urban allotments were popularized to provide locally grown food, but also spaces where people could meet to chat, have a laugh together and exchange ideas on how best to cook the foods they grew. Similar ideas are being endorsed by the United Nations' Food and Agriculture Organization (FAO). Rusciano, Civero and Scarpato (2017) describe one such example in Naples, Italy, where unemployed people and poor people are using FAO's ideas to grow food which will save them money in cash-strapped homes and enable them to engage in healthy activities during the day.

Ku and Dominelli (2017) describe how organic gardening can bridge the rural–urban divide and involve an entire community in organic farming, social enterprises and buildings that bring people together to reduce the *left-behind* migrant nexus in China. Such transdisciplinary initiatives enable communities to build intergenerational solidarity and revive earthquake-stricken settings by promoting traditional crafts, skills and knowledge still held by older people who remain in the countryside when working adults migrate to the cities. This particular project near Ya'an City also encouraged some of the migrant workers back into the rural community.

Conclusion: ways forward for green social work in urban spaces

Urban spaces do not have to be grey, concrete deserts that are soulless and destructive of human aesthetic capacity and appreciation. Green social workers should challenge the view that small, box-like apartments that cost the earth are appropriate habitats for poor, marginalized people while wealthy individuals appropriate the best, greenest and healthiest landscapes for their personal use. The way forward is to work in partnership with local communities to protect human beings, the earth's flora and fauna and physical ecosystem from the predations of a capitalist system interested only in the bottom line – more and more profits from less and less monetary investment. Growing plants together and celebrating this by sharing the consumption of home-grown foods can also facilitate multicultural activities and fusion cuisine.

Green social work has captured the imagination of many social workers across the world and offers models that can be examined and considered for their transferable skills to diverse settings, but especially those in which urban cityscapes cater for the needs of the wealthy few, not the many.[3]

Reflection questions

- How might you become involved in greening your neighbourhood?
- How would you put together an interdisciplinary team to turn a derelict building site into recreational space?
- What processes would you use to co-produce a response to a motorway that will divide a small village in two and lacks easy access for pedestrians to cross it?
- How would you encourage a poor neighbourhood to recycle materials and eliminate fly-tipping?
- How would you mobilize a community to preserve water during drought conditions?

References

BBC News (2016) 'UN admits role in Haiti's deadly cholera outbreak.' 19 August. Accessed on 20/12/2016 at www.bbc.co.uk/news/world-latin-america-37126747.

---

3   *The Routledge Handbook of Green Social Work* (Dominelli 2018) contains examples of green approaches to social work from across the world, and provides an invaluable resource for those who wish to develop their understanding of this area of practice.

Besthorn, F. (2012) 'Deep ecology's contributions to social work: A ten year retrospective.' *International Journal of Social Welfare 21*, 3, 248–259.

Brundtland, G. (1986) *The World Commission on the Environment and Development*. New York, NY: United Nations.

Busch, C. and Huang, C.C. (2015) *Cities for People: Insights into the Data*. Accessed on 12/05/2016 http://energyinnovation.org/wp-content/uploads/2015/05/C4P-Insights-from-the-Data.pdf

Button, C. (2017) 'Domesticating water supplies through rainwater harvesting in Mumbai.' *Gender and Development 25*, 2, 269–282.

Campbell, S. (1996) 'Green cities, growing cities, just cities?' *Journal of the American Planning Association* Summer, 1–30.

Carter, S., Dietrich, L. and Minor, O. (2017) 'Mainstreaming gender in WASH: Lessons learned from Oxfam's experience of Ebola.' *Gender and Development 25*, 2, 205–220.

Chmiell, Z. and Battacharyya, S. (2015) 'Analysis of off-grid electricity system at Isle of Eigg (Scotland): Lessons for developing countries.' *Renewable Energy 81*, 578–588.

Dominelli, L. (2009) *Social Work in a Globalising World*. Cambridge: Polity Press.

Dominelli, L. (2012) *Green Social Work*. Cambridge: Polity Press.

Dominelli, L. (ed.) with Nikku, B. and Ku, H.K. (2018) *The Routledge Handbook of Green Social Work*. London: Routledge.

Garner, B. (2017) '"Perfectly positioned": The blurring of urban, suburban and rural boundaries in a southern community.' *The Annals of the American Academy 672*, 3, 46–63.

Gladdis, K. (2012) 'Safari Boy shambles.' *Mail Online*. Accessed on 12/5/2016 at www.dailymail.co.uk/news/article-2172454/Safari-Boy-Mark-Hook-sent-month-holiday-steer-away-crime-clocks-113th-offence.html.

Ku, H.B. and Dominelli, L. (2017) 'Not just eating together': Space and green social work intervention in hazard affected area in Ya'an, Sichuan, China.' *British Journal of Social Work* (online early access). https://doi-org.ezproxy.massey.ac.nz/10.1093/bjsw/bcx071.

Kulkarni, S., O'Reilly, K. and Bhat, S. (2017) 'No relief: Lived experiences of inadequate sanitation access of poor urban women in India.' *Gender and Development 25*, 2, 167–183.

Mama, R. (2018) 'Community Gardening.' In L. Dominelli (ed.) *The Routledge Handbook of Green Social Work*. London: Routledge.

Marx, B., Stoker, T. and Suri, T. (2013) 'The economics of slums in the developing world.' *The Journal of Economic Perspectives 27*, 4, 187–210.

Pentland, W. (2015) 'Top 16 U.S. cities for solar power.' *Forbes* 22 May, 1–12.

Rogge, M. (2000) 'Social development and the ecological tradition.' *Social Development Issues 22*, 1, 32–41.

Rusciano, V., Civero, G. and Scarpato, D. (2017) 'Urban gardening as a new frontier of wellness: Case studies from the city of Naples.' *The International Journal of Sustainability in Economic, Social, and Cultural Context 13*, 2, 39–49.

Schumpeter, E.F. (1973) *Small is Beautiful: Economics as if People Mattered*. London: Blond and Briggs.

Sharifi, A. (2016) 'From garden city to eco-urbanism: The quest for sustainable neighbourhood development.' *Sustainable Cities and Societies 20*, 1–16.

Sharifi, A. and Murayama, A. (2014) 'Neighbourhood sustainability assessment in action.' *Building and Environment 72*, 243–258.

Stott, K. (2009) 'Remote village turns to the sun for power.' *Vancouver Sun* 26 October, p.B4.

Ungar, M. (2002) 'A deeper more social ecological social work practice.' *Social Services Review 76*, 3, 480–497.

Wheeler, S. (2004) *Planning for Sustainability: Creating Liveable, Equitable, and Ecological Communities*. London: Routledge.

WHO (World Health Organization) (2015) *Progress on Sanitation and Drinking Water: 2015 Update and MDG Assessment*. Paris: WHO and UNICEF.

Chapter 9

Social Work and Disasters

KATHRYN HAY

Introduction

Disasters have been a feature of the lives of individuals and communities since time immemorial and effects may be felt locally, nationally and globally. Multiple actors across government, non-government and private sectors intersect with the different phases of disaster management, and social workers internationally have an established history in delivering aid and support following disasters (Dominelli 2014; Pelling 2003).

It is perhaps unsurprising that social workers can be effectively involved in disaster work, given their daily engagement with individuals, groups and communities – often the most vulnerable members of society (Mapp 2008; Whitmore and Wilson 2005). At an international level, the global agenda for social work signals that the social work profession recognizes the inequalities and unsustainable environments that affect people's wellbeing due to disasters (International Association of Schools of Social Work and International Federation of Social Workers 2014). Given that disaster management has a similar goal to social work in that its focus is on promoting the development of safer, less vulnerable communities, it can be assumed that social workers should be significant actors in this field. A shift in the disaster literature from a traditional focus on hazards to vulnerability and resilience, key foci for social workers, consolidates the importance of social work within this domain (Gillespie and Danso 2010). Despite this, the literature about social work practice, relevant theoretical constructs and, importantly, the visibility of the social work profession in the disaster field, remains limited (Dominelli 2014; Gillespie and Danso 2010).

This chapter provides a discussion on social work and disasters. Contemporary theoretical frameworks are explored and an argument is presented for the involvement of social work in each stage of the disaster cycle. Two case studies are presented prior to an exploration of several challenges and opportunities associated with greater inclusion of social work practice in disaster management. The chapter concludes with questions to stimulate ongoing reflection.

Understanding the landscape
Hazards, disasters and disaster management

Some brief definitions are necessary. In the disaster literature, a distinction is commonly drawn between a hazard and a disaster. A hazard is generally regarded as a threat or possibility of an extreme event, rather than the event itself. Hazards are therefore potential or existing conditions that may cause harm to people, their property or the social, cultural, natural and economic environments (Ministry of Health 2016). A hazard only becomes a disaster (whether natural or human-made) in response to the capacity of individuals or the community to manage any impacts (Paul 2011). As Pelling (2003, p.4) asserts, 'translation into risk and potential for disaster is contingent upon human exposure and a lack of capacity to cope with the negative impacts that exposure might bring to individuals or human systems'.

Hazards are often precipitated by people – for instance, a bushfire may be either deliberately or accidentally started by humans – and an event may be constituted a hazard depending on factors such as culture, age, socio-economic status, social and political structures. For example, flooding may be either a necessary and expected element of farming or a hazard depending on location, annual farming cycles and risk to people and their property (Gillespie and Danso 2010). Additionally, hazards may be viewed as a consequence of climate change, industrial development and technology (Paul 2011).

In contrast, disasters are 'actual threats to humans and their welfare' (Paul 2011, p.7). The word *disaster* is literally defined as bad (*dis*) star (*astrum*) thus 'connoting bad luck or the result of a misalignment of the astral heavens' (Kelman and Stough 2015, p.5). The New Zealand Ministry of Health (2016) outlines three distinct categories:

1. Natural disasters (for example, tsunami).

2. Human-made, non-intentional technological disasters (for example, nuclear accidents).

3. Human-made, intentional acts (for example, terrorism).

True (2013), however, emphasizes that there is no such thing as an inevitable or *natural* disaster as such events are shaped by previous and current political and economic decisions. This questioning of the *naturalness* of a disaster enables a reframing from a hazard focus to a broader consideration of political, social, economic and cultural influences on extreme events (Marlowe 2014). This socio-political focus aligns with the social work view of individuals being situated within a wider system. The broader perspective also enables understanding of what may cause a disaster and shapes government and humanitarian responses in each of the disaster phases (Mathbor 2012). Although conceptual debates continue, there is certainty that disasters do, at least temporarily, cause significant damage and interrupt everyday individual and community life (Marlowe 2014; Paul 2011).

Disaster management is the managerial and organizational function that is responsible for creating frameworks that can reduce the community's vulnerability to hazards and support them in coping with emergencies (Mathbor 2012). Internationally, comprehensive disaster management includes:

1. Risk reduction

2. Readiness

3. Response and

4. Recovery.

(Civil Defence 2015)

These phases are alternatively referred to as the disaster cycle or disaster management cycle (Paul 2011). The cycle offers a framework for how disaster management actors, including government, the private sector, non-government organizations, and communities, may plan for and mitigate against disasters, ensure rapid and effective responses and support any processes of recovery and renewal. The phases are not distinct, but the categories do assist with conceptualizing and understanding the process and activities commonly required in disaster management.

Terminology relating to disasters varies across countries and within government and non-government sectors. In Aotearoa New Zealand, for example, *disaster* is used interchangeably with *emergency*. Australian and United States policy adheres to a disaster discourse (Gillespie and Danso 2010; Kelman and Stough 2015; Winkworth *et al.* 2009). For the purposes of this chapter, the term 'disaster' will be adopted.

Social work

Founded on principles of human rights and social justice, social work is a profession that seeks to address injustice and oppression thereby enabling a more inclusive and supportive society (Allan 2009). The global definition of social work has an overarching goal of empowering people to face the obstacles that may be obstructing their wellbeing (International Association of Schools of Social Work and International Federation of Social Workers 2014). Building resilience – that is, supporting people to adapt to adverse situations – is a common aspect of social work practice and, along with the notion of vulnerability, has become a more frequently used concept in the disaster literature (Briggs and Heisenfelt Roark 2013; Mathbor 2012; True 2013; Zakour 2012). The inclusion of micro and macro perspectives in social work theoretical and practice approaches underpins the global definition, thus widening the spectrum of fields and populations with whom social workers practise.

Despite historical accounts of social work practice going as far back as the early 20th century, there is a continuing struggle to carve out its identity and standing as a profession (Beddoe 2017; Mapp 2008). Generally speaking, there is limited understanding among the public of what social workers do and this is especially so in the disaster context (Mathbor 2012), as highlighted by Dominelli (2010, p.2):

> Nor does the general public know about practitioners' heroic and innovative interventions in some of the most horrendous situations brought about through natural and (hu)man-made disasters, where they are among the many professionals who provide emergency relief responses.

There has been ongoing concern about disproportionately negative media portrayals of the social work profession that are often based on biased or limited understanding of the professional role of the social worker (Stanfield and Beddoe 2013). This may not only undermine individual practitioners but also limit the understanding of other professionals as to the valuable contribution social workers can make to disaster work. From the available literature, there is little indication as to what disaster management personnel understand about social work, which raises questions as to the effective inclusion of social work in this field of practice (Hay and Pascoe 2018). Social workers do, however, have an important role in addressing inequities in disasters.

Inequity in disasters

People's lived experiences of disaster varies (Marlowe 2014) although it is well known that individuals and groups with 'lesser capabilities, resources and opportunities' (True 2013, p.80) are disadvantaged further during times of disaster (Neumayer and Plümper 2007; Zakour 2012). Social vulnerability theory offers a useful construction of disaster by emphasizing the importance of focusing on 'vulnerable situations' rather than 'vulnerable people' (Phillips 2015, p.32) and recognizes that some people are placed more at risk than others due to economic, political and cultural factors (Alston 2007; Hugman 2010). The impact of disasters then is felt unevenly across different populations as pre-existing inequities and inequalities and other forms of exclusion and marginalization are exacerbated (Adamson 2014; Marlowe 2014; Phillips 2015). These inequalities limit the recovery process and highlight vulnerable members of the community.

While immediately after a disaster a strong sense of community identity, connection and service can be apparent, existing structural disparities also become evident (Maidment and Tudor 2013). The more disadvantaged members of society, such as children, older people, those who are less educated or on a low income, and disabled people, may be more affected by the disaster (Good, Phibbs and Williamson 2016; Maidment and Tudor 2013).

Paul (2011) argues that women are frequently more vulnerable in disasters. He emphasizes the importance of recognizing existing gender issues and the influence of patriarchy in communities as part of the risk reduction and emergency planning phases. Gender-based and sexual violence has been associated with disasters and therefore women in male-dominated societies may be more susceptible to violence and other discrimination following a disaster event (Cupples 2007; Paul 2011). Similarly, True (2013) purports that women's unequal status in relation to men must be addressed in disaster risk reduction and planning phases if the vulnerability of girls and women post-disaster is to be mitigated. Gender-sensitive disaster planning and decision making are critical not only post-disaster but also in the earlier phases of the disaster cycle.

Hugman (2010) suggests that children and young people also deserve particular attention post-disaster as the established world in which they lived and trusted has become unstable. During the response and recovery phases they may find it more difficult to adjust and process what has occurred. The increased stress experienced by other family members, particularly caregivers, also exacerbates this uncertainty and can lead to further distress.

Disabled people and those with mental health conditions are frequently marginalized and our societal and built environment does not typically consider or accommodate the needs of these sizeable populations (Alexander 2015). A disaster may generate further disadvantage as infrastructure can be destroyed or disrupted, companion animals may be hurt or traumatized, and usual support systems can be affected (Evans and Perez-y-Perez 2013; Good et al. 2016). Mental health conditions may be triggered by traumatic events and with rates of diagnoses increasing post-disaster, further pressure can be placed on already compromised services. Mental health is viewed differently across cultures and so in some countries inadequate support pre-disaster may become more apparent after an extreme event. There is growing evidence that disabled people and people with mental health conditions must be included in risk reduction, planning and response phases so that appropriate, timely and targeted actions are developed (Alexander 2015; Good et al. 2016; Kelman and Stough 2015).

Planning for the needs of diverse people, and especially those considered to be at most risk, will reduce barriers, increase independence and prevent adverse effects post-disaster. The inclusion of groups that may be considered to be more vulnerable in the disaster cycle phases may also lead to an increase in understanding of disaster management personnel as their capabilities and resilience factors may also be enhanced (Maidment and Tudor 2013). These considerations are relevant for social workers as they are well situated to work alongside diverse groups in the disaster space due to their established relationships with these populations.

Social work engagement in the disaster cycle

Social workers can become involved in the disaster cycle through their normal roles in social service organizations or perhaps quite unexpectedly, such as being seconded to work in a welfare centre after an event (Hugman 2010). Many social workers, however, will have had minimal training or previous engagement in disaster work. That said, as a generalist profession, social work draws on myriad theories that enable effective practice with individuals, groups and communities in the four phases of the disaster cycle: planning, preparation, response and recovery (Whitmore and Wilson 2005; Zakour 2012). Although multiple theories may contribute to the knowledge base of social workers in disaster work, four have been selected for particular attention in this chapter.

Systems approaches

Social workers are familiar with a systems orientation that takes a holistic approach to understanding personal as well as structural elements in a situation (O'Connor *et al.* 2008; Phillips 2015). Social workers understand the connections between relationships and context; the public and the private spheres (Adamson 2014). This recognition of the interdependence between human and physical systems offers a useful framework for understanding individuals in their environment, including in disaster responses (O'Connor *et al.* 2008; Pelling 2003).

At the micro level, Alexander (2015) emphasizes that emergency respondents should be specifically trained in how to support people with particular needs or conditions and how to gain a clear understanding as to what kind of assistance will be most useful during a disaster. Assessing risk, formulating policy and implementing programmes prior to a disaster are all essential components of disaster management; importantly, psychosocial factors are being progressively incorporated into the planning and mitigation phases of disaster management rather than being seen primarily in the domains of response and recovery (Flynn 2011). Social workers understand these factors and have the necessary skillset to train other responders around particular conditions and needs assessment. They can also be involved in the post-disaster phases with their clients and others requiring assistance. Social workers recognize the importance of individuals being involved in their own decision making and can encourage the development of personal and collective strengths (O'Connor *et al.* 2008).

There is a growing literature on the importance of preparing communities for disasters, and social workers bring important knowledge about engaging with planning and action at the local and national government levels, the primary spaces in which disaster planning and risk reduction occur (Appleby, Bell and Boetto 2015; Dominelli 2014). Alexander (2015, p.20) suggests that '...the ideal situation is one in which volunteer organizations, local authority social services, local emergency planners, and local health districts are all involved in the preparations'. He does, however, caution that a lack of integration and cooperation between organizations may limit discussions and coordinated responses. Social workers have a long history of working across professional and organizational boundaries and can have a pivotal role as alliance-builders and community advocates (Flynn 2011). Working alongside other professionals not only enables opportunities for policy development and community capacity-building but may also lessen the impact of stress on emergency responders, especially if they are themselves survivors of the disaster (Benveniste 2006; van Heugten 2013).

Globally, the international social work organizations all engage in activities with the United Nations on matters concerned with disasters. Activities involve: 'capacity-building initiatives, training, professional interventions, policy statements, letters, and press releases' (Dominelli 2010, p.47), as well as awareness-raising and the lobbying of politicians at international, national and local levels. The effects of such actions may not be noticeable to many social workers working locally but are important nonetheless.

Whether at the local, national or international level, social workers can act as a conduit and encourage a whole-system and *person-in-environment* approach to foster supportive environments that enable people to be active participants in the planning and risk reduction phases as well as to manage and thrive following disaster (Briggs and Heisenfelt Roark 2013).

Human rights and social justice

Human rights and social justice are fundamental principles in social work practice. A human-rights approach accepts that all people are entitled to the basics of life, to self-determination, to equal opportunities and to equality under the law (Mapp 2008). Moreover, rights-based practice takes a collective view on social justice rather than focusing only on individuals (Healy 2008; Mapp 2008). A challenge for social workers in Western countries lies in the entrenchment of neoliberal policies that endorse fragmented services, ever-decreasing resources, burgeoning bureaucracy and involvement of private services (Ferguson and Lavalette 2005). Dissatisfaction with the neoliberal agenda may, however, lead to increased cross-sector activity, the development of alliances and a renewed emphasis on rights-based work (Ferguson and Lavalette 2005).

From a social work perspective, rights-based approaches to disaster require that anyone who needs assistance has their needs met (Dominelli 2010). This is not dissimilar to a disaster management discourse which holds to the same standard (Ministry of Health 2016). To achieve this goal, social workers can actively promote social justice outcomes and support transformation in communities, particularly as part of the post-disaster response and recovery phases (Dominelli 2010; Maidment and Tudor 2013; Marlowe 2014). As an example, Alexander (2005) argues that many forms of discrimination become apparent post-disaster. Some service users may encounter 'physical barriers, obstacles to communication, and other barriers to accessing essential services' (Alexander 2015, p.15).

Other forms of discrimination may occur, such as temporary housing not having wheelchair access. Social workers can engage in advocacy and lobbying work to address these kinds of inequities (Alexander 2015; Good *et al.* 2016).

Environmental rights are inseparable from human rights and there is an increasing acceptance that social workers have a responsibility to also uphold these (Dominelli 2010). Environmental justice issues, such as the sharing of natural resources, responding to environmental hazards, supporting sustainability and responding to climate change, can become part of a broader response within disaster management (Dominelli 2014). Disaster risk reduction could, for example, include the facilitation of interdisciplinary dialogue to promote the development of sustainable lifestyles that may reduce the chances of future disasters, especially those caused by environmental hazards precipitated by climate change (Appleby *et al.* 2015; Dominelli 2010). Social work, at least in the Western world, needs to continue to broaden its traditional focus on locally based, chiefly individual practice, and proactively contribute to ameliorating the challenges that these issues may contribute to disasters (Appleby *et al.* 2015).

Community development

Within the social work literature there is an acknowledgment that community development aligns with an emancipatory social work approach that is person-centred and empowering and that also involves challenging political structures and inequitable resource distribution (Adamson 2014). Community development enables social workers to work alongside local communities in finding their own solutions, advocate for change, assist with mobilizing both affected and unaffected groups and individuals, and encourage the promotion of new policy initiatives (Cooper-Cabell 2013).

Shevellar and Westoby (2014) suggest that community development traditions fall along a spectrum of conservatism and liberalism. More conservative forms of community development align with concepts of self-reliance, self-help and encouraging individual responsibility. Liberal perspectives may include orientation towards advocacy and lobbying work, challenging social norms, raising consciousness of affected communities and challenging inequalities. In a neoliberal environment, it could be suggested that the more conservative approaches in disaster work would be aligned with disaster management discourses currently favouring an emphasis on individual and community self-reliance (Civil Defence 2015).

However, liberal approaches are important and social workers can also have a key role in promoting these either alongside or as an alternative to conservative activities.

Community development approaches have been used in a number of settings. For example, Puig and Glyn (2003) offer an example of a group of social work students from the United States who accompanied workers from a non-government organization to support relief and reconstruction work in Honduras after Hurricane Mitch in 1998. These students participated in the assessment of families' needs, provided counselling and also assisted the work of local non-government organizations (Hugman 2010). By staying with families who had not been directly affected they could quickly learn about aspects of the local culture, including political and social differences, and, importantly, how their own country was perceived by the people in Honduras (Hugman 2010).

In October 2011, there was a significant oil spill in Aotearoa New Zealand. Social work students explored the experiences of some of the community volunteers involved in the significant clean-up effort. In class they considered the responses of the indigenous people and issues of human rights, community development, social and environmental justice and the disproportionate effects of disasters on particular communities (Hunt *et al.* 2014).

Social workers may be engaged across a spectrum of community development activities within the different disaster phases. For instance, they can assist in disaster preparedness by supporting the development of social capital so that post-disaster a community has resources among themselves from which to draw (Marlowe 2014; Pelling 2003). Disaster-informed community development can also consider how a crisis might impact on existing community dynamics and the way communities may exhibit positive behaviours post-disaster such as pooling resources and practical collective responses (Maidment and Tudor 2013). There is also a strong argument for communities to be involved in disaster planning so that lessons learned from previously affected groups can be implemented as part of the ongoing planning and mitigation for future events (Hugman 2010).

Psychosocial approaches

In the disaster literature, there is an increasing acknowledgment that trauma and psychosocial factors are significant and are sustained effects of disasters (Du Plooy *et al.* 2014; Flynn 2011). Understanding how people respond to stress and how they can best be supported, not only in the short term, but perhaps for several years after a disaster, is essential.

Social workers are able to be active workers in this space with their understanding of individual and collective grief, mental health conditions (that may be exacerbated or triggered by disasters) and recognition that certain populations may be at particular risk (Alexander 2015). Further, social workers are trained to promote individual and community resilience and transfer their skills across multiple fields of practice.

A functional approach to disaster planning and mitigation that focuses on what communication, medical care, independence, supervision and transportation may be helpful for different populations when a disaster strikes may assist with preventing considerable stress on individuals and families (Phillips 2015). Incorporating social workers into this planning may prevent additional vulnerability for groups with whom they work.

Speaking about their experience of working at a hospital immediately after the 2011 earthquake in Canterbury, Aotearoa New Zealand, Briggs and Heisenfelt Roark (2013) suggest that the provision of early psychological support following a disaster can prevent stress reactions from becoming chronic. At this early stage, social workers can also identify people who may require more specialized support (Briggs and Heisenfelt Roark 2013). Similarly, the provision of psychosocial support as a key aspect of an effective emergency response was highlighted in a study on the 2003 earthquake in Iran which resulted in over 30,000 deaths (Mathbor 2012).

Immediately following a disaster, the response phase focuses on the safety of people and property (van Heugten 2013). Social workers can support people, both in practical and psychological ways, at welfare centres or by door-knocking in affected areas and checking on people's safety and wellbeing (Maher and Maidment 2013; Milner 2013). After a disaster, social workers also continue to work alongside their own clients to ensure their physical and emotional safety and to maintain a sense of normality among the chaos created by the disaster (Milner 2013). Assisting people to continue to manage their daily affairs is a key priority.

Systems approaches, human rights and social justice, community development and psychosocial approaches offer valuable theoretical contributions to disaster management. Social workers also bring myriad skills that are transferable to the disaster management arena, including those identified by Mapp (2008, p.163):

- Social workers are trained to consider a problem at different systems levels.

- Social workers are task-oriented and know how to develop and implement solutions in full partnership with the client.

- Social workers understand the role of culture.

- Social workers can analyse a situation and use all variables to effect change.

- Social workers have the ability to bring the human element to planning, policy and service development. They understand the connection between a client's wellbeing and the political, economic and social context in which he or she lives.

- Social workers have the training to bring all the actors and elements together to develop strategies and plans and implement programmes.

This comprehensive skillset, as well as the foundational theoretical constructs described above, clearly illustrates the suitability of social workers to be engaged in all phases of disaster management.

The following case studies offer two scenarios for readers to consider as they reflect on their transferable social work skills and the gaps in their current knowledge about disaster work. The case studies invite reflection on the connections between theory and practice, ethics and values, working with clients and colleagues and recognizing diversity.

Case study: Mere

Mere is a Māori (indigenous) registered social worker at a non-government social service organization that primarily works with families. She is at work with three of her colleagues when the magnitude 7.0 earthquake strikes her provincial town, Middlesville. Her manager is not on site. Although none of the staff are physically hurt in the event, there appears to be significant damage to the building, with cracks visible in the walls, furniture broken, windows shattered and parts of the ceiling collapsed. The electricity is not working.

Mere is shaken by the event and immediately afterwards she talks with her colleagues and they discuss the experience, their feelings and what needs to happen next, for them individually as well as for the organization. They are mindful that five clients are due to arrive shortly for a weekly group session on parenting and will likely have been travelling, many by public transport, during the earthquake. Mere is also concerned about her whānau/family and particularly her daughter in high school. Mere has not been able to contact anyone by mobile phone as the lines are overloaded. Her other colleagues are in a similar situation and all of them are starting to feel overwhelmed by the situation.

1. What are the challenges for Mere and her colleagues in this scenario?

2. What resources, ideas or strategies could Mere and her colleagues draw on to assist their decision making?

3. What actions should Mere and her colleagues take next?

Case study: Toby

Toby is a registered social worker. He is in a new role in a primary school that has recognized that a significant proportion of children are exhibiting behaviours that indicate anxiety and stress. Toby lives in a city where three years previously there had been a significant disaster. The majority of the children in the school had experienced the event themselves, many had left their homes due to extensive damage, and some had had family members or friends die as a result of the disaster. Toby had also experienced the event but had not had significant damage to his home or his workplace. His aunt and uncle, whom he was close to, had died as a result of the disaster.

After working in the school for several weeks, Toby now has an awareness of some of the ongoing physical and psychological impacts of the disaster on the children, including sleep disturbances, worry, anxiety, attachment issues and physical and behavioural regression. Toby has built positive relationships with the children and now he is focused on supporting them to find hope, recognize their strengths, engage in hobbies and activities that could bring a sense of joy, while cultivating their self-confidence and sense of self-worth.

1. What might Toby need to consider about his own wellbeing in this scenario?

2. In thinking of Toby's role, what elements are likely to be satisfying or challenging?

3. In what ways might Toby's work be considered multidisciplinary?

Social work engagement in disaster management is important but a range of challenges and opportunities also require consideration.

Challenges and opportunities for social work

Social work as a profession is often associated with low status and a focus on specific practices rather than its breadth and diversity (Dominelli 2010; Hugman 2010). In the disaster management field, do emergency responders even recognize who is a social worker and what part they can play in planning, mitigation, response and recovery efforts? Crucial to a greater inclusiveness and involvement of social workers in each disaster phase is the need for a significant increase in the visibility of the social work profession.

Raising awareness of the professional role of the social worker will assist with increasing this understanding of what social workers can provide, how and where they can be accessed and what contribution they can make to short-term, immediate and long-term disaster efforts. Documenting evidence-based practice in disaster work will also increase visibility of the social work profession and, importantly, equip other social workers to undertake necessary tasks. A deliberate inclusion of theoretical and practice constructs that connect with disaster work in the training of social work students will further strengthen the positioning of social work practice in the disaster phases (Marlowe 2014).

Indigenous knowledge can add particular value to social work practice in the disaster phases. For Māori, the indigenous peoples of Aotearoa New Zealand, there is an obligation to protect and sustain human and natural environments for the benefit of future generations (Durie 1998). This high regard for the connection between people and their natural environment is a core tenet of indigenous knowledge and practice (Ruwhiu 2013). Social workers are tasked with being culturally competent and to have an awareness of the impact of social inequalities, especially on marginalized and minority groups. Indigenous peoples are overrepresented in negative social indicators and therefore may be more susceptible to the impacts of disasters. Social workers can add value by working alongside indigenous leaders and community members in ensuring that their voices can be heard at all levels of disaster management. They can also bring their own understanding of indigenous theories and models into their practice environments, including in the response and recovery disaster phases. Strengthening the inclusion of indigenous approaches such as cultural values and practices in disaster work will limit the current marginalization of these groups in the disaster management space and be likely to produce better outcomes for indigenous peoples in times of disaster (Phibbs, Kenney and Solomon 2015).

As identified earlier, social workers have extensive networks and relationships across disciplines and are trained to advocate and build alliances. For these reasons, they have an important role in building and sustaining relationships across government, non-government and private sectors whether pre-, during or post-disaster. Many scholars (for example, Christoplos 2003; Cooper-Cabell 2013) have argued that the neoliberal agenda, and especially decentralization and bureaucratic emergency management models, have led to local institutions having greater responsibilities to deal with disasters. Although local and national governments are expected to be actively planning and reducing risk for future disasters, gaps are often evident because the prospect of disaster seems remote (Christoplos 2003). However, disasters cause an increased demand in social work services, although resources to support these needs may not always be forthcoming (Cooper-Cabell 2013; Zakour 2012). Strengthening partnerships across government and non-government organizations and among the community can assist with service delivery that may not fit with government's core business in a disaster (Huang, Zhou and Wei 2011). Gaining a clearer understanding of how other actors, including social workers, can effectively contribute to the disaster phases is important so that duplication is avoided and effective use of scarce resources is ensured (Christoplos 2003; Pelling 2003).

The incorporation of disaster interventions in social work curricula has been well canvassed in the social work literature (Adamson 2014; Dominelli 2014; Hunt *et al.* 2014). A more deliberate inclusion of environmental social work, culturally appropriate responses in disaster work and the needs of minority and vulnerable populations is timely (Briggs and Heisenfelt Roark 2013; Hunt *et al.* 2014). There is less agreement as to whether specific courses on disaster work should be established given the transferability of social work skills and knowledge in areas such as 'crisis intervention, problem-solving, practice skills, networking, community development, mobilizing and utilizing local resources' (Maher and Maidment 2013, p.75).

Social work curricula also require a strong focus on trauma and its impacts. Van Heugten's study of the challenges experienced by 43 service workers in Christchurch, Aotearoa New Zealand, illustrates the stressful nature of working to address the needs of service users while also being a survivor of a disaster. The shared trauma added additional emotional weight to the already difficult environment, which often faced reduced resources. An increased number of ethical dilemmas and moral distresses were also identified as specific challenges in the post-disaster context (van Heugten 2013). Through the use of scenarios, students can begin to appreciate the complexity associated with being a social worker as well as a survivor of a disaster (van Heugten 2013). Further, social workers need to establish support systems and strong professional boundaries in the response and recovery phases, and students should be well prepared around these matters (Briggs and Heisenfelt Roark 2013). In addition to the current transferable curricula, the literature suggests that students could receive better preparation around managing the media, ensuring privacy in a crisis situation, negotiating boundaries within interdisciplinary teams and recognizing the specific impacts of disaster work (Du Plooy *et al.* 2014).

Conclusion

As reflective practitioners, social workers are encouraged to question the role and purpose of social work practice and the boundaries in which it operates as a profession. As an emerging, and often unanticipated, field of practice, social workers are encouraged to consider their actual or potential interaction in the disaster space. Social workers have transferable skills that can be utilized during the four phases of disaster, including individual counselling, policy writing, alliance building, advocacy, structural analysis, organizing, administration and management (Hugman 2010). Systems theory as well as human rights and social justice, community development and psychosocial approaches have been identified as being especially applicable to social work practice in disaster work.

Although social workers have already been essential actors during many disasters, it is questionable whether disaster management personnel understand the breadth of work they can effectively undertake. Raising the profile and understanding of the professional role of the social worker is important if the social work profession is to contribute most effectively across all four phases of disaster management and, in tandem, continue to develop relevant theory and practice ideas.

Reflection questions

- What social work theoretical frameworks and models of practice might be relevant in the four phases of disaster management?

- What might be ongoing impacts on social workers who are working with clients affected by a disaster and who have been survivors themselves?

- How can codes of ethics and conduct inform social work practice in the disaster management field?

References

Adamson, C. (2014) 'A social work lens for a disaster-informed curriculum.' *Advances in Social Work and Welfare Education 16*, 2, 7–22.

Alexander, D. (2015) 'Disability and Disaster: An Overview.' In I. Kelman and L.M. Stough (eds) *Disability and Disaster: Explorations and Exchanges*. New York, NY: Palgrave Macmillan.

Allan, J. (2009) 'Theorising New Developments in Critical Social Work.' In J. Allan, L. Briskman and B. Pease (eds) *Critical Social Work: Theories and Practices for a Socially Just World*. Crows Nest, Australia: Allen and Unwin.

Alston, M. (2007) '"It's really not easy to get help": Services to drought affected families.' *Australian Social Work 60*, 4, 421–435.

Appleby, K., Bell, K. and Boetto, H. (2015) 'Climate change adaptation: Community action, disadvantaged groups and practice implications for social work.' *Australian Social Work 70*, 1, 78–91.

Beddoe, L. (2017) 'Field, Capital and Professional Identity: Social Work in Health Care.' In S. Webb (ed.) *Professional Identity in Social Work*. Abingdon: Routledge.

Benveniste, D. (2006) *Crisis Intervention After Major Disasters*. Carter-Jenkins Website. Accessed on 07/08/2017 at www.thecjc.org/pdf/benveniste_crisis.pdf.

Briggs, L. and Heisenfelt Roark, M. (2013) 'Personal reflections: What happens when disaster hits?' *Aotearoa New Zealand Social Work 25*, 2, 98–104.

Christoplos, I. (2003) 'Actors in Risk.' In M. Pelling (ed.) *Natural Disasters and Development in a Globalizing World*. London: Routledge.

Civil Defence (2015) *The Guide to the National Civil Defence Emergency Management Plan*. Accessed on 22/11/2017 at www.civildefence.govt.nz/assets/guide-to-the-national-cdem-plan/Guide-to-the-National-CDEM-Plan-2015.pdf.

Cooper-Cabell, N. (2013) 'Mind the gap: Post earthquake community wellbeing?' *Aotearoa New Zealand Social Work 25*, 2, 27–34.

Cupples, J. (2007) 'Gender and Hurricane Mitch: Reconstructing subjectivities after disaster.' *Disaster 31*, 2, 155–175.

Dominelli, L. (2010) *Social Work in a Globalizing World*. Cambridge: Polity Press.

Dominelli, L. (2014) 'Learning from our Past: Climate Change and Disaster Interventions in Practice.' In C. Noble, H. Strauss, and B. Littlechild (eds) *Global Social Work: Crossing Borders, Blurring Boundaries*. Sydney, Australia: Sydney University Press.

Du Plooy, L., Harms, L., Muir, K., Martin, B. and Ingliss, S. (2014) '"Black Saturday" and its aftermath: Reflecting on post-disaster social work interventions in an Australian trauma hospital.' *Australian Social Work 67*, 2, 274–284.

Durie, M. (1998) *Te Mana, Te Kāwangatanga: The Politics of Māori Self-Determination*. Melbourne, Australia: Oxford University Press.

Evans, N. and Perez-y-Perez, M. (2013) 'Will Marley come home? An exploration of the impacts of the Canterbury earthquakes on people's relationships with their companion animals.' *Aotearoa New Zealand Social Work 25*, 2, 7–17.

Ferguson, I. and Lavalette, M. (2005) '"Another World is Possible": Social Work and the Struggle for Social Justice.' In I. Ferguson, M. Lavalette, and E. Whitmore (eds) *Globalisation, Global Justice and Social Work*. Abingdon: Routledge.

Flynn, B.W. (2011) 'Community and Organizational Responses to Disasters.' In R. Kaufman, R.L. Edwards, J. Mirsky and A. Avgar (eds) *Crisis as an Opportunity: Organizational and Community Responses to Disasters*. Lanham, MD: University Press of America.

Gillespie, D.F. and Danso, K. (2010) *Disaster Concepts and Issues: A Guide for Social Work Education and Practice*. Alexandria, VA: Council on Social Work Education.

Good, G., Phibbs, S. and Williamson, K. (2016) 'Disoriented and immobile: The experiences of people with visual impairments during and after the Christchurch, New Zealand, 2010 and 2011 earthquakes.' *Journal of Visual Impairment & Blindness 111*, 6, 425–435.

Hay, K. and Pascoe, K.M. (2018) 'Where is social work in emergency management? Exploring visibility in New Zealand online media.' *Australasian Journal of Disaster and Trauma Studies 22*, 1, 3–10.

Healy, L. (2008) *International Social Work: Professional Action in an Interdependent World* (2nd edition). Oxford: Oxford University Press.

Huang, Y., Zhou, L. and Wei, K. (2011) 'Wenchuan earthquake recovery: Government policies and non-governmental organizations' participation.' *Asia Pacific Journal of Social Work and Development 21, 2,* 77–91.

Hugman, R. (2010) *Understanding International Social Work: A Critical Analysis.* Basingstoke: Palgrave Macmillan.

Hunt, S., Sargisson, R.J., Hamerton, H. and Smith, K. (2014) 'Integrating research on the impact of volunteering following the Rena oil spill into the University of Waikato social work teaching curriculum.' *Advances in Social Work and Welfare Education 16, 2,* 36–45.

International Association of Schools of Social Work and International Federation of Social Workers (2014) *Global Definition of Social Work.* Accessed on 04/09/2017 at www.ifsw.org/what-is-social-work/global-definition-of-social-work.

Kelman, I. and Stough, L.M. (2015) '(Dis)ability and (Dis)aster.' In I. Kelman and L.M. Stough (eds) *Disability and Disaster: Explorations and Exchanges.* New York, NY: Palgrave Macmillan.

Maher, P. and Maidment, J. (2013) 'Social work disaster emergency response within a hospital setting.' *Aotearoa New Zealand Social Work 25, 2,* 69–76.

Maidment, J. and Tudor, R. (2013) 'Editorial.' *Aotearoa New Zealand Social Work 25, 2,* 1–6.

Mapp, S.C. (2008) *Human Rights and Social Justice in a Global Perspective.* Oxford: Oxford University Press.

Marlowe, J. (2014) 'A social justice lens to examine refugee populations affected by disasters.' *Advances in Social Work and Welfare Education 16, 2,* 46–59.

Mathbor, G.M. (2012) 'Disaster Relief and Management: Readiness, Response and Recovery.' In L.M. Healy and R.J. Link (eds) *Handbook of International Social Work: Human Rights, Development, and the Global Profession.* Oxford: Oxford University Press.

Milner, V. (2013) 'In the zone: Keeping hope alive through shaky times.' *Aotearoa New Zealand Social Work 25, 2,* 45–57.

Ministry of Health (2016) *Framework for Psychosocial Support in Emergencies.* Wellington, New Zealand: Ministry of Health.

Neumayer, E. and Plümper, T. (2007) 'The gendered nature of natural disasters: The impact of catastrophic events on the gender gap in life expectancy, 1981–2002.' *Annals of the Association of American Geographers 97, 3,* 551–566.

O'Connor, I., Wilson, J., Setterlund, D. and Hughes, M. (2008) *Social Work and Human Service Practice.* Frenchs Forest, Australia: Pearson Education.

Paul, B.K. (2011) *Environmental Hazards and Disasters: Contexts, Perspectives and Management.* Chichester: Wiley-Blackwell.

Pelling, M. (2003) 'Emerging Concerns.' In M. Pelling (ed.) *Natural Disasters and Development in a Globalizing World.* London: Routledge.

Phibbs, S., Kenney, C. and Solomon, M. (2015) 'Ngā Mōwaho: An analysis of Māori responses to the Christchurch earthquakes.' *Kōtuitui: New Zealand Journal of Social Sciences Online 10, 2,* 72–82.

Phillips, B. (2015) 'Inclusive Emergency Management for People with Disabilities Facing Disaster.' In I. Kelman and L.M. Stough (eds) *Disability and Disaster: Explorations and Exchanges.* New York, NY: Palgrave Macmillan.

Puig, M.E. and Glynn, J.B. (2003) 'Disaster responders: A cross-cultural approach to recovery and relief work.' *Journal of Social Service Research 30, 2,* 55–66.

Ruwhiu, L.A. (2013) 'Making Sense of Indigenous Issues.' In M. Connolly and L. Harms (eds) *Social Work: Contexts and Practice.* South Melbourne, Australia: Oxford University Press.

Shevellar, L. and Westoby, P. (2014) '"Perhaps?" and "Depends!" The possible implications of disaster related community development for social work.' *Advances in Social Work and Welfare Education 16, 2,* 23–35.

Stanfield, D. and Beddoe, L. (2013) 'Social work and the media: A collaborative challenge.' *Aotearoa New Zealand Social Work 25*, 4, 41–51.

True, J. (2013) 'Gendered violence in natural disasters: Learning from New Orleans, Haiti and Christchurch.' *Aotearoa New Zealand Social Work 25*, 2, 78–89.

van Heugten, K. (2013) 'Supporting human service workers following the Canterbury earthquakes.' *Aotearoa New Zealand Social Work 25*, 2, 35–44.

Whitmore, E. and Wilson, M.G. (2005) 'Popular Resistance to Global Corporate Rule: The Role of Social Work (with a little help from Gramsci and Freire).' In I. Ferguson, M. Lavalette and E. Whitmore (eds) *Globalisation, Global Justice and Social Work*. Abingdon: Routledge.

Winkworth, G., Healy, C., Woodward, M. and Camilleri, P.J. (2009) 'Community capacity building: Learning from the 2003 Canberra bushfires.' *The Australian Journal of Emergency Management 24*, 2, 5–12.

Zakour, M.J. (2012) 'Natural and Human-Caused Disasters.' In L.M. Healy and R.J. Link (eds) *Handbook of International Social Work: Human Rights, Development, and the Global Profession*. Oxford: Oxford University Press.

• Part 3 •

PRACTICE APPROACHES

Chapter 10

Te Whakapakari Ake i te Mahi: Mana-Enhancing Practice: Engagement with Social Work Students and Practitioners

PAULÉ RUWHIU

Introduction

This chapter draws on the experiences in Aotearoa New Zealand and explores the central role that culture has in social work practice. In all countries there are diverse cultural groups living together and communication is important for ensuring that these groups can achieve mutual respect for one another. In Aotearoa New Zealand, we have a particular focus on two groups: Māori as Tangata Whenua (people of the land) and Tauiwi (non-Māori, New Zealanders).[1] This relationship is bound by the Treaty of Waitangi (Te Tiriti O Waitangi) signed in 1840 where the intention was to form a respectful bicultural partnership.

In social work practice mana-enhancing practice is one way that respectful cultural relationships can be promoted. Mana-enhancing practice was first introduced in a book chapter by Dr Leland Ruwhiu[2] (L. Ruwhiu 2009). Ruwhiu (2009) cites three recognition points that are

---

1   It is noted that te reo Māori is an official language of Aotearoa New Zealand; however, common terms and concepts used throughout this chapter have been translated loosely into English as a guide for international readers. It is acknowledged that te reo Māori (the indigenous language) is complex and has multiple meanings. The English translations in this chapter denote a fair representation of interpretation.

2   Dr Ruwhiu presented mana-enhancing practice in 2009; since then he has extended his work in other publications. The chapter in Connolly and Harms by Dr Ruwhiu (2009) provides a comprehensive discussion of this concept.

fundamental in working with Māori[3] and their whānau[4] (kinship) in Aotearoa New Zealand. The recognition points signpost cultural awareness markers that facilitate responsiveness to cultural complexities (L. Ruwhiu 2009). Furthermore, the Social Work Registration Board in Aotearoa New Zealand utilizes the term 'mana-enhancing' in the Kaitiakitanga Framework (Social Work Registration Board 2017). The Kaitiakitanga framework is 'proposed as the core concepts to assess social workers' competency to work with Māori in Aotearoa New Zealand' (Social Work Registration Board 2017, p.6).

Mana encompasses many meanings and is seen as a link to the human and natural environment. Mana appears through the essential dimensions of te ao Māori (the world of Māori, including our own traditional philosophies) and celebrates the link to our Ātua (our ancestral influences and deities) such as Papatūānuku (our earth mother) as mana whenua (power from the land). With regard to social work education, a focused reflection exercise can be used to teach social work students about mana through the lens of te ao Māori. This means that the way in which we see mana is from a cultural system of knowledge derived from the world of Māori.

With this in mind, this chapter endeavours to provide some strategies for practitioners to use when developing their knowledge of mana-enhancing practice. The chapter is also designed for social work educators to use as a teaching resource for social work students. In addition, the relevance for practice internationally is in the recognition of indigenous knowledge in informing social work practice and consideration of the experience of other indigenous cultures. The ideas presented in this chapter have relevance for all social work practitioners as the lessons outlined require that practice remains relevant and respectful and incorporates ongoing reflective processes.

This chapter extends the recognition points developed by Ruwhiu (2009) and describes how mana-enhancing practice can be used in practice. The examples do not express the breadth of te ao Māori knowledge but do provide an understanding of how one might engage with Māori concepts.

The three recognition points are: the significance of history, narratives as promoters of identity and Māori concepts of wellbeing (L. Ruwhiu 2009).

---

3   The term Māori is used throughout this chapter as is Tangata Whenua and both meanings refer to the indigenous peoples of Aotearoa New Zealand.

4   Whānau is commonly used to demonstrate a group of people who are related through a genealogical connection as a kinship group. However, it is acknowledged that this includes people who are not related but are support people who may live with the kinship group, people who are fostered into the whānau, and people who are connected to the whānau by marriage and common law partnerships.

The recognition points inform the structure of this chapter and include a discussion of emerging literature and application to practice. The challenges of mana-enhancing practice are discussed with both Tangata Whenua and Tauiwi practitioners in mind, and reflection questions for further consideration are given at the end of the chapter.

Recognition point 1: the significance of history

L. Ruwhiu (2009, p.108) describes this recognition point as 'the historical relationship between Tangata Whenua and Tauiwi' and the need for social workers to build an understanding of this relationship.

When entering into social work education, students have perceived ideas and worldviews about the history of Aotearoa New Zealand. These worldviews are formed through influences in their lives that may not be reliable or healthy (Ruwhiu 2017). For the first time, tertiary education exposes many students to information that provides diverse or alternative perspectives to what they have understood in their earlier education experiences. This information includes the historical events that formed the relationship between Tangata Whenua and the British Crown through the binding documents of the Treaty of Waitangi in 1840. Reid (2011, p.37) notes that 'students develop a personal position about the Treaty' and therefore to strengthen their understanding of the Treaty, students are encouraged to reflect on the events which occurred after the signing of the two documents and which disadvantaged Tangata Whenua. Examples of these events include: the confiscation of iwi(tribe)-owned land for public purposes, legislative decisions that were detrimental to the indigenous peoples, and warfare that dislocated hundreds of whānau (kinship) and hapū (sub-tribes). One example is the New Zealand Settlements Act (1863) which 'enabled the Crown to confiscate land and property from any Māori who were believed to be in rebellion' (Consedine and Consedine 2005, p.94). As a result, 1.3 million hectares were confiscated. This meant that many whānau and hapū were forced to seek refuge elsewhere.

Learning about this historical information can bring an emotional response for students, particularly if they have similar narratives within their own whānau and hapū. There is also a direct link to historical trauma where what happened in the past has an impact on future generations (Walters 2012).

Historical trauma

Historical trauma theory has been explored by indigenous writers such as Karina Walters (2012) and Eduardo Duran (2006), who focus on the impact of cultural assimilation and the generational effects on the wellbeing of indigenous peoples. 'Historical trauma is held personally and is transmitted over generations. Thus even a family member who has not directly experienced the trauma can feel the effects of the event generations later' (Evans-Campbell 2008, p.320). This means that the trauma that was experienced historically has had a profound effect on future generations (Brave Heart 2003). Pihama *et al.* (2014) suggest that this perspective on trauma has relevance for the experiences of Tangata Whenua of Aotearoa New Zeland. One such impact was after the signing of the Treaty of Waitangi when there was a 'large-scale land confiscation that amalgamated the destruction of entire communities and their livelihood' (Wirihana and Smith 2014, p.199). Many lives were lost and many whānau and hapū were displaced in the bid for the establishment of British colonies. In addition, Christianity influenced assimilation as part of civilizing Māori and this included the teaching of the English language in schools. Colonization had a negative impact on Māori identity (Moeke-Pickering 1996) that changed the landscape of how Māori interacted within their own communities. As a result, there are Māori who have grown up outside their iwi boundaries and who have taken on Christian values that have impacted on their Māori identity.

Houkamau and Sibley (2010, p.12) note that 'Māori identity is assumed to be a multidimensional construct involving the feelings, attitudes, beliefs, knowledge and behaviours individuals associate with being Māori in their everyday experience and social representations'. Social work educators in Aotearoa New Zealand encourage students to explore these constructs and learn to work with others from cultural groups different from their own. The need to explore the impact of colonization triggers emotional responses of anger, grief, guilt, sadness and shame. A process of de-colonization is used to address these mixed emotions. De-colonization is 'a process by which people peel away the psychological and spiritual effects of colonization through a facilitated journey of learning the truths of their history' (Bell 2006, p.14). This process is important for all students of social work as it assists with developing an understanding of the bicultural relationship of Tangata Whenua and Tangata Tiriti (non-indigenous to Aotearoa New Zealand). De-colonization also supports students to think about their own position within the relationship of Tangata Whenua and Tangata Tiriti.

The Tangata Whenua and Tangata Tiriti relationship

The Tangata Whenua and Tangata Tiriti relationship has been contentious throughout the years but mana-enhancing practice allows the communication between the two cultural groups to be negotiated. This means that the acknowledgment of the history between the two groups needs to be the key in understanding each other's cultural position. Under recognition point 1, it is important to know the significance of the Treaty of Waitangi as a document that is part of a binding relationship. What students discover is that this relationship is laden with mistruths.

It is also important to note the international influence as a colonizer and the impact it has had on the colonized. For example, while many of the students who choose to undertake social work may not be direct descendants of the British (the colonizers), they will have histories with the colonizers or have been colonized in their own countries of origin. The students should then be able to locate themselves and learn to understand the constructs of what this means in history, which determines how they will work with Tangata Whenua (the colonized). In learning about these relationships the students start to question their own position in Aotearoa New Zealand and what that looks like as Tangata Whenua or as part of Tangata Tiriti. Prior to participating in social work education, the students may have labelled themselves as *New Zealanders* or *kiwi*, which according to Mikaere (n.d.), denies their own international links and place of origin. For instance, their ancestors may have come from Italy or Africa but there is no personal connection to these places because they are the third or fourth generation to be born in Aotearoa New Zealand. Seeing for themselves that their connection to Aotearoa New Zealand is just as important as their international cultural heritage is essential to understanding the link to their own heritage. Nevertheless, working in Aotearoa New Zealand as Tangata Tiriti requires social workers to have an understanding of the indigenous peoples and how to work with them in a mana-enhancing way (L. Ruwhiu 2009).

The link to social work practice

When a social worker walks into a home of whānau Māori[5] (kinship group) the acknowledgment of the social worker should be to the tūpuna (ancestors) of the whānau Māori and the historical discourses the tūpuna experienced. Acknowledgment should also be with the whānau Māori that

---

5   Whānau Māori in this instance refers to all members in a household who are seeking assistance from a social worker.

may not be from the iwi they reside in. This means that the whānau Māori have moved from the iwi boundaries they can directly genealogically connect to, they may have no knowledge of their own iwi connections nor the connections of the iwi they reside in and they have chosen to move away from their own iwi because of financial, employment or whānau Māori reasons. By acknowledging these key aspects of the whānau Māori, the social worker can connect with the iwi history and tūpuna of the whānau Māori. This is significant because it means that the social worker is acknowledging the historical impact of colonization and historical trauma inside the home even before there is any work done.

To be able to recognize the impact of colonization when in practice as a social worker opens up an understanding of what the whānau Māori have endured inside their whakapapa (genealogy). For instance, if the whānau Māori the social worker is working with has whakapapa connections to the North Island of Aotearoa New Zealand but resides in the South Island, there may be a historical story behind this geographical location. For example, to keep safe, their whānau Māori or hapū may have been forced to move location at the time of the land wars in the 1800s. In more recent times, the whānau Māori may have sought employment away from their place of origin as part of the urbanization drift in the 1980s. The stories told are significant as they provide an important foundation for working with whānau.

Recognition point 2: narratives as promoters of identity

L. Ruwhiu (2009) indicates that recognition point 2 identifies the elements that contribute to a strong sense of identity. These include: te reo Māori (the indigenous language of Aotearoa New Zeland) and access to ancestral land and whakapapa. These factors promote both individual and collective wellbeing and influence Māori ways of knowing (Durie 1997). Attached to these key factors are stories or narratives that endorse the right to be Tangata Whenua. The sharing of these narratives helps create an understanding from others who are of another culture. Recognition point 2 requires that the two cultural groups of Aotearoa New Zealand negotiate how these stories are retold and are shared with each other. There are two types of stories that are important to know: collective stories and individual stories.

Collective stories

Collective stories are commonly shared knowledge and are based on historical events that have been woven into contemporary times. The stories exist as part of Tangata Whenua as a whole but are not homogenous because there are diverse versions of the stories. For example, our great-grandparents, our grandparents and parents were physically punished for speaking te reo Māori under the Native Schools Act 1867 (Penetito 2010; Selby 1999; Walker 1990). Mainstream schooling was a tool to assimilate Māori into the Western system of education. This example shows the collective stories that Tangata Whenua have as a shared history. There are also stories and narratives that are specific to an individual's lived experiences and perspectives.

Individual stories

Individual stories are stories that are told as a lived experience where an individual has a memory of an event that has had a profound and traumatic effect in their lives. To demonstrate this, I provide an example from my own experience. I attended a same-sex high school for three years in the 1980s; during my fifth-form year (year 11) I witnessed a lot of my Māori friends leaving school and accessing the unemployment benefit. The day came when I turned 16 and I went to see the guidance counsellor for advice on my future career choices. The guidance counsellor said that I should leave school and register on the unemployment benefit to receive $78.00 a week because it would be more productive for me to do this instead of staying at school and failing. I took her offer and the next week signed up to receive the unemployment benefit.

This story contributes to my journey through the education system at a young and vulnerable age. The story describes my removal from school, labelling me as a failure and setting me up to enter a system of dependence. The options of pursuing a career or further study were not offered to me and there was an expectation that the unemployment benefit would serve my needs as a young Māori woman.

While this story may resonate with others who have had a similar experience, it is also a personal encounter that had implications for my wellbeing and for my identity as Tangata Whenua. Linking this individual story to mana-enhancing practice demonstrates the importance of communicating our lived experiences with others from another cultural group. The significance of knowing the historical context places into perspective contemporary issues; in this case the education experiences of Māori in the 1800s and the connections between the lived experiences of Māori in the 21st century are examples of the lasting effects of colonization.

The link to social work practice

Recognition point 2 promotes the significance of narratives as contributing to the construction of identity. One of the most important attributes of social work is communication and this is taught within degree programmes as verbal and non-verbal skills. This requires social workers to share their stories of their cultural position and to listen to the stories of the whānau Māori with whom they are working. This will enable engagement and build trust within the helping relationship. The sharing of collective and individual stories promotes a secure and respectful relationship where clients and social workers build an understanding of who each other is and their position in Aotearoa New Zealand. L. Ruwhiu (2009, p.114) notes, 'Social workers seeking to develop culturally responsive practice need to be aware of the ways in which such narratives can contribute to building a strong cultural identity for Māori and to provide a sense of belonging and connection with the world.'

Drawing from my own individual story, at a young age I became a user of the welfare system and had thoughts of failure consistently through my teen years. It was not until I met positive role models that I started to believe in myself as an indigenous woman and the right to be me and what that represented as part of my own iwi, hapū and whānau. Stories are powerful and have an impact on the way people see and hear the person they are communicating with. Recognition point 2 allows that connection to develop successfully through a de-colonization process as part of social work education and social work practice.

Recognition point 3: Māori concepts of wellbeing

Recognition point 3 determines culturally responsive practice that embraces the concepts of Māori wellbeing (L. Ruwhiu 2009). The significance of this recognition point is to learn about Māori wellbeing and the effective healing processes that can be used in social work practice with Māori. In Aotearoa New Zealand, social workers who hold a different cultural worldview and lens on healing can be given opportunities to learn about these areas from the perspective of Māori.

L. Ruwhiu (2009) identifies four Māori concepts that are central to understanding Māori healing and a holistic perspective on wellbeing: wairuatanga (wairua) is described as encompassing spirituality, ideology, paradigms, perspectives, values and beliefs (Ruwhiu 2003); whakapapa is about our ancestry and connectedness; tikanga and kawa ensure we embrace our customs and protocols as a way of doing the right things and engaging with others; and, the fourth concept is mana, which is described as encompassing power, prestige, authority and humility and this was introduced at the beginning of the chapter as a foundation for mana-enhancing practice.

While the meaning of these concepts can be loosely translated into the English language, there is a risk of them being taken out of context and practised from the understanding of the interpreter's perspective – for example, wairua being described as only meaning spirituality or being seen as just about religion. Social work education needs to support social workers to learn the complexity of these concepts and how they can be applied to practice, including the challenges that arise when utilizing them in practice – for example, seeing them from their own cultural lens rather than the lens of Māori, applying them from a Western organizational standpoint or taking them out of context by thinking from an individual view and not from a collective perspective. The four concepts will now be discussed and examples will be provided for further understanding.

Wairua

There are certain facts we need to know about wairua. First, wairua begins to exist when the eyes of the foetus are formed. Wairua is not located in any particular part of the body, for example I cannot point to my shoulder and say: 'this is my wairua' or my knee and say: 'this is where my wairua is'. It exists everywhere and is in all aspects of my body. Māori believe that our wairua is immortal, that it exists after our physical body is deceased. The existence of our wairua in this realm allows us to connect with our tūpuna in the spirit world. The spiritual connection to our tūpuna also exists in certain portals of communication with them. For example, through karanga (a formal ceremonial call to visitors when entering the marae–a place of cultural significance), we call to our tūpuna to help guide and protect us (Hibbs 2006), and we acknowledge those who have gone before us when we feel their presence through a physiological reaction in our bodies. When we hear and see the haka (a dance performance that embodies cultural meaning), our body reacts in a way that can be described as a shiver or an overwhelming surge of energy (L. Ruwhiu 2009).

Wairua is also an indicator for us to take notice when we are feeling safe and warm or when we feel that something is not quite right in our environment. The physiological reaction can be likened to what many call our intuition. Wairua is part of our worldview, our values and our beliefs, therefore wairua is developed by the influences we have as we grow. If we are born into a loving and caring environment with a healthy value base, then our wairua is healthy. The reverse also applies: if we are born into or exposed to an unhealthy environment, surrounded by negative experiences and beliefs, our wairua becomes dysfunctional and unhealthy. At this point and to demonstrate the effects of wairua being damaged, a childhood story is told.

When I was six years old, I remember walking through the long grass at the back of our house. I came home and walked inside. My mother stopped me short and said, 'Look at your pants; you are not coming into the house with that all over you. You can sit down outside and pick them off.' I looked down and saw small green seed balls that were known as biddy-bids. I remember sitting down on the front step and arduously taking one biddy-bid off at a time. An hour passed and I had made a dent in my task but there still remained hundreds of the little seed pods stuck to the bottom of my pants, on my socks and in the inside sleeve of my jersey. The frustration of this task was that I would pull one off and discard it but it would stick back on me somewhere else. The task would have been much more effective if I had had help to pull the biddy-bids off so I could go inside the house.

This story describes the painstaking task of a child removing seed pods from her clothes because of the scorn of her mother. I never got all of them off but remembered feeling very irritated at the thought that so many had attached themselves to me. Let us now relate this story to wairua and the negative actions or experiences we have in our lives such as drug abuse, domestic violence, sexual abuse, unhealthy lifestyles, self-identity issues and institutional/personal racism. If each negative experience or action represents one biddy-bid and we are responsible for pulling it off by ourselves this would take a long time, we would be at risk of it re-sticking, and there would also be a strong likelihood that we would become frustrated with ourselves.

This analogy is valuable for social workers in their work with Māori. There are whānau who are covered in biddy-bids and need a lot of time to pull each one off. There is no guarantee that the whānau will not return to the same place where the biddy-bids will re-attach themselves, nor is there a guarantee that the whānau will be completely clean from the negative experiences or actions that have happened to them. Perhaps there is also a risk of the biddy-bids being transferred to others who are close to the whānau. So how does the social worker safely assist with each biddy-bid and how do they get pulled off? Central to this is finding safe places where connections can be made between people and also with the environment.

Matāmua (2016) presents the intrinsic connection to our environment and the places of comfort we seek out which will assist our wairua to heal. The four walls of an office may not be one of those places and perhaps the stress of the whānau home may also not be a place to talk safely. Matāmua (2016) shares insight on this when he acknowledges that some Māori find solace in the forest where their physiological reaction to the plants, trees and forest floor ignites a place of healing. For some, the sea gives a connection to their wairua as a place where they can reflect and tune into the sounds and sight of the mighty Tangaroa (Ātua or guardian of the sea). For others, it might be next to their loved ones at the ūrupa (cemetery), where they feel safe and close to their tūpuna. Whatever that chosen place may be, there is an opportunity for the social worker to assist in pulling off some biddy-bids and start to heal the wairua.

Whakapapa

Whakapapa (genealogy) is also connected to our wairua where our worldviews are formed from those who have passed on and who guide us from the spirit world. The connection is also with those to come. L. Ruwhiu (2009, p.114) states, 'the notion of whakapapa also strengthens the basic belief that one's future is linked with one's past so knowledge of that heritage needs to be firmly implanted to ensure whānau members would know who and what they are'. With this in mind, the social worker needs to know the reluctance Māori may have when asked about their whakapapa. While it is important to seek information to form a clear picture of who is in the whānau and where they come from to assist with making those connections, the importance from an organizational standpoint can look completely different. Where does this information go? Where is it stored? What happens to it when it is no longer needed by the organization?

The fear of exploitation may also mean that one is reluctant to share one's whakapapa. For instance, my great-great-grandfather is Kamariera Te Hau Takiri Wharepapa, a well-known Ngāpuhi (my tribal name) chief who travelled to England in the 1800s. He is seen in many of the homes of my whānau hanging on the wall as a Lindaeur (a renowned artist) painting and treasured in our whakapapa. In the 1970s, my great-great-grandfather's face was made into a postal stamp. If we think about this for a moment and ask ourselves what is the purpose of a postal stamp, the answer would be that we lick the back of it and stick it on a letter as proof that we have paid for its travel and then post it away for many hands to fondle through its journey.

While this is but one example, there are many more; it is a demonstration of a disregard for our tūpuna. What this example tells us is that what may be trivial to others is sensitive to the whānau of our tūpuna. Whakapapa connects to recognition point 1– the significance of our history and to recognition point 2 – narratives as promoters of identity.

Tikanga and kawa

L. Ruwhiu (2009) highlights the binding link of tikanga and kawa. Where there is tikanga, there needs to be kawa. L. Ruwhiu (2009, p.115) offers an explanation that informs working with whānau Māori: 'the principles that guide practice and the actual practice deliverables need to be aligned with tikanga and kawa'. The challenge for social workers is to determine what tikanga is and what kawa is. Tikanga is flexible, pragmatic and open ended, so tikanga can change according to the circumstances. Kawa are rigid processes and procedures that are followed for the best outcome. According to Mead (2003, p.14), 'there are several aspects of tikanga' and our guide for this is the learning and understanding of tikanga that is performed on a marae (a place of cultural significance). This comes from our kaumātua (our elderly), kuia (our elderly women) and whānau leaders.

Tikanga includes the word *tika*, which loosely translated means *to do right*. There are certain protocols that have been passed down from our tūpuna that are practised on a marae. There is also tikanga that is put in place inside a household which is established by the whānau themselves. 'Some tikanga provide guidelines of behaviour for individuals and for family groups and the practices are more personal in many cases' (Mead 2003, p.15).

Kawa are rules that are put into practice to ensure the household is run efficiently. An example of this is separating the household washing such as bedding and clothing into one pile and cloths associated with food into a different pile (Mead 2003). Another example is to remove outside footwear before entering the home. This is to prevent dirt and germs being carried into the house. Both examples indicate issues with personal hygiene where cross-contamination can occur, thus placing people in the household at risk of sickness.

Explanation of kawa in our household did not occur but as children when we were told not to do something we figured there was a reason for this and did not question it. My dad told me a few times in my younger days not to sit on the table; I reluctantly got off and did not question it.

It was not until I was much older that I worked out that my backside was making contact with a place where food was consumed. The same can be said when people sit on desks at an education institution and insist that it is not where food is eaten.

Resistance to following such tikanga and kawa may come from people stating that they are not Māori and it is a *Māori thing* to take your shoes off or not to sit on tables, so they do not need to follow these practices and rules. However, these people can be challenged to think about the reasons for tikanga and kawa, such as ensuring personal hygiene in order to prevent the spreading of germs. Tikanga and kawa determine the health and wellbeing of people.

Mana

As stated in the previous discussion, mana underlines a direct relationship between human beings and their environment. Māori acknowledge the significance of their environment and the implications for a person's wellbeing. To demonstrate this, if we imagine a person standing in isolation with nothing around them, what would be our thoughts? If we then imagine the same person standing in the same position but seeing their tūpuna, their grandparents, their parents, their partners and children, what do we see? If we also see that person with their mountain, their river and their home, what does this mean? If we visually see that person with their belief systems and their worldviews such as how they see their connection to ngā Ātua (ancestors with continuing influence, deities), Papatūānuku (earth mother), Ranginui (sky father), Tawhirimatea (Ātua of the wind), Tangaroa (Ātua of the sea), Haumietiketike (Ātua of uncultivated food) and Tāne Mahūta (Ātua of the forest), what does this mean?

The person that we have imagined possesses mana in the form of Mana Tangata (mana of the people), Mana Whenua (mana of the land) and Mana Ātua (mana of ancestral links) (Ruwhiu and Eruera 2015). There are other explanations of mana; however, this example shows that Māori do not stand alone and have many dimensions that contribute to their mana. If any of these dimensions of mana are diminished or inaccessible, there will no doubt be issues that need addressing. The lens in which you see this person is from a collective perspective where no person stands alone.

The link to social work practice

The concepts explored here open up a range of options to assist whānau Māori to utilize cultural systems of knowledge from te ao Māori to heal and achieve wellbeing. Wairua is the essence of a person; whakapapa celebrates our ancestral inheritance and our own identity; tikanga and kawa indicate the right things to do; and mana gives us our innate connection to the environment. All of the concepts have a purpose and are important to our wellbeing as Māori. Social workers can critically reflect on these concepts and seek guidance on the proper use of these in their practice. This is particularly important for social workers who have a different lens and worldview and where these concepts have not been part of their own lived experience.

The challenges of mana-enhancing practice

Two challenges will be explored in this section: the challenges Tangata Whenua face and the issues that arise for Tauiwi social workers when working with whānau Māori.

Tangata Whenua social work students have an opportunity in their social work journey to be able to reclaim, revitalize and reconnect with who they are as Māori (Ruwhiu 2017). Mana-enhancing practice allows a process of de-colonization where they are able to work through issues that have prevented them from embracing their identity as Tangata Whenua, including their own understanding of the Treaty of Waitangi, their own collective and individual stories and their own ways of ensuring wellbeing and healing. The challenge for these social work students occurs when they take on a position in an organization that may not be fully open to kaupapa Māori social work (a Māori approach with Māori principles and philosophies). This means there is a risk of being re-colonized.

Mana-enhancing practice ensures Tangata Whenua social workers remain securely in their position and can enact the right to be who they are as Tangata Whenua. The recognition points outlined in this chapter enable all social workers to make connections within their collective stories and have an opportunity to share individual stories, thus moving forward into a place of healing where they are comfortable in their position and practice.

Mana-enhancing practice is also a way forward for Tauiwi social work students and enables them to develop a close relationship with the whānau Māori and Māori colleagues they will work with in practice. The challenge for these social workers is that their de-colonization journey rests with their own authenticity and humility in being able to understand and embrace their cultural position as Tangata Tiriti. This journey may start when the students connect with their own international heritage and learn about the roles they pursue in Aotearoa New Zealand with

Tangata Whenua. Mana-enhancing practice is so much more than its title, and students and practitioners should be aware of its intricacies. While it is often associated with strengths-based approaches, it cannot be directly compared to Western approaches. It comes in its fullest form where students and practitioners take time to work with each recognition point. This includes putting thought into how to implement these in practice, including thinking about what impact they may have for whānau Māori and also the social worker who embraces this approach to practice.

Conclusion

This chapter has extended the work of Dr Leland Ruwhiu[6] on mana-enhancing practice and has explored three recognition points. The chapter has provided practical examples and illustrations of contemporary social work practice with whānau Māori. The chapter can be used as guide for practitioners and for the teaching of social work students. It provides an opportunity for social work students and practitioners to critically reflect on their lived experiences and on how these inform their practice. Each recognition point in mana-enhancing practice encourages the social worker to think about how the element relates to their practice and how it can be effectively implemented in building successful relationships with the whānau with whom they are working.

Examples are provided throughout the chapter and encourage social work students and practitioners to consider other perspectives and relate these to their own experiences. Despite the challenges of utilizing mana-enhancing practice, being able to connect with other diverse cultures is a rewarding achievement. Mana-enhancing practice should be lived and felt because when it is, the relationship between two cultural groups will be fully recognized as an honest partnership that can generate new understanding for both groups. While this chapter has focused on social work practice in Aotearoa New Zealand, it is hoped that social workers internationally will find the ideas relevant to their practice as they work to build respectful relationships with their clients. The ideas in this chapter can be used as a framework for critically reflecting on practice and the place of indigenous and cultural knowledge in social work practice.

---

6   E taku tungāne, e tūmanako ana kua kaha tautoko au i āu mahi kia ora tonu tō wawata. Ā, he hōnore nui kia mahi tahi me tō tuhinga i runga i te mōhio i tōku taha koe ā wairua nei (A message to my cousin).

Reflection questions

- Recognition point 1: How do you see the relationship between Tangata Whenua (people of the land) and Tangata Tiriti (non-indigenous to Aotearoa New Zealand)? What are the parallel experiences in your own cultural experiences?

- Recognition point 2: What narratives are specific to your own whānau and families and how are these related to the impact of colonization?

- Recognition point 3: Why is it important to learn about Māori and indigenous concepts of wellbeing as part of healing processes and how can these be incorporated into your practice?

References

Bell, H. (2006) Exiting the Matrix: Colonisation, Decolonisation and Social Work in Aotearoa. Unpublished thesis for Master of Philosophy. Palmerston North, New Zealand: Massey University.

Brave Heart, M. (2003) 'The historical trauma response among Natives and its relationship with substance abuse: A Lakota illustration.' *Journal of Psychoactive Drugs 35*, 7–13.

Consedine, R. and Consedine, J. (2005) *Healing our History: The Challenge of the Treaty of Waitangi*. Auckland, New Zealand: Penguin Books.

Duran, E. (2006) *Healing the Soul Wound: Counselling with American Indians and Other Native People*. New York, NY: Teachers College Press.

Durie, A. (1997) 'Te Aka Matua.' In J. Te Whaiti, M. McCarthy and A. Durie (eds) *Mai i Rangiatea: Maori Wellbeing and Development*. Auckland, New Zealand: Bridget Williams Books.

Evans-Campbell, T. (2008) 'Historical trauma in American Indian/Native Alaska communities: A multilevel framework for exploring impacts on individuals, families and communities.' *Journal of Interpersonal Violence 23*, 3, 316–318.

Hibbs, S. (2006) 'The uniquely female art of karanga.' *Te Kōmako IX, Social Work Review 18*, Winter, 1–8.

Houkamau, C. and Sibley, C. (2010) 'The multi-dimensional model of Māori identity and cultural engagement.' *New Zealand Journal of Psychology 39*, 1, 8–28.

Matāmua, R. (2016) *EIT Public Lecture*. Eastern Institute of Technology, Hawkes Bay. Accessed on 21/09/2017 at www.youtube.com/watch?v=hfuEkqz8v3k&t=1385.

Mead, H. (2003) *Tikanga Māori: Living by Māori Values*. Wellington, New Zealand: Huia Publishers.

Mikaere, A. (n.d.) *Are We All New Zealanders Yet? A Māori Response to the Pākehā Quest for Indigeneity*. Accessed on 10/03/2015 at www.converge.org.nz/pma/iwi-am04.pdf.

Moeke-Pickering, T. (1996) Māori Identity Within Whānau: A Review of Literature. Unpublished paper. Hamilton, New Zealand: Māori and Psychology Unit, University of Waikato.

Penetito, W. (2010) *What's Māori about Māori Education?* Wellington, New Zealand: Victoria University Press.

Pihama, L., Smith, C., Reynolds, P., Smith, L., Reid, J. and Te Nana, R. (2014) 'Positioning historical trauma theory in Aotearoa New Zealand.' *AlterNative: An International Journal of Indigenous Peoples 10*, 3.

Reid, P. (2011) 'Good Governance: The Case of Health Equity.' In V. Tawhai and K. Gray-Sharp (eds) *Always Speaking – The Treaty of Waitangi and Public Policy.* Wellington, New Zealand: Huia Publishers.

Ruwhiu, E. (2003) Kei te Huehue te Puna e Kotokoto. Unpublished thesis for Master of Arts. Otaki, New Zealand: Te Wānanga O Raukawa.

Ruwhiu, L. (2009) 'Indigenous Issues in Aotearoa New Zealand.' In M. Connolly and L. Harms (eds) *Social Work: Context and Practice.* Melbourne, Australia: Oxford University Press.

Ruwhiu, L. and Eruera, M. (2015) 'Na te Rauroha, na te Rangiātea i tuku iho Tiaki Mokopunam – Actioning Transformative States of Māori Children in Aotearoa New Zealand.' *Cultural Responsiveness in a Multi-agency World Conference,* 29 March–1 April 2015, Auckland, New Zealand. Accessed on 28/09/2017 at www.youtube.com/watch?v=6zymKgzeMW8.

Ruwhiu, P. (2009) Kā Haere Tōnu te Mana o ngā Wahine Māori: Māori Women as Protectors of te ao Māori. Unpublished thesis for Master of Social Work. Palmerston North, New Zealand: Massey University.

Ruwhiu, P. (2017) Wetekia te Mauhere o te Hinengāro, ma tātou anō e Whakaora, e Whakawātea te Hinengāro–Emancipate Yourself from Mental Slavery, None but Ourselves Can Free Our Minds. Unpublished paper. Palmerston North, New Zealand: Massey University.

Selby, R. (1999) *Still Being Punished.* Wellington, New Zealand: Huia Publishers.

Social Work Registration Board (2017) *Core Competence Standards.* Accessed on 21/09/2017 at http://swrb.govt.nz/for-social-workers/competence-assessment/core-competence-standards.

Walker, R. (1990) *Kā Whawhai Tonu Matou – A Struggle Without End.* Auckland, New Zealand: Penguin Books.

Walters, K. (2012) *Yappalli: To Walk Slowly and Softly in a Growing Community – Researcher Partnerships Addressing Historical Trauma and Micro-aggressions.* Historical Trauma Research Centre. Accessed on 12/05/2016 at http://mediacentre.maramatanga.ac.nz/content/historical-trauma-research-seminar-professor-karina-walters.

Wirihana, R. and Smith, C. (2014) 'Historical trauma, healing and wellbeing in Māori communities.' *Mai Journal 3,* 3, 198–210.

Chapter 11

Social Work with Pacific Communities

TRACIE MAFILE'O

Introduction

Contemporary social work is becoming increasingly international and intercultural in nature. Increased mobility across borders, diversifying populations, and the perpetuation of racial and structural inequalities urge social work to forge new responses. Indigenous perspectives are becoming more visible in social work theory, practice, policy, education and research. This chapter examines social work with Pacific communities, illustrating emerging indigenous non-Western perspectives for contemporary social work.

Pacific communities refer to people who are indigenous to Pacific nations across Polynesia, Melanesia and Micronesia, and who live in either their homelands or the diaspora. A history of colonization throughout the Pacific, together with extensive migration in the post-war period, has contributed to the Pacific diaspora. Taking Tonga as an example, more people of Tongan ethnicity live outside of Tonga (mostly in Aotearoa New Zealand, Australia and the USA) than within the nation of Tonga. The Pacific is diverse, with linguistic, cultural and geographic differences both within and across Pacific nations. Across some 23 Pacific Island nations, there are over 1200 indigenous Pacific languages and, given colonization in the region, English and French are national languages across much of the Pacific. Transnationalism is another characteristic of Pacific communities, with identity and relationship to homeland centred on the concept of reciprocity (Nakhid 2009).

In addressing social work with diverse, transnational, indigenous Pacific communities, this chapter contributes to broader conversations around international social work, intercultural practice, cultural competency, anti-racism, decololoniality and indigenization.

Pacific indigenous ways of being, knowing and doing are emerging to inform social work practice and service development across the Pacific (Autagavaia 2001; Crichton-Hill 2018; Faleolo 2013; Lawihin 2017; Mafile'o and Vakalahi 2016; Ministry of Social Development (MSD) 2015; Mulitalo-Lauta 2000; Newport 2001; Ravulo 2016; Vakalahi and Godinet 2014; Yeates 2013). Nonetheless, the predominance of Western theoretical models and assessment tools in social work, compared with indigenous theoretical models, is a recognized challenge in the Asia-Pacific region (Shek, Golightley and Holloway 2017). This challenge is addressed in this chapter by profiling, applying and discussing key principles within Pacific indigenous social work perspectives.

Three Pacific social work practice principles – love, relationship and humility – are discussed in the first section. The principles derive meaning within Pacific cultural perspectives and represent points of alignment across various ethnic-specific Pacific social work frameworks. Two case studies, illustrating the application of Pacific social work principles, are presented next. One case study is a micro practice example, while the other is a macro practice, community development example. The final section discusses key challenges in Pacific social work theory and practice: promoting indigenous knowing amid the evidence-based debates; questioning the cultural competency discourse; and de-coloniality, anti-racism and environmentalism.

Pacific social work theory and practice

The Pacific social work principles discussed here – love, relationship and humility – illustrate Pacific social work theory and practice which contributes to global knowledge and, importantly, benefits the lives of Pacific families and communities. Even so, the selected principles are more illustrative than exhaustive. An inherent limitation of this discussion is its conception and expression primarily in English, as nuances rooted in Pacific languages and cultures cannot be fully captured in this space.

Love

Love is perhaps the most fundamental Pacific practice principle. 'Ofa – the Tongan word depicting love, care or compassion – has been pinpointed as the philosophy underpinning Tongan society (Bennardo 2008; Kavaliku 1961) and a cornerstone for Tongan social work practice (Mafile'o 2008; MSD 2015). The fact that translations of love are part of a number of Pacific language greetings suggests the centrality of love as a principle in

Pacific cultural perspectives. For example, *fakaalofa*, the root word in the Niue greeting *fakaalofa lahi atu*, and the Hawaiian greeting *aloha* both mean to show compassion, love and kindness. *Alofa* (love, compassion) is a key value within *faʼasamoa*, the Samoan culture (Mulitalo-Lauta 2000), and one of the strands within the *Tautua Framework*[1] (MSD 2015) developed within the Aotearoa New Zealand statutory child protection and youth justice agency for social work with Samoan families. *Alofa*, Mulitalo-Lauta (2000, p.22) explains, is defined in the Samoan saying ʼ*e le naʼo upu ma tala, aʼo mea e faʼatino e iloa ai le alofa* – it is not just words, but action and commitment which truly demonstrate love, compassion and concern for othersʼ.

Other centredness was nuanced in a qualitative study with Tongan social workers practising in Aotearoa New Zealand, exploring the Tongan values, skills and processes used in their contemporary practice (Mafileʼo 2008). As a practice principle, Tongan social workers reflected on love in the following ways:

> Itʼs an unselfish giving of oneʼs self, possession[s], time, everything, and never thinking that Iʼm going to get anything good out of it. (p.124)

> The more successful [Tongan] social workers are the ones who can convince the people that you are not doing it for a job; youʼre doing it because of your personal passion…and itʼs not money… I believe that they are people who have a genuine love for people. (p.124)

> I was in…the jail for eight hours with one of the clients [who was accused of a stabbing]. They said, ʼWhat about your safety? … Arenʼt you scared?ʼ I said, ʼNo…if you go there because you really love them, they wonʼt mind… Here is…your mind together with your heart and then you can do the work properly…ʼ If not, you just come here to work for money. (p.124)

The social work principle, love, as reflected by these practitioners, means not just *doing* social work as a job or profession. Rather, *being* a social worker as a life calling, a way of life, is important within Pacific social work (Pacific Island Community and Social Workers Auckland 1986). From within a Fiji context, George (2005) observes three types of service: volunteering part time in human service work; undertaking social service as a full-time profession; and, finally, he advocates devoting oneʼs entire life to service so ʼlife is service before selfʼ (George 2005, p.38).

---

1 *Tautua* is a distinctive Samoan cultural framework, which is outlined within the broader *Vaʼaifetu* framework document.

Love, while being a core principle in Pacific cultural frameworks, is emerging as an ethical and practice principle in social work literature more generally (Godden 2017; Morley and Ife 2002; Walker 2015). A common theme within this literature is consideration of love at the humanity level, suggesting that Pacific perspectives hold relevance for practice beyond social work with Pacific communities. The love of humanity, according to Morley and Ife (2002), connects diverse groups despite limitations imposed by privilege and under-privilege. Promoting fully human practice, Walker (2015, p.47) proposes that 'love in the context of professional relationships within the social work process is at the heart of a 21st century emancipation of...oppressed groups'. That love is profoundly emancipatory and important for the future of social work is also an underpinning of Godden's (2017, p.415) argument:

> The love ethic can guide the personal and professional behaviour of radical social workers... Love-based practice involves opposing policies, structures, and practices that perpetuate injustice – becoming activists in all aspects of our lives... As a framework of interconnectedness, the love ethic provides hope for our collective future, and is worthy of consideration by social work theorists and practitioners.

Centring love as a social work concept resonates with conversations taking place in other fields such as healthcare (Barsade and O'Neill 2014) and education (Palmer 1993). A culture of companionate love was shown in a longitudinal study in a USA long-term healthcare facility (Barsade and O'Neill 2014) to be associated with positive organizational outcomes (including employee satisfaction and clients' outcomes).

In education, Palmer (1993) posits that knowing is essentially relational and is, potentially, an act of love. He states:

> The act of knowing is an act of love, the act of entertaining and embracing the reality of the other, of allowing the other to enter and embrace our own. In such knowing we know and are known as members of one community, and our knowing becomes a way of reweaving that community's bonds. (Palmer 1993, p.8)

Love, 'ofa, alofa, aroha and so forth are foundation concepts in Pacific social work frameworks. This concept of love infers selfless service, and a commitment to community and others beyond a job or profession. It is principally about our human connectedness. Pacific concepts of love resonate with non-Pacific literature asserting love as an important principle within social work and further afield. The love principle makes relationships central to Pacific social work, which is the principle explored next.

Relationship

Relationship is a key principle in Pacific social work. Nurturing, tending to and navigating the *va* – the space between that relates (Mila-Schaaf 2006; Wendt 1996) – is a core concept addressed by several Pacific social work authors (Autagavaia 2001; Mafile'o 2008; Mila-Schaaf 2006). *Va* as a key Pacific concept is also promoted in applied disciplines such as education (Anae 2010; Reynolds 2016; Tuagalu 2008), counselling (Pala'amo 2017) and architecture ('Ilaiu 2009). Autagavaia (2001) explains that within *fa'asamoa* (the Samoan culture) the self does not exist in isolation, and identity stems from *aiga* (family) and land. *Va* is a central organizing concept in Tongan traditional culture (Mahina 1992) and in contemporary transnational Tongan realities (Ka'ili 2017). Ka'ili (2017, p.1) portrays *tauhi va* (tending to the *va*) as an 'indigenous artistic device that uses symmetry to reconcile sociospatial conflicts and create harmonious and beautiful sociospatial relations'. Nurturing sociospatial relations is evident in such practices as all-night funeral wakes, and the performance of social duties such as the roles of the *'ulumotu'a* (oldest male in the extended family) or the *fahu* (honored female role). In Pacific social work perspectives, practice is anchored in the nurturing of relationship spaces.

Relationship is one of eight principles in the *Va'aifetu* framework (MSD 2015) developed in Aotearoa New Zealand for culturally responsive statutory child protection and youth justice social work with Pacific families. According to the *Va'aifetu* framework: the Pacific child has a right to belong with people who will love, protect, defend and nurture them; for Pacific families, good relationships are a form of social currency; and for the practitioner, collective effort is needed to achieve and sustain best outcomes for children (MSD 2015, p.7). Relationship, then, is a key principle for social work practice with Pacific children and families and must be central to the way practitioners conceptualize and engage with Pacific communities. In application to Pacific social work, the child is always considered as part of an extended family (MSD 2015), and a collective, community development approach is an integral aspect of Pacific-based social work practice (Mafile'o 2005).

Understanding diverse Pacific family and social structures (or hierarchies) and having the ability to skilfully engage and interact with such hierarchies are important practice requirements of Pacific relationship-based social work. For example, the *Va'aifetu* framework (MSD 2015) explains that the Cook Islands society has a hierarchical, collective, tribal structure, including: *ngutuare tangata* (household family), *kopu tangata* (extended family), *makakeinanga* (people from the same village), *enua tangata* (people from the same island) and *ipukarea* (people from the

Cook Islands). In child protection or youth justice social work, these multiple layers of connections must be considered not only for a full understanding of the issues for a child, but, more importantly, for a fuller range of solutions derived within the family, community and cultural context to emerge. As another example, Tongan social structure includes *tu'i* (King/royalty), *hou'eiki* and (nobility) and *kakai tu'a* (commoners); within traditional Tongan family structure, status and roles within families pivot on seniority and gender. Awareness of one's one position in relation to others and the ability to navigate successfully within and around the family and social structures will largely determine the outcome of social work assessment and intervention in a Tongan setting (Mafile'o 2008).

In Pacific social work, the social worker–client relationship is overlaid with family-like concepts as a way to respectfully and authentically engage. This is understood within Tongan social work as *matakainga* – being like family (Mafile'o 2006) or behaving with mutual respect (MSD 2015). For Tongan social workers, use of inclusive language portrays *matakainga*. For example, despite there being no biological connection between a practitioner and service user, a practitioner may refer to *our children* or *our daughter* when speaking with parents, or use the Tongan language terms for *father* or *uncle* when referring to an older male (Mafile'o 2006). Inclusive language effectively facilitates *fakafehokotaki* (engagement) between a social worker and a client (MSD 2015). Similarly, Mulitalo-Lauta (2000) relates the example of a Samoan female prison officer referring to Samoan men inside the prison as *brother* or *uncle*.

Use of such inclusive, family-like, language diminishes stigma associated with having a social worker involved and works to destabilize the power associated with a professional social work role. Inclusive language, therefore, is effective in positioning the practitioner on the same level as clients and opens up a more humane, compassionate social work practice by harnessing Pacific concepts of relationship. Challenging conventional constructions of social work relationship boundaries, Pacific relationship-based social work resonates with the promotion of mutuality and connection, rather than separation, in social work professional boundaries (Lynn 2001; O'Leary, Tsui and Ruch 2013).

Respect is closely connected with the notion of relationship in Pacific social work. *Matakainga* (being like family), expressed through the use of inclusive language, builds social work relationships based on Pacific notions of respect. The Tongan word for respect is *faka'apa'apa*, which is also a key Tongan social work practice concept (Mafile'o 2008; MSD 2015). For example, within the Tongan world, respect between a brother and sister relationship is pronounced. In Tongan tradition, a sister holds higher social status than her brother and brothers have a duty to honour, serve and respect their sisters. On this basis, a young female Aotearoa New Zealand-born Tongan social worker stated the following:

> A lot wasn't Tongan too traditionally, but I wouldn't call that not being Tongan. Like I sat in a forum with six guys for 12 weeks and gave anger management. That's not Tongan. But…I came across as their sister and they respected me in that sense. (Mafile'o 2008, p.122)

Finally, the broad basis on which connections are made in social worker–client relationships is a key aspect of emerging Pacific social work approaches. For a Pacific social worker, relationship building with clients from the same ethnic group may include reference to the social worker's extended family, village and island, and could also include schools attended and the religious affiliation of the social worker (Mafile'o 2004). Within Tongan social work, this has been referred to as *fakafekau'aki* (Mafile'o 2004) or *hohoko* (MSD 2015).

Important differences exist between relationship-based social work within emerging Pacific frameworks and the relationship-based social work that has undergone a recent resurgence within Western social work. With its roots in psychoanalytic theory (Ward, Turney and Ruch 2010), Western relationship-based social work is primarily focused on a social worker–client therapeutic relationship that does not explicitly and directly involve the families and communities of the individuals concerned. That is, social workers and clients are more or less perceived as individuals. Within the Pacific world, however, the relational self is based on a social worker and a client being integral representatives of families and communities and this being an integral part of social work practice (Pacific Island Social Workers 1986).

Humility

Humility is the final Pacific practice principle discussed here to illustrate emerging frameworks for Pacific social work. Pacific notions of 'humility' have all been used extensively in relation to Pacific social work (Mafile'o 2004; MSD 2015; Mulitalo-Lauta 2000; Talaimanu 2006).

Tongan social workers shared the following reflections about humility (*fakatokilalo*):

> We are always crawling…crawl into the family, and they will take you up – instead of you coming from up-down.

I use my Tongan humility to get through because our people are proud people...when they see...humility in the person who is approaching them...then they will open up to you... fakatokilalo...I am lucky to have that island thing with me because I can work with my other counterparts and I can see that they are really high up. (Mafile'o 2004, pp.250–251)

A vivid illustration of the potential of humility in Pacific social work is that of the *ifoga* process within a Samoan cultural context. The *ifoga* is a public forgiveness ceremony where, in cases of serious offence, the offending party pleads pardon from the offended (Efi 2003). Efi (2003) explains how *ifoga* involves the offender and their extended family coming to the residence of the offended at sunrise (signifying harmony with the peace and refreshing of the new day), and the offender sitting on the ground covered by a traditional fine mat. The offended party, when ready, can respond. The *ifoga* ceremony is a form of art therapy, where processes of storytelling, poetry, chanting, prayer, metaphor and drama move victims, family, community and offenders to healing and transformation (Mulitao-Lauta and Menon 2006). According to Efi (2003, p.60), 'three elements sustain ifoga: a sense of remorse and shame by the perpetrator, accountability by the family and village, and forgiveness by the victim's family'. Humility is an underlying element of the *ifoga* process.

In summary, humility, is a concept informing the position and approach of the social worker, but is also a concept that informs intervention strategies engaging individual, family and community change.

Case studies

So far, this chapter has introduced three Pacific social work principles – love, relationship and humility. The discussion has explained how social work with Pacific communities can draw on indigenous values and processes emanating within Pacific worldviews. Doing so challenges the definition of social work as a discipline and a profession, moving towards a more whole-family, whole-community and whole-life conception of social work.

The way in which love, relationship and humility nuance Pacific social work theory and practice is further developed here through a consideration of two case studies. The first case study illustrates how a non-Pacific social worker aligns with and draws on Pacific social work principles in a micro practice example with a Pacific young person in a school setting. The second case study, while still focused on Pacific young people in the education context, illustrates how Pacific social work principles can inform a community development in a macro practice context.

Case study 1: Micro practice

Sara is a non-Pacific school social worker in an area where, over the last several years, there has been a substantial increase in students of Pacific ethnicities as new families moved into the area. She has received a referral from the Principal for Michael, a 16-year-old boy of Tongan/Niue ethnicity. Michael has had multiple unexplained absences from school over the last six months. Four days ago, Michael had an altercation with another student, threw a chair at the wall, and left school. He has not returned to school since that incident. The school has been unsuccessful in engaging with Michael's parents through letters sent home and phone calls.

Sara begins her preparation to engage with Michael and his family, thinking about Michael in the context of his family and community relationships. From her own involvement in community sports, she is aware there are a few different Pacific churches which have a range of spiritual, creative and sports activities for their youth. She wonders how Michael and his family might be connected to any of these groups. She talks with some of Michael's teachers and finds out that Michael is the oldest of five children, the father had grown up in Tonga while the mother was Aotearoa New Zealand-born Niuean, and the family moved to the area about a year ago.

Sara and a colleague visit the family home. On arrival they meet Bev, Michael's mother, and Sara greets the mother with *fakaalofa lahi atu*. Sara apologizes for her visit, explains who she is and what her role is, and asks for permission to meet with the family to discuss how the family and the school can work together to support Michael's education and wellbeing. Bev explains that she has been unwell over the past few months and Michael has been a big help looking after his younger siblings. Michael's father, Sione, is away for work during most weeks, but has next week off. Sara also asks if she can talk with Michael. When she speaks with Michael, he is remorseful about his part in the altercation with the other student.

A meeting takes place the following week at a community centre close to the family home. The family know this venue as they have attended cultural community events there. Sara also advises the family that she will invite her agency's Pacific cultural liaison, who is Tongan, to attend the meeting.

Sara prepares some light refreshments for the meeting. Sione, Bev, Michael and Mele, the paternal grandmother, arrive at the meeting and Sara greets them with handshakes. To begin the formalities, Jim, the Pacific cultural liaison, welcomes the family in the Tongan language, acknowledging where the family are from in Tonga, the grandmother's presence and the love they show for their son Michael by being present today. After translating what he said into English, he invites Mele to open the meeting with *lotu* (prayer). Sara then introduces herself (explaining her role and talking about her own background, including that she is a mother of three young children). She explains the concerns from the school's perspective (truancy and behaviour), and her hope that today a good working relationship can be established around understanding what is happening for Michael and the family and making a plan for his education and wellbeing. She invites the family to share aspirations and concerns.

Reflection on Pacific social work principles: relationship and humility

In her preparation, Sara seeks to understand the young person in the context of their family and community relationships. Although not being of Pacific ethnicity herself, Sara considers how she might link to the family as a community member through her sport connections. There is a subtle yet powerful difference in viewing clients as *other* and viewing clients as part of one's own community; by positioning herself in community with the young person at the outset, Sara is more able to adopt a position of humility in her engagement. Initial in-person contact, to set up the family meeting, is another way in which humility and respect for relationship are demonstrated. Sara apologizes for her visit and asks permission for a family meeting, both further aligning with humility as a practice principle.

Reflection questions

- As a practitioner, what would influence your decision about engaging an external person with cultural and language skills as part of your social work approach?

- How useful are Pacific social work principles (love, relationship, humility) when working with resistant, involuntary clients?

Case study 2: Macro practice ·······························

Pasifika Fusion is an annual secondary school Pacific Festival in Palmerston North, a provincial Aotearoa New Zealand town. Involving around 20 schools, it is the largest pan-Pacific community event in the region.[2] Pasifika Fusion is run by Pacific community volunteers.

A group of Pacific community members initiated Pasifika Fusion over a decade ago. They mostly grew up and attended schools in the area, and many were educators from early childhood through to tertiary. The group understood that the Pacific population in Aotearoa New Zealand was increasing, was mostly Aotearoa New Zealand-born (second or third generation migrants), and was youthful (Sorensen *et al.* 2015). Further, there was a shared concern about the engagement of Pacific learners in a largely mono-cultural education system and about the wellbeing of Pacific young people, including cultural identity and learning about their Pacific cultures and heritage.

Students enter a range of categories addressing the year's theme. Examples of recent themes are:

- Polynesian impact: How do Pacific people/Islands contribute to the wider global community?

- Building self-worth and resilience.

- Pacific leadership.

- Communities of learning: It takes a village to raise a child.

Categories invite cultural, academic (essay writing, speech – English and Pacific languages, science, quiz and debate) and artistic (poetry, talent, drama, wearable art, cinematography, visual art) contributions. Each school presents a cultural performance involving all members of the Pacific club, typically including traditional cultural songs, dance and costume from a selection of Pacific cultures. Pacific students from local primary or intermediate schools perform an opening item and are part of the audience throughout parts of the event. Information booths are set up during the day by organizations such as universities and health and youth services. The event culminates in a community concert with selected items performed, a guest speaker addressing the theme, and the announcement of category winners and an overall winner.

The success of the event relies heavily on Pacific parent, family and community support to teach and mentor the Pacific young people, particularly for the cultural performances and Pacific language speeches. Many weeks, or months, are committed to practice and preparation. Each school has a largely student-led Pacific or *Poly* club, providing leadership development opportunities. The event

---

2   For pictures and video clips of *Pasifika Fusion* visit www.facebook.com/PaSifika-FuSion-104136386297938.

occurs as a partnership between local government (funding), schools, families and Pacific communities.

Reflection on Pacific social work principles: love and relationship

The initiators of Pasifika Fusion demonstrate *'ofa* or *alofa* (love) with their voluntary contribution to organize and to keep improving and developing the event for well over a decade. Pasifika Fusion developed out of a shared love, concern and commitment by community members for the wellbeing of their Pacific young people. The community initiative reflects love by providing positive space and affirmation for Pacific young people in their academic, performative and artistic skills, centred within Pacific worldviews. Love also underpins Pasifika Fusion in speaking back to negative educational and social statistics in relation to Pacific young people through the celebration and nurturing of Pacific cultural and community strengths.

The relationship principle is also evident, with parents and families of students being central to this high point in school and Pacific community life. Urging younger students to offer an item and to observe positively harnesses the relationship principle, providing inspiration and cultural pride for them when they see their older siblings, cousins and community members participating and excelling. Finally, the event is both successful and sustainable due to relationships built over time and the collective effort among diverse parties (local government, families, schools and community).

Reflection questions

- What type of agency and policy contexts would best enable a social worker to support community development initiatives such as Pasifika Fusion?

- How comfortable and committed are you are to working collectively across diverse groups (such as ethnic minority groups and local government)?

- How can you work collectively and innovatively to create sustainable change in your local community with a different cultural community to your own?

Challenges for Pacific social work theory and practice

The case studies give examples of how Pacific principles – love, relationship and humility – inform individual, family, group and community level social work practice with Pacific peoples. The following section extends the consideration of social work with Pacific communities by discussing challenges and debates in the field of Pacific social work: promoting indigenous knowing in the context of the evidence-based debates; questioning the cultural competency discourse; and de-coloniality, anti-racism and environmentalism.

Promoting indigenous knowledge amid the evidence-based debates

What counts as legitimate social work knowledge and ways of knowing is contested (Karki 2016; Kumsa 2016). The current political and professional context in which social work with Pacific communities is practised is one where empirical evidence and big data modelling are emphasized as a basis for policy and programme decision making (Crichton, Templeton and Tumen 2015; Gillingham and Graham 2017). While positivist science is one source of knowing, Pacific social work theory necessarily draws from Pacific epistemologies (Gegeo and Watson-Gegeo 2001; Nabobo-Baba 2006; Ravulo 2016) and is concerned with the de-colonization of research and knowledge (Suaalii-Sauni and Fulu-Aiolupotea 2014). Pacific epistemology is integrally connected to the natural environment, and the expression and transmission of knowledge takes place in a relational context via geographic and oceanic features and in stories, chants and songs and includes spiritual dimensions (Gegeo and Watson-Gegeo 2001; Nabobo-Baba 2006; Newport 2001; Pala'amo 2017; Suaalii-Sauni and Fulu-Aiolupotea 2014).

Indigenous authors (Durie 2004; Weaver 2015) argue the benefits of intersecting indigenous and non-indigenous knowledge in ways that value the contribution of each, although doing so is not without its challenges (Ravulo 2016). Weaver (2015) encourages the intersection between indigenous ways and social work in a manner that makes the differences between them 'synergistic rather than antagonistic' (Weaver 2015, p.8). The intersection between Pacific knowing and dominant discourses, such as the debates on what constitutes evidenced-based practice, will be a tension needing negotiation in the advancement of Pacific social work.

Questioning the cultural competency discourse

Ironically, efforts to assure cultural competency in the training, licensing and employment of social workers presents a challenge for Pacific social work. Essentialist notions of cultural competency focus on the attainment of skills and knowledge related to the culture of 'others' (Nadan 2017). Essentialism is problematic since no one can ever be fully competent (skilful and knowledgeable) in every culture; clients will ascribe to various aspects of traditional and ethnic cultures and not to others in their day-to-day lives; and it can be harmful when a practitioner is unaware of their unknowing. With the degree of linguistic and cultural diversity under the label of *Pacific*, it is a misnomer to believe any one individual could be fully competent to practise across every Pacific population and context. Culture is lived and changes in the process of being lived. While a family may be Tongan, their expression of Tongan values may differ substantially from another Tongan family in the same neighbourhood. Similarly, if a social worker has extensive experience working with Samoan clients, it would be unwise to assume work with other Pacific families will be the same.

Nadan (2017) advocates for a social constructionist approach to cultural competency which gives due consideration to context and cultural fluidity. In a social constructionist perspective, unequal power relations in the broader society, which influence client realities and are present in the social worker–client relationship, are accounted for. Cultural humility is an appropriate alternative, which, instead of focusing on mastery of skills and knowledge, keeps a social worker's lack of knowing in view, requiring ongoing critical self-reflection and accountability at individual and institutional levels (Fisher-Borne, Cain and Martin 2015). Pacific perspectives for social work – illustrated with the principles of love, relationship and humility – align well with a social constructionist perspective and a position of cultural humility. Cultural humility is responsive to Pacific diversities and the structural inequalities affecting Pacific realities. Furthermore, cultural humility compels social work practitioners and institutions, Pacific and non-Pacific alike, to engage in an ongoing process of learning, engagement and accountability in relation to social work with Pacific communities.

De-coloniality, anti-racism and environmentalism in Pacific social work

To achieve deep, sustainable change for the wellbeing of Pacific communities, Pacific social work must join forces with more generic movements of de-coloniality, anti-racism and environmentalism. Colonialism is a pervasive challenge in Pacific social work, as it is in social work more broadly (Hart *et al.* 2016; Johnson and Yellow Bird 2012). De-colonization of social work requires confronting 'the ways in which the profession continues to participate in colonial projects... [and] acknowledgement and incorporation of Indigenous communities' strengths within social work theory and practice' (Johnson and Yellow Bird 2012, p.212). For example, indigenous resistance to American colonization and militarization in the Marianas is utilizing the indigenous Chamoru cultural framework of *inafa' maolet* (to make things good for each other), a foundation of Chamoru culture, to organize and strategize (Na'puti and Bevacqua 2015) while creating solidarity beyond the archipelago via social media (Frain 2016). Balancing a focus on ethnic-specific indigenous Pacific social work in its own right and a focus on theoretical, political and interdisciplinary alliances is essential in Pacific social work.

Anti-racism (Dominelli 2018) is an important, and convergent, theoretical perspective when working from a Pacific perspective. Outcomes for Pacific peoples are affected by structural, institutional, cultural and personal racism, particularly in the diaspora (Harris *et al.* 2006; Teaiwa and Mallon 2005; Vakalahi and Godinet 2014). Dominelli (2018, p.232) explains that in anti-racist practice, social workers change social work agencies, transform professional practice and contribute to and sustain anti-racist social relations in all communities.

Finally, the potential of alignment of Pacific social work with environmental social work (Boetto 2017; Dominelli 2013) is yet to be fully realized. Certainly, contemporary issues facing Pacific communities connect to broader environmental issues, such as climate change impacts in the Pacific Islands (Keener *et al.* 2012). The ontological position of identity as interconnectedness with nature as a basis for culturally sensitive community-based methodologies within Boetto's (2017) transformative eco-social model, for example, reflects what has been at the heart of indigenous Pacific approaches to social development since before the conception of social work as a profession. The challenge for Pacific social work is to consider the politics in the social construction of social work theory (Payne 2014) and to leverage engagement with international movements in social work theory and practice for the benefit of Pacific communities.

Conclusion

Indigenous knowledge, as well as Western social science knowledge, must inform social work (Hart *et al.* 2016; Lynn 2001; Mafile'o and Vakalahi 2016; Weaver 2015) to achieve 'social change and development, social cohesion, and the empowerment and liberation of people' (International Federation of Social Workers 2014). Emerging Pacific perspectives for social work – illustrated by the principles of love, relationship and humility – are contributing to the social construction of social work. The principle of love constructs social work as a way of life, which is compassionate and other-centred. Pacific relationship-based practice flows from Pacific collectivism and focuses on tending to the *va*, the space that relates. The humility principle shapes social work engagement, as well as intervention options.

Advancing Pacific social work involves addressing a number of challenges. Development of Pacific social work requires navigation of epistemological challenges, negotiating indigenous epistemologies amid the emphasis on evidence within a positivist paradigm, which defines much of the neoliberal practice context. A social constructionist perspective of cultural competency, and the more apt approach of cultural humility, is important for social work with Pacific communities. De-coloniality, anti-racism and environmentalism align for the advancement of Pacific social work. Pacific social work principles of love, relationship and humility, while rooted in Pacific worldviews, dynamically speak into global-level conversations on social work and social development and are relevant for informing contemporary intercultural social work.

Reflection questions

- From your own cultural worldview, how do you relate to the Pacific social work concepts of love, relationship and humility presented in this chapter?

- In what ways can you practise cultural humility when working interculturally?

References

Anae, M. (2010) 'Research for better Pacific schooling in New Zealand: Teu le Va – A Samoan perspective.' *MAI Review 1*, 1–24.

Autagavaia, M. (2001) 'Social Work with Pacific Island Communities.' In M. Connolly (ed.) *New Zealand Social Work: Contexts and Practice*. Melbourne, Australia: Oxford University Press.

Barsade, S.G. and O'Neill, O.A. (2014) 'What's love got to do with it? A longitudinal study of the culture of companionate love and employee and client outcomes in a long-term care setting.' *Administrative Science Quarterly 59*, 4, 551–598.

Bennardo, G. (2008) 'Metaphors, source domains, and key words in Tongan speech about social relationships: 'Ofa "Love" is giving.' *Anthropological Linguistics 50*, 2, 174–204.

Boetto, H. (2017) 'A transformative eco-social model: Challenging modernist assumptions in social work.' *British Journal of Social Work 47*, 48–67.

Crichton-Hill, Y. (2018) 'Pasifika Social Work.' In M. Connolly, L. Harms and J. Maidment (eds) *Social Work: Contexts and Practice*. Melbourne, Australia: Oxford University Press.

Crichton, S., Templeton, R. and Tumen, S. (2015) *Using Integrated Administrative Data to Understand Children at Risk of Poor Outcomes as Young Adults. Analytical Paper 15/01*. Wellington, New Zealand: New Zealand Treasury.

Dominelli, L. (2013) 'Environmental justice at the heart of social work practice: Greening the profession.' *International Journal of Social Welfare 22*, 431–439.

Dominelli, L. (2018) *Anti-racist Social Work*. London: Palgrave Macmillan Education.

Durie, M. (2004) 'Understanding health and illness: Research at the interface between science and indigenous knowledge.' *International Journal of Epidemiology 33*, 5, 1138–1143.

Efi, T.A.T.T.T. (2003) 'In search of meaning, nuance and metaphor in social policy.' *Social Policy Journal of New Zealand 20*, 49–63.

Faleolo, M.M. (2013) 'Cultural Authentication in Social Work Education: A Balancing Act.' In C. Noble, M. Henrickson and I.Y. Han (eds) *Social Work Education: Voices from the Asia Pacific*. Sydney, Australia: Sydney University Press.

Fisher-Borne, M., Cain, J.M. and Martin, S. (2015) 'From mastery to accountability: Cultural humility as an alternative to cultural competence.' *Social Work Education: The International Journal 34*, 2, 165–181.

Frain, S.C. (2016) 'Resisting political colonization and American militarization in the Marianas archipelago.' *AlterNative: An International Journal of Indigenous Peoples 12*, 3, 298–315.

Gegeo, D.W. and Watson-Gegeo, A. (2001) 'How we know: Kwara'ae rural villagers doing indigenous epistemology.' *The Contemporary Pacific 13*, 1, 55–88.

George, P.J. (2005) 'Service before self.' *The Fiji Social Workers' Journal 1*, 1, 38–39.

Gillingham, P. and Graham, T. (2017) 'Big data in social welfare: The development of a critical perspective on social work's latest "electronic turn".' *Australian Social Work 70*, 2, 135–147.

Godden, N.J. (2017) 'The love ethic: A radical theory for social work practice.' *Australian Social Work 70*, 4, 405–416.

Harris, R., Tobias, M., Jeffreys, M., Waldegrave, K., Karlsen, S. and Nazroo, J. (2006) 'Racism and health: The relationship between experience of racial discrimination and health in New Zealand.' *Social Science & Medicine 63*, 6, 1428–1441.

Hart, M., Burton, A.D., Hart, K., Rowe, G., Halonen, D. and Pompana, Y. (2016) *International Indigenous Voices in Social Work*. Newcastle upon Tyne: Cambridge Scholars Publishing.

'Ilaiu, C. (2009) 'Tauhi va: First space.' *Interstices: Journal of Architecture and Related Arts 10*, 20–31.

International Federation of Social Workers (2014) *Global Definition of Social Work*. Accessed on 04/09/2018 at www.ifsw.org/what-is-social-work/global-definition-of-social-work.

Johnson, J.T. and Yellow Bird, M. (2012) 'Indigenous Peoples and Cultural Survival.' In L.M. Healy and R.J. Link (eds) *Handbook of International Social Work: Human Rights, Development, and the Global Profession*. New York, NY: Oxford University Press.

Ka'ili, T.O. (2017) *Marking Indigeneity: The Tongan Art of Sociospatial Relations*. Tucson, AZ: University of Arizona Press.

Karki, K.K. (2016) 'Walking the complexities between two worlds: A personal story of epistemological tensions in knowledge production.' *Qualitative Social Work: Research and Practice 15*, 5/6, 628–639.

Kavaliku, S.L. (1961) An Analysis of 'Ofa. Unpublished Bachelor of Arts with Honors thesis. Cambridge, MA: Harvard University.

Keener, V.W., Marra, J.J., Finucane, M.L., Spooner, D. and Smith, M.H. (2012) *Climate Change and Pacific Islands: Indicators and Impacts: Report for the 2012 Pacific Islands Regional Climate Assessment*. Washington, DC: Island Press.

Kumsa, K.K. (2016) 'Thinking about research.' *Qualitative Social Work: Research and Practice 15*, 5/6, 602–609.

Lawihin, D. (2017) Building a Culturally Relevant Social Work Curriculum in Papua New Guinea: Connecting the Local and Global in Field Education. Master of Social Work (research) thesis. Clayton, Australia: Monash University.

Lynn, R. (2001) 'Learning from a "Murri Way".' *British Journal of Social Work 31*, 6, 903–916.

Mafile'o, T. (2004) 'Exploring Tongan social work: Fakafekau'aki and fakatokilalo.' *Qualitative Social Work: Research and Practice 3*, 3, 239–257.

Mafile'o, T. (2005) 'Community Development: A Tongan Perspective.' In M. Nash, R. Munford and K. O'Donoghue (eds) *Social Work Theory in Action*. London: Jessica Kingsley Publishers.

Mafile'o, T. (2006) 'Matakainga (behaving like family): The social worker–client relationship in Pasifika social work.' *Social Work Review/Tu Mau 18*, 1, 31–36.

Mafile'o, T. (2008) 'Tongan social work practice.' In M. Grey, J. Coates, and M. Yellow Bird (eds) *Indigenous Social Work Around the World: Towards Culturally Relevant Education and Practice*. Williston, VT: Ashgate Publishing.

Mafile'o, T. and Vakalahi, H.F.O. (2016) 'Indigenous social work across borders: Expanding social work in the South Pacific.' *International Social Work* (advance online publication). doi:10.1177/0020872816641750.

Mahina, 'O. (1992) The Tongan Traditional History Tala-ē-Fonua: A Vernacular Ecology Centred Historico-Cultural Concept. PhD dissertation. Canberra, Australia: Australian National University.

Mila-Schaaf, K. (2006) 'Va-centred social work: Possibilities for a Pacific approach to social work.' *Tu Mau/Social Work Review 18*, 1, 8–13.

Ministry of Social Development (MSD) (2015) *Va'aifetu: Guardians and Guardianship of Stars. Principles, Cultural Frameworks, Guidelines – Part II*. Accessed on 17/09/2018 at https://practice.orangatamariki.govt.nz/assets/documents/knowledge-base-practice-frameworks/working-with-pacific-peoples/vaaifetu-part-2-final.pdf.

Morley, L. and Ife, J. (2002) 'Social work and a love of humanity.' *Australian Social Work 55*, 1, 69–77.

Mulitalo-Lauta, P.T. (2000) *Fa'asamoa and Social Work within the New Zealand Context*. Palmerston North, New Zealand: Dunmore Press.

Mulitalo-Lauta, P.T. and Menon, K. (2006) 'Art therapy and Pacific Island peoples in New Zealand: A preliminary observation and evaluation from a Pacific Island perspective.' *Tu Mau/Social Work Review 18*, 1, 22–30.

Nabobo-Baba, U. (2006) *Knowing and Learning: An Indigenous Fijian Approach*. Suva, Fiji Institute of Pacific Studies, The University of the South Pacific.

Nadan, Y. (2017) 'Rethinking "cultural competence" in international social work.' *International Social Work 60*, 1, 74 –83.

Nakhid, C. (2009) 'Conclusion: The Concept and Circumstances of Pacific Migration and Transnationalism.' In H. Lee and S.T. Francis (eds) *Migration and Transnationalism: Pacific Perspectives*. Canberra, Australia: ANU Press.

Na'puti, T.R. and Bevacqua, M.L. (2015) 'Militarization and resistance from Guåhan: Protecting and defending Pågat.' *American Quarterly 67*, 3, 837–858.

Newport, C. (2001) 'Knowing practice Pasifika.' *Social Work Review/Tu Mau 13*, 3, 6–9.

O'Leary, T., Tsui, M.S. and Ruch, G. (2013) 'The boundaries of the social work relationship revisited: Towards a connected, inclusive and dynamic conceptualisation.' *British Journal of Social Work 43*, 1, 135–153.

Pacific Island Community and Social Workers Auckland (1986) 'Good social work practice: A Pacific Island perspective.' *New Zealand Social Work Journal 11*, 2, 6–9.

Pala'amo, A.F. (2017) Fetu'utu'una'i le Vā – Navigating Relational Space: An Exploration of Traditional and Contemporary Pastoral Counselling Practices for Samoans. Unpublished PhD thesis. Palmerston North, New Zealand: Massey University.

Palmer, P.J. (1993) *To Know as We Are Known: Education as a Spiritual Journey*. San Francisco, CA: Harper.

Payne, M. (2014) *Modern Social Work Theory*. Houndmills: Palgrave Macmillan.

Ravulo, J. (2016) 'Pacific epistemologies in professional social work practice, policy and research.' *Asia Pacific Journal of Social Work and Development 26*, 4, 191–202.

Reynolds, M. (2016) 'Relating to va: Re-viewing the concept of relationships in Pasifika education in Aotearoa New Zealand.' *AlterNative: An International Journal of Indigenous Peoples 12*, 2, 190–202.

Shek, D.T.L., Golightley, M. and Holloway, M. (2017) 'Editorial: A snapshot of social work in the Asia-Pacific Region.' *British Journal of Social Work 47*, 1–8.

Sorensen, D. Jensen, S., Rigamoto, M. and Pritchard, M. (2015) *Pacific People in New Zealand: How Are We Doing?* Auckland, New Zealand: Pasifika Futures.

Suaalii-Sauni, T. and Fulu-Aiolupotea, S.M. (2014) 'Decolonising Pacific research, building Pacific research communities and developing Pacific research tools: The case of the talanoa and the faafaletui in Samoa.' *Asia Pacific Viewpoint 55*, 3, 331–344.

Talaimanu, F.U.W. (2006) 'Youth social work enhanced by fa'asamoa imperatives: Patience, humility and balance.' *Social Work Review/Tu Mau 18*, 1, 42–46.

Teaiwa, T. and Mallon, S. (2005) 'Ambivalent Kinships? Pacific People in New Zealand.' In J.H. Liu, T. McCreanor, T. McIntosh and T. Teaiwa (eds) *New Zealand Identities: Departures and Destinations*. Wellington, New Zealand: Victoria University Press.

Tuagalu, I. (2008) 'Heuristics of the Va.' *AlterNative: An International Journal of Indigenous Peoples 4*, 1, 108–126.

Vakalahi, H.F.O. and Godinet, M.T. (2014) *Transnational Pacific Islander Americans and Social Work: Dancing to the Beat of Another Drum*. Atlanta, GA: National Association of Social Workers.

Walker, S. (2015) 'New wine from old wineskins, a fresh look at Freire.' *Aotearoa New Zealand Social Work 27*, 4, 47–56.

Ward, A., Turney, D. and Ruch, G. (2010) *Relationship-Based Social Work: Getting to the Heart of Practice*. London: Jessica Kingsley Publishers.

Weaver, H. (2015) 'Social Work, Indigenous Ways, and the Power of Intersection.' In C. Fejo-King and P. Mataira (eds) *Expanding the Conversation: International Indigenous Social Workers' Insights into the Use of Indigenist Knowledge and Theory in Practice*. Darwin, Australia: Magpie Goose Publishing.

Wendt, A. (1996) 'Tatauing the post-colonial body.' *Span 42–43*, 15–29.

Yeates, D.B. (2013) 'Pacific Social Work and its Functional Alternative.' In A. Sasaki (ed.) *(Professional) Social Work and its Functional Alternatives*. Tokyo: Social Work Research Institute, Asian Center for Welfare in Society, Japan College of Social Work and Asian Pacific Association for Social Work Education.

Chapter 12

Cross-Cultural Social Work Practice

ROSALEEN OW

Introduction

This chapter explores cross-cultural social work practice. In cross-cultural social work, the term *cultural diversity* is a central idea and encompasses a range of definitions of cultural and social groups. These include: people who are associated with their race (inherited membership by descent), and groups defined by culture (behavioural expression of a preferred lifestyle), religion (affiliation to a set of transcendental beliefs), gender affiliations (identity related to sexuality) and ethnicity (identity that is socially constructed or legal). This chapter will focus on cultural diversity from the perspective of ethnic diversity. The term *ethnicity* used in this chapter refers primarily to the description of groups of people in terms of identity (Williams and Johnson 2010) which is socially constructed and *political*. Ethnicity is used as a means or a label for negotiation and recognition in administrative statistics, and has implications for social policy, specialist welfare and legal rights.

Cross-cultural social work has been conceptualized in a number of ways, partly because of the different ways in which culture is defined. It is important to try to understand what the term culture means in the context of cross-cultural social work. According to Spencer-Oatley (2012), the term culture is difficult to define but there are some key characteristics of culture shared across the different definitions. These characteristics include the way in which culture manifests, such as in observable artefacts, values and underlying assumptions or worldviews related to nature, time and space and to human activities and relationships. Definitions of culture typically include references to differences in ancestry and language, traditions and way of life and particular cognitive maps or worldviews. Lum (2011, p.18), for example, summarized culture as a way of life involving 'shared meanings and behaviors in a social activity setting with external and internal learning patterns that are constantly changing'. The emphasis here is that culture is not only about shared meanings and behaviours, but is dynamic and may change over time and setting. Since culture is learned and not something a person is born with, it is specific to a group and a result of socialization. Individuals in society are organized in many different social groups (such as family, school, friends, religion, career and recreation) so in a sense people can potentially belong to several different cultural groups at the same time, that is, possess multiple identities. In the context of diversity, culture has also been conceptualized from an ecological perspective as 'a site of differences and power differentials and as relational and dynamic' (Ling 2014, p.9) among different groups of people, such as disadvantaged and marginalized minority groups.

Culture changes when there is diffusion and borrowing of ideas and artefacts from one culture to another (for example, through the increasing use of digital devices in communication and the sharing of thoughts through social media). Therefore, it is always helpful to define the culture of a social group with reference to the possible changes that have taken place over time, that is, the chronosystem from the ecological perspective in human development. 'A chronosystem encompasses change or consistency over time not only in the characteristics of the person but also of the environment in which the person lives' (Bronfenbrenner 1994, p.1646).

Lastly but of immense importance is that culture is a descriptive concept and not an evaluative one. Terms such as *high and low culture* or *primitive and civilised culture* are unhelpful as culture relates to a society or a social group and not to individuals who are deemed to exhibit the characteristics that may be associated with such terms. A more helpful approach is to view culture as something that is similar within a particular social group or different among different groups of people (Spencer-Oatley 2012).

The remainder of the chapter will explore the literature and emerging theories in cross-cultural social work. It will present case studies to illustrate the key elements of practice and it will identify some tensions in this field of practice. The chapter concludes with some questions for further reflection.

Cross-cultural social work

In the context of social work literature, diverse approaches to the definition of culture are also evident. Beyond ethnicity and race, Fong and Furuto (2001) in the USA argued that the traditional focus of social work on helping the oppressed and vulnerable also involved recognizing that the culture of the help-seeker is embedded in the multiple and complex relationships among the individual help-seeker, the family and the community. Hugman (2013), for example, discussed culture in the context of values and ethics embedded in everyday life such as in relation to the expression of care of vulnerable children and the definition and treatment of neglect and abuse. In New Zealand, Walker and Eketone (2014) added another dimension to the definition of culture in the context of social work with Māori, the indigenous population. Culture is not just about language and beliefs but is a way of life that is closely associated with indigenous knowledge and meaning, including the use of land and spaces and natural resources. Culture, therefore, can be conceived as a cognitive map that guides the interpretation of experiences and behaviour and the way in which behaviour is interpreted.

The strengths and the challenges in working with the *person-in-environment* in problem definition and resolution are also closely related to the culture of the help-seeker as well as the helper. For example, in an Australian study on the loss and bereavement experiences of employees and managers in Aboriginal health and education services in South Australia and New South Wales, Anderson *et al.* (2011) illustrated practices that are culturally safe and supportive. In the 12-month study, more than half of the Aboriginal employees attended seven or more funerals, with one-third attending between 12 and 30 funerals. Having managers and colleagues who had shared knowledge and experiences of issues related to grief and loss among Aboriginal people helped in the flexible interpretations of policy guidelines within the system, such as the rules guiding bereavement leave.

Since the definition of culture is a complex endeavour, it is not surprising that the definition of cultural competence as a construct in working across cultures is equally challenging. Cultural competence is one of a number of concepts, such as cultural awareness, cultural sensitivity, cultural safety and, more recently, cultural humility in cross-cultural practice (Danso 2016). Cultural competence is conceptualized as having three major elements, namely: the cultural awareness of the worker's own cultural values, beliefs and attitudes; cultural knowledge of diverse groups, their needs, values and beliefs; and the worker's skills in using knowledge about others to provide culturally appropriate services (Chiu *et al.* 2013; Hendricks 2003). Walker and Eketone (2014, p.75) described the three elements of cultural competency as: cognitive knowledge, affective competency and behavioural competency, involving knowledge of the other culture; understanding and an ability to identify with some aspects of the other culture; and, the ability to behave in an appropriate manner in different cultural settings.

According to Lum (2011, p.3), 'cultural competence is a relational, dialogical process (a dialogue rather than worker's competence) between the worker and the client, between cultures, and between people and context'. Hence, apart from building the cultural competence of the worker, the emphasis in cultural competence should be on building the competence of the worker and the help-seeker together so that they can be proficient in using cultural ways of coping with the needs and problems of daily living in a participatory relationship.

There are also overlapping theoretical models of what constitutes culturally competent practice. Diverse approaches to what is considered appropriate cross-cultural social work include models that emphasize the strengths perspective, and empowerment theories that address working with marginalization and social justice (for example, Fong and Furuto 2001). Other models emphasize cultural awareness and ethnic sensitivity, such as the impact of multi-culturalism and the impact on welfare policies and the delivery of social services (for example, Devore and Schlesinger 1999; Sue and Sue 2008). In addition, the concern with cultural awareness extends to the professionalization of the social worker embracing the sub-culture of the profession itself, as described by Green (1998). Green's (1998) discussion on help-seeking behaviour in the human services posited that there are differences in the conceptualization of the help-seeking process between social work professionals and help-seekers as a result of the utilization of different *stocks of knowledge*, and among minority social workers and their clients arising from both cultural and professional socialization.

In a more recent discourse, Yan (2008a), in a study with 30 practitioners in Canada, found that social workers experienced at least three different modes of crossing in cross-cultural practice. First, most study participants saw crossing as unilateral where the workers entered the client's cultural frame in a unilateral way with the focus on the client's culture but where the worker's culture was blocked from the client. Second, there was bilateral crossing where cross-cultural engagement was a two-way process. The client had access to the worker's culture when the worker through self-disclosure allowed the client to have some access into the worker's cultural boundaries. The control over the amount of mutual crossing remained in the hands of the worker. Last, a higher level of crossing appeared to be one of blending and merging of two cultural views, which resulted in the construction of a new form of understanding in problem definition and resolution. Yan (2008a, p.285) summarized this process as 'searching for the commonality and vantage point [which] is important for a common goal or solution that is acceptable to both cultures' and not whose culture is more important.

Emerging theory and literature

From the discussion above on culture and cross-cultural social work we can understand why cross-cultural social work is increasingly being recognized as an emerging issue in social work practice. The latest online information shows that the International Federation of Social Workers (IFSW) (2018) currently has 116 member organizations across five regions of the world (Africa, Asia and Pacific, Europe, Latin America and North America). Social work across the globe is concerned with the wellbeing of many different peoples and cultures. With the increase in immigration (for various reasons), almost every country has a population that comprises individuals with different ethnic, religious and socio-economic backgrounds. Cross-cultural social work represents ethically sound practice.

From a cognitive-humanistic perspective, social work has a responsibility to engage the whole person in problem solving. Goldstein (1986) described this as engaging the various *persons* of the self, namely, the *person of the mind*, the *person of community*, the *person of faith*, and the *person of principle*, who influence how a problem is defined and resolved. Seen through a phenomenological lens, these *persons* of the self are largely a product of socialization and hence are culturally embedded.

Hugman (2013) discussed in depth the assumptions underlying the idea of universal values and ethics. In recent years, following the critique of Midgley (1981) that the internationalization of social work is a form of professional imperialism, there had been similar questions about the relevance of transporting Western values and ethics to other countries in the non-Western context (Ling, Martin and Ow 2014; Osei-Hwedi, Ntseane and Jacques 2006; Yip 2004). Current globalization and migration challenge the development and delivery of welfare services, particularly in the allocation of resources in welfare-oriented states such as the UK (Williams and Johnson 2010) where new population groups may present a different set of needs from the more mono-cultural service-seekers of the past. A diverse population therefore calls for diversity in the social work workforce and cultural competence in the provision of professional social services.

In addition to existing ethnic diversity in many societies, new communities emerging as a result of humanitarian immigration may pose different challenges in terms of the needs arising from experiences of loss, trauma, grief and experiences or the witnessing of atrocities in their home country. Initial adjustment for these new communities might also be complicated by difficulties with language and other social factors such as shame and fear in seeking and receiving assistance (Abraham and Martin 2014). There is some similarity in the accessing of health and social services for such new communities with that of other minority groups such as indigenous groups that may be smaller in numbers in the wider population, for example, indigenous people in New Zealand, Australia, Canada and other parts of the Asia Pacific. Ramsden (1990) first raised the notion of *cultural safety* for such groups in the context of nursing as a result of the negative experiences that Māori patients had when using health services in New Zealand. The Nursing Council of New Zealand (2005, amended 2011, p.7) refers to cultural safety as 'the experience of the recipient of nursing service and extends beyond cultural awareness and cultural sensitivity'. An individual who feels alienated, humiliated or discouraged when accessing services may not feel safe in help-seeking.

The idea of cultural safety thus extends beyond cultural awareness and cultural competence to the underlying unequal relationships that exist between the environment and the service user in cross-cultural encounters. An individual's lived experience of personal troubles is compounded by historical, political, economic and social factors wherein the troubles are located. Williams (1999, p.212) describes cultural safety as an environment that is safe for people and where there is no assault, challenge or denial of their identity and what they need. Cultural safety includes the need for both practitioner and institutional cultures to avoid victim-blaming in the provision and delivery of services. Cultural safety is perceived as choosing the client's perspective as the norm in the helping process and definition of outcome. McEldowney and Connor (2011) further elaborated on this through an ethic of care approach, which involved collaborative working relationships within a collectivist framework. Yeung (2016) conceptualized cultural safety as emphasizing transfer of the power to the patient (client), recognizing the feeling of safety during care, reducing the emphasis on the professional's knowledge of indigenous culture and recognizing the structural threats that are in the system as a whole.

An emerging concept arising from the critique of cultural competence is that of cultural humility. In a schematic representation of the terminology that is generally used to describe culturally appropriate care, Yeung (2016, p.5) defined cultural humility as practice where the provider of care does not assume their norms are *correct* or universal. The provider acknowledges that they also bear cultural values that impact on the care provided. In contrast to cultural humility, cultural competence assumes that the care provider has sufficient cultural awareness, skills and knowledge about different social groups to deliver appropriate services in a diverse population. Cultural competence also assumes that there are universal norms within a particular social group but this may not always be the case. For example, the Chinese are not just people whose ancestors were from China but they are also members of the many provincial and dialect groups in China with linguistic differences and sub-cultural family norms and values. Similarly, among indigenous people in Canada, the USA and the Asia Pacific (including Australia and New Zealand), there are differences (and similarities) across tribal groupings. Hence, it is important to recognize that there is diversity within diversity in the move towards developing cultural competence.

Perhaps it is this recognition of the complexity within diversity and the myth of universal norms even within identified social groups that has resulted in recent criticisms of cultural competence and a move to replace cultural competence with cultural humility. However, Danso (2016, p.2) argued that 'although cultural humility sounds semantically appealing and politically correct, it appears not to have greater practice advantage over cultural competence'. He further argued that the fundamental underpinnings of cultural humility had already been developed and were key principles in anti-oppressive social work and education, and it was essentially a rebranding of anti-oppressive practice. Regardless of whether one accepts Danso's (2016) conclusion, the idea of rebranding can actually be a positive one. Seen from the perspective of the more paternalistic and collectivist social and political systems, in many parts of Asia a collaborative rather than a confronting stance in advocacy may actually be more culturally acceptable. In cultures such as those among the Chinese where *face* behaviours and interpersonal relationships (*guanxi*) are important in working relationships (Bond and Hwang 1988; Ow 1991), many decisions are made based on trust and goodwill arising from the nature of the encounter.

Intercultural communication is essential for an interdependent global society (Samovar *et al.* 2017), especially in the face of mass migration because of poverty and economic opportunities, political oppression and conflict amid competition for natural and economic resources. In addition, overseas travel to experience other cultures and lifestyles for most millennials is part of growing up and an existential search for purpose and direction, compounding the significance of intercultural encounters. People use language to communicate ideas, feelings and experiences. It is also a vehicle for social interaction. Imagine an interpersonal encounter in a foreign land where you do not understand a word spoken by the other party and have to depend entirely on your interpretation of non-verbal behaviour. What do you think could be the nature and consequence of such an encounter? Language is also a means to develop and maintain collaboration and social cohesion within and across groups of people. Prolonged intercultural communication where people interacting do not really understand each other may result in conflict arising from misunderstanding of meanings and intent in verbal or non-verbal expressions, and internal conflict when confronted with culturally different beliefs, values or behavioural protocols that make it difficult to negotiate and co-construct acceptable meanings and outcomes.

These observations and questions are relevant for cross-cultural social work. In an early study with American and Japanese students, Barnlund (1975) found that the willingness to disclose information was associated with what could be conceptualized as the *public* and *private* self of the individual. In most cases, the amount and type of personal information that both groups of students were willing to disclose verbally and non-verbally were closely associated with the norms of the cultural environment within which they were socialized. While generalization needs to be avoided, understanding that the concept of the *public* and *private* self does exist in reality could help in preventing intrusion and misunderstanding in intercultural encounters involving engagement and problem-solving in cross-cultural social work.

Nye (2006) illustrated how the subtle and complex differences in the client's affective worlds can challenge the worker's capacity to understand people who are culturally different when there is a lack of verbal understanding. The following example is about Nye, an American academic who worked in partnership with a Thai medical social worker Suwanrang Dansawan at Suan Dok Hospital in Chiang Mai, northern Thailand. Nye (2006, p.305) illustrates the importance of verbal proficiency by noting that:

> Because I did not know Thai well enough to follow the content of the sessions accurately, during our debriefing, I relied on Suwanrang to translate, to relay the actual content of what had been said. During the session, I had to rely on other sources of information, on other cues – body language, gestures, tone, intonation – and on my clinical intuitive skills, my capacity to read affective communication. My experience in these sessions, my struggle to understand what was going on in the room between Suwanrang and her clients, brought the challenge of understanding across cultures into stark relief.

Similarly, a study (Pierce 2007) on cross-cultural communication differences between northern, remote indigenous community members in

Canada and service providers and professionals found that language and translation, and professional terms and jargon were among the factors that created misunderstanding in cross-cultural communication. For example, in translation there could be instances where two languages do not have terms for a similar experience or where one language does not have terms that can accurately express the feelings or experiences of the other culture. In the professionalization process, social workers are trained to think and speak in line with the theories and models of practice taught in the curriculum. The terms that social workers may use, such as resistance, defensive, motivation, learned responses and problem definition, might be quite alien to the clients who may use only lay language to tell their story and to express the help and support they are seeking.

An associated practice issue is how social workers incorporate cultural beliefs and values into their practice. Understanding the place of spirituality in practice is an example of this challenge. In social workers' drive towards being non-partisan, non-judgemental and non-imposing as a profession, the topic of spirituality and the significance of the spiritual resources that many clients may depend on have not always been adequately addressed in social work education and practice. However, in recent years, there has been growth in the development of conceptual frameworks that include spirituality – an aspect of being that aligns with the worldviews of many of the clients that social workers serve. For example, Fukuyama and Sevig (1999, p.156) wrote about a holistic, integrative model 'for psychological, multicultural, and spiritual growth' that linked psychological development to spiritual evolution and vice versa in the context of counselling. Spirituality is associated but not synonymous with religion and is 'concerned with transcending self and opening to the cosmos (God, Mystery, Ground of Being, or the Sacred)' (Fukuyama and Sevig 1999, p.157).

The body, mind and spirit connection has been developed by Boone (2014), Chan (2001), Gold (2010) and Lee et al. (2009) as training manuals which illustrate this integrative approach from an Eastern perspective. In particular, the body–mind–spirit approach is found to be relevant in the context of death, dying and bereavement, life events that are both cultural and personal in nature (for example, Chan and Chow 2010; Kellehear 2000; Mun and Ow 2017; Ow 2014).

Two case examples below from a qualitative study with Chinese mothers in Singapore illustrate the importance of spirituality in the adjustment to the bereavement of young children through maintaining some form of continuing bond (Mun and Ow 2017, p.15):

Having their ashes in the house makes me feel that they are still part of the family. I don't want to deny their existence. They had indeed been part of the family. … They are still very much alive inside my heart…even though you (deceased children) are up there (in heaven), you will always be remembered by me and missed by me. (Catholic mother who lost two children: a son at 45 days old and a daughter at 3 years old)

After he passed away, he returned to me in my dreams and he told me 'Can you do me a favour? Just for three years, do good deeds.' I said ok, what do you want? Then he said, 'I see all the children in the hospital, they are very pitiful. They have no Children's Day celebration, no Christmas Day celebration, no Chinese New Year celebration. On any of these days, you can go there, just go and make them happy.' I have done so for two years, there is still one more year to go. (Taoist mother who lost a 12 year-old son)

In developing responsive practice that recognises the central role of cultural values and beliefs, social workers will mediate the tensions and challenges of this practice.

Cross-cultural practice: opportunities, tensions and challenges

Social workers are at the centre of multi-faceted tensions arising from cultural similarities and differences among them and clients, organizations and society. Some of these tensions may exist between cultural competence and cultural humility; cultural awareness and diversity; and, the co-existence of biculturalism and multiculturalism.

Singapore is an example of a multicultural society where social workers need to develop knowledge and skills to manage the tensions in working across cultures. For example, the following scenario provides an example of cross-cultural social work practice. Inter-ethnic marriages have increased over the years among its own multicultural population along with international marriages between Singapore citizens and foreigners. In 2016, 21.5 percent of total marriages were inter-ethnic, up nearly threefold from 7.6 percent in 1990 (Department of Statistics Singapore 2016). International marriage trends in Singapore also showed a certain class hierarchy, with highly educated women marrying men from advanced Western economies and less educated men marrying women from lower-income countries such as China, Vietnam and Indonesia (*Straits Times* 3 January 1999 cited in Yeoh *et al.* 2013*)*.

Commercially matched marriage migrants (mainly women) from lower-income countries have been viewed as contributing to the social problems of the society because of low-income generation, lack of fit in an urban environment, and language difficulties. However, these women also perform much-needed services, such as helping care for elderly persons; they increase the fertility rate and take care of what might have continued to be a low-income bachelor home. These women hold multiple identities: as a wife and mother in the Singapore context, as a daughter with filial responsibilities to parents in their home country, as a *foreigner* in the local community and, in terms of social policies, as a non-citizen with few rights to social benefits and old age savings, being totally dependent on the husband. Social work with such transnational families involves understanding the multiple identities of these women, whose vulnerability is mainly a result of immigration laws where marrying a Singapore citizen does not automatically qualify them for permanent resident status (PR), let alone Singapore citizenship (Yeoh *et al.* 2013). Cross-cultural social work in such situations involves working with the individual at the micro level (individual and family), systemically at the meso level to harness community resources, and at the macro level for case advocacy in the event that the woman is not granted a visit pass. The following case study (Yeoh *et al.* 2013, p.1933) illustrates the complexities and challenges in working with such individuals.

Case study: Thach

Thach (20 years old) had been married to a 55-year-old widowed truck driver for ten months. She had serious glaucoma and was in need of surgery, without which she felt she would become blind. Being a foreigner in Singapore, she was dependent on her husband to finance her medical expenses. When she approached her husband to request an eye examination with a specialist, he repeatedly tried to avoid the issue, giving the excuse that 'he [didn't] see any problem with her eye'. Disappointed by his tight-fisted nature, Thach was anxious to secure PR status so that she would be able to work to support herself. She had also hoped to be able to send money back to her family in Vietnam, which had been struggling to make ends meet.

Thach shared that she was careful not to breach the relationship with her husband. While he was *a good man*, Thach revealed that she hated sex with him, because she could not stand the thought that an *old man* was that passionate for sex [every night]. Despite feeling both reluctant and uncomfortable, she confessed: 'If I don't do that, he won't love me anymore. So everything he does to me, I do the same for him... But honestly, it was very disgusting to me.' She noticed that every time she consented to him sexually, he became generous to her the following day. It was a case of *no sex, no money*.

In such cases, tensions for the social worker include: understanding the role and authority of the husband in a traditional hierarchical Asian family; the difficulty in discussing intimate issues such as sexual behaviour, especially across gender; and, the sensitivity required in the discussion of financial matters given that a person's financial status may be considered as part of the *private self* not easily accessible to an outsider. In addition, in cross-cultural social work practice, the social worker often has to work with the non-citizen client within the constraints of structural issues such as the immigration laws of the country, and to resolve potential tensions in casework with the individual and case advocacy within the wider macro-system.

Another challenge in cross-cultural social work practice may present itself in the development of cultural awareness. To what extent is this really possible? Spencer-Oatley (2012, pp.16–17) in discussing the core concepts of the term and meaning of culture concluded that there are at least six mutually related ideas about culture that are inadequate if used to define culture and for understanding social action, conflict and resolution. These six ideas include the belief that culture is homogenous, it is a thing that can act independently of human action, it is evenly distributed among group members, that an individual possesses only one culture, culture is synonymous with tradition or customary ways of behaving, and culture is timeless, non-changing over the years. In challenging these ideas, researchers have identified the difficulty in determining what is specific and unique and what is universal among population groups. Weaver (2001, pp.178–182) illustrated this difficulty in discussing organization and community assessment with indigenous people in the USA. For example, there seems to be no total consensus about terminology in identifying the indigenous community. Some groups might prefer one term over another, such as Native Americans or First Nations People or just broad tribal affiliations (for example, the Cherokee, the Navajo, the Anishnabeg or the Dakota). Although there are commonalities among the groups, such as the importance of community, and the belief that ancestors and future generations are equally relevant in considering actions in the present, the use of a collective term in identifying the groups may obscure the diversity among them. This fact may also be equally relevant for other indigenous communities across the globe such as in Australia, New Zealand, Malaysia, Vietnam, China and the Pacific Islands.

The challenge explored above foregrounds the importance of social workers building an understanding of the self as a socially constructed entity with multiple identities that exist in situated interactions rather than one self-defining identity that is independent of the social contexts surrounding it. Multiple identities may develop from living in a multi-ethnic environment such as New Zealand (Keddell 2007). Inter-ethnic marriage is the most common micro, meso, and macro context for the development of multiple identities. The practical implications of accepting that people can have, and are allowed to decide on, multiple identities rather than one ascribed identity through descent or ethnicity are social and political.

Socially, decentred and multiple identities can be manifested in how an individual talks and behaves with different people according to age cohort, gender and in communication such as the use of slang and accent. In New Zealand, Keddell (2006), in a study that examined whether there is a *true* Samoan identity among persons with one Pākehā parent and one Samoan parent, cited an example of tensions that may arise in social interactions for people with multiple identities or ethnicities from a study with children of inter-ethnic marriages in Samoa, as follows:

> This dynamic has an impact on my participants. It was one of the influences that resulted in them mostly identifying as being Samoan, especially if the enquirer is Pākehā. Even the one participant (A) who identified as mostly Pākehā felt he could not baldly state 'I'm Pākehā' without further explanation. (Keddell 2006, p.48)

Another source of tension comes from within the term cultural competence, where there is an assumption that it is possible for a social worker within one particular cultural context to understand the meanings and behave appropriately in another culture in which they have not lived as part of that community. Recent discourse highlights the need for cultural humility, where expert knowledge and problem-solving resources are perceived to be located in the clients and within their communities. This discourse suggests that social workers should therefore no longer see their role as knowing enough to help *fix* the problem but rather to facilitate and seek to empower the clients to resolve their needs in the context of their cultural knowledge and resources (which may include the spiritual).

In addition, Yan (2008b) found that being a minority social worker in a multicultural context may create its own tension because sharing the same background or experience can be both beneficial and problematic. The benefits had largely been expounded under the development of the cultural awareness and cultural competence agenda but the problems that may arise when working with clients from the same community had not been as fully discussed. Yan (2008b) found that some minority social workers felt that being the same caused extra burdens because clients could have unreasonable expectations of the worker in terms of change.

Some clients may resist working with a worker from the same community for fear of gossip or losing face in the community, or holding a view that the minority worker may not be as effective as a worker from the mainstream community. Workers themselves may experience countertransference as a response to the client's struggles or experience. In view of such conceptual and practice tensions, there is therefore a need to search for coherence among social workers in the context of cross-cultural social work (Yan 2008b).

Conclusion

The literature on cross-cultural social work practice can be categorized under three main areas: cultural awareness (of one's own culture and that of the other); cultural competence (the ability to translate knowledge about another culture into an effective and respectful process of help-giving); and cultural safety (providing a service where the recipient feels safe, dignified and accepted in the interface of the cross-cultural encounter). Cultural tensions may arise when social workers, in an attempt to develop cultural awareness, fail to understand and acknowledge the *diversity* that exists within populations, resulting in the use of stereotypical images and behaviours in their practice, contradicting (perhaps unconsciously) their national professional code of ethics.

A strict line between the West and the non-West reflects the boundaries of the past (Chow 1987; Midgley 1981), However, new paradigms consist of an integration of the traditional West and the non-West in a multicultural context where people embrace something from each other, thus creating a new world citizen seeking to be comfortable with multiple identities. These identities encompass diverse worldviews aligned with the different contexts wherein people live and work. The challenge for cross-cultural practice is for social workers to work together with service users to find an accepted cultural space to explore intercultural relations and practice that embraces respect for diversity and the practice of self-determination and social justice.

Reflection questions

- Reflect on an experience of a cross-cultural encounter. How did you feel about that encounter, for example in learning about cultural awareness and cultural safety? To what extent is the concept of multiple identities relevant in integrating your understanding with that particular experience?

- Given the heterogeneity of human groupings in most societies, would the term multicultural social work be more appropriate than cross-cultural social work?

- To what extent do you think social, economic and political structures affect the acceptance and practice of cross-cultural social work?

- How is the concept of *multiple identities* relevant to your own experience of identity formation? In your opinion, how would this concept of multiple identities influence your social work practice with people from other cultures?

References

Abraham, N. and Martin, J. (2014) 'Cultural Safety with New and Emerging Communities: Older Refugee Experiences of Health and Welfare Services in Australia.' In H.K. Ling, J. Martin and R. Ow (eds) *Cross-Cultural Social Work: Local and Global.* South Yarra, Autralia: Palgrave Macmillan.

Anderson, M., Bilney, J., Bycroft, N., Cockatoo-Collins, D. *et al.* (2011) 'Closing the gap: Support for indigenous loss.' *Australian Nursing Journal 19,* 10, 25–27.

Barnlund, D.C. (1975) *Public and Private Self in Japan and the United States.* Tokyo: Simul Press.

Bond, M.H. and Hwang, K.K. (1988) 'The Social Psychology of Chinese People.' In M.H. Bond (ed.) *The Psychology of the Chinese People.* New York, NY: Oxford University Press.

Boone, M.S. (2014) *Mindfulness and Acceptance in Social Work: Evidence-Based Interventions and Emerging Applications.* Oakland, CA: Context Press.

Bronfenbrenner, U. (1994) 'Ecological Models of Human Development.' In T. Husen and T.N. Postlethwaite (eds) *International Encyclopedia of Education* Vol. 3 (2nd edition). Oxford: Pergamon Press.

Chan, C.L.W. (2001) *An Eastern Body-Mind-Spirit Approach: A Training Manual with One-Second Techniques.* Department of Social Work and Social Administration, the University of Hong Kong, Hong Kong: Hong Kong University Press.

Chan, C.L.W. and Chow, A.Y.M. (2010) *Death, Dying and Bereavement: A Hong Kong Chinese Experience.* Hong Kong: Hong Kong University Press.

Chiu, C.Y., Lonner, W.J., Matsumoto, D. and Ward, C. (2013) 'Cross-cultural competence: Theory, research, and application.' *Journal of Cross-Cultural Psychology 44,* 843–848.

Chow, N.W.S. (1987) 'Western and Chinese ideas of social welfare.' *International Social Work 30,* 1, 31–41.

Danso, R. (2016) 'Cultural competence and cultural humility: A critical reflection on key cultural diversity concepts.' *Journal of Social Work* (online first). doi: 10.1177/146817316654341.

Department of Statistics Singapore (2016) *Singapore in Figures 2016.* Singapore: Department of Statistics.

Devore, W. and Schlesinger, E.G. (1999) *Ethnic-Sensitive Social Work Practice* (5th edition). Boston, MA: Allyn and Bacon.

Fong, R. and Furuto, S. (2001) *Culturally Competent Practice: Skills, Interventions, and Evaluations*. Boston, MA: Allyn and Bacon.

Fukuyama, M.A. and Sevig, T.D. (1999) *Integrating Spirituality into Multicultural Counselling*. Thousand Oaks, CA: Sage.

Gold, J.M. (2010) *Counseling and Spirituality: Integrating Spiritual and Clinical Orientations*. Hoboken, NJ: Pearson Education.

Goldstein, H. (1986) 'Education for social work practice: A cognitive cross-cultural approach.' *International Social Work 29*, 149–164.

Green, J.W. (1998) *Cultural Awareness in the Human Services: A Multi-Ethnic Approach* (3rd edition). Boston, MA: Allyn and Bacon.

Hendricks, C.O. (2003) 'Learning and teaching cultural competence in the practice of social work.' *Journal of Teaching in Social Work 23*, 1–2, 73–86.

Hugman, R. (2013) *Culture, Values and Ethics in Social Work: Embracing Diversity*. London and New York, NY: Routledge.

International Federation of Social Workers (IFSW) (2018) *Our Members*. Accessed on 10/05/2018 at http://ifsw.org/membership/our-members.

Keddell, E. (2006) 'Pavlova and pineapple pie: Selected identity influences on Samoan-Pākehā people in Aotearoa/New Zealand.' *Kōtuitui: New Zealand Journal of Social Sciences 1*, 1, 45–63.

Keddell, E. (2007) 'Cultural identity and the Children, Young Persons, and their Families Act 1989: Ideology, policy and practice.' *Social Policy Journal of New Zealand/Te Puna Whakaaro 32* (online). Ministry of Social Development/Te Manatu Whakahiato Ora.

Kellehear, A. (2000) *Death and Dying in Australia*. New York, NY: Oxford University Press.

Lee, M.Y., Ng, S.-M., Leung, P.P.Y. and Chan, C.L.W. (2009) *Integrative Body–Mind–Spirit Social Work: An Empirically Based Approach to Assessment and Treatment*. New York, NY: Oxford University Press.

Ling, H.K. (2014) 'Social Work Across Cultures: Contexts and Contestations.' In H.K. Ling, J. Martin and R. Ow (eds) *Cross-Cultural Social Work: Local and Global*. South Yarra, Australia: Palgrave Macmillan.

Ling, H.K., Martin, J. and Ow, R. (2014) 'Introducing Cross-Cultural Social Work: Local and Global.' In H.K. Ling, J. Martin and R. Ow (eds) *Cross-Cultural Social Work: Local and Global*. South Yarra, Australia: Palgrave Macmillan.

Lum, D. (2011) *Culturally Competent Practice: A Framework for Understanding Diverse Groups and Justice Issues* (4th edition). Belmont, CA: Thomson Brooks-Cole.

McEldowney, R. and Connor, M. (2011) 'Cultural safety as an ethics of care: A praxiological process.' *Journal of Transcultural Nursing 22*, 4, 342–349.

Midgley, J. (1981) *Professional Imperialism*. London: Heinemann.

Mun, S. and Ow, R. (2017) 'Death of a child: Perspective of Chinese mothers in Singapore.' *Journal of Religion and Spirituality in Social Work: Social Thought 36*, 3, 306–325.

Nursing Council of New Zealand (2005, 2011) *Guidelines for Cultural Safety, the Treaty of Waitangi and Māori Health in Nursing Education and Practice*. New Zealand.

Nye, C. (2006) 'Understanding and misunderstanding in cross-cultural practice: Further conversations with Suwanrang.' *Clinical Social Work Journal 34*, 3, 303–317.

Osei-Hwedie, K., Ntseane, D. and Jacques, G. (2006) 'Searching for appropriateness in social work education in Botswana.' *Social Work Education 25*, 6, 569–590.

Ow, R. (1991) 'Social Behaviour in an Asian Cultural Setting.' In M. Clare and L. Jayasuriya (eds) *Issues of Cross-Cultural Practice*. Occasional Paper Anniversary Edition, Department of Social Work and Social Administration, University of Western Australia, Perth, Australia: Fineline.

Ow, R. (2014) 'End-of-Life Issues: Perspectives in Multicultural Societies.' In H.K. Ling, J. Martin and R. Ow (eds) *Cross-Cultural Social Work: Local and Global*. South Yarra, Australia: Palgrave Macmillan.

Pierce, J. (2007) Cross-Cultural Communication in Social Work Practice, An Interpretative Descriptive Approach to Cross-Cultural Communication Difficulties. Thesis submitted in partial fulfilment of the requirements for the degree of Master of Social Work, The University of Northern British Columbia. Ottawa: Library and Archives Canada, Heritage Branch.

Ramsden, I. (1990) 'Cultural safety.' *The New Zealand Nursing Journal: Kai Tiaki 83*, 11, 18–19.

Samovar, L.A., Porter, R.E., McDaniel, E.R. and Roy, C.S. (2017) *Communication Between Cultures* (9th edition). Boston, MA: Cengage Learning.

Spencer-Oatley, H. (2012) *What is Culture? A Compilation of Quotations. GlobalPAD Core Concepts*. Available at GlobalPAD Open House, http://go.warwick.ac.uk/globalpadintercultural.

Straits Times (1999) 'They help to groom Singapore.' 3 January, p.2.

Sue, D.W. and Sue, D. (2008) *Counseling the Culturally Diverse: Theory and Practice* (5th edition). Hoboken, NJ: Wiley & Sons.

Walker, S. and Eketone, A. (2014) 'Biculturalism as an Approach to Social Work.' In H.K. Ling, J. Martin and R. Ow (eds) *Cross-Cultural Social Work: Local and Global*. South Yarra, Australia: Palgrave Macmillan.

Weaver, H.H. (2001) 'Organization and Community Assessment with First Nations People.' In R. Fong and S. Furuto (eds) *Culturally Competent Practice: Skills, Interventions, and Evaluations*. Boston, MA: Allyn and Bacon.

Williams, R. (1999) 'Cultural safety – what does it mean for our work practice?' *Australian and New Zealand Journal of Public Health 23*, 2, 212–214.

Williams, C. and Johnson, M.R.D. (2010) *Race and Ethnicity in a Welfare Society*. Berkshire: McGraw-Hill Education.

Yan, M.C. (2008a) 'Exploring the meaning of crossing and culture: An empirical understanding from practitioners' everyday experience.' *Families in Society: The Journal of Contemporary Services 89*, 2, 282–292.

Yan, M.C. (2008b) 'Exploring cultural tensions in cross-cultural social work practice.' *Social Work 53*, 4, 317–328.

Yeoh, B.S.A., Chee, H.L. and Baey, G.H.Y. (2013) 'The place of Vietnamese marriage migrants in Singapore: Social reproduction, social "problems" and social protection.' *Third World Quarterly 34*, 10, 1927–1941.

Yeung, S. (2016) 'Conceptualizing cultural safety: Definitions and applications of safety in health care for indigenous mothers in Canada.' *Journal for Social Thought 1*, 1, 1–13.

Yip, K.S. (2004) 'A Chinese cultural critique of the global qualifying standards for social work education.' *Social Work Education 23*, 5, 597–612.

• Chapter 13 •

Integrative Body-Mind-Spirit Social Work Practice: Achieving Holistic Wellbeing

SYLVIA HONG YAO, CECILIA LAI WAN CHAN AND CELIA HOI YAN CHAN

Introduction

Traditionally, social workers have adopted psychotherapeutic or systems models when designing psychosocial interventions for clients, families and communities. The medical model and deficit approaches have had a major influence on social work theories and practice approaches but current thinking challenges these approaches and focuses on client capacities and strengths. Interventions that are informed by the medical model focus on dysfunction or problems, take a deficit approach to practice and aim for symptom reduction, using remedial actions to decrease harm. Clinicians may also assume that their clients lack capacity for self-help. The reality is, however, that most social work clients actively search for effective coping and survival strategies when confronted by life challenges. This reflects their knowledge of the complex reality in which they usually live, where their responses to life challenges are predisposed by their stage of biological development, health and illness, diet and lifestyle, upbringing and socialization, economic, political and cultural contexts, emotions, thoughts and ways of coping, and adjustment and resolution of stress and conflicts. Moreover, deficit approaches rarely adopt interventions that incorporate concepts of spirituality, meaning-searching, or activities such as prayers and meditation (Canda and Furman 2010; Lee *et al.* 2016).

Recognition of the power that clients bring to interventions underpins an alternative perspective, the classic biopsychosocial social work model, which takes account of common mind–body changes that are associated with identity formation challenges over the lifespan (infancy, childhood, adolescence, puberty and school, work and homemaking, marriage and pregnancy, social engagement and parenthood, menopause, retirement, old age, bereavement and death). This model positively focuses on clients' capacities (not their deficits), and supports them to consider active integrated healing approaches to regain health and wellbeing. Biopsychosocial interventions incorporate exercise, diet, acupuncture, massage, prayers, meditation, dance, arts, aromatherapy, and self-help and support groups. Those clients who transcend their difficulties often become advocates and lay volunteers, reflecting the extent of their personal growth. Many inspiring stories of how clients grow to help others have encouraged social workers to develop interventions that are strengths-focused and empowering, rather than focused on weaknesses and vulnerabilities.

This chapter outlines the Integrative Body-Mind-Spirit approach (IBMS), which is underpinned by the social work biopsychosocial model. In the IBMS model, social workers adopt a systemic perspective of *person-in-environment* as a core principle in person-centred practice. IBMS social work interventions consolidate theories of psychology, sociology, anthropology; family and cultural studies; network analysis; ecology and environmental science; organization development; Chinese and Western medicine; and resilience, capacity building and resource mobilization in order to understand human behaviour. The IBMS social work model (developed by the authors) integrates Eastern philosophies and health-promoting practices with relevant Western biopsychosocial psychotherapeutic techniques. It places emphasis on a *total person* orientation, dynamic balance framework, spiritual teachings on the meaning of life, health practices and exercises, guided by traditional Chinese medicine.

This chapter describes the philosophical underpinnings and theoretical framework of the IBMS model, and the process model underpinning clinical intervention (Engaging, Nurturing, Shifting, Integrating, Transforming (ENSIT)). Clinical intervention tools commonly used in IBMS social work practices are explored. Exemplar case studies are provided and the chapter concludes with reflection questions.

Emerging theories of psychosocial and spiritual care
The mind–body connection
The classic biopsychosocial social work model is underpinned by a range of theories. Piaget described different stages of cognitive development of children; Freud proposed theories on psychosexual development; Werner included the importance of genetic influence; while Bronfenbrenner

included the micro, meso, exo, macro and chrono levels in ecological systems theory (Bronfenbrenner 1994; Killam and Degges-White 2017). Individuals' responses to lifespan challenges are believed to be influenced by their bio-genetic code; physiological and physical development; somatic and cognitive maturation; socio-economic-cultural upbringing (as defined by social expectations); and norms and morality of families and societies (Lee *et al.* 2018).

Traditional Eastern and Western wisdom emphasizes reciprocal relationships between physical and psychological health, as well as mind–body connections. Social interaction analysis in Western societies focuses on the attainment of independence, autonomy and self-expression of individuals, while Eastern scholars are more likely to pursue notions of interdependence, harmony, relatedness and social connection (Chan, Chan and Chan 2014b). These are characterized by broad attention to wholeness in social relationships, and a collective existential experience (Varnum *et al.* 2010). Increasing recognition of the complexity of mind–body interactions has renewed efforts to produce scientific evidence of how these connections relate to holistic population wellbeing (Josefsson, Lindwall and Archer 2014; Oh *et al.* 2010; Yao *et al.* 2017). Holistic orientation is a unique feature in the IBMS approach, as Eastern wisdom often focuses on the liberation of individuals from physical and emotional suffering through spiritual cultivation and inward exploration of the mind. Individuals are thus empowered to identify their deeper existential meaning in a larger context, which may ultimately lead to improved relationships with self, others, community and nature.

A large volume of research has been published on how Eastern exercises such as qigong, tai-ji and yoga can improve quality of life and reduce depression, anxiety, obesity, pain, fatigue and insomnia (Lee, *et al.* 2018; Chan *et al.* 2016; Chan *et al.* 2017a). For people who are unwilling, or unable, to share their emotions with a counsellor, use of exercise may be a good entry point to biopsychosocial social work interventions. It is thus essential for social workers to be equipped with basic knowledge of the ways to exercise the body to reach the spirit and the mind, in order to holistically engage clients. All exercise techniques should be simple to learn and perform, and enjoyable, in order to encourage participation. No matter what the exercise, or how it is performed, the very action of embracing it has been reported as helpful to individuals with physical, psychological, social and emotional issues (Ho *et al.* 2012; Ho *et al.* 2016a; Ho *et al.* 2016b). IBMS social work supports clients to practise body movements and physical exercises in order to stimulate the connections between body, mind and spirit. The following discussion explores these techniques.

Considering fine motor body movements: One Second Body Techniques are hand and body movement exercises developed by the IBMS team, which integrate qigong exercises and meridian massage within a self-help framework. They are freely available online.[1] Regular practice of *One Second Body Techniques* can improve mood, quality of life and levels of anti-ageing protective blood markers; and reduce physiological stress (measured as stress hormones or inflammatory markers). Examples of individual techniques include healing hand movements and massage, concentrating on breathing and sound, and face massage.

Considering gross motor body movements: Gross movements exercise the whole body, and can be undertaken individually or with others. They can include unstructured activities such as walking, hiking, swimming or cycling, or more structured activities such as boxing, tai-ji or tai-chi, ballroom dancing, and muscle training for balance and strength.

Integrated body movements: Activities that integrate fine and gross motor skills have been shown to reduce negative mood and increase emotional and spiritual resilience (Ho *et al.* 2012; Ho *et al.* 2016a; Ho *et al.* 2016b; Lee *et al.* 2018). These can be undertaken individually or in a group, and can include a range of activities, such as social dancing, choir singing, karaoke, calligraphy, needle work, expressive art and clay modelling.

The following case study illustrates one person's progression from emotional suffering to spiritual awareness and empowerment by attending daily yoga sessions at a local community club with others in similar situations.

Case study 1: Shella

Shella used to run her own fashion boutique. She was a cheerful person, full of energy. She started suffering from insomnia and fatigue soon after her husband's death, three months after an end-stage liver cancer diagnosis. She reported low energy throughout the day, muscle aches, knee joint pain, loss of appetite, poor concentration and frequent tears. She closed her shop and mostly lay in bed. She developed muscle wastage and chronic pain, and eventually consulted a social worker regarding a potential move to residential care. Shella's symptoms were clear manifestations of bereavement. She blamed herself for not spending more time with her husband, and not paying attention to his liver conditions despite knowledge of his Hepatitis B carrier status since childhood. As a migrant with poor

---

1   See https://learning.hku.hk/ibms/home/e-learning/ibms-worksheet.

mastery of the local language, no children and no social support, Shella's health deteriorated quickly. The social worker recognized imbalance in her mind–body connection and referred Shella to a community yoga club for daily exercises. Other bereaved ladies attended this club, and Shella made friends. Within six months, Shella reported sleeping better and having a daily routine. She was rebuilding her social network, along with her sense of self-efficacy, self-care capacity and muscle strength. Ultimately, she withdrew her application for residential care.

Shella's experience illustrates how regular integrated mind–body exercise (in this instance, yoga), undertaken in the company of others with similar life challenges, assisted her to work through her bereavement and reach a higher level of understanding of herself within her social, emotional and physical environment. IBMS techniques of yoga and group interaction were applied in this situation to reintegrate Shella's pathway to health and wellbeing.

Spirituality in social work practice

Edward Canda founded the Society for Spirituality and Social Work to raise general awareness among social workers of the importance of mind, body and spirit integration in their practice (Canda and Furman 2010). Spirituality has been defined as 'the search for meaning, purpose, and morally fulfilling relations with self, other people, the encompassing universe, and ultimate reality, however a person understands it' (Furman *et al.* 2004, p.772). There is empirical evidence of important connections between mind, body and spirit (Peterson and Seligman 2004). Over the past decade, there has been a large volume of research into the effectiveness on health and wellbeing outcomes of interventions such as mindfulness and meditation, and spiritual practices of appreciation, gratitude, forgiveness and compassion. Despite general professional concerns regarding the diffusion of religious faith into clinical practices, spirituality can take a prominent role in many social work practices in response to clients' demands, unmet needs and feedback.

Influenced by Western Judeo-Christian traditions, individual coping strategies of prayers and church attendance are not new to social work practice. Generally, to respect ethnic and cultural diversity, social workers usually avoid discussion of religion in professional practice. Yet, faith and spirituality are fundamental to existential human wellbeing. For much of the 20th century, social workers have been encouraged to engage meaningfully with clients with spiritual struggles, and to help them with meaning-searching behaviours (Crisp 2017). Under the IBMS framework, spirituality focuses on attaining peace of mind and articulates individual meaning of life.

In recent years, Eastern philosophies and practical techniques such as Confucianism, Buddhism, Daoism and Traditional Chinese Medicine have been integrated successfully into biopsychosocial social work practices (Chan *et al.* 2012). Eastern philosophies teach appreciation of human spirituality, such as acceptance of vulnerability, letting go of hang-ups, being humble and relaxed with the flow of nature (including illness and death), embracing adversity and suffering, and being grateful for everyday experiences. In the IBMS model, spirituality is defined by the state of mind.

Individuals seeking spiritual wellness acquire peace of mind, which enables them to find meaning in life. Individuals with spiritual strengths develop the capacity to accept life's adversities with equanimity, be at ease with ups and downs in life, face losses and hardship without resentment and blame, and be willing to embrace trauma and suffering as a test for resilience and perseverance (Peterson and Seligman 2004). Thus they learn to transcend bitterness, obtain life wisdom and faith in humanity, and use simple self-nurturing activities such as getting in touch with mother nature, having an animal companion, gardening (no matter how small), consciously counting daily blessings, and making a habit of showing appreciation and gratitude.

The promotion of strengths-based qualities in psychosocial social work interventions (for example, love, forgiveness, compassion, gratitude, hope, creativity, fairness and humour) can enhance clients' self-knowledge, as well as teamwork and leadership abilities. Consequently, IBMS social work practices have adopted values of altruism, unselfishness, conscientiousness, personal sacrifice and continuous self-cultivation into interventions to create a positive experience in spiritual transcendence.

Transcendence in suffering

The IBMS model promotes personal growth that facilitates transcendence in suffering. Suffering takes root from an individual's inability to acknowledge impermanency, often seen as ambivalence in accepting suffering as part of life's journey. However, ambivalent feelings are not necessarily problematic, as they can be part of the pathway towards self-awareness. Thus they deserve recognition, tolerance and contemplation. Consciously taking this approach is an integral element of the IBMS model.

In Buddhist teaching, suffering is associated with features of the life course (birth, old age, sickness, death), as well as with features of attachment and expectations. Suffering is inevitable in life, and individuals who suffer most appear to have an aversion to pain in life, and an over-attachment to sensory gratification, relationships and pleasure.

> When Heaven is about to confer a great responsibility on any man, it will exercise his mind with suffering, subject his sinews and bones to hard work, expose his body to hunger, put him to poverty, place obstacles in the paths of his deeds, so as to stimulate his mind, harden his nature, and improve wherever he is incompetent. (*The Book of Mencius*, annotated by Tu 1998, p.62)

Confucianism promotes the notion that experience of suffering is a blessing in disguise, as it can be followed by transcendence: *no pain, no gain* (Chan, *et al.* 2014a; Ng *et al.* 2005). Personal ordeal is not just a test, it is an opportunity for growth, where sufferers can learn forbearance, courage, kindness, faithfulness and self-transcendence through dealing with pain. The IBMS model assists clients to overcome an initial crisis and adjust positively to suffering. Social workers using the IBMS model can empower clients to strive conscientiously to exercise mind and body and realize their full holistic potential through a meaning-making and reconstruction process.

On a daily basis, individuals can be traumatized by unexpected adverse experiences (for example, divorce, job dismissal, miscarriage, suicide in the family). By working through and overcoming such adversities, most people grow spiritually and emotionally. They become more sensitive and empathetic to the needs and vulnerabilities of others, and more willing to offer help. When working with clients in need, the IBMS model assists social workers to apply mind–body–spirit strategies that channel greater empathy and compassion to their clients. Many influential networks and organizations, such as Save the Children and Mothers Against Drunk Driving (MADD), have their genesis in traumatic experiences where sufferers have turned grief into compassionate actions that have transformed the world. However, the pathway to transcending suffering may not be linear, or readily attained. It may involve iteration, ambivalence, questioning, creating balance and revisiting past steps.

Ambivalence and dynamic balance perspectives

There is increasing discussion on the concept of ambivalence in both the East and the West (Connidis 2015; Lee *et al.* 2018; Tighe, Birditt and Antonucci 2016). Ambivalence reflects a difficult situation in making decisions and choices in everyday life when individuals are torn by conflicting emotions and thoughts such as love–hate, persevere–give up, accept–deny, and faith–mistrust. Ambivalence can be intergenerational, interpersonal or intrapersonal. According to Chinese culture, ambivalence can be described as a *mixed bag* of complex emotions; it is represented as an entanglement of emotions (Guo, Chi and Silverstein 2013) that creates approach–avoidance conflicts. Ambivalence is difficult to manage when feelings cannot be untangled, or even named properly (Pillemer and Suitor 2008). When individuals are locked into difficult choices, ambivalence and suffering generally follow.

Ambivalence is often characterized by the yin–yang symbol, which represents continuous oscillation, seeking a balanced and harmonious state that may never exist. In daily life, people often subconsciously engage in dynamic balancing processes to deal with opposing forces, such as optimism versus pessimism, hopefulness versus hopelessness, health versus ill-health and so on. The Chinese wisdom of yin–yang balance represents a holistic, dynamic and dialectical worldview (Fang 2012) that supports social workers to see problems encountered by clients as a unity of paradoxes. By adopting a dynamic self-correcting stance, IBMS approaches value the co-existence of yin and yang within the processes of unfolding events and changes in daily lives (Chan *et al.* 2017b). When a crisis occurs, IBMS interventions can teach individuals to trust that there will always be light at the end of the tunnel and that they can transform risks into opportunities by using available resources and support.

The word *crisis* in Chinese consists of two words: *danger* and *opportunity*. Crisis can indeed offer opportunity to stimulate significant changes and transformation through a disruptive process. Anxiety can enhance motivation to prepare for stressful events, such as a job interview or university entrance examination. Frustration and sadness associated with failures can discourage people, but can also assist them to reflect deeply on future directions and strategies. A primary goal of IBMS social work interventions is to regain a dynamic balance between physical, mental and spiritual subsystems. This means accepting ambivalence and being comfortable even when in a state of being *out of balance*. The IBMS intervention focuses on the individual's capacity to embrace vulnerability and adversity and to trust in potential strengths and abilities in a dynamic balancing process while seeking harmony and peace. Figure 13.1 demonstrates the oscillation between ambivalent states for someone suffering from psoriasis, assisting them to constantly make and remake meaning in their life (Chan *et al.* 2017b).

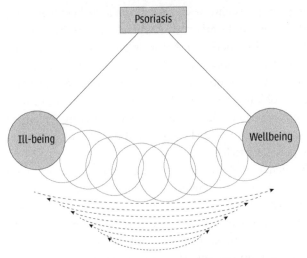

Figure 13.1: Ambivalent oscillation between ill-being and
wellbeing when a person is coping with psoriasis

The following case study outlines an example of ambivalence. Daniel's
situation could aptly be described as *torn between two obligations.*

Case study 2: Daniel

Daniel moved from his marital home to live with his elderly mother who had
dementia. He had ambivalent feelings towards his mother. He loved her and
recognized the enormous sacrifices she had made to take care of him when he
was young. But he was frustrated by her, as she no longer recognized him and
had temper tantrums directed at him. Furthermore, he was ambivalent towards
his situation. Despite fulfilling his filial obligations, he resented having to leave
his wife, who refused to move with him to take care of his mother.

Daniel would benefit from participating in an IBMS social work intervention
where he could be assisted to understand his dilemma, recognize the paradoxes
within his situation, celebrate the processes of unfolding events and prioritize
his decisions using short- and longer-term strategies to ensure that he was not
torn apart, and that the women he loved (his mother and his wife) were part of
the solution.

Application of the IBMS model in social work practice

The IBMS model is an evidence-based intervention which empowers
clients to foster their innate capacity to change, and to build resilience in all
aspects of mind, body and soul. It includes elements of interconnectedness

of body, mind and spirit; spirituality as a core domain of human existence; attaining growth and transformative changes instead of focusing on symptom reduction; and setting multiple goals of healing, empowerment, love, forgiveness and capacity building (Chan, Ho and Chow 2002). The IBMS model requires that social workers pay attention to the context of *person-in-environment* (Lee *et al.* 2018). The core principles of the IBMS social work model are outlined in Figure 13.2 and Table 13.1.

Figure 13.2: Core elements of the IBMS model
Adapted from Lee et al. 2018.

Table 13.1: Core principles of the IBMS model

Strength-based	• Belief in intrinsic healing capacity of human beings and the potential of individual. • Expanding horizon through meaning reconstruction. • Empowerment is the goal.
Meaning focused and transformation oriented	• Exploring alternative meanings through cognitive restructuring and spiritual teaching. • Focus on spiritual transformation of self. • Encouraging integration of the transformed identity through commitment to help, serving as role models, and advocating for the wellbeing of others.
Multi-modal approach	• Emphasis on body–mind–spirit connectedness. • Change can start from any domain of the body, mind, spirit entity of an individual.
Experiential-based	• Body is often the vehicle for shifting and transformation as it bypasses the conscious and logical mind. • Developing appreciation of nature and self through mindfulness practice and experiential encounter.

Adapted from Integrative Body-Mind-Spirit Fidelity Checklist and Observational Protocol. Unpublished protocol, Centre of Behavioural Health, The University of Hong Kong, HK.

IBMS-based social work interventions have been used with individuals and groups and in community programmes. There are an increasing number of clinical trials with promising outcomes for divorced women, people with eczema, bereaved persons, cancer patients, insomnia sufferers, those with chronic fatigue or depression, and women undergoing in-vitro fertilization (IVF) (Chan *et al.* 2012; Chan *et al.* 2017a; Lee *et al.* 2018). More studies are required, however, with other groups of people with specific needs, to further explore the effectiveness of IBMS social work interventions.

Applying the IBMS to practice with individuals

The following contrasting case studies illustrate how people suffering from terminal heart failure can take different pathways when dealing with the same life challenges. The first case study highlights how the IBMS model might assist Adrian to face his health challenges with equanimity.

Case study 3: Adrian and Brian

Adrian and Brian were both cared for in a long-stay care home.

Adrian was frail and dependent. His physical, social, emotional, spiritual distress included being overwhelmed by death anxiety, fear and resentment; frustrated by physical symptoms of breathlessness and oedema; depressed by his loss of mobility and having to stay in a residential care facility; angry with the failure of the healthcare system to find a cure; and blaming God for putting him into such chaos and shame. Reflecting his irritability and anger, his family members experienced high caregiver stress, helplessness and guilt for not being able to help him. His family members lodged complaints and made unrealistic and unreasonable demands on the care home staff.

Brian was peaceful, and grateful for living a life worth living. Despite his heart and renal failure, Brian accepted impending death gracefully, found life meaningful and interesting, treasured every moment with his loved ones and focused on finishing unfinished business so that his loved ones had no issues to resolve after his death. Brian was appreciative of the dedication of the staff and the love from his family members. His positive attitude towards his impending death, his gratitude to life and his effort in sharing his life wisdom by writing cards gave meaning to his experiences. The sharing of these with care home staff also strengthened those relationships.

The end-of life journey for Adrian was very different from the one experienced by Brian. A key question for Adrian is: 'How can I realign my life priorities?' Is this possible? Certainly! The IBMS intervention framework provides social workers with a process that supports clients to fully embrace their situation and appreciate personal growth and their contribution to others, even on an end-of-life journey.

In taking a holistic lens, social workers can assist their clients to reach beyond biopsychosocial symptom reduction and attain emotional, existential and spiritual transformation. Positive and transformative changes not only happen in the physical, cognition, emotional and social domains, but they also impact on core values and meanings and reinforce spiritual connections with one's inner self and a higher being.

Applying the IBMS to a group setting

An illustration of how the IBMS model might be applied in a group setting can be seen in the IBMS-based Cancer-fighter Training Course for lung cancer patients. These patients were given an end-stage diagnosis and many were overwhelmed by the thought of their imminent death. They were at a loss as to what to do in their remaining lifetime. The IBMS Cancer-fighter Training Course intervention consisted of eight three-hour group sessions:

1. Be a cancer-fighter: gain holistic wellness through IBMS

2. Dynamic balance between body and mind: regulate your emotions

3. Learn to appreciate self: emphasis on mind–body connection

4. Loss and found: transcendence from sufferings

5. Positive psychology: peer and family support

6. Self-care: appreciation and gratitude

7. Inner peace and life wisdom: life lessons

8. Resilience and awakening: life goes on.

The programme aimed to empower participants to cope effectively with their health status, reduce death anxiety, foster family communication and promote physical exercise, meaning in life and optimism, despite deteriorating physical conditions.[2] The strong sense of helplessness among participants at programme enrolment was linked to a belief that there was

---

2   Details of the programme can be found at: https://learning.hku.hk/ibms.

nothing that they could do to help themselves. The participants found, however, that by following the IBMS programme they regained a sense of control and rediscovered meaning in their lives. Being able to share their fears and anxieties with others in similar situations was empowering. Life-transforming outcomes that occurred as a result of the IBMS Cancer-fighter Training Course are exemplified in Mary's story.

Case study 4: Mary

Mary was a middle-aged divorced woman diagnosed with an end-stage lung cancer.

> I see it [the cancer] as a test from Heaven. Heaven used it as a test on my faith... The Heaven (God) was testing my mind to see if I would yield to the disease. I think my willpower is strong. I won't be defeated. I have to face it... The greater the challenge, the stronger my will to fight... I have been working so hard and totally forgot my parents and my children. This diagnosis reminds me of my most important people in my life. I ended my business and am spending more time on exercise, with my family members, and volunteering with the Cancer Centre in the hospital... I started my painting lessons, which I had no time for when I was running my own business. Painting gives me enormous joy and satisfaction in connecting my mind and soul. You may not believe me but I am a much happier person since my cancer diagnosis. Although I do not know how much time I am going to live, the cancer has given me a new life.

Being able to accept cancer and her limited time to live, freed Mary from attachment to earthly possessions and life's material successes. She re-aligned her priorities, established new connections with self, family members, and her higher being.

In the midst of suffering, meaning-searching can help individuals to regain a sense of self, and to maintain normalcy in their lives. For patients with lung cancer, death is a topic that brings suffering physically, emotionally and spiritually. Although most patients in the IBMS Cancer-fighter Training Course experienced denial, anger, bargaining, depression and acceptance as described by Kübler-Ross (2009), the coping process itself was filled with complex emotions which often led to relationship conflicts and ambivalence among family members. Ambivalent attitudes of death denial versus death acceptance are common for people who are confronted by cancer, chronic illness, infertility and other uncontrollable adversities. Among all the helpful strategies that these people with lung cancer used to cope with the emotions surrounding their imminent death, meaning reconstruction played a pivotal role in activating their inner strengths and being able to utilize external resources to cope with the emerging challenges of a diagnosis of end-stage cancer (Neimeyer 1994).

The IBMS process model: Engaging, Nurturing, Shifting, Integrating and Transforming (ENSIT)

The IBMS scholars and practitioners have designed a process model of Engaging, Nurturing, Shifting, Integrating and Transforming (ENSIT) to assist social workers to effectively implement the IBMS model. The ENSIT steps are outlined in Figure 13.3.

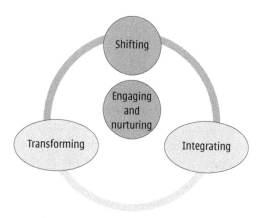

Figure 13.3: The IBMS process model (ENSIT)
Adapted from Integrative Body-Mind-Spirit Fidelity Checklist and Observational Protocol. Unpublished protocol, Centre of Behavioural Health, The University of Hong Kong, HK.

Engaging

The IBMS intervention starts with engaging the client and creating a nurturing therapeutic environment. The therapeutic alliance significantly impacts on clinical efficacy in social work practice. Being able to engage clients quickly helps to establish this alliance. In the initial contact, the social worker builds alliances, undertakes a body–mind–spirit assessment and outlines intervention goals. Social workers develop connections and collaborative relationships with clients in order to explore concerns, problems, strengths and resources. Engagement involves the establishment of contracts around mutually agreed goals. Establishing trust and collaborative engagement helps clients to prepare for exploration and experimentation, as well as supporting them to embrace challenges that may emerge in the transformative change process.

Nurturing

Social workers who adopt IBMS approaches believe in the innate healing capacities and strengths of individuals and support clients to recognize and utilize their potential and capacity to achieve self-awareness and self-acceptance. Transformative change may require a disruption to the existing status quo of the body–mind–spirit. Social workers create a nurturing environment where clients feel supported to take risks, venture into new horizons, be in touch with unresolved issues and explore their inner sense of vulnerability. Nurturing in the IBMS model is about creating a *holding environment* to facilitate unconditional self-acceptance and self-appreciation, as well as educating clients on techniques to nourish their body, mind and soul.

Shifting

IBMS interventions aim to produce synergy in the physical domain (body), cognition and emotional state (mind), core values and meaning, as well as connection with the divine and self (spirit). Problems can arise because of disconnection or imbalance in one or more of these domains. Therefore, social workers facilitate reconnection, normalization and validation, expanding and moving the status quo to attain a new body–mind–spirit wellbeing, balance and harmony.

Integrating

Integrating involves anchoring learning and incorporating changes in physical, mental and spiritual domains into total wellbeing. This is a critical process in the IBMS intervention, as it puts a spotlight on how individuals benefit from this change process and integrate IBMS learning into their everyday lives, particularly when confronted by future life challenges.

Transforming

Transforming is a continuous process, which occurs throughout the IBMS intervention. The transforming process facilitates clients to search for their idiosyncratic meanings and purposes in life, foster their ability to embrace adversities and suffering, live in the moment (the *here and now*) and deepen connections with their authentic self. As individuals expand into their higher levels of consciousness, they can transform their roles and identities from being victims to survivors, and convert their pain into empathy, loving kindness and compassion for others.

The ENSIT process rarely occurs in a linear fashion. Engaging and nurturing play central roles during the initial phases of IBMS interventions. Shifting, integrating and transforming are more closely linked and usually emerge throughout the intervention process. There are necessarily (and anticipated) individual differences in the sequence of ENSIT processes. Social workers can be creative in responding to the interests and preferences of clients throughout the therapeutic process. The experience of Anita demonstrates how clients are coached to move through the transformation process, a process that responds to their unique needs and capacities for change.

Case study 5: Anita

Anita is a primary school teacher who suffered anxiety and depression after a miscarriage. Anita was married for five years and badly wanted a child. The extended family were overjoyed when they learned of her pregnancy after going through IVF. The subsequent miscarriage smashed her dreams and sense of purpose in life. She was constantly fearful and anxious, suffered from insomnia and could not return to work for two years. She came to the social work clinic despite not being sure if the social worker could help her, because she had already tried many types of healing. The social worker supported her by normalizing her experience of mood swings after her miscarriage, telling her it was common among women going through rapid hormonal changes associated with reproductive events of pregnancy, miscarriage, post-partum and menopause.

By focusing on her strengths, Anita revisited her passion for painting. Being a dedicated Catholic, Anita referred her suffering to the pain of Holy Mary losing her child Jesus Christ. By prayers, Bible reading, painting, and reflection on her priorities in life, Anita gradually regained her inner peace and accepted the loss. She joined the United Nations Children's Fund (UNICEF) as a volunteer by painting cards for fundraising. By focusing on the pain and suffering of children in war zones and disaster-affected areas, Anita regained her energy in compassionate action and moved out of her self-pity after six months. The IBMS processes of Engagement and Nurturing were accomplished in one session, while the Shifting, Integrating and Transforming processes took three more sessions. Anita discovered that volunteering and church-going were a means of shifting her attention to helping others. She embraced the experience of her miscarriage, was willing to let go of her indulgence in her pain and shift her focus on to helping mothers and children in war zones.

The IBMS model offers an effective social work intervention that engages the mind, body and spirit in integrated healing, such that individuals are empowered to deal with their circumstances, and achieve significant change. The case studies illustrate that IBMS interventions can improve the holistic wellbeing of clients who face a range of complex challenges (Chan *et al.* 2012; Chan *et al.* 2017a; Chan, Wong and Tam 2015; Liu *et al.* 2008; Ng *et al.* 2016; Sreevani *et al.* 2013). However, applying IBMS interventions is not without its challenges, which means that the self-care of social workers is an important component in this process.

Self-care

Social workers practising IBMS interventions need knowledge, skills and commitment to activate the innate potential of their clients. However, it is essential that they take care of themselves in order to nurture others. With high stress levels and large caseloads, social workers may experience compassion fatigue and professional burnout. Organizations have a key role in supporting social workers to develop strategies for looking after themselves physically, emotionally and spiritually. As with safety instructions while flying, adults (social workers) should put on oxygen masks before helping others (clients). Social workers can use a range of self-care tools, including spiritual and contemplative exercises (meditation, listening to inspiring music, art appreciation, reading, sleeping and resting, praying) and somatic exercise (daily physical exercise, mindful walking, sports, yoga/qigong/martial arts, dancing, singing, laughing). The supervision of practice and professional development also has a central role in self-care.

Challenges

The therapeutic mechanisms of IBMS interventions require ongoing research. Unlike single modal interventions oriented to specific phenomena, IBMS interventions attempt to elicit integrated changes in the mind, body and spirit. The IBMS model has produced exciting effects for clients (Chan *et al.* 2016), which are supported by significant changes in physiological effects such as stress and immune system biomarkers (Chan *et al.* 2017a; Ho *et al.* 2012). More research is needed to identify the best outcome measures from IBMS interventions, under different circumstances for different clients and client groups. Furthermore, ongoing research into best practice, organizational issues and quality service delivery will support social workers to establish stronger therapeutic alliances with clients and to promote multidisciplinary collaboration across service settings. This will ensure the consistent provision of valued, comprehensive, seamless and holistic biopsychosocial spiritual care for clients and their families.

Conclusion

IBMS social work practice incorporates mind–body, strengths-based, meaning-focused empowerment interventions, which focus on transformation through pain and suffering. This chapter has outlined the principles of IBMS and has introduced the ENSIT process model, which enables social workers to transfer the principles into practice in diverse settings. Exemplar case studies were provided that illustrated the IBMS model in action. The reflection questions encourage social workers to consider how they could implement the model into their practice with diverse issues and populations.

Reflection questions

- What are the guiding principles of IBMS social work practice?

- What are the five components of the ENSIT process model?

- What should social workers focus on when designing IBMS interventions that draw on the ENSIT process?

- What can social workers do to ensure self-care and to make themselves more sensitive to their own body-mind-spiritual needs?

Websites and other resources

- Instruction manual, workbook, video and audio demonstration, PowerPoint presentation, guided meditation for mindfulness practices: https://positivepsychologyproducts.com/mindfulness-x-48percentoff.

- Concepts, video and worksheets to promote integrative body–mind–spirit social work intervention: https://learning.hku.hk/ibms.

- Spirituality and social work (outlining Edward Canda's detailed information on adopting spirituality into social work practice): http://spiritualdiversity.ku.edu/resources (updated 2014) and http://data.socwel.ku.edu/users/canda (updated 2010).

- Video demonstration of One Second Techniques: https://learning. hku.hk/ibms.

- Values in Action (2017): www.viacharacter.org/www/Character-Strengths/VIA-Classification.

References

Bronfenbrenner, U. (1994) 'Ecological Models of Human Development.' In In T. Husen and T.N. Postlethwaite (eds) *International Encyclopaedia of Education*, Vol. 3 (2nd edition). Oxford: Pergamon Press.

Canda, E.R. and Furman, L.D. (2010*) Spiritual Diversity in Social Work Practice: The Heart of Helping* (2nd edition). New York, NY: Oxford Universtiy Press.

Chan, C., Wong, S. and Tam, M. (2015) 'Effectiveness of a self-help integrative Body-Mind-Spirit Intervention (I-BMS) in reducing infertile women's anxiety during their in-vitro fertilization (IVF) treatment result awaiting period.' *Fertility and Sterility 104*, 3, e358.

Chan, C.H.Y., Chan, T.H.Y. and Chan, C.L.W. (2014a) 'Translating Daoist concepts into integrative social work practice: An empowerment program for persons with depressive symptoms.' *Journal of Religion and Spirituality in Social Work 33*, 1, 61–72.

Chan, C.H.Y., Chan, T.H.Y., Leung, P.P.Y., Brenner, M.J. *et al.* (2014b) 'Rethinking well-being in terms of affliction and equanimity: Development of a holistic well-being scale.' *Journal of Ethnic and Cultural Diversity in Social Work 23*, 289–308.

Chan, C.H.Y., Chan, C.L.W., Ng, E.H., Ho, P.C. *et al.* (2012) 'Incorporating spirituality in psychosocial group intervention for women undergoing in vitro fertilization: A prospective randomized controlled study.' *Psychology and Psychotherapy 85*, 356–373.

Chan, C.H.Y., Ji, X.W., Chan, J.S.M., Lau, B.H.P. *et al.* (2017a) 'Effects of the Integrative Mind-Body Intervention on depression, sleep disturbances and plasma IL-6.' *Psychotherapy and Psychosomatics 86*, 1, 54–56.

Chan, C.H.Y., Yao, S.H., Fung, Y.L., Ji, X.W. and Chan, C.L.W. (2017b) 'Dynamic balancing in illness coping: An interpretive phenomenological analysis on the lived experience of Chinese patients with psoriasis.' *Health Science Journal 11*, 4, 515.

Chan, C.L.W., Ho, P.S.Y. and Chow, E. (2002) 'A body–mind–spirit model in health: An Eastern approach.' *Social Work in Health Care 34*, 261–282.

Chan, J.S.M., Yu, N.X., Chow, A.Y.M., Chan, C.L.W. *et al.* (2016) 'Dyadic associations between psychological distress and sleep disturbance among Chinese patients with cancer and their spouses.' *Psycho-Oncology 26*, 6, 856–861.

Connidis, I.A. (2015) 'Exploring ambivalence in family ties: Progress and prospects.' *Journal of Marriage and Family 77*, 1, 77–95.

Crisp, B.R. (2017) *The Routledge Handbook of Religion, Spirituality and Social Work.* London: Routledge.

Fang, T. (2012) 'Yin Yang: A new perspective on culture.' *Management and Organization Review 8*, 1, 25–50.

Furman, L.D., Benson, P.W., Grimwood, C. and Canda, E. (2004) 'Religion and spirituality in social work education and direct practice at the millennium: A survey of UK social workers.' *British Journal of Social Work 34*, 6, 767–792.

Guo, M., Chi, I. and Silverstein, M. (2013) 'Sources of older parents' ambivalent feelings toward their adult children: The case of rural China.' *Journal of Gerontology – Series B Psychological Sciences and Social Sciences 68*, 3, 420–430.

Ho, R.T.H., Chan, J.S.M., Wang, C.W., Lau, B.W.M. *et al.* (2012) 'A randomized controlled trial of qigong exercise on fatigue symptoms, functioning, and telomerase activity in persons with chronic fatigue or chronic fatigue syndrome.' *Annals of Behavioral Medicine 44*, 2, 160–170.

Ho, R.T.H., Fong, T.C.T., Wan, H.Y.A., Au-Yeung, F.S.W. *et al.* (2016a) 'A randomized controlled trial on the psychophysiological effects of physical exercise and Tai-chi in patients with chronic schizophrenia.' *Schizophrenia Research 171*, 1, 42–49.

Ho, R.T.H., Ng, S.M. and Chan, C.L.W. (2007) 'Effects of dance movement therapy on improving mental health in cancer patients.' *Psycho-Oncology 16*, 9, S225.

Ho, R.T.H., Wan, A.H.Y., Chan, J.S.M., Ng, S.M., Chung, K.F. and Chan, C.L.W. (2016b) 'Study protocol on comparative effectiveness of mindfulness meditation and qigong on psychophysiological outcomes for patients with colorectal cancer: A randomized controlled trial.' *BMC Complementary and Alternative Medicine 17*, 390–397.

Josefsson, T., Lindwall, M. and Archer, T. (2014) 'Physical exercise intervention in depressive disorders: Meta-analysis and systematic review.' *Scandinavian Journal of Medicine and Science in Sports 24*, 2, 259–272.

Killam, W.K. and Degges-White, S. (2017) *College Student Development: Applying Theory to Practice on the Diverse Campus.* New York, NY: Springer.

Kübler-Ross, E. (2009) *On Death and Dying* (40th anniversary edition). Abingdon: Routledge.

Lee, J.E., Zarit, S.H., Rovine, M.J., Birditt, K. and Fingerman, K.L. (2016) 'The interdependence of relationships with adult children and spouses.' *Family Relations 65*, 2, 342–353.

Lee, M.Y., Chan, C.H.Y., Chan, C.L.W., Ng, S.M. and Leung, P.P.Y. (2018) *Integrative Body–Mind–Spirit Social Work: An Empirically Based Approach to Assessment and Treatment.* New York, NY: Oxford University Press.

Liu, C.J., Hsiung, P.C., Chang, K.J., Liu, Y.F. *et al.* (2008) 'A study on the efficacy of body–mind–spirit group therapy for patients with breast cancer.' *Journal of Clinical Nursing 17*, 2539–2549.

Neimeyer, R.A. (1994) *Death Anxiety Handbook: Research, Instrumentation, and Application.* New York, NY: Taylor and Francis.

Ng, A.H.N., Boey, K.W., Mok, D., Leung, E.K.T. and Chan, C.L.W. (2016) 'An Integrative Body-Mind-Spirit Intervention Program for enhancing holistic well-being of young people in emerging adulthood.' *International Medical Journal 23*, 3, 214–218.

Ng, S.M., Yau, J.K., Chan, C.L.W., Chan, C.H.Y. and Ho, D.Y.F. (2005) 'The measurement of body–mind–spirit well-being: Toward multidimensionality and transcultural applicability.' *Social Work in Health Care 41*, 33–52.

Oh, B., Butow, P., Mullan, B., Clarke, S. *et al.* (2010) 'Impact of medical Qigong on quality of life, fatigue, mood and inflammation in cancer patients: A randomized controlled trial.' *Annals of Oncology 21*, 3, 608–614.

Peterson, C. and Seligman, M.E.P. (2004) *Character Strengths and Virtues: A Handbook and Classification.* New York, NY: Oxford University Press and Washington, DC: American Psychological Association.

Pillemer, K. and Suitor, J.J. (2008) 'Collective ambivalence: Considering new approaches to the complexity of intergenerational relations.' *The Journals of Gerontology Series B: Psychological Sciences and Social Sciences 63*, 6, S394–S396.

Sreevani, R., Reddemma, K., Chan, C.L.W., Leung, P.P.Y., Wong, V. and Chan, C.H.Y. (2013) 'Effectiveness of integrated body–mind–spirit group intervention on the well-being of Indian patients with depression: A pilot study.' *Journal of Nursing Research 21*, 179–186.

Tighe, L.A., Birditt, K.S. and Antonucci, T.C. (2016) 'Intergenerational ambivalence in adolescence and early adulthood: Implications for depressive symptoms over time.' *Developmental Psychology 52*, 5, 824–834.

Tu, W. (1998) *Humanity and Self-Cultivation: Essays in Confucian Thought.* Boston, MA: Cheng & Tsui.

Varnum, M.E., Grossmann, I., Kitayama, S. and Nisbett, R.E. (2010) 'The origin of cultural differences in cognition: The social orientation hypothesis.' *Current Directions in Psychological Science 19,* 1, 9–13.

Yao, S.H., Ji, J.X.W., Chan, C.H.Y. and Chan, C.L.W. (2017) 'Body-mind connectedness: Integrative Body-Mind-Spirit group work for depressed persons with salient somatic disturbances.' *In Depression* (InTech), 91–100.

Part 4

INFORMED AND ETHICAL PRACTICE

Chapter 14

Supervision and Evidence-Informed Practice

KIERAN O'DONOGHUE

Introduction

The theory and practice of social work supervision has been strongly influenced by social work practice theories since the early 20th century (Kadushin and Harkness 2014). This chapter reviews supervision theory from the early 20th century through to the present day and explores the recent development of evidence-informed practice as it applies to social work and supervision. A fictional case example is used to illustrate the application of an emerging evidence-informed supervision model. The chapter concludes with a discussion of the challenges for an evidence-informed approach to supervision and questions for reflection.

The development of social work supervision theory

At the beginning of the 20th century, theories of supervision were developed through supervisors reflecting on their experiences and deriving understanding and new practices from these experiences. These theories were shared through publications and oral transmission at conferences. Brackett (1903, p.4) demonstrates this when he notes that the individualized form of social casework supervision started to emerge as the result of 'observation, comparison and study' and the formulation of casework methods. The primary focus of these early conceptualizations of supervision practice was to identify the elements within supervision and to understand the purpose and practice of supervision (Burns 1958; Munson 1979). This in turn contributed to the development of emergent theories about the purpose and methods of supervision, which were focused on teaching the social casework method

(Burns 1958). One example of this is found in Mary Richmond's (1917) classic text, *Social Diagnosis*, where supervision involves the comparison and review of the casework record with supervisors being encouraged to use questionnaires as an educative tool to help their supervisees.

The adoption of psychoanalytic theory within casework coupled with the advent of formal social work education set the foundation for practice theory to also provide the theoretical underpinnings for supervision (Burns 1958). The advent of formal social work education, particularly the supervision of students' field experience, became the medium for the transmission of casework practice theory into supervision. The application of psychoanalytic theory to supervision influenced the structure, format and processes of supervision, as well as reinforcing an individualized session-based approach. The therapeutic emphasis of psychoanalytic theory influenced supervision to the extent that it was conceptualized as therapy for the caseworker, and the supervision relationship was for a time conceived as a therapeutic one (Rabinowitz 1987). This therapeutic element did not endure and between 1937 and 1950 it disappeared from the social work supervision literature. Burns (1958) attributes the reasons for its demise and disappearance to the depression of the 1930s, when the focus of practice shifted from clients' psychological needs to their welfare needs, and to the emphasis of supervision's role in the training and development of social caseworkers.

Robinson (1936) advanced the educational focus of supervision by defining supervision from an educational perspective and emphasizing the role it had in the professional development of practitioners. Robinson (1936) also provided a unified conceptualization of social casework supervision, which consisted of administration, teaching and helping components, together with a theory of learning. This enabled a consolidation to occur across all three components of supervision.

Over time, there were changes to social work's connection with psychoanalytic theory (Munson 2002). These mirrored those occurring in counselling psychology, which were due to the influence of other psychodynamic schools, as well as the emergence of behaviourist and humanist approaches in counselling psychology and changes in society (O'Donoghue 2010). Munson (2002) notes that in the 1950s there was a backlash against psychoanalysis within social work, which contributed to social workers preferring a social science theory base to conceptualize their practice rather than a psychological one. During this time, social science and social psychological theories (for example, functional theory, role theory and communication theory) gained influence in social work. The social science theories changed the emphasis towards the influence of the social environment and systems, which was in stark contrast to the psychological emphasis that had been prevalent through the influence of the psychodynamic schools (Munson 2002). A stronger psychosocial approach to social work and supervision developed through this period, with examples of this being apparent in models that integrated social science theories, such as Perlman's (1957) problem-solving approach and Hollis's (1966) psychosocial therapy. The changes in practice theory were reflected in supervision to the extent that the emerging theoretical pluralism from practice theory was reflected in the supervision literature, which incorporated ideas from transactional analysis, task-centred practice, role and interactional theory (Kadushin 1968, 1976; Munson 1979; Pettes 1979; Shulman 1982).

Moving forward to the 21st century, this situation continues, with supervisors using ideas drawn from strengths-based (Cohen 1999; Thomas and Davis 2005), task-centred approaches (Caspi and Reid 2002), and solution-focused (Thomas 2013), social constructionist (Hair and O'Donoghue 2009; O'Donoghue 2003) and indigenous theories (Eketone 2012; Eruera 2012). Alongside the use of specific practice theories, O'Donoghue and Tsui (2012) found evidence that supervisors, like practitioners, integrated personal, professional and technical concepts drawn from their experiences and used these within their practice. These supervisors applied these concepts reflexively in response to the practice setting, content and process of supervision, and the person they were supervising. From their findings, O'Donoghue and Tsui (2012) proposed an emergent knowledge map consisting of a combination of the supervisors' experiential wisdom, conceptual interpretive reasoning abilities and their personal and interpersonal sensitivity. This map included foundational knowledge about supervision for understanding the supervision process and relationship; working principles, frameworks, theories and methods for interpreting and making sense of what was presented and discussed in supervision, and what transpired; and the emotional intelligence needed within sessions to engage effectively as a supervisor. O'Donoghue and Tsui (2012) noted that none of the supervisors in their study specifically identified that they were informed by research, or evidence-based practice, or practice evidence, and that further research is needed in regard to use of research within supervisory practice.

Evidence, practice and supervision

Evidence-based practice entered social work from medicine at the dawn of the 21st century, by way of several highly cited social work articles (for example, Gambrill 1999, 2001; Gibbs and Gambrill 2002; McNeece and Thyer 2004; Webb 2001), which drew from the definition of evidence-based medicine (Hodge, Lacasse and Benson 2012). Sackett *et al.* (1996, p.71) defined evidence-based medicine as 'the conscientious, explicit, and judicious use of current best evidence in making decisions about the care of individual patients'. Over the course of the last 16 years there has been debate about what constitutes evidence and evidence-based social work. Witkin and Harrison (2001) argued that *evidence* is just a word and that its meaning is derived from its use in any particular context. They asserted that 'evidence is the name given to a culturally preferred reason for an existential claim or the performance of an action' (p.295), with evidence being concerned with the establishment of factual proof in one instance and in another with the credibility of an authoritative justification. Factual proof is established through direct evidence derived from the credible reporting of personal experience, or the credible observation or recording of an experience. The credibility of the witness or the report is derived from its reliability, the reputation of the witness, and its degree of corroboration with other evidence.

In contrast, the notion of evidence as an authoritative justification pertains to the authorizing and justifying of a particular action. In other words, evidence authorizes decision making and subsequent actions. It is this meaning of evidence that is used in evidence-based practice, with evidence from research providing the authorization for assessment and intervention in practice with clients. Gray, Plath and Webb (2009) argue that evidence is one form of knowledge used in social work, and they note that there are a range of views within social work about what counts as evidence for practice. This range includes those who adopt the scientific research hierarchy of systematic reviews, random controlled experimental trials, quasi-experimental studies, single-system case-study designs, surveys, and qualitative research (McNeece and Thyer 2004). In contrast, there are those, like Rosen (2003), who acknowledge the limitations of the evidence-based approach and propose that the application of generalist knowledge to a specific client situation needs to be critically weighed against practice wisdom and local knowledge, as well as reflexively evaluated in terms of its contribution to practice outcomes. Mullen (2016) advances this point further when he reconsiders the idea of evidence in order to establish a more nuanced understanding. He proposes a more pragmatic approach wherein the hierarchy of evidence is replaced by assessing evidence in terms of its relevance, credibility and strength. In other words, Mullen (2016) argues that we give serious consideration to the question of the relevance of the evidence as well as its quality.

The limitations of evidence-based practice together with the challenges of implementing this approach have seen the emergence of evidence-informed social work practice (Epstein 2009). According to Nevo and Slonim-Nevo (2011), in evidence-informed social work evidence is used to *inform* practice. It does not form the *basis* for practice, because in social work there is not enough conclusive evidence on which to base practice and there are other factors to consider, such as the client's situation, the client's wishes, the dynamics of interactive practice, the availability of resources and the complexity of modern social problems. For Nevo and Slonim-Nevo (2011), evidence-informed social work is more inclusive than evidence-based practice because it is the client's needs and the dynamics of interactive social work practice that influence how evidence contributes and enriches practice. They contrast this with evidence-based practice where it is the evidence that shapes the practice.

Their evidence-informed approach is also not limited by the scientific research hierarchy or the five-stage evidence-based model comprising: a) an individual assessment and well-formulated practice question, b) searching for the best evidence, c) critically appraising the evidence, d) application of the evidence, and e) an evaluation of the outcome (Epstein 2009; Nevo and Slonim-Nevo 2011). Instead, the approach taken is dialogical and reflexive, involving a systematic and interactive conversation about the application of knowledge in practice. This conversation involves the critical consideration of the available research, while at the same time valuing all forms of knowledge (for example, professional ethics, practice theory and cultural wisdom) with the aim of achieving a best-fit professional response to the client and their situation (Epstein 2009; Nevo and Slonim-Nevo 2011).

Evidence-informed supervision

Evidence-informed supervision is an emerging theory within social work. The work to date includes significant attempts to make social work supervision research more accessible through several research reviews (Carpenter *et al.* 2012; Carpenter, Webb and Bostock 2013; Mor Barak *et al.* 2009; O'Donoghue and Tsui 2015). These reviews have each explored specific aspects of social work supervision research but none of them has specifically addressed the application or translation of the research evidence into an evidence-informed approach or model (O'Donoghue 2014a; O'Donoghue, Wong Yuh Ju and Tsui 2017). The first approach taken towards the formal inclusion of evidence in supervision was by Shulman (2010), who discussed the supervision of three evidence-based practice models, namely, motivational interviewing, solution-focused practice and cognitive behavioural therapy. His focus was the supervision of empirically supported interventions rather than the development of an evidence-based or evidence-informed model for supervision. The next development was O'Donoghue (2014a), who advanced the case for adopting an evidence-informed approach for clinical social work supervision based on the research reviews referred to above.

O'Donoghue *et al.* (2017) have taken this one step further by constructing an evidence-informed social work supervision model derived from an analysis of the results of 130 peer-reviewed journal articles written in the English language between 1958 and 2015. These articles were systematically summarized and analysed in terms of the research design, type of participants, location, sampling and response rate, and the focus and results of the study. O'Donoghue *et al.* further analysed the focus and the results of each study with the view to how they may be applied to supervisory practice.

The evidence-informed model that was developed is concerned with the process and tasks of supervision. The aspects of the model concerned with the process of supervision pertain to the construction of supervision, the supervision alliance or relationship and the interactional process. The outcome of these processes is the development of shared understanding, purpose and expectations, a trusting relationship and constructive communication within supervision. The two tasks of supervision the model addresses concern the supervision of the practitioner and the supervision of their practice. These tasks aim to: a) enhance the performance, wellbeing and development of the practitioner; and b) enable better practice with clients and better outcomes for clients. Figure 14.1 below illustrates the interrelationship between the processes and tasks of supervision.

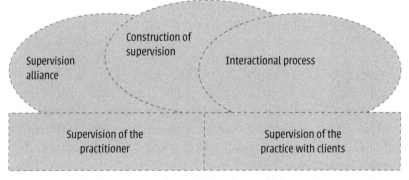

Figure 14.1: An evidence-informed supervision model

Application of processes and tasks in supervisory practice

The application of the processes and tasks of the evidence-informed model in supervisory practice require the supervisor to draw from summaries of the key findings from social work supervision research to inform their practice. The processes within the model are integral and enabling for the effective supervision of both the practitioner and their practice with clients. In other words, the interdependencies of the process and task aspects are such that they form a dynamic, integrated model. That said, for the purpose of this chapter, and to elaborate on the model, each aspect will be discussed separately with the application in practice illustrated by the use of a fictional case example.

Construction of supervision

The research evidence summarized by O'Donoghue *et al.* (2017) found that supervision is both socially and personally constructed. It is socially constructed by the contexts within which it is embedded and personally constructed by the participants' expectations, experiences and enactment. Supervision is composed of the administrative, educative and support functions and routinely practised through individual meetings or sessions, with group sessions being either a supplementary addition or substitute. How supervision is arranged in any particular setting is subject to the social, cultural, organizational, professional and practice context within which it occurs, and the supervisors' and supervisees' understanding of supervision derived from their experiences.

The research evidence also shows that there are clear indications that supervisees prefer supervision that is focused on their practice, education and support rather than on administrative matters. The research evidence also shows that supervisors construct and understand supervision differently from supervisees. They see it as a relational and reflective process concerned with organizational and professional accountability, development and support. The implications of this for supervisory practice are that supervisors in their work with supervisees need to negotiate and maintain a shared understanding of the social, cultural, organizational, professional and practice context within which supervision is immersed and how supervision is constructed within their particular setting.

To illustrate the application of this process in practice we join Dannielle (supervisor) and John (supervisee) at the start of their supervision relationship. Dannielle welcomes John to supervision and after checking in with him about his day and how his work is going generally, their conversation turns to what supervision will involve. Dannielle leads this conversation by asking John, 'What are your expectations of supervision?' She listens to his responses about 'wanting to be supported in his practice', 'to develop professionally', 'to have a space to reflect safely and confidentially'. Dannielle also clarifies with John the meaning of what he wants, and then explores his past experiences of supervision regarding what was helpful and less helpful to him. From there, the conversation progresses to John's understanding of the agency's supervision policy, guidelines, their respective roles, responsibilities, practical arrangements, accountabilities, and the mandate (both organization and professional) that sanctions their supervision.

Having explored the agency's policy and guidelines, Dannielle introduces the supervision agreement template and outlines her expectations regarding preparation for, participation in and the process of supervision. She then checks with John what his understanding is of what will happen in supervision, what may happen, and what does not happen. Dannielle is mindful and responsive to John's preferences for a focus on his practice, development and support. She also clarifies with him that her role involves supervising both John *and* his practice. Dannielle emphasizes that supervision is both a relational and reflective practice that involves having a shared understanding of its purpose and expectations in order to meet their personal, organizational and professional expectations and responsibilities. They conclude this conversation by making a plan to complete the supervision agreement and to revisit their shared understanding of supervision when they review the draft agreement.

Supervision alliance

According to O'Donoghue *et al.* (2017), the supervision alliance is essential for effective supervision. The characteristics of a strong supervision alliance are trust, support, honesty, openness, and the ability to collaboratively navigate power relations, as well as respecting social and cultural differences. For supervisors, their ability to demonstrate well-developed personal and professional qualities and attributes (particularly empathy and emotional intelligence) as well as practice expertise and relationship skills, contributes to their standing within the relationship. This in turn contributes to their supervisees having a secure base from which to participate fully.

Where the supervision relationship or alliance is not strong and supervisors have both clinical and managerial roles, supervision has the potential to become predominantly concerned with administrative compliance and surveillance. The effect of this on supervisees in these relationships is that they become less engaged in supervision and may act to avoid being supervised by saying they are too busy. They may subvert and undermine the authority of the supervisor and the process of supervision by not bringing or raising practice issues, or challenges, or seeking to divert the supervisor's enquiries into such matters by discussing organizational issues or personal matters.

Overall, the research highlights that for supervisors, the supervision alliance concerns establishing and sustaining a constructive, considerate, culturally competent and caring relationship with supervisees based upon empathy and emotional intelligence, expertise in practice and relationship skills.

To illustrate how this occurs in practice, let us revisit Dannielle and John who have established a supervision agreement and completed several sessions of supervision together. Over the course of these sessions, Dannielle has attended to John and focused on establishing a trusting relationship. This has involved checking in about what is happening for him and his work, as well as acknowledging the social and cultural differences between them, including exploring how John's needs in regard to gender and cultural differences can be met. Dannielle has also tuned into John's body language and is sensitive to whether the tone of voice, his body language and the language he uses changes or differs from her previous experiences. Dannielle pays particular attention to indicators of vulnerability, for example whether his voice is strained, there is a change in pitch, the words he uses, his facial expression, such as whether he is flushed or tearful. Dannielle also reflects back his emotional responses to show her understanding of his situation and experience. She also tailors her intervention to respond to what she has picked up, and intervenes by saying, 'I've been noticing this', or 'I've heard you saying these comments and it has really concerned me. I am wondering what is happening for you?' Depending on John's response and the nature of the concern, she decides whether to discuss the matter further or give him time to think about her comments. Throughout her time with John, she is working to maintain the alliance and connection as well as emphasizing that supervision is something that they are engaged in together.

Interactional process

The interactional process is reflective of the quality of the supervision alliance and has been described metaphorically as the dancing that produces the dance of supervision – with how well the dancers dance depending on each person doing their part and how in sync they are with each other (O'Donoghue 2014b). The research evidence related to this shows that the interactional process is formal and mirrors the social work helping process (O'Donoghue *et al.* 2017). The supervision session, like the social work interview, has a structure and engages the supervisee in an interactive, reflective, problem-solving process (O'Donoghue 2014b; Tsui 2006). The structure varies according to the type of supervision, the people involved, cultural and ethnic diversity and the dynamics of the process (Itzhaky and Rudich 2003/2004; O'Donoghue 2014b; O'Donoghue *et al.* 2017; Tsui 2004). The evidence also indicates that where the interactional process is unstructured and unproductive, supervisees are disorientated and dissatisfied with supervision (Kadushin 1992; O'Donoghue 2008; O'Donoghue 2014b; O'Donoghue *et al.* 2017). Nonetheless, the overall message concerning the interactional process is that it is progressive and moves through the phases of preparation, engagement, planning, working and ending. It also involves constructive, interactive, discursive exchanges between the supervisee and supervisor.

For the practice application of this aspect let's now return to our supervisor Dannielle, who is mindful that she has a session starting soon with John. In her preparation for this session, Dannielle reviews the notes from their last session and identifies items and actions to follow up with John. She also thinks about John, particularly, what she has noticed about his behaviour over the week and she ponders questions such as, 'How is he in his role?' and 'What might he bring to the session?' Dannielle also attends to her setting – she diverts her phone, switches her mobile phone to silent and puts the 'do not disturb' sign on the door. She also gets a glass of water for herself and John. When John arrives, she greets and welcomes him. They have an agreement that they will start their sessions with a centring exercise in which they feel the ground beneath their feet, attend to their bodies in the chair and tune into their breathing and being present in the here and now. After this exercise, Dannielle engages John by asking, 'How has today been?' She listens, reflects back and then checks with John about his work generally, his feelings about his work, about being here in supervision and what's currently on top.

After exploring these issues, Dannielle focuses the agenda for the session by asking John what is on his list for today. Dannielle then shares the couple of items from her list that she had noted from their previous session. Having agreed on the agenda and the priority of the items, John then outlines a recent experience with a client whom he believes is at risk. Dannielle listens to John's story and then, after he has given the initial overview, she asks clarifying questions, summarizes and helps John reflect and explore the situation and his role and understanding of it, as well as demonstrating that she has an understanding of what he is presenting, what his concerns are and his reasons for discussing them. Having demonstrated this, Dannielle then uses a range of problem-solving strategies, such as circular questioning, identifying exceptions and strengths, the pros and cons, mapping using the whiteboard, the application of theory and research to the situation, and reframing. After working through the issues together to the point where John is having an 'ah hah' moment, Dannielle then advances the matter through questions such as, 'What would you like to come out of this?', 'Would you like to look at some strategies now, or…do you see any pattern in here?', 'Do you see any learning here?' Following John's responses, Dannielle then assists him to develop an action plan of agreed tasks from the exploration of possible outcomes and strategies.

Following this, Dannielle and John then discuss the remaining items on their agenda until they get near to ending their session. At this point, Dannielle reviews what has been covered in the session. She also summarizes the decisions and agreed actions and they arrange a date and time for the next session. Dannielle closes off the session by asking John, questions such as, 'How are you?', 'How did you find the session?' and 'Where will you be going next?' They then close the session with a moment of silence before John gets up and goes. After the session, Dannielle writes up the notes and shares these with John via email. She also ponders any learning for her and what she might take to her own supervision.

Supervision of the practitioner

One of the most consistent findings from supervision research is that when supervisees are helped with their work and their professional development, and given social and emotional support, they are more likely to be satisfied and effective in their work, committed to the organization, and well psychologically (Mor Barak *et al.* 2009; O'Donoghue and Tsui 2015; O'Donoghue *et al.* 2017). The task of supervising the practitioner involves first creating and sustaining a safe relational space for the supervisee to process and learn from their emotions and perceptions, particularly those pertaining to their safety, vulnerabilities and fears (O'Donoghue *et al.* 2017). It then requires attending to the development of the supervisee's professional competence through reinforcing their learning and role-modelling ethical professional standards, as well as ensuring that supervision matches the developmental level of the supervisee. The third aspect of the supervision of the practitioner is a focus on the supervisee as a person and taking an active interest in their wellbeing, emotions and professional development.

For Dannielle, the task of supervising John involves mindfully exploring what the experience is like for him, how it has affected him personally and professionally and what he needs in regard to this situation in order to grow and develop as a practitioner. What will help him learn and grow at this point in his career? In other words, Dannielle imagines what it is like for John to be in supervision discussing his concerns with her, and she considers his strengths and areas of development as a practitioner and as a human being. In terms of the session outlined above in the previous section, Dannielle's supervision of John as a practitioner initially involves picking up on John's anxiety and fear about the client. In doing this, she validates his concerns and explores with him what it is like for him to work with this challenging situation. Dannielle also explores with John the strengths he has at his disposal and the assistance available to him from others that he can draw on. Dannielle creates a holding environment which reinforces the importance of bringing his concerns and fears to supervision in order to contain them, problem solve and learn from them together with the situation from which they arose. In doing this, Dannielle focuses her questions towards John's learning from this client in relation to at-risk situations and for himself as a developing practitioner. Having worked through the impact of the situation on John, his learning and development from it and how he will implement this learning, Dannielle then attends to John's feelings about what transpired between them and whether there was anything else that she could do to assist him in his professional development.

Supervision of the practice with clients

The evidence concerning the supervision of the supervisee's practice with clients is not as well developed as the other areas within the evidence-informed model. Nonetheless, the available evidence indicates that focusing attention on the client's problems within supervision is more likely to result in better client outcomes and that an emphasis on clinical practice within supervision and organizations results in better practice outcomes (O'Donoghue and Tsui 2015; O'Donoghue *et al.* 2017).

For our supervisor Dannielle, the supervision of John's practice with clients starts when she engages him in a reflective dialogue exploring the client's issues and situation. In doing this, Dannielle aims to assist John in envisioning the best possible outcomes for the client he believes to be at risk. Dannielle does this in the problem-solving phase of her session after she has shown him that she has heard his story about the concerns he has regarding the client. We rejoin the session with John outlining the client's situation and talking about how the client is being pressured by peers to get back into synthetic drugs. John is concerned on the one hand about the impact that using drugs would have on the client's health and life and, on the other hand, about the effect that these peers are having on the client's goal of representing Aotearoa New Zealand at rugby at a youth grade. John describes how over the past six months the client has made great strides with their education and sporting achievements, including gaining enough credits for entry to university and selection in the North Island age group rugby squad.

In exploring this issue with John, Dannielle starts by asking about the client's background, culture, family, significant relationships, day-to-day life, strengths and supports, and what has changed for the client. Dannielle also asks John about how he works with youth who use psychoactive substances and about his use of motivational interviewing in his practice (Lundahl *et al.* 2010). In doing this, Dannielle also explores with John some effective ways of working with youth and the issue of substance use. They draw from research guides available in the organization and from social work journals. Part of this exploration includes a discussion about how a positive youth development approach and supportive youth-centred relationships have a positive impact on client outcomes and how John could use these ideas in his ongoing work with the client to facilitate attainment of the client's goals (Sanders and Munford 2014; Sanders, Munford and Liebenberg 2017). From their discussions, they agree to a set of strategies that draw on motivational interviewing and positive youth development ideas and they also agree they will revisit how John gets on with the client at their next session.

Challenges

The evidence-informed approach offers supervisors an integrated research-informed model for the supervision of social workers in a field where there is an absence of empirically supported models (O'Donoghue and Tsui 2015; O'Donoghue *et al.* 2017). The model presents a revised theoretical understanding of supervision that connects the processes and tasks of supervision and is responsive to the plurality of supervision arrangements found internationally (O'Donoghue 2015). The model also provides supervisors with an integrated approach to supervision practice in which they can:

- establish a shared understanding of supervision within their supervisees, and clarify roles, responsibilities and accountabilities

- effectively engage with the relational and interactional processes involved in supervision

- attend to the professional development and emotional needs of their supervisees as practising social workers

- seek to improve the supervisee's practice with clients.

In doing this, the model challenges the neoliberal and managerial influences within social work that seek to bureaucratize and reduce the role of supervision to staff surveillance and procedural compliance (Harlow *et al.* 2013). In other words, the model provides social work supervisors with a way to reconceptualize supervision within a professional framework by attending to the processes, tasks and the people involved in supervision (Brashears 1995). In order for supervisors to do this, they need to be supported through their own supervision and by organizational and professional infrastructures that support best practice.

Internationally, there is a significant challenge in regard to building supervisory capability through post-qualifying education that assists supervisors in developing their knowledge, skills and attributes in relation to the processes and tasks of supervision within the model. O'Donoghue *et al.* (2017) argue that the development of an evidence-informed supervision model has the potential to contribute to a curriculum for supervisor training, because it both summarizes the social work supervision research and translates this into principles and practices for supervisors to use in their practice. Additionally, they assert that each of the five aspects of the model could be used as modules in an education programme that assists social workers and supervisors to deepen their understanding of: the nature of social work supervision, the supervisor–supervisee alliance, the interactional process of supervision, and the effective supervision of practitioners and their social work practice.

The final challenge pertaining to this model is that it continues to be further refined in light of the latest research, and evaluated in terms of its effectiveness. This involves the training of supervisors, the development of a manual and measures, the setting of a baseline, and then a period of implementation of the model with quarterly evaluation.

Conclusion

This chapter has explored social work supervision and evidence-informed practice by reviewing the historical relationship between social work practice theory and supervision theory and providing an overview of the theory of evidence-informed social work and its application in the form of an emerging evidence-informed model of social work supervision. This model revises the theoretical understanding of supervision and connects the processes and tasks of supervision. It is also responsive to challenges of 21st-century social work. For the model to be effective there is a need internationally for investment in supervisors and the organizational and professional infrastructure supporting supervision and social work practice.

In conclusion, the most important message of this chapter is the importance of strengthening social work practitioners and their practice through supervision that embodies a shared understanding and purpose, a constructive relational and interactive process and a focus on the needs, aspirations and goals of the people we work with, be they our colleagues or clients.

Reflection questions

- Why is it important for supervisors to develop with their supervisees a shared understanding of supervision and the organizational and professional setting within which it occurs?

- What are the key aspects of a strong supervision alliance?

- What does a constructive interactional process involve?

- What are some useful questions to keep in mind when undertaking the task of supervising a practitioner?

- Why is it important to focus on client outcomes within supervision?

- What have you learned from the case example about how to practise supervision?

References

Brackett, J.R. (1903) *Supervision and Education in Charity.* New York, NY: MacMillan. Accessed on 05/09/2018 at https://archive.org/details/supervisioneduca00bracrich.

Brashears, F. (1995) 'Supervision as social work practice: A reconceptualization.' *Social Work* 40, 5, 692–699.

Burns, M. (1958) The Historical Development of the Process of Casework Supervision as Seen in the Professional Literature of Social Work. PhD dissertation. The University of Chicago, Ann Arbor, MI: University Microfilms International.

Carpenter, J., Webb, C., Bostock, L. and Coomber, C. (2012) *Effective Supervision in Social Work and Social Care* (SCIE Research Briefing 43). London: Social Care Institute for Excellence. Accessed on 05/09/2018 at www.scie.org.uk/publications/briefings/files/briefing43.pdf.

Carpenter, J., Webb, C.M. and Bostock, L. (2013) 'The surprisingly weak evidence base for supervision: Findings from a systematic review of research in child welfare practice (2000–2012).' *Children and Youth Services Review 35*, 11, 1843–1853.

Caspi, J. and Reid, W. (2002) *Educational Supervision in Social Work: A Task-Centred Model for Field Instruction and Staff Development*. New York, NY: Columbia University Press.

Cohen, B. (1999) 'Intervention and supervision in strengths-based social work.' *Families in Society 80*, 5, 460–466.

Eketone, A. (2012) 'The purposes of cultural supervision.' *Aotearoa New Zealand Social Work 24*, 3/4, 20–30.

Epstein, I. (2009) 'Promoting harmony where there is commonly conflict: Evidence-informed practice as an integrative strategy.' *Social Work in Health Care 48*, 216–231.

Eruera, M. (2012) 'He kōrari, he kete, he kōrero.' *Aotearoa New Zealand Social Work Review 24*, 3/4, 12–19.

Gambrill, E. (1999) 'Evidence-based practice: An alternative to authority-based practice.' *Families in Society: The Journal of Contemporary Social Services 80*, 4, 341–350.

Gambrill, E. (2001) 'Social work: An authority-based profession.' *Research on Social Work Practice 11*, 166–175.

Gibbs, L. and Gambrill, E. (2002) 'Evidence-based practice: Counterarguments to objections.' *Research on Social Work Practice 12*, 452–476.

Gray, M., Plath, D. and Webb, S. (2009) *Evidence-Based Social Work: A Critical Stance*. New York, NY: Routledge.

Hair, H. and O'Donoghue, K. (2009) 'Culturally relevant, socially just social work supervision: Becoming visible through a social constructionist lens.' *Journal of Ethnic and Cultural Diversity in Social Work 18*, 1/2, 70–88.

Harlow, E., Berg, E., Barry, J. and Chandler, J. (2013) 'Neoliberalism, managerialism and the reconfiguring of social work in Sweden and the United Kingdom.' *Organization 20*, 4, 534–550.

Hodge, D.R., Lacasse, J.R. and Benson, O. (2012) 'Influential publications in social work discourse: The 100 most highly cited articles in disciplinary journals: 2000–09.' *British Journal of Social Work 42*, 4, 765–782.

Hollis, F. (1966) *Casework: A Psychosocial Therapy*. New York, NY: Random House.

Itzhaky, H. and Rudich, V. (2003/2004) 'Communication and values in the cross-cultural encounter and their influence on supervision in social work.' *Arete 27*, 2, 50–64.

Kadushin, A. (1968) 'Games people play in supervision.' *Social Work 13*, 3, 23–32.

Kadushin, A. (1976) *Supervision in Social Work*. New York, NY: Columbia University Press.

Kadushin, A. (1992) 'Social work supervision: An updated survey.' *The Clinical Supervisor 10*, 2, 9–27.

Kadushin, A. and Harkness, D. (2014) *Supervision in Social Work* (5th edition). New York, NY: Columbia University Press.

Lundahl, B.W., Kunz, C., Brownell, C., Tollefson, D. and Burke, B.L. (2010) 'A meta-analysis of motivational interviewing: Twenty-five years of empirical studies.' *Research on Social Work Practice 20*, 2, 137–160.

McNeece, C.A. and Thyer, B.A. (2004) 'Evidence-based practice and social work.' *Journal of Evidence-Based Social Work 1*, 1, 7–25.

Mor Barak, M.E., Travis, D.J., Pyun, H. and Xie, B. (2009) 'The impact of supervision on worker outcomes: A meta-analysis.' *The Social Service Review 83*, 1, 3–32.

Mullen, E.J. (2016) 'Reconsidering the "idea" of evidence in evidence-based policy and practice.' *European Journal of Social Work 19*, 3/4, 310–335.

Munson, C.E. (1979) *Social Work Supervision: Classic Statements and Critical Issues*. New York, NY: Free Press.

Munson, C.E. (2002) *Handbook of Clinical Social Work Supervision* (3rd edition). Binghamton, NY: Haworth Social Work Practice.

Nevo, I. and Slonim-Nevo, V. (2011) 'The myth of evidence-based practice: Towards evidence-informed practice.' *British Journal of Social Work 41*, 1176–1197.

O'Donoghue, K. (2003) *Restorying Social Work Supervision*. Palmerston North, New Zealand: Dunmore Press.

O'Donoghue, K. (2008) 'Towards improving social work supervision in Aotearoa New Zealand.' *Aotearoa New Zealand Social Work Review 20*, 1, 10–21.

O'Donoghue, K. (2010) Towards the Construction of Social Work Supervision in Aotearoa New Zealand: A Study of the Perspectives of Social Work Practitioners and Supervisors. PhD thesis, Massey University, Palmerston North. Accessed on 09/05/2018 at http://hdl.handle.net/10179/1535.

O'Donoghue, K.B. (2014a) 'Towards an Evidence-Informed Approach to Clinical Social Work Supervision.' In M. Pack and J. Cargill (eds) *Evidence, Discovery and Assessment in Social Work Practice*. Hershey, PA: IGI Global.

O'Donoghue, K.B. (2014b) 'Towards an interactional map of the supervision session: An exploration of supervisees' and supervisors' experiences.' *Practice 26*, 1, 53–70.

O'Donoghue, K. (2015) 'Issues and challenges facing social work supervision in the twenty-first century.' *China Journal of Social Work 8*, 2, 136–149.

O'Donoghue, K.B. and Tsui, M.S. (2012) 'In search of an informed supervisory practice: An exploratory study.' *Practice: Social Work in Action 24*, 3–20.

O'Donoghue, K. and Tsui, M.S. (2015) 'Social work supervision research (1970–2010): The way we were and the way ahead.' *British Journal of Social Work 45*, 2, 616–633.

O'Donoghue, K., Wong Yuh Ju, P. and Tsui, M.S. (2017) 'Constructing an evidence-informed social work supervision model.' *European Journal of Social Work 1–11*. doi:1 0.1080/13691457.2017.1341387.

Perlman, H. (1957) *Social Casework: A Problem-Solving Process*. Chicago, IL: University of Chicago Press.

Pettes, D. (1979) *Staff and Student Supervision – A Task-Centred Approach*. London: Allen and Unwin.

Rabinowitz, J. (1987) 'Why ongoing supervision in social casework: An historical analysis.' *The Clinical Supervisor 5*, 3, 79–90.

Richmond, M. (1917) *Social Diagnosis*. New York, NY: Russell Sage.

Robinson, V. (1936) *Supervision in Social Casework*. Chapel Hill, NC: The University of North Carolina Press.

Rosen, A. (2003) 'Evidence-based social work practice: Challenges and promise.' *Social Work Research 27*, 197–208.

Sackett, D.L., Rosenberg, W.M.C., Gray, J.A.M., Haynes, R.B. and Richardson, W.S. (1996) 'Evidence-based medicine: What it is and what it isn't.' *British Medical Journal 312*, 7023, 71–72.

Sanders, J. and Munford, R. (2014) 'Youth-centred practice: Positive youth development practices and pathways to better outcomes for vulnerable youth.' *Children and Youth Services Review 46*, 160–167.

Sanders, J., Munford, R. and Liebenberg, L. (2017) 'Positive youth development practices and better outcomes for high risk youth.' *Child Abuse & Neglect 69*, 201–212.

Shulman, L. (1982) *Skills of Supervision and Staff Management*. Itasca, IL: F.E. Peacock Publishers.

Shulman, L. (2010) *Interactional Supervision* (3rd edition). Washington, DC: NASW Press.

Thomas, C. and Davis, S. (2005) 'Bicultural Strengths-Based Supervision.' In M. Nash, R. Munford and K. O'Donoghue (eds) *Social Work Theories in Action*. London: Jessica Kingsley Publishers.

Thomas, F. (2013) *Solution Focused Supervision – A Resource-Oriented Approach to Developing Clinical Expertise.* New York, NY: Springer.

Tsui, M.S. (2004) 'Supervision models in social work: From nature to culture.' *Asian Journal of Counselling 11,* 1/2, 7–55.

Tsui, M.S. (2006) 'Hopes and dreams: Ideal supervision for social workers in Hong Kong.' *Asia Pacific Journal of Social Work and Development 16,* 1, 33–42.

Webb, S. (2001) 'Some considerations on the validity of evidence based practice in social work.' *British Journal of Social Work 31,* 57–79.

Witkin, S.L. and Harrison, W.D. (2001) 'Whose evidence and for what purpose?' *Social Work 46,* 293–296.

• Chapter 15 •

Repositioning Ethical Theory in Social Work Education

DONNA MCAULIFFE AND LESLEY CHENOWETH

Introduction

There is a resounding consensus in social work practice literature that at its heart, social work is essentially a moral endeavour. The many definitions of what social work *is* carry a message that social workers have a responsibility to uphold important principles of social justice and human rights, act with integrity in all dealings with others, speak up against injustice and structures that oppress and discriminate, and promote systems that are based on compassion and care. Social workers make important decisions every day of their working lives. Decisions need to be justified and based on sound knowledge. Theory is key to social work in its purpose and practice as it provides a foundation for rationale of actions and interventions.

Social work programmes devote considerable time and resources to covering the requisite knowledge and theories that social workers draw on in their practice. Social work education can be conceptualized in three core foundational areas: first, knowledge of and engagement with social work theory and other theories from social sciences, sociology, psychology and humanities; second, core social work values and ethics; and third, skills required for practice. These three pillars are interlinked and integrated in the learning journey through employing processes of reflective practice of the theory–practice nexus in the classroom and in the field. Ultimately, knowledge, values and skills come together in a holistic framework for practice that will carry a graduating student into the field with a well-integrated sense of professional identity, and the competence to work with people in a way that will uphold the values of the profession (Chenoweth and McAuliffe 2018; Trevithick 2012).

For the purposes of this chapter, we will focus on the value that knowledge of ethics and ethical theory brings to honing the skills of robust and principled decision making. We will explore the key ethical theories that underpin social work ethics and ethical decision making and illustrate how this sometimes neglected body of theory can be critical for attaining a deeper understanding of motivations and actions of self and others at a moral level. We are motivated by three main questions in this chapter:

1. Do social work students and practitioners have a solid understanding of ethical theories from the field of moral philosophy more broadly? If not, should they?

2. Would a deeper engagement with these theories at an earlier stage of the education process be helpful to students in developing their knowledge and skills for effective decision making?

3. What might be the most effective approach in educating students about the various theories of ethics in the context of a social work programme?

The chapter is divided into three main sections. The first presents some of our own experiences that have prompted thinking about the current status of the teaching of theory in social work. We explore a selection of some of the most referenced and recommended texts in general social work theory with a view to determining the extent to which ethical theories are covered within the broader area of social work theory, that is, theories *of* social work and theories *for* social work. The second section focuses more specifically on the teaching of ethics in social work programmes and how earlier engagement with ethical theory could potentially provide an additional lens through which to view decisions made from the individual to much higher levels. While we are primarily focused on Australia and Aotearoa New Zealand in this chapter, there are similar issues and experiences in teaching ethics internationally (see, for example, Pugh 2017; Reamer 2014). This second section considers how ethical theory can inform an understanding and in some cases appreciation (although not always agreement) of the position of others, when such positions appear at odds with social justice principles. In the third section, the gaps in ethical theory and education are outlined and proposals as to what might be the most effective approach to address them are offered through a series of case studies. Finally, comment is offered on some of the future challenges for both educators and practitioners.

Current state of theory in social work education

Throughout our work in social work education and in our engagement with practitioners over many years, we have often pondered the extent to which social workers know and understand ethical theories. After all, as a profession strongly guided by theory for practice and also so deeply guided by ethical practice, it would seem a fair and reasonable assumption that social workers would be very aware of ethical theory and why it is important – just as they are aware of psychological, sociological, social science and social work theories. We provide an example from our own practice to illustrate that this knowledge of ethical theory is not always able to be well articulated.

Teaching ethics – the moral continuum

Over the years, we have conducted many workshops on ethical decision making for practitioners in a range of settings. These workshops are based on the *inclusive model of ethical decision making* (McAuliffe and Chenoweth 2008). As a lead-in to discussion of ethical theory, we often set up a *moral continuum* activity where we ask participants to position themselves on a line where they can move up and down the continuum as a case unfolds. The participants need to decide where to position themselves as more information about the case is provided and decisions need to be made about what should happen as more details are revealed in sequence. We have used a range of cases, including child protection scenarios; health-related cases with a focus on end-of-life, suicide or negligent practice; criminal justice cases with a focus on capital punishment or mandated therapeutic interventions; and relationship-based scenarios involving family violence, infidelity, secrets, and confidentiality breaches. The cases are tailored to the participant audience and their field of practice.

This activity allows participants a space to explore their own value positions on controversial topics, and also to hear the justifications of others for their positions, which may substantially differ. It gives space for dialogue, and opportunity for consideration of deeply held moral beliefs and how these might impact on personal and professional decisions. At the conclusion of the activity, participants are asked to identify and reflect on their own process and what factors might have resulted in them taking a firm stance at particular points in the case. Typically, participants are able to do this well; however, when it comes to putting ethical theory language around the decision-making justifications, our experience has been that this is much more difficult and much of the terminology is foreign to them unless they have specifically been exposed to this language in an educative context.

For example, if a participant took a firm position on the basis of adherence to law, rules or a policy in an end-of-life case, elected to act on the basis of a standard in a code of ethics, or held a religious position against the taking of life (for example, in the case of euthanasia) then their rationale might be in accordance with the ethical theory of *deontology*. This theoretical position dates back to Immanuel Kant (often known as Kantian ethics) and is based on duty and reliance on rules rather than consequences. If a position taken was on the basis of *the greatest good for the greatest number*, this could be a *utilitarian* position, and would have involved a weighing up of consequences for a range of stakeholders, perhaps clients, their families or the broader society, including the distribution of healthcare resources. Utilitarianism is known as a teleological or consequentialist theory and one of the primary criticisms of it is its propensity to further marginalize disenfranchised voices.

A *communitarian* ethical position could also be relevant if the concerns were for the collective good above those of the individual, perhaps in a community context. If a participant found themselves constantly asking what a a compassionate response would entail or what the implications would be for relationships and connections with others, perhaps including an analysis of power relations, this could be viewed as an *ethic of care* response from within the feminist perspective. More contemporary literature has adopted the concept of *relational ethics*, which focuses on the importance of the relationships between people rather than on what is *right* or *wrong*. Similarly, if there was contemplation on what professional attributes might be upheld, or what a person who was of good moral character would do, this may show a rationale based in *virtue ethics*. This theoretical position dates back to Aristotle and is person rather than action based, meaning that the focus is on what virtues or character traits the person demonstrates (such as honesty, fidelity, loyalty) as opposed to what actions they take or decisions they make.

In addition to these classic groupings of ethical theory, there are important concepts such as *moral absolutism* and *ethical relativism* that twist and weave through the debates about right and wrong, good and bad. In a world where cultural considerations are increasingly at the forefront of many social issues, an understanding of these positions is also critical. While many ethical theories have their roots in Western moral philosophy, there are a range of *Eastern philosophical positions* and *indigenous worldviews* that make up a complex philosophical landscape and provide depth to reflective practice (McAuliffe 2014). Inclusion of these ideologies and perspectives has been for too long absent from ethics literature, and students have been confused as to why philosophies from Buddhism, Hinduism, Confucianism and Judaism have been relegated to second place, if present at all. This is particularly noticeable when many of these Eastern philosophies speak more clearly to the values of social work in their focus on harmony, balance, compassion, respect, awareness and social and collective responsibility.

Yip (2016, p.126) sets out a compelling argument for a shift from rights-based discourse to responsibility-based language, stating that:

> Most social work leaders in western countries are familiar with rights in terms of advocacy, the strengths perspective and empowerment. But they may fail to have a deep theoretical underpinning of the philosophical debate concerning the language of rights. From such a view of rights, they do not look deeper into other cultures that may not anchor the language of rights. In these countries such as China, Korea and Japan, the language of responsibility is rooted in tradition and culture.

In cases where a clear ethical dilemma for a practitioner forms part of the scenario, and may include many cultural considerations, the moral continuum activity demonstrates that what might be an ethical dilemma for one person may not be so for another. Or one person might construct an ethical dilemma using different conflicting principles. For example, an ethical dilemma about whether or not a sensitive discussion should be recorded in a case file might be framed by one practitioner as autonomy (the right of the practitioner to not disclose some things told to them by a client) versus duty of care (for the client or others); or by another as privacy (for the client) versus organizational mandate (that full disclosure in case files is expected as part of policy). This is one of the most important points that needs to be understood before any ethical decision-making process can be contemplated. If a person does not identify a situation as an ethical dilemma (x versus y), they *will* be able to make a decision about what to do and should go forth and make that decision, as there will not be competing ethical principles to have to deal with. This does not mean that the decision itself might not be difficult and hard to make (so there is still an ethical problem that should be acknowledged), but the direction is clear and the action justifiable. It would not, however, technically be an ethical *dilemma* in accordance with the definition of this term (Banks 2012; Beckett, Maynard and Jordan 2017; McAuliffe 2014).

Reviewing ethics in key social work texts

Our experiences with social work and other health and human services practitioners who appear unfamiliar with ethical terminology (many of them very experienced workers) leads us to question whether ethical theory has perhaps been a neglected body of knowledge in the teaching of theories of and for social work. It is not that these practitioners lack knowledge of ethics or of appropriate conduct, as we have been constantly impressed with the depth of thought and willingness to explore complex issues. There does, however, seem to be a lack of connection to knowledge that comes from moral philosophy. To pursue this line of questioning, we explored the extent to which major ethical theories and their roots in philosophy are covered in some of the most popular and widely cited social work and human service texts currently used in social work education. While this was very much a preliminary exploration, it did yield some interesting findings and prompted further areas for inquiry.

A total of nine texts that are widely used in social work programmes in Australia and Aotearoa New Zealand were reviewed for content on ethical theory. Texts that specifically pertain to social work theory were selected for review, though some more general introductory texts were also included for the purpose of comparison. The texts included author-only and edited texts. We first reviewed the tables of contents for chapters or sections addressing the topic and then checked the indices and glossaries for entries on ethics, ethical theory, ethical decision making, and the terminology most commonly used in referring to different ethical theories as previously described.

The edited text by Mel Gray and Stephen Webb, *Social Work Theories and Methods* (2013), illustrates the role of theory in explanation of social phenomena and social structures and is focused on *thinking about social work*, which is clearly specified by the editors at the outset. While the term *ethics* has only a small number of mentions, it is of interest that the book focuses intentionally on theorists like Habermas, Foucault, Bourdieu, Butler and Giddens, who have played a major role in influencing contemporary philosophical thought about social relations. Major ethical theories are not explored in the traditional way in this book; however, there is a section on the *ethic of care* and reference to the influence of Carol Gilligan in the chapter on feminist theory, as would be expected.

There are four texts that are commonly used in teaching social work theory courses, these being Mary Nash, Robyn Munford and Kieran O'Donoghue's text *Social Work Theories in Action* (2005); Marie Connolly and Louise Harms's text *Social Work: From Theory to Practice* (2015); Karen Healy's text *Social Work Theories in Context* (2014); and Malcolm

Payne's text *Modern Social Work Theory* (2014). In all of these texts there is limited content on ethical theory, although Connolly and Harms do set out a clear relationship-based foundation from which to explore practice. Nash, Munford and O'Donoghue provide an edited text that has a strong cultural base and relies on the ecological perspective to explore cross-cultural practice. Healy does not cover ethical theory, although there is a philosophical foundation of commitment to ethical and accountable practice. Payne covers the *ethic of care* in some detail within his chapter on feminist theory, but does not make mention of any other ethical theories. The most recent addition to the social work theory literature in this region is the text by David Hodgson and Lynelle Watts, *Key Concepts and Theory in Social Work* (2017), which does not include content on ethical theory per se, but does include a chapter on decision making and professional judgement.

The generalist text *Social Work: Contexts and Practice,* edited by Marie Connolly, Louise Harms and Jane Maidment (2017), has one chapter on social work theory and a separate chapter on social justice and critical reflection. Ethical theories are not covered in the theory chapter but in later chapters Sharlene Nipperess provides reference to John Rawls and the Theory of Justice, and Charlotte Williams clearly defines the complex concept of cultural relativism. There is a strong values-based thread throughout the 19 chapters of this book, with clear attention to the multitude of cultural and practice issues that will inevitably confront and challenge social workers. In a similar vein, the critical perspective text *Engaging with Social Work*, written by Christine Morley, Selma Macfarlane and Phillip Ablett (2014), also has a chapter on social work theory and a separate one on values and ethics, with the content of this ethics chapter covering ethical theories, including utilitarianism, deontology, virtue ethics and ethical decision making.

Finally, it is of note that our own text on generalist introductory social work and human services, *The Road to Social Work and Human Service Practice* (Chenoweth and McAuliffe 2018) follows the same structure of separating out a chapter on ethics that does, like the Morley, Macfarlane and Ablett book, include a range of ethical theories in a discrete chapter. These theories include deontology, teleology/utilitarianism, virtue ethics, ethic of care, communitarianism and contractarianism. In reflecting on ethics education literature and the dialogue we have engaged in to prepare this chapter, we have come to question the wisdom of the disconnect of general social work theories from ethical theories that have so much to offer social work. Perhaps there are possibilities for expanding the theory to practice linkages by formally housing ethical theory where it may better belong – within courses dedicated to exploration of all that falls under *theory*.

In summary, it would be true to say that there is scant attention paid to ethical theory in generic social work theory texts. The reviewed texts offer comprehensive content on social work theories and are excellent resources for students and practitioners. Different frameworks are used to explore and analyse these theories but the essential theories for practice, including psychodynamic, systems/ecological, cognitive-behavioural, strengths, solution-focused, anti-oppressive, are covered in most texts. Most also mention or discuss codes of ethics, although the degree to which these are interrogated varies. Literature that is specifically targeted at social work values and ethics, of course, always has chapters dedicated to the foundations of ethical theory and generally explores codes of ethics and ethical decision making in detail (Banks 2012; Beckett *et al.* 2017; Gray and Webb 2010; Hugman 2005a; McAuliffe 2014). The problem is that not all social work programmes have courses dedicated specifically to ethics, so where these courses combine ethics with law, human rights or policy, attention to ethical theory may be more minimal as other content dominates. Incorporating ethical theory at an earlier stage of a curriculum, where social work theory courses generally sit, may give better opportunity for the foundations to be set before students engage more specifically with the study of ethics and professional practice. This leads us to an exploration of how ethics is generally taught, and what the possibilities might be for clearer integration of ethical theory in other parts of a social work curriculum.

Teaching ethics in social work

Ethics is fundamental to social work. The International Federation of Social Workers (IFSW) (2018) requires all member organizations to have a code of ethics or at a minimum adopt the IFSW ethical principles that are set out on a platform of social justice and human rights. Accreditation standards for social work programmes in most countries require the inclusion of courses or course components on ethics. For example, the Australian Association of Social Workers (AASW) *Education and Accreditation Standards* (2012) specifically require that social work education programmes cover content that results in knowledge of social work ethics, and one of the graduate attributes is to ensure sound understanding of and commitment to social work values and ethics to guide professional practice. The process of ethical decision making is a fundamental element of social work practice and a core component of social work programmes. Although the AASW *Code of Ethics* (2010) includes a specific section on ethical practice and decision making, we now question the extent to which this has become more of a technical exercise, that is, included in skills for social work rather than a deep philosophical engagement with ethical theories that can then inform and explain the technical processes of decision making. It is the integration between the technical and the moral that will firm up confidence in working with the many challenging situations that social workers face in practice.

Values and ethics have been a central feature of social work education and professional development from the early beginnings of the profession. Students encounter ethics through their initial engagement in understanding the role and purpose of social work and through discussion of social work values and founding principles to implementation in practice as ethical decision making. Reamer (1998) acknowledges that social work ethics have shifted through history from the early morality period, to engagement with values and the goals of social work, to the focus on ethical decision making and currently the management of risk and malpractice through ethical standards. Social work ethics education reflects that history. For example, in more recent decades there has been attention in the literature to the more technical and practical aspect of ethics for social work practice, especially in the processes of ethical decision making and associated models (Groessl 2015; Reamer 2012).

There are now so many ethical dilemmas that confront practitioners that attention needs to be paid in ethics education to setting out content, including (but not limited to) confidentiality and privacy, informed consent and assessment of capacity, boundary issues and dual/multiple relationships, duty of care and duty to warn, collegial and workplace relationships, disclosures, competence and impaired practice. In the context of field education, Reamer (2012) outlines the need to focus on: 1) value base; 2) ethical dilemmas; 3) ethical decision making; and 4) ethics risk management for field education. In more recent literature, Reamer (2017) has sounded a warning that social workers need to pay close attention to ethical dilemmas arising from the digital age, as advances in technology are resulting in a host of new ethical dilemmas not previously encountered.

Boland-Prom and Anderson (2013) outline three approaches to the teaching of ethics. The process model covers broad ethical issues within the context of social work values and principles and focuses on self-analysis and reflection through decision making. The technical model has more of a focus on codes of ethics, ethical decision making applied to case examples and application of the codes. The third approach is the comprehensive model, which uses both process and technical approaches.

The question of how ethics is best taught in social work also extends to the debates about whether ethical content should be infused through a curriculum or taught as a discrete course. Sanders and Hoffman (2010) advocate caution in using a predominantly infused model on the basis of incoherence in ensuring that all relevant material is covered. It has only been in the last two decades that most social work programmes in the Australian and Aotearoa New Zealand context have shifted to a discrete ethics course model and there is still evidence that many courses combine ethics with other content areas such as law and policy. It is interesting to note that there has been very little evaluation of the effectiveness of these approaches to the teaching of ethics. However, there have been debates in the literature about what Hugman (2005b) called the *paradox* of teaching ethics. This includes an inherent tension of understanding ethics as a rules-of-conduct exercise with possible correct answers against an understanding of the ambiguities of social work practice as an intrinsically moral endeavour. This leads us towards a proposal for new approaches to the teaching of ethics in social work.

New approaches to ethics education

It is beyond the scope of this inquiry to make the definitive claim that social work educators never include the teaching of ethical theory, within a context of moral philosophy, in introductory courses on social work theory. While theoretical paradigms are broad ranging and cover the spectrum of the human experience from individual through to structural, it is proposed that an important theoretical body of knowledge that sheds light on *why* and *how* individuals, groups and organizations make the decisions that they do at a deeper moral level should not be sidelined. The language and concepts that sit within a moral philosophy framework are often avoided, perhaps because of their complexity, and should be introduced in the early years of social work education, rather than relegated to inclusion in courses more aligned with ethical practice that typically sit later in a curriculum.

The inclusion of ethical theory in an early stage social work theory course could potentially go further than the traditional focus on the moral theories of development as part of the life course. In their first year of study, students are generally introduced to psychoanalytic, evolutionary and cognitive theories of moral development to illustrate how behaviours are learned, how altruism develops, and how a sense of right and wrong shifts with emotional and cognitive growth. These are very important platforms of psychological knowledge for social work practice and should be included in the social work curriculum at an early stage, generally within courses on human behaviour and development across the lifespan. They could, however, also be revisited in more specific social work theory courses so that students can make the links from these moral development theories to other theories that draw on systems, ecological and critical approaches. It is easy to see how the suite of ethical theories might struggle to find a place in a social work theory course. However, the problem with not incorporating the ethical terminology at an early stage is that students may not be able to integrate this as well as other theory, as they see it as a different set of knowledge related only to ethical conduct. The application to analysis of systems, perhaps using a utilitarian approach, and to students' own sense of developing professional autonomy and proficiency in decision making based on relational ethics may not be as well understood.

So what are the ethical theories that could ideally be included in a social work theory course, and how can these be explained in a way that links theory to practice? One of the difficulties with ethical theories is their undeniable complexity, and the shifts and developments over the course of a history that extends back to the time of early Greek philosophers. The very nature of moral philosophy relies on debate and refutal, rather than necessarily on consensus and agreement that there is a true and correct path to follow and a right answer to be found. The very definition of the term *philosophy* is the rational investigation of truths and principles of being, knowledge or conduct. It is the investigation that is of importance, not the outcomes. This can be difficult for social work students to grasp. The fact that there are many shades of grey in ethics, where much depends on situational factors, often leaves students who seek *black and white* answers in an uncomfortable quandary.

The logical starting point for any discussion of moral philosophy and ethical theory is to set out the historical timeline of ethical theory and locate developments in social work theory alongside this. The work by Reamer (1998, 2017) referred to earlier in this chapter sets out the historical evolution of values and ethics in social work and the periods of time in which there was different emphasis on defining values, establishing how ethical theory was useful for social work practice, establishing standards of conduct, developing models of ethical decision making and formalizing codes of ethics. There are a number of examples of how developments in ethics line up with developments in social work theory. In the 1930s and onwards, social work was highly influenced by the medical model with an emphasis on social casework, positivism and scientific evidence.

Advances in bioethical thinking travelled a parallel track with development of the 'four principles approach' as outlined by Beauchamp and Childress (1979), specifying beneficence, non-maleficence, autonomy and justice as the unrivalled platforms that would result, if followed, in medical practitioners doing no harm. The Hippocratic Oath, and the codes of ethics of many professions that took its lead, were documents designed to impose rules and sanctions, thus falling into the deontological camp.

Another example was in the 1970s, with the rise of critical and radical social work that was heavily influenced by feminist perspectives. Alongside and within feminist theory was the *ethic of care* that dictated a relational response to ethical decision making antithetical to theories of justice that called for individualist approaches which did not take relationships into account in any meaningful way. Shifts towards postmodern ideologies and poststructural theories that became influential in social work in the 1990s were reflected in emerging theories of ethical and moral pluralism that held that conflicting values may all be equally valid and worthy of respect, and that truth may lie in many places.

If we look at the respective timelines of social work theory and the developments in ethical theory, it is possible to draw the connections and in so doing, weave together a more comprehensive theoretical framework that will ultimately provide students with more robust knowledge on which to base their skills and interrogate their values. When students come to study a discrete course on ethics and professional practice – a position that we strongly advocate – they will be able to integrate and draw on this theoretical knowledge and apply it to case scenarios designed specifically to explore ethical dilemmas and develop skills in ethical decision making.

The following quote by Beckett *et al.* (2017, p.33) sums up much of the arguments so far in this chapter well:

> We do not suggest that scholarly debates about the relative merits of utilitarianism and deontology are a common occurrence in the normal working day of a social worker, but debates about what is the right thing to do are common and, if you look under the surface of these debates, you will find differences of view, not only about what is right and wrong in a given situation, but about the nature of right and wrong themselves. Social workers do take deontological and utilitarian positions even if they do not use those words, and do advocate various types of virtue ethics even if they never mention Aristotle.

We move on now to present three cases that serve to illustrate how a situation that might originally be presented for exploration using traditional social work theories can be viewed through a more expansive lens with the inclusion of relevant ethical theory.

Case study 1: The National Disability Insurance Scheme: social justice, neoliberalist or utilitarian response? ....

The National Disability Insurance Scheme (NDIS) was launched in Australia in 2015 with the promise of more choice and control for people with disabilities. In responding to the findings of the Productivity Commission that the current support system gave people with disability little choice and no certainty of access to appropriate supports, Australia introduced an insurance model for disability support – the NDIS. The NDIS is based strongly on the United Nations Convention on the Rights of Persons with Disabilities (CRPD), which advocates a person-centred approach to the provision of services for people with disabilities (United Nations 2006). The NDIS therefore is regarded as having a strong social justice theme in its policies and aims. It also has a person-centred, market-driven delivery method of implementation. Undertaking a critical analysis of the NDIS makes it possible to unpack neoliberal ideologies of managerialism, individual responsibility and privatized market service delivery. Indeed, many accounts of the policy provide exactly that kind of analysis. Others argue that it represents an acknowledgment and upholding of the rights of people with disability. There is ample space for debate here. So how might ethical theory contribute to these debates?

Another perhaps less discussed aspect of the NDIS is that it also had the aim of providing more targeted support to more people. More than 400,000 people are deemed to be receiving support at the completion of the roll out – a significant increase in overall numbers nationally. So does the NDIS represent a way of providing the greatest good to the greatest number?

Another aspect of the NDIS is that it seeks to promote social inclusion and the wellbeing of people with disability and their carers through supporting these relationships in a network of social relations. So a central question for students and practitioners is: does the NDIS also represent a way of promoting practices within an ethic of care?

Case study 2: Child protection: a compassionate response? ..

Consider a situation in a child protection agency where a worker is faced with the decision of whether to remove three children from a mother addicted to crystal methamphetamine (ice) or to preserve the family. This is a common scenario for social workers across many jurisdictions. There are clear and immediate risks to the children in terms of safety and neglect, as well as long-term risks arising from disruption of the family unit and precarious care arrangements within the child safety system. Many theories inform this practice situation, such as child development and attachment, family systems, ecological theory, theories of addiction and dependency, as well as theories of resilience, strengths and power. Certainly, most practitioners in this situation would engage in a process of ethical decision making but would this also include a thorough consideration of ethical theories? Deontology would require the practitioner to consider their duties and the rules governing the situation. What is the right thing to do in accordance with duty? What are the legal obligations here and what rules are embodied in agency policies and procedures? Utilitarianism would require a focus on the consequences of the action for all parties, asking for consideration of what action would cause the most benefit over cost. Adopting a feminist ethic-of-care position would highlight the importance of interpersonal relationships and compassion or benevolence as a virtue central to moral action. So a central question for students and practitioners is: how might the focus shift if the central question asked what a compassionate response would require?

Case study 3: Cyberbullying: multiple considerations on a growing social problem

Internationally, media reports of increased cases of teenagers taking their own lives in a desperate attempt to escape online bullying are pushing mental health services into crisis. Cyberbullying has become a national social problem and responses range from shifting the responsibility back to parents, to blaming schools for perceived inaction, to government rhetoric about laws to stop young people under the age of 12 from having access to social media. Applying a critical social work lens to cyberbullying exposes the power structures that have created social media and internet addiction, and how businesses make millions out of this technology with no concern for the impact it has on young lives. Is this a utilitarian perspective where benefits outweigh costs? Do the advantages of a connected world override those who end up in the mental health system as a result of social media tragedies? Social workers might well look to use theories of human development to explain why young people turn to social media to develop peer relationships, or how strengthening family and social systems can mitigate against social isolation. So central questions for students and practitioners are: do deontological responses focused on regulation and law play any real role here? Or is the response better guided by relational ethics that value interpersonal connections, respect human dignity and worth and uphold virtues of care for others?

These three case studies, and others like them, give students and practitioners the opportunity to engage in a deep way with ethical thinking, rationale and dialogue. When ethics education is used in an interactive way, such as with the moral continuum activity detailed earlier in this chapter, reflection on moral positioning is given a more prominent place in the education context.

Future challenges

There is no disputing that the range and types of ethical dilemmas facing social workers across multiple fields of practice are becoming more complex, and the need for skills in ethical decision making is a critical part of the requirements of a work-ready graduate. Not only do social workers need to have a secure sense of their own professional identity, but they also need to have a good appreciation of the value positions of their professional colleagues who will come from a range of disciplinary backgrounds. The case for ethics to be taught in an interdisciplinary way has been made elsewhere (McAuliffe 2014). While this chapter has posed a challenge to social work educators, particularly those engaged in teaching and writing about theory for social work practice, it has also provided a way forward in suggesting that better integration of ethical theory into social work theory courses is possible and could be of benefit to students. For this to make sense to students, however, there does need to be a follow-up course on ethics and professional practice later in social work programmes so that students can focus more specifically on ethical decision making in practice.

The social work education issue is not the only one needing consideration. It has become apparent that social work practitioners and managers who may not have had the benefit of learning about ethical theory in their own education, often many years back, may not have access to this body of knowledge in an accessible way. There may be a need for professional development to focus on this area with theory revision workshops or webinars that can fill this gap for experienced practitioners, many of whom are responsible for supervising students and new graduates. Ethical theory could then be incorporated as part of a suite of theory revision so that the language of the moral endeavour in which we are all engaged can be extended and better understood.

Conclusion

This chapter has set out a series of questions relevant to social work educators and those involved in designing social work programmes and curricula. The case in point is whether social work students could benefit from an earlier exposure to a body of knowledge pertaining to ethical theory and whether this knowledge could be integrated into social work theory courses. We are of the view that practitioners are relatively unfamiliar with the basic terminology and concepts of ethical theories that provide essential foundations for ethical decision making. From our preliminary review of a range of social work theory and generalist texts commonly used in the Australian and Aotearoa New Zealand region, we suggest that there is room for the inclusion of content that more specifically focuses on ethical theory. As educators lead social work students towards the development of a framework for professional practice through the years of their study, it could be argued that a social work practice framework devoid of an ethical dimension will be missing a critical element (Weinberg 2016). If graduating students are able to articulate their knowledge, values and skills in a way that also includes their understanding of the moral dimensions of practice, they will surely have a stronger professional identity to carry them with more confidence into the workforce. Furthermore, if efforts are made to provide professional development on theory, including ethical theory, to practising social workers in the field, there is increased likelihood for social work to hold its place as an important professional stakeholder in ethical decision making.

Reflection questions

- What is the role and place of moral philosophy and ethical theory in social work education?

- What could be the potential benefits of including ethical theory in social work theory courses?

- What are the barriers to inclusion of ethical theory in courses dedicated to social work theory?

- How should professional ethics be taught in social work programmes?

- How can ethics be kept on the agenda for students when they move into practice, and how can continuing professional development incorporate exploration of ethical dimensions of practice in contemporary workplaces?

References

Australian Association of Social Workers (AASW), (2010) *Code of Ethics*. Canberra, Australia. Accessed on 09/03/2018 at www.aasw.asn.au/practitioner-resources/code-of-ethics.

Australian Association of Social Workers (AASW) (2012) *Australian Social Work Education and Accreditation Standards*. Canberra, Australia. Accessed on 09/03/2018 at www.aasw.asn.au/careers-study/education-standards-accreditation.

Banks, S. (2012, original work published 1995) *Ethics and Values in Social Work*. London: Palgrave Macmillan.

Beauchamp, T.L. and Childress, J.F. (1979) *Principles of Biomedical Ethics*. New York, NY: Oxford University Press.

Beckett, C., Maynard, A. and Jordan, P. (2017, original work published 2005) *Values and Ethics in Social Work*. London: Sage.

Boland-Prom, K. and Anderson, S.C. (2013) 'Teaching ethical decision making using dual relationship principles as a case example.' *Journal of Social Work Education 41*, 3, 495–510.

Chenoweth, L. and McAuliffe, D. (2018, original work published 2005) *The Road to Social Work and Human Service Practice*. South Melbourne: Cengage.

Connolly, M. and Harms, L. (2015, original work published 2012) *Social Work: From Theory to Practice*. London: Cambridge University Press.

Connolly, M., Harms, L. and Maidment, J. (2017, original work published 2011) *Social Work: Contexts and Practice*. London: Oxford University Press.

Gray, M. and Webb, S. (2010) *Ethics and Value Perspectives in Social Work*. London: Palgrave Macmillan.

Gray, M. and Webb, S. (2013, original work published 2009) *Social Work Theories and Methods*. London: Sage.

Groessl, J. (2015) 'Teaching Note – Conceptualization of a contemporary social work ethics course.' *Journal of Social Work Education 51*, 4, 691–698.

Healy, K. (2014, original work published 2005) *Social Work Theories in Context*. London: Palgrave Macmillan.

Hodgson, D. and Watts, L. (2017) *Key Concepts and Theories in Social Work*. London: Palgrave Macmillan.

Hugman, R. (2005a) *New Approaches for Ethics in the Caring Professions*. New York, NY: Palgrave Macmillan.

Hugman, R. (2005b) 'Exploring the paradox of teaching ethics for social work practice.' *Social Work Education 24*, 5, 535–545.

International Federation of Social Workers (IFSW) (2018) *Our Policies*. Accessed on 17/09/2018 at www.ifsw.org/what-is-social-work/global-definition-of-social-work.

McAuliffe, D. (2014) *Interprofessional Ethics: Collaboration in the Social, Health and Human Service*. London: Cambridge University Press.

McAuliffe, D. and Chenoweth, L. (2008) 'Leave no stone unturned: The inclusive model of ethical decision making.' *Ethics and Social Welfare 2*, 1, 3–49.

Morley, C., Macfarlane, S. and Ablett, P. (2014) *Engaging with Social Work: A Critical Introduction*. Port Melbourne: Cambridge University Press.

Nash, M., Munford, R. and O'Donoghue, K. (2005) *Social Work Theories in Action*. London: Jessica Kingsley Publishers.

Payne, M. (2014, original work published 1991) *Modern Social Work Theory*. London: Palgrave Macmillan.

Pugh, G.L. (2017) 'A model of comparative ethics education for social workers.' *Journal of Social Work Education 53*, 2, 312–326.

Reamer, F. (1998) 'The evolution of social work ethics.' *Social Work 43*, 6, 488–500.

Reamer, F. (2012) 'Essential ethics education in social work field instruction: A blueprint for field educators.' *Field Educator 2*, 2, 1–15.

Reamer, F. (2014) 'Ethics education in social work – transformation of a profession.' *Social Work Today 14*, 2, 14.

Reamer, F. (2017) 'Evolving ethical standards in the digital age.' *Australian Social Work 70*, 2, 148–159.

Sanders, S. and Hoffman, K. (2010) 'Ethics education in social work: Comparing outcomes of graduate social work students.' *Journal of Social Work Education 46*, 1, 7–22.

Trevithick, P. (2012, original work published 2000) *Social Work Skills and Knowledge: A Practice Handbook*. Maidenhead: Open University Press.

United Nations (2006) *Convention on the Rights of Persons with Disabilities and Optional Protocol*. Accessed on 12/05/2018 at www.un.org/disabilities/documents/convention/convoptprot-e.pdf.

Weinberg, M. (2016) 'Critical approaches to ethics in social work: Kaleidoscope not bleach.' *Social Alternatives 35*, 4, 85–89.

Yip, K. (2016) 'Shifting from a Rights-Based Social Work to a Responsibility-Based Social Work: An Initial Articulation.' In R. Hugman and J. Carter (eds) *Rethinking Values and Ethics in Social Work*. London: Palgrave Macmillan.

• Chapter 16 •

Conclusion: Emerging Theories for Effective Social Work Practice

ROBYN MUNFORD AND KIERAN O'DONOGHUE

This final chapter brings together the central ideas across the chapters and explores the key elements of effective practice. The authors have presented emerging theories for social work practice in a range of fields of practice and have illustrated these with case examples. While the issues and contexts explored are diverse, there are common themes across practice settings. Considered together they contribute to a framework for effective social work practice. The international definition of social work (International Federation of Social Workers (IFSW) 2014) provides a foundation for this practice. This definition encompasses the principles of social justice, human rights, collective responsibility and respect for diversities, and defines social work practice as working on the individual level and the wider level of groups and communities, and at a global level. The international definition reinforces a key strength of social work practice – that of the capacity for social workers to understand the connection between the personal and the structural.

We situate the discussion in this final chapter within a framework of relational practice, a key focus across all the chapters. This practice locates the client at the centre of practice and identifies the importance of the helping alliance where social workers and clients establish respectful partnerships. We begin with a discussion on relational practice followed by a discussion of integrated and evidence-informed practice and working at multiple levels. The next section explores the key foundational principles of the international definition of social work as a cornerstone of effective practice. Context and recognition of the contribution of local and indigenous knowledge in informing social work interventions are explored in the next section. The final section discusses reflection on practice as a key element of effective practice that enables social workers to respond to immediate issues and to the future challenges that are shaping social work practice globally.

Relational practice

Several chapters explore the key elements of relational practice as a cornerstone of effective practice. The discussion identifies the factors that contribute to responsive and respectful practice in work with individuals, families and groups. A key focus of relational practice is building strong helping alliances that locate the client at the centre of decision-making processes for determining plans and interventions. Effective practice begins with the social worker's ability to engage with and form meaningful relationships with clients, which, as John Pinkerton, John Canavan and Pat Dolan underline in their chapter on family support, enables practitioners to activate the psychosocial resources within a client's social ecology. As they suggest, relationships are the core component of social work practice and the personal encounter between the client and the social worker is the axis of practice.

Helping relationships have the potential to expand opportunities and possibilities for clients that can lead to better outcomes and realize different futures. Jackie Sanders and Robyn Munford explore the important role of the helping relationship in practice with young people who have experienced adverse childhood experiences. Their research showed that positive relationships with social workers created relational spaces that provided a safe space for young people to work on complex issues and hold hope for the future. The social work relationship provided a safe and secure base for young people to experience a sense of belonging and seek out opportunities for creating and strengthening positive networks.

Relational practice approaches inform interventions in diverse practice settings. For example, Polly Yeung explores two relational approaches in practice with older people: the person-centred and the capability approach. A person-centred approach ensures mutual respect in the care relationship; older people's knowledge about their context is valued and they remain at the centre of decisions about their care. The capability approach ensures that human dignity and rights are upheld and the helping relationship is a resource that promotes choice, and challenges the conditions that restrict opportunity.

Culturally responsive practice embraces the key elements of relational practice and several chapters explore these ideas. For example, in exploring the attributes of cross-cultural social work practice, Rosaleen

Ow underlines the importance of a relational and dialogical process between a practitioner and help-seeker that enables the development of a shared understanding of needs and values. The cultural context of the help-seeker informs this understanding. Associated with this is promoting an *ethic-of-care* approach which focuses on a collaborative and collective approach that underlines a relational response to solution-finding, including addressing moral and ethical issues. This orientation to practice is explored in the chapter by Donna McAuliffe and Lesley Chenoweth.

Indigenous concepts of wellbeing have much to contribute to new thinking on relational and culturally responsive practice. Paulé Ruwhiu's chapter on mana-enhancing practice identifies that respectful relationships begin with humility where history and context are acknowledged, including the impacts of colonization on indigenous populations. Authentic and genuine social work relationships are established when social workers are aware of their own cultural position and understand how this informs their practice. Indigenous perspectives also remind social workers of the importance of connections across generations, with the environment, and the connections with place and where one is from.

Tracie Mafile'o, in exploring Pacific social work practice, also calls for an acknowledgment of the role of cultural values and beliefs as integral to client–practitioner relationships. Central to this practice is building a deep understanding of what clients bring to the helping relationship, including recognition of the client as a member of a family and community; these important connections are key resources to be harnessed in social work interventions. This practice occurs at multiple levels, in direct practice with the client and their family and with the wider community. Practice at multiple levels is the focus of the next section.

Integrated and evidence-informed practice: working at multiple levels

The focus of this book has been on examining emerging theories of practice in a range of fields of practice. A dominant theme is the connection between theory and practice, identifying what works in practice and responding to the diverse needs of clients (Ife 2005). Evidence-informed practice, as elucidated in Kieran O'Donoghue's chapter, is a dynamic interactive process that is informed by several factors, including the client's needs, context and wishes, resources, and the complexity of issues. Using evidence to inform practice is a dialogical and reflexive process that involves an interactive conversation about how knowledge is applied in practice and how practice informs knowledge development. Evidence-informed practice values all forms of knowledge including research, cultural and practice wisdom and ethical issues. Practice decisions are informed by a desire to achieve the best fit for the client and their situation.

Achieving the best fit and the best outcomes for clients may require social workers to work at multiple levels – at the micro, meso and macro levels. This integrated and intentional practice draws on an understanding of the connections between individual lived experience and the structural conditions that shape clients' daily lives. The international definition of social work (IFSW 2014) embraces an ecological approach; a *person-in-environment* orientation and a 'dual commitment to *both* agency and structure' (van Breda 2018, p.2). This means that social workers support individuals to address life challenges and enhance wellbeing while working on the structural issues and social conditions that impact on their daily lives (van Breda 2018). Ecological approaches enable analysis of clients' interactions and circumstances at multiple levels, but, as van Breda (2018, p.3) argues, such approaches do not only enable learning about these but also seek to 'change, the social conditions that impede human flourishing'.

Several chapters explore interventions that support clients to address immediate issues while working to transform structures and policies. For example, Robyn Munford and Jackie Sanders provide examples of transformative social work practice where social workers in partnership with clients worked to transform policies and systems that excluded and marginalized children and families. Lena Dominelli, in her chapter on green social work practice, identifies how change at the micro level can have a powerful effect and contributes to change at the global level. The compelling message here is that what we do locally is strongly connected to wider movements such as the global goal of saving the planet and protecting the environment for future generations. Other chapters also illustrate that this practice involves clients taking control of social change initiatives such as those explored in the chapters by Garth Bennie and Sara Georgeson and Malcolm Golightley and Gloria Kirwan, which illustrate the ways in which disabled people and people living with mental illness take on leadership roles in decisions about policy development and service provision. Social work practice at multiple levels is informed by the principles of social work practice and the international definition of social work, the focus of the next section.

Key principles

The key principles of the international social work definition inform social work practice globally. All of the chapters, in some way, foreground practice that gives effect to these principles. We focus on social justice and human rights as important principles of the international definition of social work (IFSW 2014) and as dominant themes in several of the chapters. Working to challenge social injustice is a key theme in many of the chapters in this book. This takes various forms across the chapters, but a common thread concerns social work practice that challenges marginalization, exclusion and social inequality, and, alongside this, working to achieve participation and inclusion.

Donna McAuliffe and Lesley Chenoweth position social work as a moral endeavour; central to this is a commitment to speaking up against injustice and oppressive structures and promoting practice that is based on compassion and care. Social justice practice occurs on both a global level and at the level of practice with individuals and communities. With regard to the global level, Lena Dominelli explores green social work practice and the important role for social workers in contributing to the realization of environmental justice. Kathryn Hay locates environmental justice in the context of disaster management and advocates for practice that adopts a collective view on social justice alongside work with individuals. These interventions can transform communities by actively promoting social justice outcomes.

Social justice practice is to be found in interventions with specific population groups, which, given their particular circumstances and history, face complex challenges. Jay Marlowe, in his chapter on practice with resettled refugees, posits that a commitment to social justice involves social workers building an understanding of how human rights are enacted for populations which have been displaced. This work focuses on building enduring connections and a sense of belonging; a key role for social workers is to activate practical and emotional resources that facilitate safety, inclusion and participation in community life.

A commitment to upholding human rights and facilitating opportunities for promoting citizenship has always been at the core of social work practice. Social workers take on advocacy roles and in partnership with clients develop strategies for achieving citizenship. This involves challenging invisibility and providing meaningful support for individuals to actively participate and contribute to their communities. Several of the chapters demonstrate how social work practice is informed by rights discourses. Polly Yeung, in her discussion on social work practice with older people, advocates for a focus on justice, human rights, empowerment and advocacy. This practice challenges structural barriers and inequalities, including private business models of healthcare provision that may compromise the level of care, restrict older people's choices and undermine their ability to participate in community life. At the core of this practice is respect for diversities, another key principle of the international definition of social work, which recognizes that meaningful support for older people incorporates respect for their diverse lived experiences and their right to choose where and how they want to live.

John Pinkerton, John Canavan and Pat Dolan explore rights discourses in the context of family support practice. The United Nations Convention on the Rights of the Child (UNCRC) informs child welfare practice with children and young people (United Nations 1989). It grants a set of rights to all children and young people, including being guaranteed care and protection to ensure their wellbeing and access to support and resources that enable them to participate in cultural and community activities.

The chapter by Jackie Sanders and Robyn Munford on PARTH approaches explores the experiences of young people who have faced adversity and impoverished social and material conditions. These young people have not had opportunities throughout their childhood to have the *ordinary* experiences of their better-resourced peers. Social workers have a key role in supporting these young people to seek out resources and support, and alongside this to challenge systems and policies that exclude these young people from being able to fully participate in community life. This includes, for example, challenging school personnel to find pathways that enable young people to return to school.

The idea of social workers advocating for clients to experience *ordinary* life, everyday life in everyday places, such as school, recreational and cultural activities, is a key theme in practice in mental health and disability support services. Malcolm Golightley and Gloria Kirwan suggest that developments at the international level focus attention on the right of people living with mental illness to be free from discrimination and to be supported to engage fully in social life including having access to important resources such as education and employment.

The chapter by Garth Bennie and Sara Georgeson provides an example of practice where rights discourses inform policy and system transformation. They describe an innovative project, Enabling Good Lives, where partnerships between disabled people, families, practitioners and policy makers are engaged in a transformational change project that upholds the rights of disabled people to fully participate at all levels of community life. This example provides an illustration of key principles of the international definition of social work, that of promoting social change and collective responsibility, which involves practice on a wider level to uphold clients' rights and to transform systems and policies.

Robyn Munford and Jackie Sanders also underline the important role of social workers in facilitating collective action to challenge exclusion, inequality and marginalization. They explore transformative social work practice and, in particular, community-led approaches that involve building connections and forming partnerships to challenge the structural conditions that shape everyday lives and future possibilities.

The examples of social justice and rights practice underline the important role social workers have in challenging power relations and in working in partnership with clients to effect change processes. A core element of this practice is building an understanding of context and the foregrounding of local and indigenous knowledge in social work interventions; this is the focus of the next section.

Context: local and indigenous knowledge

Closely associated with social justice and rights practice is the idea of context and promoting local and indigenous knowledge to inform practice. Context-sensitive practice encourages social workers to build an understanding of the key factors that inform clients' experiences, including historical events that impact on current experiences (for example, colonization, displacement and marginalization); cultural belief systems; power relations within families and communities; and, local wisdom and networks. Central to this understanding of context is recognition that practice is firmly rooted in the relational, social and interpersonal realities of diverse client groups, and the recognition of the grounding of practice in local wisdom, knowledge and experience (Gray, Coates and Yellow Bird 2008a). Internationally, it is recognized that where 'local culture is used as a primary source for knowledge and practice development, social work practice can become culturally appropriate, relevant and authentic' (Gray, Coates and Yellow Bird 2008b, p.5).

Indigenous social work practice is a key example of reclaiming knowledge in a process of challenging colonization and adopting practice models that generate 'knowledge and practice models from the ground up, drawing on the values, beliefs, customs and cultural norms of local and indigenous helping practices' (Gray *et al.* 2008b, p.5). As illustrated in the chapter by Paulé Ruwhiu, social workers in Aotearoa New Zealand have drawn on the expertise of Tangata Whenua (indigenous population) and on the numerous perspectives that derive from traditional practices to develop integrated and holistic practice frameworks. These frameworks move from deficit approaches that have a primary focus on problems and issues, to those that focus on strategies for promoting wellbeing and positive development for whānau (families). Such approaches have an affinity with strengths perspectives that underscore the importance of supporting clients to find solutions within their own cultural contexts.

Other examples of context-sensitive practice involve practitioners working with local communities to address global issues and to work collectively to identify a vision and goals for more sustainable futures. Both Lena Dominelli and Kathryn Hay, in their respective chapters on green social work practice and social work in disasters, identify the importance of practitioners working with communities to use local wisdom to identify solutions to complex issues.

The chapters also foreground other examples of reclaiming practice knowledge. For example, Tracie Mafile'o identifies three Pacific social work practice principles – love, relationship and humility – that inform responsive practice with Pacific families and communities. Sylvia Yao, Cecilia Chan and Celia Chan present an Integrative Body-Mind-Spirit (IBMS) model to achieve holistic wellbeing and demonstrate the contribution of Eastern philosophies and health-promoting practices to biopsychosocial psychotherapeutic techniques. Rosaleen Ow advocates for responsive cross-cultural social work practice that embraces the cultural beliefs of clients as central to intervention processes that contribute to emerging theories and models of practice. This orientation to practice that recognizes the important role of cultural beliefs and values in practice is also relevant for social work practice in resettlement processes with refugees, as Jay Marlowe outlines in his chapter on effective practice with refugees.

Social workers also have a key role in supporting service users to have a voice and to have their lived experience recognized as important knowledge to be harnessed in interventions. This involves disrupting and shifting the professional hegemony that prioritizes the practitioner's expertise over that of the service user. Garth Bennie and Sara Georgeson explore the shift in thinking that promotes consumer-driven and consumer-led services where clients direct interventions in partnership with practitioners.

Malcolm Golightley and Gloria Kirwan also explore the shift in service provision, including the emerging focus on recovery and participation-based approaches that have developed out of the experiences of people living with mental illness. This challenges the discourses around being defined solely in terms of a psychiatric diagnosis and brings new knowledge to thinking about mental illness. In similar ways that have seen disability being reframed in the context of social, economic and political factors, which determine how impairment is manifest in a disabling society, definitions of mental illness have also been reframed. Malcolm Golightley and Gloria Kirwan explore the recasting of *psychiatric patients* as agentic, self-determining *mental health service users*, which replaces prior conceptualizations of *patients* as passive and incapable of making informed decisions about their care. These changes in the ways in which clients are defined impact on the way in which social work practice is constructed. In order to respond to these emerging challenges, social workers need to engage in critically reflective processes that enable them to think deeply about what constitutes effective practice with diverse client groups. We now turn to a discussion of reflection on practice.

Reflection on practice

We conclude this chapter with a discussion on reflection on practice and the need for social workers to incorporate critical reflection as an essential component of their practice. In his chapter on supervision and evidence-informed practice, Kieran O'Donoghue outlines a process for ongoing critical reflection and for reviewing practice and the practice context. This critical reflection also focuses on the practitioner, including exploring what they require in order to be well prepared to work effectively with clients and to develop strategies for self-care. Reflection on practice and the practice context includes an assessment of the available knowledge, including social work theories, practice wisdom, local knowledge and solutions, cultural knowledge, and the knowledge that clients bring to the helping relationship. While social workers carry out reflection on practice with supervisors and colleagues, it is important that they also do this in partnership with clients. This a core element of relational practice where clients and social workers engage in a genuine dialogical process to share knowledge and reflect together on interventions (Ife 2005, p.12). This process also involves reflection on how clients' immediate issues are shaped by wider contexts and how social workers and clients may work together at a number of levels to not only address immediate issues, but also become involved in social change projects.

Reflection on practice also includes reflection on *use of self* and involves strategies for ensuring that practitioners are well equipped to engage effectively with clients. Donna McAuliffe and Lesley Chenoweth suggest that a key element of practice is learning about ethical theories and practising robust and inclusive ethical decision making. This, like all other aspects of practice, is informed by cultural beliefs and values and these will influence how ethical matters, including rights and responsibilities, are perceived.

Self-care is an important contributing factor to effective practice and, as Sylvia Yao, Cecilia Chan and Celia Chan emphasize, to achieve this social workers can use techniques that align with their own cultural values and beliefs.

Ongoing reflection on practice requires a commitment from social workers to make this an integral component of their practice. Reflection on practice is a critical element in the construction of effective practice. Organizations also need to consider how they give effect to critical reflection. Importantly, organizations can support social workers to engage in critical reflection by incorporating this into practice guidelines and by providing time and resources. Finally, critical reflection is underpinned by the key principles of the international definition of social work, including a commitment to social justice practice.

Conclusion

This chapter has explored the key elements of effective social work practice. We have distilled insights on emerging theories of practice from the chapters to identify how effective and responsive practice is constructed at multiple levels and in diverse contexts. Historically, social workers have responded to global challenges, and the chapters have explored the current challenges social workers are facing and the ways in which social work practice has responded to these. Globally, they will confront complex future challenges including the damaging effects of climate change; the effects of displacement and forced migration; the lasting effects of trauma and abuse; and the consequences of inequality and marginalization. The challenge for social workers is to develop theory and practice frameworks that are able to effectively respond to these challenges. This practice is informed by a commitment to upholding human rights and to social justice practice.

The chapters explore how social workers work at the individual level to address immediate issues and mediate the impacts of these global challenges. Social workers also work at the meso and macro levels in partnership with clients and communities to confront these challenges and to develop strategies for transforming the societal conditions that create inequality and marginalization. As the discussion across the chapters has shown, social workers will continue to think deeply about what constitutes effective and responsive practice, including how they can contribute to social change movements. Guiding these reflections are questions about their role as agents of change, including how social work interventions create possibilities for those they work alongside to realize different futures.

References

Gray, M., Coates, J. and Yellow Bird, M. (2008a) *Indigenous Social Work around the World: Towards Culturally Relevant Education and Practice*. Aldershot: Ashgate Publishing.

Gray, M., Coates, J. and Yellow Bird, M. (2008b) 'Introduction.' In M. Gray, J. Coates and M. Yellow Bird (eds) *Indigenous Social Work Around the World: Towards Culturally Relevant Education and Practice*. Aldershot: Ashgate Publishing.

Ife, J. (2005) 'Foreword.' In M. Nash, R. Munford and K. O'Donoghue (eds) *Social Work Theories in Action*. London: Jessica Kingsley Publishers.

International Federation of Social Workers (IFSW) (2014) *Global Definition of Social Work*. Accessed on 04/09/2017 at www.ifsw.org/what-is-social-work/global-definition-of-social-work.

United Nations (1989) United Nations Convention on the Rights of the Child (UNCRC). Accessed on 21/03/2018 at www.ohchr.org/EN/ProfessionalInterest/Pages/CRC.aspx.

van Breda, A.D. (2018) 'Reclaiming resilience for social work: A reply to Garrett.' *British Journal of Social Work* (online advanced access). doi:10.1093/bjsw/bcy010.

Authors' Information

Editors

Robyn Munford is Director of the Research and Practice Development Hub and Professor of Social Work in the School of Social Work at Massey University, Aotearoa New Zealand. She co-leads the Pathways to Resilience and Successful Youth Transitions research programmes, which examine patterns of risk and resilience in the lives of vulnerable young people and the ways in which formal and informal systems of support facilitate positive development.

Kieran O'Donoghue is Associate Professor in the School of Social Work at Massey University, Aotearoa New Zealand, and a Research Associate of the Department of Social Work, Stellenbosch University, South Africa. His research is in social work supervision and social work theory and practice.

Authors

Garth Bennie is Chief Executive of the New Zealand Disability Support Network (NZDSN), a national membership organization representing agencies and people involved in disability service provision across Aotearoa New Zealand. NZDSN provides advice and guidance to government on disability-related policy and service design and supports innovation and service quality through a variety of training activities and research. Garth has a PhD in Social Policy and Social Work; he has worked in the disability sector in management, evaluation, training, policy and research, and in the public sector and in non-government organizations.

John Canavan is joint founder and Associate Director of the UNESCO Child and Family Research Centre at the National University of Ireland, Galway. His main research interests are family support, children's policy and service delivery and evaluation theory. John is currently leading a major study on prevention, early intervention and family support with Ireland's Child Protection and Welfare Agency.

Cecilia Lai Wan Chan is Chair Professor in the Department of Social Work and Social Administration at the University of Hong Kong. Her primary research focus is empowerment practices on transformation through pain and suffering. She has developed physiological outcome indicators in measuring the impact of her innovative East–West Integrative Body-Mind-Spirit interventions on different population groups. She is a pioneer in adapting Traditional Chinese Medicine and qigong practices for clinical social work interventions. Her leadership in palliative care, psychosocial oncology, disaster and bereavement care is well recognized.

Celia Hoi Yan Chan is Associate Professor in the Department of Social Work and Social Administration at the University of Hong Kong. As a social work researcher and practitioner in healthcare settings, Celia integrates best research evidence with clinical experience by applying the Integrative Body-Mind-Spirit intervention model. She has extensive clinical experience in working with different populations, including patients with cancer, insomnia, psoriasis, infertility, depression and anxiety.

Lesley Chenoweth AO is Professor Emeritus in the Menzies Health Institute of Queensland, Griffith University, Australia. She was a social work educator and researcher for almost 30 years, focusing on disability and rural and remote practice. Lesley continues to research in the disability and community sectors.

Pat Dolan is joint founder and Director of the UNESCO Child and Family Research Centre at the National University of Ireland, Galway. He holds the prestigious UNESCO Chair in Children, Youth and Civic Engagement, the first to be awarded in the Republic of Ireland.

Lena Dominelli is a Professor at the University of Stirling and was most recently the Professor of Applied Social Sciences and Academician in the Academy of the Learned Societies for Social Sciences at Durham University, UK. She is also Co-Director of the Institute of Hazard, Risk and Resilience Research with specific responsibility for the Vulnerability and Resilience Programme. Lena has published extensively in the fields of sociology, social policy and social work. She has argued passionately for the realization of human freedom from social inequalities and has recently been awarded an honorary doctorate from Malmö University, Sweden, for developing green social work as a new paradigm for the profession.

Sara Georgeson is a policy analyst with the New Zealand Disability Support Network, a national membership organization representing agencies and people involved in disability service provision across Aotearoa New Zealand. She is also working with the Open Polytechnic as a co-course leader to develop a new online programme on disability sector leadership. Sara's background is in social work, tertiary education, and disability support and policy development. Sara is a disabled woman with an interest in disability rights and strategic issues. She has lengthy experience with managing her own individualized funding, including employing her own support workers.

Malcolm Golightley is a professor in the School of Health and Social Care, University of Lincoln, UK, and has worked in the mental health field for over 20 years. He has many publications on social work practice in the mental health field, has served as a Mental Health Act Commissioner and carried out inspections on behalf of the Healthcare Commission. He is currently co-editor of the *British Journal of Social Work.*

Kathryn Hay is a senior lecturer in the School of Social Work at Massey University, Aotearoa New Zealand. Her research interests include social work and disaster management, field education, and readiness to practise of newly qualified social workers.

Gloria Kirwan is Assistant Professor of Social Work in the School of Social Work and Social Policy at Trinity College Dublin, Ireland. She is a registered social worker. Her main research interests include mental health, group work and social work education.

Tracie Mafile'o identifies as an Aotearoa New Zealand-born Tongan; her father was from the village of Te'ekiu in the Pacific nation of Tonga. She is a senior lecturer in the School of Social Work, Massey University, Aotearoa New Zealand. Her professional career has involved work in Aotearoa New Zealand, Australia and Papua New Guinea. With practice experience in child and family, women's refuge, counselling and youth work, she focuses her research on Tongan/Pacific social work, youth development, HIV prevention and Pacific research strengthening.

Jay Marlowe is Associate Professor of Social Work at the University of Auckland, Aotearoa New Zealand. His research focuses on refugee settlement; he has written about transnationalism, working with trauma, disasters and the way in which refugees can participate as peers in civil society. He has many publications on this work, including a 2018 book entitled *Belonging and Transnational Refugee Settlement.*

Donna McAuliffe is Professor and Head of School of Human Services and Social Work at Griffith University, Australia. She has a social work background and has been an academic and educator for over 20 years, specializing in the field of professional ethics in both teaching and research. She led the last review of the Australian Association of Social Workers' Code of Ethics (2010).

Rosaleen Ow is a senior lecturer at the Department of Social Work, National University of Singapore. Her research interests are in cross-cultural social work, mental health and resilience.

John Pinkerton is Professor of Child and Family Social Work in the School of Sociology, Social Policy and Social Work at Queen's University Belfast, Northern Ireland. His areas of research, publication and teaching are leaving care services, family support and the process of relating research to policy and practice. His most recent publication is the co-authored book, *Understanding Family Support: Policy, Practice and Theory* (2016).

Paulé Ruwhiu is a lecturer in the School of Social Work, Massey University, Aotearoa New Zealand. She is currently completing her PhD on 'The Process of Decolonisation and the Experiences of Māori Social Work Students and Māori Social Workers'. Paulé's research interests include intergenerational patterns of Māori, de-colonization and the transmission of knowledge.

Jackie Sanders is Professor of Children's and Youth Studies in the School of Social Work at Massey University, Aotearoa New Zealand. She co-leads the Pathways to Resilience and Successful Youth Transitions research programmes, which examine patterns of risk and resilience in the lives of vulnerable young people and the ways in which formal and informal systems of support facilitate positive development.

Sylvia Hong Yao is a social worker and PhD student in the Department of Social Work and Social Administration at the University of Hong Kong. She has practised the Integrative Body-Mind-Spirit intervention model with the clinical population for many years, including psychosocial interventions for infertile couples, cancer patients and people with chronic illness.

Polly Yeung is a senior lecturer in the School of Social Work at Massey University, Aotearoa New Zealand. She is a member of the Health and Ageing Research Team at Massey University. Her research is on ageing, disability and quality of life.

Subject Index

Author Index